# FBI Files on Mexicans and Chicanos, 1940–1980

# FBI Files on Mexicans and Chicanos, 1940–1980

## The Eagle Is Watching

José Angel Gutiérrez

LEXINGTON BOOKS
*Lanham • Boulder • New York • London*

Published by Lexington Books
An imprint of The Rowman & Littlefield Publishing Group, Inc.
4501 Forbes Boulevard, Suite 200, Lanham, Maryland 20706
www.rowman.com

6 Tinworth Street, London SE11 5AL, United Kingdom

British Library Cataloguing in Publication Information Available

**Library of Congress Cataloging-in-Publication Data**

Names: Gutiérrez, José Angel, author.
Title: FBI files on Mexicans and Chicanos, 1940–1980 : the eagle is
    watching / José Angel Gutiérrez.
Description: Lanham : Lexington Books, [2021] | Includes bibliographical
    references and index. | Summary: "FBI Files on Mexicans and Chicanos,
    1940–1980 is a multi-chapter book that examines the FBI files on multiple, well
    known Mexican and Chicanos, as well as the Texas Farm Workers Union and the
    American G. I. Forum, and the Zoot Suit police riots in Los Angeles, California,
    during the 1940s."—Provided by publisher.
Identifiers: LCCN 2020047062 (print) | LCCN 2020047063 (ebook) |
    ISBN 9781793624536 (cloth) | ISBN 9781793624550 (pbk) |
    ISBN 9781793624543 (epub)
Subjects: LCSH: United States. Federal Bureau of Investigation—Sources. |
    Mexican Americans—History—20th century—Sources. | Mexican
    Americans—Political activity—20th century.
Classification: LCC E184.M5 G8683 2021 (print) | LCC E184.M5 (ebook) |
    DDC 973.046872—dc23
LC record available at https://lccn.loc.gov/2020047062
LC ebook record available at https://lccn.loc.gov/2020047063

# Dedication

I dedicate this work, first, to Dariana and Elder [surnames redacted], brave and courageous daughter and father, from Honduras. Dariana, nine years old, was among the first of migrant children separated from parents at the El Paso border with Mexico by the US Border Patrol. She does not remember when. She was then placed in detention 20 miles from El Paso near Clint, Texas, along with hundreds more of such "unaccompanied minor, separated" children as they are labeled by the Trump administration officials in charge of this practice. When national publicity about the horrible conditions under which the children were warehoused reached a crescendo, Dariana was relocated to a similar facility in New York City. While there for three months, she was able to appear before an immigration judge and ask to be sent back to Honduras. Her father had also been detained for months before being deported to Honduras. The two are now together again in the country they fled from to be safe.[1]

Second, to those of Mexican and Puerto Rican origin who were erased as heroes and loyal, patriotic US soldiers during World War II. Specifically, to those who were part of the 10,000 survivors of the cruel Bataan "Death March," of which 25 percent were Mexican Americans among the 6,000 who perished in that 85-mile forced march. They were erased in 1998 by the likes of Stephen Spielberg (*Saving Private Ryan*), Ken Burns (*The War*), and in 2007 by Tom Brokaw (*The Greatest Generation*) in their works on this period of US history.[2] Also to the Chicanas who served in the Women's Army Auxiliary Corps (WAAC), Women Accepted for Volunteer Emergency Service (WAVES), and Women's Air force Service Pilots (WASP) such as nurse Rafaela Muñoz Esquivel from San Antonio, Texas, and air-traffic controller Anna Torres Vasquez of East Chicago, Indiana. Also, to the unknown dozens of Chicanas who were deemed guilty by association during the arrests and trial of the Sleepy Lagoon defendants. The girls were imprisoned and held at the Ventura School for Girls by the California Youth Authority. Eight of them—Dora Barrios, Lorena Encinas, Frances Silva, Josefina Gonzales, Juanita Gonzales, Betty Zeiss, Berta Aguilar, and Guadalupe "Lupe" Ynostroza—were charged with rioting but never tried and kept imprisoned until they turned twenty-one years of age.[3]

Lastly, I want to dedicate this work to my wife, Natalia Verjat, *mi preciosa Colorada*, who gives me space, time, room, attention, and affection that keeps me going and writing at age seventy-five.

Redlands, California, USA
*Rosarito, Baja California, Mexico*

## NOTES

1. Patrice Taddonio, FRONTLINE, January 6, 2020. Her story and that of others is depicted at https://www.pbs.org/wgbh/frontline/person/patrice-taddonio/ and the documentary, *Targeting El Paso*, premiered on January 7m 2020 on PBS and steaming at https://www.pbs.org/wgbh/frontline/film/targeting-el-paso/ Accessed January 10, 2020.

2. Rodolfo F. Acuna, *Occupied America: A History of Chicanos*, New York: Pearson, 2020: 241.

3. *Ibid.*, 246.

# Contents

Acknowledgments     ix

Introduction     xi

1   Luisa Moreno, the Guatemalan Mexican     1

2   Ernesto Galarza, the First Chicano Activist Scholar     41

3   Ramón "Raymond" Telles, First Chicano Ambassador of the United States, and His Wife, Delfina Navarro     65

4   Salvador Buruel Castro of the Los Angeles School District Student Walkouts of 1968     95

5   Balde from San Benito, Texas, a.k.a. Freddy Fender     129

6   Francisco "Pancho" Medrano: The Chicano UAW Union Man     141

7   The American G.I. Forum and Joe Molina's Case     151

8   The Border Coverage Program, the US Intervention in Mexico's Internal Affairs     181

Conclusion     205

Bibliography     211

Index     235

About the Author     249

# Acknowledgments

To my reviewers who made important suggestions to improve this work; Jason Parry and Alison Keefner, my editors, who had to put up with my tantrums over editing instructions and deadlines; and, to Henry Flores, who also listened to my concerns and brokered them with the folks at Lexington Books of Rowman and Littlefield to make this into a book, Volume II of hopefully III volumes about the FBI surveillance of La Raza.

# Introduction

A major contribution of the Chicano Movement, beginning in the late 1950s, was nation building. My generation of Chicano people learned to accept the historic segregation within US communities of the South and Midwest in employment, housing, education, health, cemeteries, and even the "Spanish" Mass celebrated on Sundays by many Catholic churches. The adherents and activists of the Chicano Movement flipped the negative connotation of not being wanted and kept apart, however, into a positive vision and goal. They sought to build a Chicano nation within this nation. They fought for the right to self-determination. Programs, projects, protests, movements, and organizations that became institutions were created to build the Chicano Nation in the United States: Aztlan. During all these years, the Federal Bureau of Investigation (FBI) was watching all the activists and protests held during the Chicano Movement. Some of those histories of FBI surveillance are in this volume.

## COMMEMORATIONS AND CELEBRATIONS

Looking back from 2020, we can see and experience the many celebrations and commemorations of this type of nation-building activity 100, 50, and 25 years ago. Chicano anniversaries are the current standard as I write this piece. A huge marker into the future is 2020. Back in 1880s, for example, the United States was a white man's country and rapidly becoming a world power. By 1930, the Mexican Revolution had pushed the Mexican-origin population in the United States over 3 million.[1] In 2020, the projection is that nonwhite children will become the majority of the nation's 74 million children, according to noted demographers. And, whites of all ages will become a minority in the United Sates around 2045.[2]

A major contributing factor to there being large family size among Mexican origin people is the influence of the Catholic Church on contraception, abortion, and childbearing. In 2018, Mexican women had a fertility rate of 62 births for every 1,000 women in the United States ages 15–44 compared to 59.1 for all women. White and Asian women in the United States, however, only had a fertility rate of 56.3 and 55.6, respectively.[3] Mexicans, as well as many other Spanish-speaking ethnic groups, are predominantly Catholic in their faith and religious practices. On Christmas Eve 1969, a Chicano group formed by Ricardo Cruz, a law student at Loyola Law School, *Catolicos Por La Raza*, peacefully picketed Mass at St. Basil's Church in Los Angeles. The Los Angeles County Sheriff's deputies arrested twenty-one demonstrators and twelve were ultimately convicted. They were protesting the nearly 4-million-dollar expenditure by Archbishop and Cardinal James Francis McIntyre in the building of St. Basil's Church in the exclusive Wilshire Boulevard district of Los Angeles while shutting down Our Lady Queen of Angels Girls' High School, predominantly attended by Chicana girls. The subsequent trial, convictions, and jail sentences led to the formation of two important organizations, PADRES and HERMANAS. The former was an organization of Chicano priests and the latter an organization of Chicana nuns. Chicano clergy had been a minority compared to whites since the removal of Mexican and Spanish priests and nuns following the incorporation of the Southwest as US territory in 1848.[4] A fiftieth anniversary celebration of this event to reform the Catholic Church was held at Church of the Epiphany in Los Angles, California, of this movement on January 11, 2020, which this author attended.

In Texas, namely Crystal City and San Antonio, the famous Chicano student walkout of 1969 celebrated with a public commemoration at the Crystal City High School of that event on December 9, 2019. On January 9, 2020, the local newspaper *The Zavala County Sentinel* ran an opinion editorial commemorating the founding of La Raza Unida Party in Texas and subsequently the national formation in El Paso, Texas, over Labor Day weekend in 1972.[5] These two events took place fifty years ago.

The Vietnam War also caused many Chicanos, among others, to protest that military engagement in Southeast Asia. Most famous of protests was the Los Angeles-based National Chicano Moratorium. Beginning in 1968–1969, Rosalio Muñoz, the first Chicano student body president at the University of California Los Angeles, began organizing anti-war protests. The largest held was in August 29, 1970, and this protest led to a police riot which resulted in several Chicanos killed by police, including the only Chicano newspaper columnist Ruben Salazar.[6] Coming up in August 2020 will be the commemoration of these protests and police killing.

## THE BEGINNINGS OF STUDENT PROTESTS

The effort to institutionalize these histories of struggle began with the many Chicano student protests over the lack of equal opportunity and education in the nation's public schools. The largest consecutive number of these school boycotts, so named because students did not attend classes, thereby hurting the state allocation not sent to individual school districts due to loss of daily enrollment, began in 1968 in Texas and California. The most reported and commercialized into an HBO movie *WALKOUT!*, which premiered March 18, 2006, were the Chicano walkouts at five East Los Angeles high schools and the one at San Antonio, Texas, at Lanier High School followed by others in the city's West Side, the Chicano barrio. Common to all these walkouts were student demands for reform, and central to each list of demands was for the teaching of Chicano history, Spanish, and, generally, culture. From these demands were created Chicano Studies programs, which grew in numbers over time, and the National Association of Chicano Studies, later renamed National Association of Chicana and Chicano Studies.[7] In the case of Chicano Studies, there have been many anniversary celebrations at different times and locations depending on the founding of each program and department from 2018 to the present time. But, these events also took place fifty years ago more or less.

## MORE UGLY STORIES IN 2020

There are too many historic events that took place decades ago that make for a comprehensive history of Chicano struggle for civil rights. Let me close with just a couple of more examples. *Baja News*, the English newspaper for Anglo ex-pats who have settled in Baja California for retirement and dollar stretching, headlined "Trump vs. Pancho Villa."[8] The article traced the invasion of Francisco "Pancho" Villa of US soil at Columbus, New Mexico, some 104 years ago on March 9, 1916. It was the first such invasion before the 9/11 Twin Towers attack. Villa was sending a message that this raid into occupied Mexico was more symbolic than an act of war. He was busy with his revolution within Mexico and resented US interference against him in that conflict. Moreover, he just needed guns, money, and horses. Earlier the United States had violated Mexican sovereignty by bombing and occupying the port of Vera Cruz to destroy an arms shipment into Mexico to Francisco Madero's top military commander-turned-assassin, Victoriano Huerta. The United States killed some 300 Mexicans as a result. After the Columbus raid, the United States sent more than 14,000 soldiers into Mexico to hunt down "Pancho" Villa. Commanding

Brigadier General John "Black Jack" Pershing, while in pursuit spent over $100 million and several months. He and his top aide, Lt. Joseph Swing, later to resurface as the Immigration and Naturalization Service (INS) Commissioner in charge of Operation Wetback in 1954, never found Villa much less capture or kill him. President Woodrow Wilson stationed 140,000 US Army and National Guard troops along the US-Mexico border signaling yet another imminent US invasion of Mexico. It did not happen but for the United States declaring war on Germany and entering World War I. The troops and General Pershing were recalled away from the Mexican border to Europe.[9]

On December 23, 2019, President Donald Trump called on the new Mexican President Andres Manual Lopez Obrador to allow US troops into Mexico to stop the drug activity and violence of the cartels. He had made the same request to the prior Mexican President Enrique Peña Nieto in 2017. Whereas in 1916, the newly imposed Mexican President Venustiano Carranza allowed US troops into Mexico in exchange for US support, economic and military, for his regime. President Andres Manuel Lopez Obrador declined the offer as had Peña Nieto.[10]

When twenty-one-year-old Patrick Crusius of Allen, Texas, traveled across Texas to El Paso, his motive and intent were made clear by the manifesto he posted online just before he opened fire on innocent Mexicans, men, women, and children, at the Cielo Vista Mall's Walmart store. He killed at least twenty-two persons and left another twenty-four seriously maimed from his shooting spree. Texas Governor Greg Abbott called him mentally ill. President D. Trump called him a coward. The El Paso Mayor, a Republican by the name of Donald "Dee" Margo, chastised the shooter for "surrendering like a coward." None labeled this massacre a hate crime perpetrated by a racist white man.[11] By way of contrast, the shooting of nine Mexican citizens with dual US nationality in Northern Mexico by an alleged drug cartel on November 5, 2019 is what prompted President Trump to ask President Obrador for permission to send US troops into Mexico and hunt down the killers. The dead were members of the Church of the Latter Day Saints, better known as Mormons, whose roots in Mexico, the states of Chihuahua and Sonora more specifically, date back to the time of polygamy being a religious practice among the faithful.[12] The delay in ratifying Utah as a state on January 4, 1896, was tied to this unlawful practice under US law. The United States acquired Utah as part of the Mexican territory ceded in 1848 under the Treaty of Guadalupe Hidalgo. US Senator Mitt Romney's (R-Utah) father, George Romney, former governor of Michigan and US presidential contender, was born in Mexico to his grandparents who left Utah after 1890 when the Mormon Church officially banned polygamy to obtain US statehood.[13]

## WELCOMING 2020

The second decade of the twenty-first century did not begin with all "Happy New Year" stories nor did the *Dia de los Reyes Magos* on January 6 bring gifts of joy and happiness to all; only for some. The Alliance for Retired Americans began circulating a petition for signatures to be forwarded to Congress calling for an expansion of Social Security coverage by increasing the share the wealthier among US taxpayers pay into the fund. The Alliance claims the richest Americans, more than 1,000 of them, have stopped paying into the fund as of January 2, 2020, and most of the other rich members of our society "are paying a lower percentage of their income to Social Security than working Americans."[14]

The Gallup polling organization has been taking surveys for decades. One such survey undertaken the past seventy-one years is the "Happiness" measure. The 2019 survey indicated that 44 percent of Americans reported being "fairly happy" and 42 percent claiming they were "very" happy. This combined 88 percent is "the lowest overall percentage happy Gallup has recorded in periodic readings taken since 1948." This is the fifth time the happiness mark has dropped below 90 percent. And, the highest "not too happy" response was reported by 14 percent of those polled; the highest measured to date. According to this poll, nonwhites report being less happy (77 percent) than whites. Republicans, 53 percent, also reported being very happy compared to only 29 percent of Democrats. Worldwide happiness is also measured by Gallup for the United Nations and has found the US happiness rating dropping from fourteenth place among other nations in 2014 to eighteenth place in 2018 and was measured at nineteenth place in 2019.[15]

## THE FORMAT OF UNTOLD HISTORIES IN THIS VOLUME

After my last books utilizing FBI files obtained under the Freedom of Information and Privacy Acts, as amended, on Cesar E. Estrada and Reies Lopez Tijerina, I changed my book format from a single individual to a multi-chapter book on several individuals, two organizations, and one event. *The Eagle Has Claws* was the first volume in this series. This work, *The Eagle Is Watching*, is my second volume. I hope to finish three volumes to leave a legacy of production on how extensive, both in range of targets and chronology, the FBI surveillance of people of Mexican origin has been. My contribution is to add information to the history of US oppression of La Raza, specifically those of us of Mexican origin in the United States. In the scholarship generated by other scholars on this specific topic and those focused on US history, our contributions have been purposely skipped, erased, ignored, revised, and sanitized. In *The Eagle Has Claws*, I posit that the surveillance is based on the perception of Mexicans and their progeny as the historic enemy. I continue to make that argument with more examples in this work but add another feature, that of "pinning the tail on the donkey," if you will, and to name those who are maintaining this paradigm of exclusion by skipping evidence in the historical record. Best put by Michael Nava, in "Big Lit Meets the Mexican Americans: A Study in White Supremacy," is the critical observation that the "big five publishers, *The New York Times Book Review* and its echo chambers in print and online media, MFA programs, independent book stores, libraries, and book festivals" skip over our history.[16] His conclusions, based on research, are detailed in the five parts of his essay. In summary, the Big Lit cabal is a "whites-only country club" that imposes market hegemony. The Big Lit comprises Penguin Random House, HarperCollins, Macmillan, Hachette, and Simon and Shuster.[17] Nava's lengthy Part 2 repeats my Chicano-centered review of our history of conquest, domination, land theft, settler colonization, and impoverishment over centuries, first by the Spanish and Catholic Church then, by the US government and its monopoly capitalist economic system. This physical repression of all dissent and protest by Chicanos is presented earlier in this Introduction to *The Eagle Has Claws*. But, Nava goes further by documenting the biased, racist, stereotypical, and outright sick caricature of Mexicans as lazy, dirty, ignorant, cowardly, sexually immoral, and stupid. He cites articles in *Scribner's Magazine* and *The Atlantic* of 1894 and 1899, respectively, that reflect those signifiers of Mexicans. This view has been ingrained in the white and black American psyche by sheer repetition in popular media and instruction in the public schools. Currently, I can add another layer to those in existence that of Mexicans being "illegal aliens." This charge has been levied for the past seventy years, at least, beginning with Operation Wetback in the 1950s and the massive deportations of Mexican-origin persons; about one-third of those deported being US citizens. Earlier in the 1930s, massive deportations of Mexicans occurred as well. Again, many of those deported were US citizens. Nava claims that up to 60 percent were US citizens. Deportations of Mexicans from US soil began as early as the late 1880s.

The US policy directive then was, and still continues to be, to rid the country of "illegal" Mexicans, those crossing without authorization. Yet, the waiting period for such a lawful processing at this writing is still fourteen years for Mexicans. Who can wait while starving or fearing violence or unemployment that long? Recent US presidents from Bill Clinton, George W. Bush, Barack Obama, to now Donald Trump, each has increased the number of Mexicans being deported from the United States. And now, added targets for deportation have been made part of the list: the children of persons from Mexico that have been raised in the United States since babyhood; the children of those seeking lawful entry under political asylum criteria are not only separated from parents at the border and held in detention across the country but also the parents are now the added targets for deportation by the Trump administration; and, deportation of those who have criminal records in the United States, which has been expanded to include traffic citations and misdemeanors. Aggravating the circumstances of a person being detained and children separated is the new practice to deny visitation by advocates and family members.[18]

According to Nava in Part 3, the Chicano civil rights struggle has been placed on the back burner by Big Lit, while the Black civil rights movement makes front-page news and countless publications. The result is Mexicans have no history of civil rights struggle, only blacks, white women, and now the LGBTQ+ community have such histories. The record shows Mexican-filed civil rights cases in the 1930s, 1940s, and 1950s later to be used by blacks as precedents in their cases. Those cases are not featured in the curriculum in US law schools, the featured ones are only those involving blacks, women, and gays. Nava also provides statistics of how white the Big Lit industry is: only 6 percent of Latinos work for Big Lit; 89 percent of librarians and library administrators are white and non-Hispanic; 90 percent of books reviewed were by white reviewers and the top Chicano books were not published by any of the Big Lit mafia; as of the late 1990s, not one literary agent was Hispanic, much less Chicano; and the faculty and students of MFA programs in the country are predominantly white.[19]

In my work on the FBI surveillance, primarily, of Mexican origin people, I focus here on new subjects and their files in my possession from the FBI. In the case of Ambassador Raymond Telles and his wife, Delfina, I also utilized State Department records; other Department of Justice correspondence in the case of the Zoot Suit riot by the Los Angeles Police and US Navy personnel, I used some military records for material. Ample other secondary source material was also relied upon and is found in the Bibliography. What should be obvious to the reader as they go from chapter to chapter is how new this information is to them. I refer not to the FBI surveillance generally but specifically on the spying done on persons of Mexican origin during the many decades of the agency's existence. Even in the books and articles on the history of FBI surveillance done by others, there are empty spaces for inclusion of this type of spying on the United States' largest ethnic minority, persons of Mexican origin and Latinos. We are also skipped in this history.

## HISTORY OF SURVEILLANCE

In 1964, the dynamic journalist duo of David Wise and Thomas B. Ross, of the *New York Herald Tribune* and the *Chicago Sun-Times*, respectively, produced the first comprehensive study on what they termed "the invisible government," which became the title of their book.[20] Their focus was on the Central Intelligence Agency's (CIA) role in the various *coup-de-etat*'s occurring in that decade such as Iran (Operation Ajax), Guatemala (Operation PBSUCCESS), and others in Indonesia, Vietnam, Bay of Pigs invasion in Cuba, and Laos, for example. They exposed the CIA's funding and promotion of regime changes around the globe. The previous year, the duo published their research into the US spy plane, the U2, downed in Russia.[21] Together, they wrote three books before Wise ventured into his own writing.[22] Wise and Ross have both since passed away. The CIA tried to intimidate the authors and their publisher, Random House, into not printing the manuscript on *The Invisible Government*.[23] It did not work. *Look* magazine did succumb to this pressure and made changes to the serialization of the book chapters.[24]

As whistleblowers of the day, Wise and Ross rank up there with the Berrigan brothers, Chelsea Manning, and Edward Snowden and as researchers without the internet or the Freedom of Information and Privacy Acts (FOI/PA). It is utterly amazing to learn that their main source of information on the CIA was no less than Allen W. Dulles, founder and first director of that agency, as reported by Giylco and Wolf, previously cited above in the *Look* reference. An earlier work on the US intelligence agencies of the 1960s was done by another author but kept in-house for internal use; now reprinted and available commercially.[25] Of interest, to my work in this volume are all three of the Wise and Ross books for their early history, description, and functions of the components of the intelligence community prior to what we have now, post 9/11. While these books mentioned above are not specifically about the FBI, in *The Invisible Government* they do review the organizational structure of the military intelligence units by branch and point out that spying by the US Army dates back to WWI.[26] The FBI as part of the intelligence community is also described by its mission, organizational structure, and its operations and budget as of 1964. The FBI is credited by Wise and Ross in these words: "its counter-espionage work is vital to national security."[27]

## "WATCHING THE WORKERS"

Those are the caption words of chapter seven in Joan M. Jensen's book, *Army Surveillance in America, 1775–1980*. She details the history of an anti-labor surveillance program initiated by the US Army during the years prior to WWI.

> These were not workers suspected of espionage or sabotage, or even of the ore vague charge of disloyalty. Instead they were ordinary workers who happened to be working for companies that had government contracts.[28]

She estimated some 37,000 such companies had government contracts during World War I. Many more companies were related directly to these companies, for example, the farm and ranch producers of food products which provide the raw product for further processing, such as vegetables, fruits, and meats; the rail and truck companies that delivered these products and many others, even moving troops within the country. In short, the tentacles of the US Army involving workers in management and supervision in these companies became labeled the Plant Production Section (PPS) that reached into many sectors. One of the focuses of the PPS was labor unions as target: the Industrial Workers of the World (IWW) union, primarily. In the Southwest, West, and Midwest, the IWW was organizing farm workers, miners, lumberjacks, food-processing plants and warehouses, truckers, and rail workers. Many workers in these specific types of industries were of Mexican origin. The US Army and the agents working in the PPS went after them all. "By 1914, [IWW] leaders had emerged who concentrated on organizing farm laborers and harvest hands in the Midwest. An agricultural workers' organization formed within IWW soon boasted a membership of one hundred thousand."[29] Jensen further narrates the Army and PPS agents moving in the 1890s on miners in Coeur d'Alene mines in Idaho; coal fields of Southern Colorado; copper mines ion Arizona; and castor bean fields in Florida. In Ludlow, Colorado, the National Guard fired on a workers' tent colony, killing scores of women and children, and set fire to the camp, killing more innocent children.[30]

## THE PLANT PROTECTION SECTION SYSTEM

The PPS was a massive use of informants and volunteer snitches by the military. It developed into its own operation. Under the guise of checking into plants and companies that performed or supplied a vital function for the war effort, those charged with the first PPS actions did an inspection of a site under the ruse of fire hazards and safety measures. The military PPS inspector with company assistance would identify a plant official to be designated head of the Interior Secret Service Organization, becoming the local, in-house PPS operation. Plant officials would supply the lead man with names of the most trusted employees to act as captains of the Interior Secret Service Organization. These captains were to recruit down the line employees who could be trusted to spy on all the other workers and report any suspicious activity as described earlier, mainly unionizing. The PPS was structured like the military, top down by rank and role to unfold the first industrial war between business interests and the federal government against workers. In some of the plants deemed vital to the defense of the nation, identification cards with photographs of each employee began to be required. The individual photograph, however, was reproduced five times, a copy for the employee to use as identification, and, the others going to the company and federal government. This practice seemed to have been discontinued in 1919.

The PPS agents went overboard in their zeal to ferret out dissenters, women and workers in general. PPS agents

> made arrangements with the post office to check suspects' mail, they searched suspects' apartments, collected information from banks, obtained copies of telegrams, installed Dictaphones, investigated lawyers retained by suspects . . . eavesdropped on bar conversations and attempted to get prosecutions for disloyal remarks made after the suspect had been drinking. They made reports on "disorderly women" and "second story hotels" (brothels). They arrested bootleggers in hotel. . . . They took a census of all people, enemy alien or otherwise, residing within one-half mile of a government plant.[31]

## IS THE FEDERAL GOVERNMENT THE BIGGEST DISCRIMINATING EMPLOYER OF MEXICANS?

In the 1979, the League of United Latin American Citizens (LULAC) published, on the anniversary of their fifty years of existence, a commemorative history. Chapter XI is titled "The Struggle for Jobs." It details the efforts LULAC made to get Mexican-origin labor hired under every government contract, particularly the military defense industry. Employment discrimination was covered by federal law, not state laws. And, even then, the federal government and state governments were the most gross discriminators against Mexican-origin people. As early as summer of 1965 in Albuquerque, New Mexico, Chicanos, many of them members of LULAC, led by Bexar County Commissioner Albert A. Peña, Jr. from San Antonio, Texas, led a walkout of participants of the meeting to discuss this issue with Commissioners of the Equal Employment Opportunity Commission (EEOC). Only one EEOC Commissioner had shown up to listen to their complaints.[32]

The Office of Personnel Management for the federal government issues reports on diversity and inclusion by race, ethnicity, gender, and civil service rank of all their employees by agency. Consistently, Hispanics are among the bottom rung of percentage of employees across the board. For example, since the LULAC days of protest in the 1940s into the 1950s on this issue, "Affirmative Action" was finally adopted as official policy by John F. Kennedy's Executive Order 10952. But nothing much beyond rhetoric has taken place.

In 2000, Hispanic employees were 6.4 percent of the federal workforce as a result of another Executive Order, 13171. In 2014, Hispanic ranks grew to 8.4 percent of all federal employees. Another Executive Order, 13583, was issued in 2017 to again address this chronic discriminatory hiring practice. Nothing much has changed because there is no will by the white vested job holders to make room for others not like them. Why, then, should private industry and state governments act any different? There is no hell to pay for discriminating against Hispanic applicants. The statistics for Hispanics in the higher ranks of government Civil Service, grade at G-S 12 and above into Senior Executive Service, are more dismal.[33]

## ORGANIZATION OF THIS VOLUME

This multi-chapter book is divided into three parts of content, featuring the surveillance of five persons of Mexican origin and a Guatemalan national, assumed to be of Mexican origin, Luisa Moreno, in the opening chapter. The other four persons featured in a chapter each in order are Ernesto Galarza, the activist scholar who organized workers and fought against the Bracero Program; US Ambassador Raymond Telles and his wife, Delfina. He was the first Chicano to be named a US ambassador. Another labor organizer from Texas is the content for chapter 4—Francisco "Pancho" Medrano of Dallas. Chapter 5 is about a musician known professionally as Freddy Fender but whose real name was Baldemar Huerta from San Benito, Texas. The next part consists of two chapters, chapters 6 and 7, on the organizers of the Texas Farm Workers Union, Antonio "Tony" and Raquel Orendain; and, the American G.I. Forum and the Joe Molina case, respectively. The last chapter is on an event: the Zoot Suit Riots by the Los Angeles Police and US Naval forces, primarily. The book ends with Conclusion, Bibliography, and Index.

## NOTES

1. Rodolfo F. Acuña, *Occupied America: A History of Chicanos*, 9th edition (New York: Pearson, 2020), 157–158.
2. Rogelio Saenz and Dudley L. Poston, Jr., "Children of Color Already Make Up the Majority of Kids in Many US States," *The Conversation blog*, January 9, 2020. See at https://theconversation.com/children-of-color-already-make-up-the-majority-of-kids-in-many-states-128499/. Accessed January 9, 2020.
3. *Ibid.*, 3.
4. Acuña, *Occupied America*, 312–313.

5. Jose Angel Gutierrez, The Making of a Chicano Militant: Lessons from Cristal, (Madison: University of Wisconsin Press, 1998), 221–225.

6. F. Arturo Rosales, *CHICANO! The History of the Mexican American Civil Rights Movement* (Houston: Arte Publico Press, 1997), 199–207.

7. For a comprehensive history of Chicano Studies, see Rodolfo F. Acuña, *The Making of Chicana/o Studies: In the Trenches of Academe* (New Brunswick: Rutgers University Press, 2011).

8. *Tijuana, Baja California, México*, 21:12:1.

9. Acuña, *Occupied America,* 165.

10. *Ibid.*, Baja: 8–12.

11. The *El Paso Times* first carried the story locally on August 3, 2019, on its front page, "El Paso Walmart Shooting by Cielo Vista Mall: What We Know About the Number of Victims, the Suspect." The story was updated and posted nationally by *USA Today* on August 5, 2019, at https://www.usatoday.com/story/news/nation/2019/08/03/el-paso-walmart-shooting-what-we-know-texas-shooting/1911030001/. Accessed January 10, 2020.

12. Mary Beth Sheridan and Brittany Shammas, *The Washington Post*, August 5, 2019, "Nine members of Mormon family, dual U.S.-Mexican citizens, killed in attack in northern Mexico; Trump offers support," at https://www.washingtonpost.com/world/at-least-seven-members-of-mormon-famil-brutally-killed-in-norther-mexico/2019/11/05/d303e448-ffbb-11e9-9518-1e76a6c088b6_story.html/.

13. For historical data on Utah becoming the forty-fifth state of the United States, see https://ilovehistory.utah.gov/topics/statehood/index.html/. Accessed January 10, 2020.

14. Reported by Action Network at https://actionnetwork.org/petitions/make-the-wealthy-pay-their-fair-share-into-social -security-2/. Accessed January 10, 2020.

15. Justin McCarthy, "Happiness Not Quite as Widespread as Usual in the U.S." *Gallup*, January 10, 2020, at https://news.gallup.com/poll/276503/. Accessed January 10, 2020. The actual questions and responses and trends are also reported on this website.

16. *The Los Angeles Review of Books*, January 2, 2020: 1. See at https://lareviewofbooks.org/article/big-lit-meets-mexican-americans-study-white-supremacy/. Accessed January 8, 2020.

17. *Ibid.*, Part I.

18. Brian Sonenstein, "ICE Retaliates Against Immigration Rights Activists by Suspending Visitation Program in Alabama," *Shadow Proof blog*, December 19, 2019. See https://shadowproof.com/ice-retaliates-activists-visitation-program-detention-alabama/. Accessed December 29, 2019.

19. Nava, Big Lit, Part 4.

20. Wise David and Thomas B. Ross. *The Invisible Government* (New York: Random House, 1964).

21. See their coauthored book, *The U-2 Affair* (New York: Random House, 1962).

22. The third coauthored book was *The Espionage Establishment* (New York: Random House, 1967). *The Politics of Lying: Government Deception, Secrecy, and Power* (New York: Random House, 1973) was his first solo work. The first lie he cites

is from Lyndon B. Johnson, as president, claiming in a speech that his great, great, grandfather had died in the Alamo battle on pages 19–22.

23. See a critical review with negative commentary by Charles E. Valpey, claiming the narrative is not based on true facts and a threat to national security for its exposé about CIA operations and programs at www.cia.gov/library/v08i4a14p_0001 .htm/. Accessed on September 30, 2019.

24. See the obituary article by David Giylco and Louis Wolf at https://covertaction magazine.com/index.php/2018/12/08/david-wise-best-seller-journalist-and historian-author-of-the-invisible-government-dead-at 88/.

25. See Jack Zlotnick, *National Security Management: National Intelligence* (Cabin John, MD: Wildside Press, 2008); previous edition was titled *National Intelligence* (Washington, DC: Industrial College of the Armed Forces, 1964).

26. Wise and Ross, *Invisible Government*: 198–200. A better source on this point is Joan M. Jensen, *Army Surveillance in America, 1775–1980* (New Haven: Yale University Press, 1991), in which she points out a much longer history of military espionage of civilians and enemy combatants dating to the pre-Revolutionary Wars of the 1770s. In addition, Jensen has a chapter on the beginnings of military surveillance in Mexico and along the US border with Mexico with the first incidents of impending revolution in Mexico, "The Mexican Border: Bringing Intelligence Home,": 111–136.

27. Wise and Ross, *Invisible Government*: 202, 200–202.

28. Jensen, *Army,* 137–159.

29. Jensen, *Army,* 137–159, 137,138.

30. Jensen, *Army,* 141.

31. Jensen, *Army,* 151–153.

32. See my Chapter 10, "The Commissioner Years, 1965–1972" in my book, *Albert A. Peña, Jr.: Dean of Chicano Politics* (E. Lansing: Michigan State University Press, 2018) for details on this protest and others including cases filed of employment discrimination by government and federal contractors against Mexican origin employees.

33. Moises Sandoval, "The First Fifty Years: Half Century of Community Leadership, 1929–1979," LULAC National Office, Washington, DC, 1979: 52–62 and for the federal statistics see www.omp.gov and go to link on Reports then Federal Workforce at a Glance or Google the individual Executive Orders cited.

*Chapter 1*

# Luisa Moreno, the Guatemalan Mexican

Jeff Smith described Blanca Rosa Rodriguez Lopez, also known as Luisa Moreno, in his two-part series this way:

> For two decades, Luisa Moreno abandoned her private life and championed the rights of workers. She zigzagged around the country, protesting, organizing, and negotiating for labor unions: garment shops in New York; cigar plants in Tampa; tuna-cannery workers in San Diego. Along with being the first Latina vice president of a union, Moreno helped found the first national civil-rights assembly for Latinos: The Congress of Spanish-Speaking Peoples.[1]

Blanca Rosa Rodriguez Lopez a.k.a. Luisa Moreno was born into a wealthy family in Guatemala City, Guatemala, on August 30, 1907. Her father was Ernesto Rodriguez and her mother was Alicia Lopez. In Spanish-speaking countries, the father's surname is after the first name or names as in Blanca Rosa Rodriguez with the mother's maiden name affixed as the last of the person's name as in Blanca Rosa Rodriguez Lopez. Her first two names in Spanish mean "White Rose," describing her very white skin. Her childhood was privileged and pampered for eight and a half years until she suffered a terrible illness. After her recovery and the political turmoil in Guatemala in 1916, the family moved to Oakland, California. Blanca Rosa attended Holy Names College, a private Catholic school for all beginning grades through high school. The family stayed in Oakland for four and a half years before returning to Guatemala. Blanca Rosa became fluent in Spanish, English, and French, with a developing affinity for writing and reading poetry.

## FIRST ORGANIZING: SOCIEDAD GABRIELA MISTRAL

Rebellious as a teenager and wanting to learn more about the world, Blanca Rosa promptly began to advocate and fight for admission to the University of Guatemala to continue her education. But she was denied admission to the university for being a woman, regardless of her family's wealth.[2] Toward that end she organized the *Sociedad Gabriela Mistral*, named after her favorite poet from Chile, to press for open admissions for women; and, eventually prevailed. She did not enroll, however.

Gabriela Mistral was a pseudonym used by Lucila Godoy Alcayaga, who was the first Latin American woman to win a Nobel Prize in literature in 1945. The pseudonym came from partial names of Lucila's favorite poets, Gabriele D'Annunzio and Frédéric Mistral. In earlier years, Lucia Godoy Alcayaga a.k.a. Gabriela Mistral was a diplomat for the Chilean government and served in various posts in Europe and the United States. During 1922, the Mexican Minister of Education José Vasconcelos invited her to help him with implementing educational reforms in the country. In the 1930s, she was a visiting professor at various private colleges for women such as Bernard, Vassar in the New York area, Middlebury in Vermont, and Mills in Oakland, California. The latter college granted her a doctorate *Honoris Causa* in 1947.[3]

## BECOMING LUISA MORENO

Blanca Rosa was heavily influenced by Gabriela Mistral; especially her poetry and passion for people. Gabriela "always took the side of the mistreated by society: children, women, native groups, Jews, war victims, workers and the poor."[4] In essence, this quote and the ones at the beginning of the chapter summarize the life work of Blanca Rosa Lopez Rodriguez, who became known as Luisa Moreno. The Moreno name either comes from that of a Mexican labor organizer, Luis Moreno, whom she greatly admired, or Luisa Capetillo, a Puerto Rican labor organizer of the time. The sources are not in agreement as to which person or the combination of both names led her to change her name.[5] As her reputation as a labor organizer and advocate grew in subsequent years, the family disapproved and objected to her politics. She changed her name to Luisa Moreno to save her family the embarrassment and harassment stemming from her political and unionizing work.

As a nineteen-year-old, she had left Guatemala City for Mexico City and soon met, her first husband, Miguel Angel De León, a cartoonist. At thirty-six years of age, he was much older than she; and, according to Luisa, a womanizer. The couple joined the *avante garde* of Mexico City that gravitated around Diego Rivera and Frida Kahlo. In May 1928 and three months pregnant, the couple left Mexico City for New York City in search of better jobs and wages. They had a daughter, Mytyl Lorraine, in November 1928. The couple's move to New York and her first job in the garment industry of the time exposed Blanca Rosa to first experiences with racism against minorities, women, the poor, and the harsh working conditions of garment workers in Spanish Harlem.[6] She and the other women worked overtime without compensation—sixteen hours a day was not unusual—and, for pennies with no benefits and filthy toilets because there was no labor union for such workers. A coworker once invited her over to her flat to see her baby. Upon arrival they could hear the baby wailing loudly. A rat had "chewed off half the baby's face."[7] Luisa began to organize *La Liga de Costureras* (League of Seamstresses) to combat this gross exploitation and repression. In 1930, she joined in support of striking workers; she was the only one protesting at Zelgreen's Cafeteria and was promptly arrested and beaten by the New York police. The only groups that openly supported minorities and workers, and opposed fascism were the members of the Communist Party USA (CPUSA). In other parts of the country, many persons were joining the Communist Party with the belief it's socialist program could end the Depression in support of President Roosevelt's alliance with Russia against Germany. In Hollywood, famous actors joined including Marlon Brandon, for example.[8] Luisa joined the CPUSA in 1930 but quit her membership by 1935.[9] In the 1930, membership in CPUSA reached 65,000, and by 1942, the highest membership figure of all time was reached, 85,000.[10]

In 1931, President Herbert Hoover had vetoed a bill passed by Congress "allowing ex-servicemen to borrow up to 50 percent of the value of their 1924 veteran certificates." The ex-soldiers began to gather in Washington, DC, to demand full payment of their veteran certificates. On July 28, 1932, President Hoover ordered General Douglas MacArthur to physically remove from Washington, DC, all the protesting veterans from World War I who were demanding they be paid their promised Cash Bonus for service to the country. The US House of Representatives had approved the relief measure to boost the economy as the Depression was in full swing, but the Senate rejected the bill. The "Bonus Marchers" as they became known grew in numbers from 1,000 to over 20,000 in the streets of the nation's capital.[11] Luisa read with horror and shame in the newspapers and listened to radio reports on the violence being inflicted by soldiers on other former soldiers. The US Army, 1,000 soldiers strong, was using tanks, tear gas, machine guns, and burning down the makeshift encampments.[12] She joined in the New York protests in support of the Bonus Marchers and against President Herbert Hoover and the US Army's actions. The general public had coined words to ridicule the president and his policies by referring to "Hoovervilles (shanty towns outside major cities where the poor and homeless lived) driving Hoovercarts (cars drawn by mules or horses), waving Hooverflags (empty pockets turned inside out) and singing 'Brother Can You Spare a Dime.'"[13] Both General MacArthur and the Secretary of War, Patrick J. Hurley, and the Department of Justice's Federal Bureau of Investigation (FBI) explained to Hoover "that the veterans who had refused to leave Washington . . . were rioters and 'insurrectionists' trying to overthrow the United States government." President Hoover believed there were "subversive influences," a communist tinge, to the actions of the Bonus Marchers.[14]

## THE UNION ORGANIZER

In 1935, her marriage was in shambles. Luisa was working many hours and trying to raise a child as a single mother. Miguel had left the home since Mytyl was three. She had met a new love, Gray Bemis, a New York cab driver and fellow communist who shared her views much better than Miguel.[15] Luisa, with child and Gray Bemis, left by bus to Florida. She began working for the American Federation of Labor (AFL), doing labor organizing in Florida and other Southern states such as Louisiana and Texas. In Florida, she legally changed her name to Luisa Moreno. After being disillusioned with the AFL bosses who watered down a negotiated settlement of a strike into a "sweetheart contract" to please the employer, she protested and agitated against ratification. She argued the sweetheart deal was nothing more than the selling out of the workers; and, as retaliation the AFL leadership ordered her transferred to Pennsylvania. She refused the reassignment and quit the AFL. In 1937, Luisa then joined the Congress of Industrial Organizations (CIO). She also finalized her divorce from Miguel Angel De Leon on October 6, 1937, in New York.[16] Shortly after, the threesome, Luisa, Mytyl, and Gray, moved to San Diego, California. In 1938, she began organizing workers for the CIO's newly formed United Cannery Agricultural Packing and Allied Workers of America (UCAPAWA). She became allied with Roberto Galvan, Ernesto Galarza, and Bert Corona, all working for similar interests in the state, laborers in the fields, sheds, and canneries of Mexican origin. Her organizing work led to her being appointed to the CIO's Labor Council, the first Latina to reach such a top position in labor union circles. In this position, she met the infamous labor leader of the International Longshoremen's Association (ILA), Alfred Renton "Harry" Bridges. For over twenty years, the FBI and the Immigration and Naturalization Service (INS) unsuccessfully sought to deport him from the United States.[17] The CIO did not merge with her despised AFL until 1955, so she had little interference from that quarter.[18] The same fate was meted out to Roberto Galvan. His family had fled the Mexican Revolution and arrived in San Diego, California, on March 13, 1918.

From 1938 to 1952, he worked for the ILA under Bridges' leadership and in the *Congreso de Pueblos de Habla Espanol* with Luisa Moreno. Like her, he had joined the CPUSA in 1944 only to quit by 1947. Many ethnic and racial minorities had joined the CPUSA only to quit over lack of support and protection of them as was the case for white members. He was incarcerated in Terminal Island like Luisa facing deportation. In 1954, he finally was deported. He walked across the border into Tijuana, Baja California and died four years later, May 12, 1958, from kidney and liver failure due to cancer.[19]

Eventually, Gray and Luisa built a home in the *Encanto* area of San Diego where the sign above their front door read: "We are created to serve others. The sad thing is we die only for ourselves." The FBI eager to keep track of her not just in public but on her personal activities at home recruited her gardener, a fellow only reported as "Manuel," to spy on her. She found him out and he confessed to be instructed to spy on her in exchange for his relatives being allowed to become US citizens.[20] Manuel, who was functionally bilingual, had looked at her collection of books, many on Marxism and Leninism; her writings and subscriptions, including *The Daily Worker*; and to report on her circle of friends, drinking, loud parties, and foreign magazines. Manuel told her the FBI had also "interviewed her neighbors and close acquaintances. The FBI agents in San Diego had asked them what kind of automobile she drove and if she was living beyond her means."[21]

Much like the mass deportations of Mexicans during the Depression, another wave of anti-Mexican hysteria hit Southern California the summer of 1943, June. Mexican youth wearing a distinctive style of clothing called Zoot Suits became the targets of violence of both police, military and civilian, and sailors, soldiers, and area Anglos, particularly member of the Ku Klux Klan. Luisa Moreno gravitated to the defense of the Mexican youth under attack and several dozen charged with murder that became known as the Sleepy Lagoon case. Carey McWilliams also joined in the defense of the Zoot Suiters and met Luisa Moreno. McWilliams was the chair of "the Sleepy Lagoon Defense Committee." McWilliams became a lifelong target for harassment by Hoover's FBI, the LAPD, and other anti-Mexican xenophobes. FBI Director "Hoover put him on the Custodial Detention list," like he had done with Luisa Moreno. California State Senator "Jack Tenney hauled him before the Committee on Un-American Activities" in California to ask if he was a Communist and in favor of interracial marriage.[22]

## THE COMMUNIST PARTY USA COINTELPRO

In 1932, Franklin Delano Roosevelt, a Democrat, succeeded Herbert Hoover in the White House. The only unchanged appointment of the new administration was that of FBI Director, J. Edgar Hoover, unrelated to the former president. Director Hoover was now in his eighth year as the second in command at the Bureau of Investigation and became head of the newly named Federal Bureau of Investigation (FBI) in 1935. In the last year of the first term, President Roosevelt met with FBI Director Hoover to discuss extremist organizations in the United States. Hoover singled out labor unions as part of communist elements, particularly the West Coast Longshoreman's union among other labor organizations, and within the US government in the National Labor Relations Board. The president summoned his secretary of state, Cordell Hull and FBI Director Hoover on August 25, 1936, to inform them he wanted a secret operation to be run by the FBI "to begin a systematic survey of subversive activities in the country," provided Secretary Hull was in accord. He was. Besides these three men, no one, not even the US attorney general, ostensibly Hoover's direct boss, knew that seeds for spying on Americans had been planted.[23] The harvest of this planting began with the initiation of the FBI's first COINTELPRO operation, the code name for the counter-intelligence activities of the FBI. In late September 1936, Hoover issued his first national directive to all FBI agents in the field according to James K. Davis on this new activity:

> Obtain from all possible sources information concerning subversive activities being conducted in the United States by communists, fascist representatives, or advocates of other organizations or groups advocating the overthrow of the Government of the United States by illegal methods.[24]

Hoover also created a new division within the FBI, the General Intelligence Section, and two new indexes: Security Index for persons to be detained in case of a national emergency and the Communist Index to include all known members of the CPUSA anywhere. In 1945, the CPUSA's membership reached perhaps 85,000 members; many FBI informants and one-third others were members of the CIO and other unions.[25] Luisa Moreno, as a member of the CPUSA since the 1930s, was now in the crosshairs of the FBI's target gun and entered in the Indexes.

## THE FBI FILE ON LUISA MORENO: NUMBER 100-50025

The San Antonio FBI office file number 100-789 dated October 23, 1941, filed by William A. Godfrey as an Internal Security (R) matter on "Luise Morena Lopez w.a., Louise Lopez, C. Frank" is the first document in the total received from the FBI based on my Freedom of Information Act (FOIA) request. The last document in the file received is dated April 25, 1956, a total period of fifteen and a half years of surveillance of a labor organizer.

This first four-page report of surveillance to be analyzed covered the period May 14–August 14, 1941. Not only is the name of the target under surveillance wrong except for the "Lopez" portion but also it is based on erroneous information supplied by a "Confidential Informant" [name redacted], who

> has advised Subject born in Mexico; active in the Communist Party . . . has continued to do organizational work for Communist Party. She arrived in San Antonio during the latter part of February, 1938 and has remained here continuously since that time. She was sent to San Antonio, Texas from the Communist Party Training School in New York City. (p.1)

The report also lists various affiliations of the Subject such as Workers Alliance, Pecan Shellers Union, Local #172, United Cannery, Agriculture, Packing & Allied Workers Union, CIO, San Antonio Industrial Council, secretary for Non-Citizens Committee of the Southwest, and organizational secretary of the Mexican Soughwest [*sic*] Political Buro, a committee of the Communist Party.

On June 28, 1941, she was sent to Los Angeles, California, following a meeting of the National Executive Committee of the Communist Party. The description of the Subject provided by the Confidential Informant in this report is as follows:

Age: About 30
Height 5'7"
Weight 110
Build Slender
Complexion Brunet
Eyes Brown
Hair Dark Brown
Education Speaks both English and Spanish fluently. She is well
    versed in Party methods of organizational work and has practical
    experience in Party methods of conspiratorial work. (p.2)

On page 3 of this report, the Confidential Informant is reported to have stated the Subject was born in Mexico to well-to-do parents and educated in Mexico City. She had married a person known as MORENO. She has a thirteen-year-old daughter living with her in San Antonio who is known as MITEL or MYTEL MORENO. The final page of the report contains the information on the future action to be taken by the San Antonio FBI field office. They are going to "conduct appropriate investigation in Subject's neighborhood for the purpose of obtaining sufficient information to racommend [*sic*] Subject for custodial detention" (p.4).

Almost a year later, on January 20, 1943, the San Antonio office filed a second report, three pages, covering the period of December 7, 1942, through January 14, 1943. The agent reporting was Thomas Ryan Walsh. The case was now characterized as "Internal Security-C; Custodial Detention." Apparently, sometime in between the prior report and this one a decision was made based on the wrong information supplied by the Confidential Informant and therefore a flawed survey about her residence in San Antonio. She was now listed and included in the Custodial Detention Index. In this report, her name is changed to "Louisa Morena Lopez, w.a.s. Louisa Lopez, C. Frank." The main thrust of the report is that "Investigation fails to determine subjects present whereabouts" (p.1). All those interviewed, which included some names redacted were Bexar County Sheriff Owen Kilday, midwife San Juana Flores, target of San Antonio file 101-9 James Sagar, Monsignor Thomas Moczygemba of St. Michael's Church, Sister Superior of St. Michael's Academy, Leonille, could not provide any information on her current whereabouts or activities in San Antonio (p.2). The report closed with information on checking with the Los Angeles Field Division as to her residence in that area (p.3).

The errors in their information should have come to light with the next one-page report filed by Vaughn I. Parry in the Los Angeles FBI office on January 28, 1943. Basically, Agent Parry wrote, "The files of the Los Angeles Field Division fail to reflect any information concerning the subject of this case." The name they searched for was "Louisa Morena Lopez." Nine months later, on September 16, 1943, a three-page report covering the period for the week of July 26–30, 1943, prepared by Hubert H. Finkel of the New York City FBI office pointed out other discrepancies. His informant stated the Subject name was Maria Perez and her alias was Louisa Morena; that she was only 5'1" tall, not 5'7", as reported by the San Antonio FBI office (p.3). New York FBI, utilizing an open source from the CPUSA, *The Daily Worker* newspaper, dated December 7, 1940, on page 5, had identified Louisa Morena [*sic*] as a CIO organizer from California known as *La Pasionaria* and director of the Spanish-speaking section of the CIO in attendance in Chicago, Illinois, on December 6, the previous day. She reportedly spoke on organizing an agricultural union for the canning industry (p.1). New York also added more speculation to the search by insisting based on his informant's tale that Maria Perez was Louisa Morena [*sic*] an organizer for the Communist Party who had been in Tampa, Florida, during the latter part of 1939 and in San Antonio, Texas, that same year working with pecan shellers. The informant also reported that she was the mistress of George Mink, a Mexican communist agitator. New York FBI pointed out that the FBI director on April 22, 1941, had a letter telling him that Mink had just returned from Tampico, Mexico, via San Antonio to pick up Maria Perez, "his mistress and paramour, and three other persons." The five were headed to Chicago or Detroit for a meeting. Other communists, some sixty-seven, including New York's Nancy Reed would be attending. New York FBI asked Gus Bkich of the Motor Vehicle Bureau of New York to check on names of operators and automobile owners under names of Louisa Lopez, Louisa Morena, and Maria Perez, with "negative results" (p.2).

The new year, 1944, began with a final and sizeable eighteen-page report from James Wimason, Los Angeles FBI, dated January 20, 1944, covering period of November 8, 1943, through January 8, 1944. Agent Wimason gave Luisa Moreno a new alias, Rose Rodriguez De Shaffer, in the tile of his report. He also gave a synopsis of facts, some correct others questionable. Agent Wimason states that the Subject was born in Guatemala City on August 30, 1907, and came to the United States in August 25, 1927, and later applied for naturalization papers in New York City. She married Jacob Shaffer in New York, a known communist member. She was married preciously in Mexico, but that marriage was annulled, and she also is divorced from Shaffer. One child was born November 8, 1928, in Brooklyn, New York (p.1). The marriage to Shaffer is not reported in any other source I consulted. The divorce is recorded, nothing on the annulment was found by this author.

The report synopsis traces her involvement with the CPUSA from consorting with known Communists, Shaffer an alleged husband, attending the Worker's Training School in New York from 1938 to 1939, Communist educational program and organizational work in San Antonio, Texas, union representative for UCAPAWA local 172 in San Antonio (p.1), attended national UCAPAWA Convention as representative of local 273, New York City, and since 1941 was UCAPAWA's international representative in Los Angeles area. Her Los Angeles address was listed as 1120 ½ West 47th Street with offices in the CIO building on 5851 Avalon Boulevard. She is a vice president of California States CIO Industrial Union Council. She has been involved with communist front organizations such as National Federation of Constitutional Liberties, Citizens Committee for Defense of Mexican Youth, and the Congress of Spanish Speaking Peoples. She subscribes to *The Daily Worker* and *The People's World*. She has been at meetings of the CIO where communist speakers such as Carl Winter, have made presentations. Winter is the secretary of the Los Angeles Communist Party. She speaks Spanish and English fluently and writes a column for the UCAPAWA News and recently attended the Communist inspired Writer's Congress at UCLA. She does not have a criminal record. "Subject in this case has been designated as a key figure in the Los Angeles County Communist Party" (p.2). The conclusion reached with this designation justified the surveillance for the next fifteen years from 1941 to April 25, 1956, which are documented here. She never had a criminal record nor committed any crime. She was deported from the United States but left the country on her own to Mexico then Cuba than back to Guatemala. She was placed under surveillance for her labor organizing and political views, which varied over time.

The Subject was under surveillance by the FBI, their informants, and other persons the FBI contacted such as neighbors and school personnel where her daughter attended. Luisa Moreno drove a 1936 Dodge coupe with California plates, 1Q1816, owned and registered under the name of Rose Shaffer whose address was 5205 Beverly Boulevard, as of January 25, 1943. This is the address the FBI found for Jacob Shaffer with various aliases as Jake Shaffer, Jacob Schaffert, Yankel Shuffer, Jankel Schuffer, and Jack Shaffer. He is the subject of a Security Matter-C investigation (p.3). An informant, Source A, reported Subject admitted to using the pen name of Luisa Moreno for a number of years. School officials at John Muir High School at 5929 South Vermont Avenue revealed the daughter was registered as Mytyl Lorraine Moreno and that her mother was Louise Moreno. Source A described her to the FBI as born in Guatemala City, Guatemala, married, white race, five feet two inches, ninety-six pounds, dark-brown hair, dark eyes and dark complexion, and her appearance was "Definite Spanish or Mexican appearance" (p.4). Prior informants have her as light-skinned, short 5′ frame at 90–110 pounds. The subsequent pages from 5 to 7 contain information repeated in earlier pages but for two items. On page 6, this statement is found: "Sheriff Owen Kilday, Bexar County, San Antonio, advised that since the raid conducted by the Sheriff's office on the Workers' School conducted by the San Antonio Communists in 1938, he had no information concerning the subject and believed she left town." This information was previously reported but this agent is stating it as if he personally learned it from the Sheriff. He does not reference any other report for this source of information. The second piece is very tempting for researchers in this area: On October 2, 1942, a confidential source informed of a meeting to be held in Los Angeles. "Motion pictures of persons attending this meeting were made by Special Agents of this field division. Individual observed coming to and going from this meeting were identified by Agents as being largely composed of local Communists. Among these individuals were . . . also observed at this meeting was LUISA MORENO" (p.7). Not only did they finally get her new legal name correct for the first time, she is on film somewhere in the national archives. On page 8 of this report, Harry Bridges, the head of the Longshoremen's Union and of the CIO, is referred to as "known Communist leaders." Similarly, Carey McWilliams, the scholar, is referred to as "an alleged Communist." By inference and innuendo, because her photo or mention is made in various labor and Communist Party publications, Luisa Moreno continues to be deemed a communist (p.8). The US Post Office in

Los Angeles by letter to Director Hoover, who had ordered a mail stop on her correspondence confirmed that Luisa Moreno Welch and Josefina Fierro received mail at a box rented under the name of the Congress of Spanish Speaking People, "Bright and Welch are both regarded as Communists" (p.9). The surname Welch is not reported in any other source for Luisa Moreno. On pages 10 through 13, a list of informants used as sources of information on Luisa Moreno are identified by letters running from A to V, a total of twenty-two plus four more identified by name, a landlord, postal carrier, columnists, and neighbor. These sources reported on mentions and photos found in other publications and newspapers including *The Peoples World* and *The Daily Worker*.

The FBI placed a mail cover to examine all her correspondence beginning November 18, 1943, at the 47th Street address; six items of interest are listed (p.13). The FBI also investigated whether the Subject had sought to register and vote in California elections; she had not (p.14).

Luisa Moreno had left her home country as a teenager only to spend more time outside her mother land than inside. She was in the United States from 1928 to 1950 before facing deportation. The FBI investigated her daughter's birth certificate records in New York; her filing for naturalization in Philadelphia (p.15) and San Antonio (p.16); and listed all the reports from various FBI field offices on the Subject (p.17–18). Hoover must have been pleased with the LA Special Agent for such a comprehensive report and compilation of sources and prior reports on Luisa Moreno. The following month Philadelphia Special Agent Ward Wight, Jr., followed up with a five-page report to FBI Director Hoover dated February 16, 1944, in which he provided the results of their investigation on the Subject. Philadelphia FBI field office named her Rose Rodriguez De Shaffer, with fifteen more aliases (p.1). It never occurred to the FBI, apparently, to investigate the use of a pseudonym used in her writings dating to her teen years in Guatemala. If she was Rodriguez Lopez then and became De Leon when first married in Mexico, where did the Luisa Moreno name come from? Director Hoover had a quick answer; she was devious and cunning attempting to hide her identity. If this had been the case, why did she keep making her writings public under Luisa Moreno once in the United States and allow photos of her image in various publications?

Philadelphia FBI confirmed she had entered the United States and provided all pertinent details to Immigration and Naturalization Service upon arrival into the Port of New York on April 27, 1928, aboard the *SS Monterey*:

> She was 20 years old-born August 3, 1907, at Guatemala City, New Mexico. Her residence for the past five years were given as: Guatemala, from birth to 1916; United States, from 1916 to 1920; Guatemala from 1920 to 1925;

Mexico from 1925 to 1928. Her mother was listed as Alicia Lopez de Macias, of Guatemala City; father deceased. Her husband was stated to be Miguel Angel De Leon, who was born at San Francisco, Zapotitlan, Guatemala, and would accompany her to the United States. A copy of her marriage certificate in Spanish is attached to the visa. Her purpose in coming to the United States was stated to be to reside indefinitely. (p.2)

Other than placing Guatemala City in the US state of New Mexico and omitting a "0" to the "3" after August for the correct birthdate of August 30, all else seems correctly verified in other sources on Luisa Moreno. There is a possibility that Luisa Moreno lied, but not likely, and these two items were not a typing error by the INS clerk or the FBI Special Agent. She was repeatedly forthcoming will all other details even listed her various names depending on marital status and use of her translated pseudonym as in Louise for Luisa, Moreno.

In Los Angeles, according to Philadelphia's investigation, on December 23, 1940, she registered as an "alien" under the folder #5761930 under the name Rosa Rodriguez Lopez, the same name she used when she entered the United States in New York. She also provided that "she was also known as Louise De Leon, Luisa De Leon, Rode De Leon, Louise Lopez Moreno, Louise Luisa Moreno." She "applied for U.S. citizenship on July 21, 1937 and her first papers were received October 20, 1937, #403306, at New York City." She also provided information on her criminal record as follows: "was arrested once for picketing in 1930 at New York, sentence suspended, and again in 1938 at San Antonio, Texas-offense unknown-released" (p.3). FBI Philadelphia also reported that the Subject submitted change of address forms to the INS authorities regularly under the name of Rose Rodriguez Lopez, no less than five times between January 7, 1941, and September 30, 1943 (p.4).

The March 7, 1944, report of six pages to Director Hoover from Los Angeles Special Agent James W. Mason provides new information on Luisa Moreno's activities in that Field Division. She was active in promoting subsides and right to vote for soldiers; writing column on the Sleepy Lagoon case; provisional chair of the CIO's Spanish-Speaking Committee, assisted in the UAW CIO Douglas Aircraft drive; promotion of vice-president [Henry] Wallace's visit to Los Angeles, and "received a letter from Carol Winter, New York defense attorney for Harry Bridges." And, that she had a new alias that of Maria Perez; "ascertained as a Key Figure in the Los Angeles Communist Party" (p.1). The next three pages summarize her organizing goals in two aircraft plants, the California citrus workers, and support for President Roosevelt's five-point program for recovery from the Depression. The mail cover imposed on her correspondence lists the intercepted items and photographs of her are the subject matter in page 4, while last page is entirely redacted but for that it contains information from two sources, A and B.

The two-page report from San Antonio, Texas, to the FBI director dated April 26, 1944, is too unintelligible to read. For some reason, many of the first pages disclosed from inception to the first few years are black background with white letters as opposed to white background with black letters. There are but a few pages composed on the latter style. Continuing with a four-page report from New York filed June 1, 1944, by Special Agent Edwin O. Haudsep to the FBI director, it concerns no birth records found on the daughter of Rose Rodriguez De Shaffer or aliases. The FBI New York office checked with five boroughs for any records between 1928 and 1929 (p.1) without success. Informants T-1 and T-2 plus the Special Squad #1, Alien Squad New York Police Department, New York Confidential Informants, all reported "they never heard of the subject under any of her known names or aliases as having resided" at the addresses the FBI provided. The FBI interviewed Mrs. Matthew Barkley, manager of the building owned by Carol King, the attorney for Harry Bridges. She stated that "no people of Spanish descent or Spanish appearance had ever resided there during the past twenty-five years" (p.2). Most peculiar was the disclosure on the last page of the actual names without redaction of informants identified earlier as T-1 and T-2 as being Hyman Hutkin, the post man, and John Morrigon, another postman (p.4).

On June 2, 1944, a five-page report from Los Angeles Special Agent George H. Scatterday to FBI director dealt with Rose Rodriguez De Shaffer attending a meeting with "certain leading Communist Party functionaries, including Carl Winter, Max Silver, Pettis Perry, George Sandy, Henry Steinberg, and Arturo Mata" on March 25, 1944, according to Source A (p.1). The main topic of discussion, according to the informants, Source B was also present, was where to send Arturo Mata to organize (p.2). Source B added a counter-argument to Luisa Moreno's communist ties. He said that she "does not have the usual books, pamphlets, and other papers which are usually maintained by active Communist Party members." She did have material on her about the People's Educational Center and her membership card to the Writers' Congress "under the name of Luisa Moreno." The FBI Special Agent preparer of this report closes this portion with these words: "It should be noted that the Writers' Congress is a Communist sponsored organization which recently met on the campus of the University of California at Los Angeles, and that the People's Educational Center is a direct outgrowth of the Writers' Congress" (p.3). The mail cover continues in place (p.4) and the identities of the informant sources, A and B are redacted (p.5).

The next four-page report from Special Agent George H. Scatterday to the FBI director, dated August 8, 1944, on Rose Rodriguez De Shaffer is about her organizing Mexican women citrus workers in the Fullerton, California area. She was now a member of the State CIO Council, Minorities Committee, and representing the UCAPAWA-CIO. An article in *The Labor Herald* of July 7, 1944, listed her in those capacities above and using the name of Louisa Morena (p.1). Oddly, two months prior in another article in the same newspaper on her she was listed as using the correct spelling of her name, Luisa Moreno, and her new nick name "Woman Dynamo." She was also credited with winning an election to certify UCAPAWA as the union of choice by the workers, 25 to 12. The mail cover in place reported on several pieces of mail received by Luisa Moreno (p.2). The last pages, 3 and 4, are almost entirely redacted and without any important content on Luisa Moreno.

Special Agent Scatterday of the Los Angeles Field office, in a four-page report on Rose Rodriguez de Shaffer with aliases, fourteen listed, to the FBI Director dated October 11, 1944, reported that the Subject had a kidney operation according to a story in *The Labor Herald*, a CIO newspaper, from August 4, 1944 (p.1). Source A is reported to have informed FBI Los Angeles that Luisa had been successful in signing a contract between UCAPAWA and the California Walnut Growers Association for the crop season of 1944. Source B reported hearsay between two men about her organizing work and one man, Max Silver, said he did not have faith in her ability to organize anyone (p.2). Los Angeles will coordinate with San Diego to verify this information given it is outside their Division; however, Scatterday nailed the Communist coffin shut with these last words: "Subject has been a member of the Communist Party for several years, has attended Workers School, and is presently an International Vice President of the UCAPAWA" (p.3). The identity of sources, A and B, is redacted (p.4).

The last report for the year is three pages long dated December 9 from Special Agent Edward J. Kirby from the FBI San Diego Field Office. He also still used the name of Rose Rodriguez de Shaffer, w.a.s. for the name of the Subject despite the FBI knowing already she went by Luisa Moreno. The content is on UCAPAWA's failure to organize the citrus workers in the Fullerton area, according to Charlene Barrett, Secretary of the Associated Farmers. Since then both the UCAPAWA and "the Subject departed Orange County for Los Angeles with the Union officials" (p.1). Confidential informant T-1 reported the same information as had been provided by Charlene Barrett. Confidential informant T-2 provided a thriller story to Special Agent Kirby which he reported without comment. This snippet could be made into a movie:

> On October 12, 1944, Confidential Informant T-2 advised that on October 10, 1944, he had boarded the California Limited Railroad Train at Kansas City, Missouri and had met one Louisa Moreno, probably identical with the Subject.

This Source stated that he became friendly with the Subject and in the course of her conversation she revealed the following information: She had married an Austrian Geologist in Europe when very young, had traveled with him all over the world and had escaped France through Casa Blanca. She stated she was a Communist and believed that the people should take over stores and businesses. She further stated that she was traveling from Chicago to Los Angeles and from there she would go to Caliente, Mexico, to deliver some important papers and from there to Havana, Cuba, which she called the Key to South America. Subject stated that the papers she was to deliver was carried in a locket that she wore around her neck and that the message was so concealed that it was necessary to use chemicals to bring it out. When questioned regarding such a paper into Mexico she said that it would not be noticed in the locket. This Source described the Locket as Heart Shape, 1" long, gold in color and hanging from a gold chain from which also hung a silver metal of some Saint. Subject at the time was accompanied by a three year old boy named Richard, who also wore a locket on a gold chain (p.2). These informant's identities are redacted. (p.3)

George H. Scatterday, special agent in the FBI Los Angeles Division, submitted his January 2, 1945, report, four pages, to FBI Director Hoover. It contained nothing new, just repeats of prior erroneous and hasty assumptions leading to false conclusions. A major one was that any labor leader or person in support of worker rights was a communist. A second one is that anyone being in support or defending Mexicans was un-American and possible subversive. Luisa and most of her friends, coworkers, superiors, and union leaders were among those ascertained to be communists. Scatterday shares with Hoover, the appearances of Luisa Moreno, articles and photographs, in labor newspapers (p.1–2) and that she would be "in attendance at the National CIO Convention in Chicago" and then "to Philadelphia to attend the UCAPAWA Convention as a representative of Local No. 3 at Los Angeles (p.2). On page 3, Scatterday writes, "will continue to follow and report on subject's Communist activities" and then the name of the source for the information, but entirely redacted (p.4). Special Agent Scatterday on July 5, 1945, filed another four-page report with sources redacted (p.4) and the usual promise to "continue to follow and report on subject's Communist activities in this field division" (p.3). The first two pages relate her new position as Director of California-Arizona Regional Council FTA (Food, Tobacco, Agricultural and Allied Workers of America-CIO).

New York, Special Agent Francis D. O'Brien on August 8, 1945, filed a four-page report to FBI Director Hoover on "Louisa Moreno, w.a.s. Louisa Marcolito, Louisa Marcel"; these being new aliases attached to Luisa Moreno. O'Brien went checking into the name of Louise Moreno as a geologist for Shell Oil Company. He did not find anyone with that name in the US operations but did find two by that name "outside of the United States." Agent O'Brien learned that no one with name of "Moreno, Marcolito, and Marcel" was employed by the Shell Oil Company as a geologist. Ralph G. Harder, Shell Oil Company manager of Tax and Compensation Division, that Agent O'Brien consulted found "no such payment had been made" as a result "of the sinking of any ship" mainly because the company does not own any of their own ships (p.1). Harder advised O'Brien to check with their San Francisco office. This inquiry was a follow-up to the alleged conversation between FBI informants and someone purporting to be Luisa Moreno traveling by train and stating she was married to a geologist; see above conversation of October 12, 1944. It turns out the informants were "two U.S. Army Lieutenants" (p.2) and the alleged husband, a geologist for the Shell Oil Company, had been killed while on a ship and she had been paid $5000 insurance (p.3). San Francisco FBI was asked to look into this matter and did. Lee M. Fallan, Special Agent, in a solo page filed October 2, 1945 confirmed "there is no record of any person with a name similar to that of the subject, under either of the three names, being employed or having been employed by the Shell Oil Company" (p.1). The last communication of 1945 is dated December 14, 1945, three pages, prepared by Special Agent George H. Scatterday in which he states having read all reports and "failed to reflect any Communist activity on the part of the subject since July of 1945," however, a source did indicate the subject had attended a meeting of the Board of Directors of the Public Labor School in San Francisco (p.1). The list of reports reviewed are on page 2 and the source information is redacted on page 3.

Only one three-page report was released for 1946 dated September 26 and filed by Special Agent Donald Wiberg Kuno on "Rose Rodriguez De Shaffer, w.a.s. Subject reported to be in contact with known Communists in San Francisco. Was elected vice president of California State CIO Council 12/11.45. Continues to reside at 156 North 5th Street, San Jose, California." This is news. According to all sources referenced in this chapter, none indicate she ever lived in San Jose, California. Supposedly, she was "conducting an organizing drive among cannery workers in the state, and the subject at that time was doing organizing work at San Jose, California (p.1). The information supplied by four different informants had her in attendance at the State CIO Convention, her appointments that never occurred with Dave Jenkins, "prominent Communist head of the California Labor School in San Francisco" and that "Aubrey Grossman, Public Relations Officer of the Communist Party in San Francisco, was desirous of having a luncheon engagement with the subject." One interesting comment made by a source was that the Subject had "criticized the People's World' for 'overplaying certain matters'" (p.2). The last page's wording is vague, unclear, and confusing: "Will attempt to develop admissible evidence of subject's affiliations and sympathies." Does this mean verify and corroborate the information supplied by the informant just cited or that the Subject is a Communist member or that more concrete "legally admissible" evidence is needed to make a criminal or civil case against her? What is known is that the US House of Representatives created the House Un-American Activities Committee (HUAC) in 1938 and lasted until 1975. A member of HUAC was Richard M. Nixon. HUAC was very busy calling witnesses and following up with prosecutions against those who lied in their testimony as was the sensational case of Whittaker Chambers. In 1948, Chambers' testimony before HUAC led to Alger Hiss being summoned and questioned. His subsequent conviction during a second trial got him a sentence of forty-four months at the Lewisburg Federal Penitentiary until 1954.[26]

Luisa Moreno was deemed a Communist and under full investigation by the FBI during these same years. On June 19, 1947, the SAC, San Francisco wrote a one-page memo to the SAC, San Diego alerting him that "Rose De Shaffer, presently using the name Luisa Mareno, [*sic*] married Gray Bemis on February 1, 1947, at Yuma, Arizona, and at the present time is with BEMIS in San Diego, where he is employed by the Plumbing Supply Company, 735 Bank of America Building." The SAC, San Francisco requested "that efforts be made to determine subject's present residence address . . . and the usual sources of information ascertain subject's Communist activities." SAC, San Diego responded with a one-page memo dated August 18, 1947, that "GRAY DAYTON BEMIS, the subject's husband is the local manager for the Consolidated Pipe and Supply Company . . . and subject and her husband recently moved into a new apartment located at 2230 Abbott Street San Diego, California." More importantly, the last paragraph is worth quoting entirely:

> Confidential informants [redacted] and [redacted] advised that neither the subject nor her husband has recontacted local Communist members in San Diego. [Redacted] who was well acquainted with BEMIS, advises that most of their former friends have left San Diego and that the party leaders had also changed during BEMIS's absence. This informant will advise the San Diego Office if either the subject or her husband takes any steps to become associated with the local Communist group.

There is another one-page letter dated September 14, 1947, from Special Agent W. H. Dettekiles. Jr. (name and entire letter are not legible). It also does not have an addressee or title of case other than a heading of "Re: CP-USA Internal Security-C" and the content has to do with some meeting held on September 12 involving eleven persons all whom have FBI files on them and are listed at bottom left of letter. The names of Bemis or Luisa do not appear on the letter.

On September 29, 1947, two transmissions were sent to Director Hoover from the San Francisco office. The first correspondence is from Harry M. Kimball at 422-Federal Office Building, Civic Center, San Francisco, California, about Rose Rodriguez Bemis, w.a.s. Security Matter-C Bureau File 100-50025 and San Diego File 100-6610. The form letter, two pages, simply lists the aliases they have on file in the Security Index for the subject beginning now with Rose Rodriguez Bemis and Mrs. Gray Dayton Bemis plus sixteen more and her San Diego address on Abbott Street. The form letter closes with a listing of all ten reports they have on file and the notice that: "In view of the fact that the San Diego Field Division has verified the present residence of the subject in its Division, this office is considering San Diego as the new office of origin, and this case is being RUC's to that office with the submission of this communication" (p.1). The last page lists eight enclosures which are photostatic copies of reports from various special agents across the country. The second correspondence is from Special Agent Donald W. Kuno, also a two-page report to FBI Director Hoover, in which he repeats the news that Luisa Moreno has married Gray Bemis and they live at the Abbott address. However, in the Synopsis of Facts, the Communist charge resurfaces with this additional language: "On August 7, 1946 (this is a year earlier) WILLIAM SCHNEIDERMAN, California Communist Party Chairman, and ARCHIE BROWN, Communist Party Labor Director, stated that subject was a Communist and was entitled to attend closed Communist Party meetings." And the last page repeats that neither Moreno of Bemis have recontacted any Communist Party members in San Diego. Moreover, it relates a hearsay conversation supplied by two informants [names redacted] between two other Communist Party leaders about inviting Luisa Moreno to a closed meeting of the California CP and "become known as a Communist Party member." Ultimately, the memo states: "They compromised on the matter by stating that they would not send LUISA MORENO an invitation to attend the meeting but that in case she arrived at the meeting place, she would be allowed to attend." How was she supposed to know about any CP meeting in San Francisco if she was not by the FBI agents in San Diego's own admission not in contact with any CP members and was not going to be specifically invited?

Beginning in 1947, copies of a postcard-type report about the Mail Cover put in place at Director Hoover's request back in 1943, began to be included in the documents released to this author. The first such postcard-type report is dated October 12, 1947. It now also includes "RE: Gray Bemis" and informs on a letter "Postmarked: Guatemala, C.A. Date: 10 x 49 From: G.M.A., G/C/P/ no. 82 Guatemala To: Mrs. Gray Bemis, P.O. Box 917 Encanto Sta. San Diego 14, Calif. Dbry Carrier." Two more such postcard-type reports dated "3/18" reporting the subject does receive mail at 2230 Abbott Street, San Diego and another on "9/1948) reporting on a photograph of subject-Louisa Bemis" being delivered.

## THE CASE OF PEDRO J. GONZALEZ

A decade earlier than the FBI and local law enforcement witch hunt aimed at Luisa Moreno and other labor activists of Mexican origin had a radio personality as the target. His crime was immense popularity, singing and broadcasting in Spanish, and ability to persuade his listeners to take social action. Beginning shortly after the raid on Columbus, New Mexico, by Francisco "Pancho" Villa, the Mexican revolutionary, in March 1916, Pedro J. Gonzalez, a messenger for Villa, deserted. He took his family and fled to Juarez, Chihuahua, and eventually made it to Los Angeles, California. Within a decade, by 1929, he had a two-hour radio program on radio station KELW, own musical band, Los Madrugadores, and a growing business featuring his recordings, jingles, and broadcasting. His dawn-breaking show like the name of his band broadcast from 4 a.m. to 6 a.m. each week-day mornings. His show was heard all over the Los Angeles area, southern California, and northern Mexico. His popularity grew to such an extent that the Los Angeles District Attorney, Buron Fitts, The DA was concerned with the amount of influence Gonzalez had over the Mexican population. He sought to have his broadcast license revoked and failed. He tried to have *Los Madrugadores* show cancelled and failed. Ultimately the DA charged Pedro with several made-up crimes; first a delinquency charge for not sending his daughter to school which was dismissed; second on a kidnapping charge which also was dismissed; third with transporting minors which was also dismissed; and, finally with having sex with two underage girls. An all-white jury found him guilty. The judge sentenced Pedro Gonzalez to fifty years in prison on March 20, 1934. Several times the DA had offered him a plea deal if he would admit to the crime and self-deport. He refused each time. Years later, one of the girls, Dora Versus, later recanted and said she was pressured by the DA to make up the story, but the trial judge refused to accept her affidavit and re-try the case. By 1936, more Mexicans were in the Los Angeles city jail than non-Mexicans. In 1939, the parole board agreed to release him if he accepted deportation to Mexico which he did.[27]

## THE CALIFORNIA SENATE FACT-FINDING COMMITTEE ON UN-AMERICAN ACTIVITIES HEARINGS

The INS office in San Diego reported by one-page letter dated June 6, 1948, and signed by U.L. Press, Officer in Charge, to the FBI San Diego office [no name provided, instead it reads "Gentlemen:"] that they had "under investigation," file 246-P-131334, "one "Rosa Rodriguez Lopez Shaffer, alias

Louise Moreno, your file No. 10-25401. She has been active in many labor activities." The local INS wanted to know if the local FBI had any objection to their continuing investigation "looking towards the possible institution of deportation proceeding under the Act of October 16, 1918, as amended."[28]

During September 8–10, 1948, the state equivalent of the US House Committee on Un American Activities held hearings in San Diego, California; day before they had concluded similar hearings in Los Angeles. A witness called for the first morning of this hearing was "Louisa Moreno Bemis." A nineteen-page report on the hearing was prepared by Special Agent Miles A. Johnsen for the SAC, San Diego and dated November 15, 1948. The opening sentence of the first page refers to "a memorandum received from [name redacted] on November 6, 1948, which is filed as 100-813-876:" and the memorandum then follows. There are two working definitions utilized by those conducting the hearing worth quoting entirely and stated in parenthesis:

(Note: As used in this memorandum, the term "Known Communist Party member" signifies an individual whose membership can be proven in a court of law, although it may not be advisable to make public the evidence at this time. The term "Acknowledged Communist' [*sic*] Party member" indicates that the individual has acknowledged membership in some public manner or had occupied an office in the Party which required public admission of Party membership in order to carry out official duties.)

Subpoenas were served "the morning of Sept. 1, 1948," on many individuals in the San Diego area by "members of the Detective Department of the San Diego Police Department" (p.1). These subpoenas required them to appear before the committee at the San Diego Chamber of Commerce Auditorium on the morning of September 8, 1948." The list of twenty names follows, which includes four Spanish-surnamed persons: Virginia Vera Goodrow, Louisa Moreno Bemis, Robert Norbert Galvan, and Philip Usquiano. There were two persons not served "because they could not be located; two more "Fellow Travelers," a third category not defined in the above Note; and, three more "friendly witnesses," a fourth category not defined in the above Note but defined in the first paragraph that identified "John Quimby" and another, as one in that category. Following all these names, the definition of "friendly witnesses" was stated as those who "had joined the Communist Party and had attended several sessions of a 'Beginners Class' *before he decided that he could not become a Communist. K.G. Bitter is Secretary-Treasurer of* the San Diego Building Trades Council, AFL. Both of these men are very anti-Communist" (p.2).

John T. McTernan, a member of the law firm of Gallagher, Margolis, McTernan and Frye, appeared at the first day's hearing and demanded that he be allowed to represent witnesses and to cross-examine all witnesses and examine all documents submitted to the Committee as evidence. He listed the individuals whom he represented as the following: (p.3)

The names of Robert Galvan and Philip Usquiano were among the twelve names he provided the Committee; not Luisa Moreno or that or Virginia Vera Goodrow. Mr. McTernan was allowed representation of his clients, "However, the Committee denied his demand to be allowed to cross-examine witnesses or to examine documents submitted in evidence" (p.3). The memorandum prepared by the special agent added his own *argumentum ad hominem*:

> Incidentally, McTernan tried to interrupt the proceedings during the hearing of Alva C. Rogers, Sr., on the first day's hearing [in Los Angeles] and was permanently ejected from the auditorium. Thereafter his clients were allowed to leave the auditorium in order to consult him in a consultation room adjoining the auditorium which was made available to McTernan. (p.3)

Virginia Vera Goodrow was called as the fifth witness of the first day (p.5). The next two days of the hearing had all of the remaining Spanish-speaking witnesses called with "LOUISA MORENO BEMIS (known Communist Party member)," who gave her address "and her occupation as a housewife" and admitted to her birth country being "Guatemala." She also admitted to having worked for UCAPAWA in 1944 but "the witness objected to answering" whether or not she did "some organizational work for the UCAPAWA in Orange County In [*sic*] June of 1944." She denied working as an instructor at the California Labor School in 1946 "in spite of the fact that the catalogue for the school for that year had so listed her (p.3). Luisa Moreno Bemis was asked "if she were an alien" which she answered as having "filed for her second papers for citizenship." Then came the killer question: "whether or not she was then or ever had been a member of the Communist Party of the Communist Political Association." But, more *ad hominem* from the reporter, "the witness used the usual Communist Party tactics to avoid an answer and after much discussion the Committee was polled and decided, unanimously, that the witness had refused to answer the question" (p.4).

The next witnesses were Robert Galvan and Phillip [this time spelled with two ll's and elsewhere as simply Phil] Usquino, both identified in the reports as "(known Communist Party member)." Both were questioned, among other issues of interest, if they "were members of the Spanish Speaking Club of the Communist party of San Diego County." Galvan specifically was asked also if he was "an applicant for citizenship" (p.15). Usquiano while on the witness stand testified "he had been born in New Mexico." He had brought an encyclopedia book from which he wanted "to read certain articles" but was "told that he would not be permitted to read anything into the record but that he could cite the reason why he refused to answer questions (p.16). Usquiano tried to argue he be allowed to read from his book but without success. He was asked direct questions as to his role with the "Workers Alliance in 1940" and "active in the Peoples World drive in San Diego County in 1939" and if he had attended the state Communist Party convention" held in "San Francisco on June 27, 1942," and "the witness continued to dodge answering the question." The Committee was "polled and unanimously voted that the witness had refused to answer the question" (p.17).

This concluded the "three day hearing of the Committee." A final note was added to the summary of the hearing proceedings to the effect that

> comparatively little information not already in the hands of the authorities was gained from this hearing, there is not any doubt but that the hearing did much to inform the citizens of San Diego as to the true character of the Communist movement in their county. In addition however the hearings have very badly disrupted the organization of the Party in San Diego County and have interfered materially with their subversive and revolutionary activities. (p.18)

On September 11, 1948, the *San Diego Tribune-Sun* ran a story with two photographs of Luisa Bemis and her testimony before the Committee. The article has no title, author or page number, but is full of descriptive verbiage of her and little on the content of the hearings or her testimony. For example, the description is "Mrs. Bemis wore a black dress, white gloves and her eyes flashed with Latin fire." The caption below one of her photos in the article reads, "Mrs. Luisa Bemis . . . filled with emotion." As to the question about her being an instructor at the California Labor School is the only germ of substance of the proceedings, "Her voice rose in power as she declared: 'I was not an instructor as you carried it in your 'little red book' (Published report of the committee for 1947). Is that clear to you." When she was admonished for not answering the direct question as to Communist Party membership and threatened with "risking the right to become a full-fledged citizen," she replied, according to this article, "Citizenship means a lot to me but the Constitution of the United States means more!"[29]

By November 9, 1948, J. Edgar Hoover is sending to the San Diego FBI office "your file 100-6619" a two-page record of FBI file no. 80 858 A on Louise Moreno/Rosa Rodriguez Lopez, which contains her criminal record for vagrancy in San Antonio, Texas, on April 15, 1938, and alien registration on December 23, 1940 (p.1), and a physical description of her along with aliases and that fingerprint records exist. Photos were not available (p.2).

## MORE MAIL COVERS AND ORDERS OF ARREST

In 1949, the Mail Cover reports continued to arrive into FBI headquarters from the superintendent of mails. Between September 29, 1949, and October 25, 1949, nineteen such reports are among the documents released to this author. The intercepted mail, and I must assume read by the FBI, came to her from Guatemala, San Francisco, Philadelphia, New York, Berkeley, Los Angeles, Worchester, Salinas, Oakland, and San Diego.

On January 24, 1949, Director Hoover requests by form letter the SAC, San Diego update their information on Rose Rodriguez Bemis, was Security Matter-C ["was" does not mean a past tense in this context; it should written with periods as in w.a.s. for "with aliases' stated"]. Hoover's form letter states no report has been had since that from Special Agent "Donald W. Kuno" dated 9-29-47 at San Francisco. Hoover closes with "This matter should receive your immediate attention." Special Agent W. Albert Stewart, Jr., on February 14, 1949, wrote to his SAC, San Diego that the subject continues to live at same address on file. He also states, "All information concerning the above Subject's Communist activities are being channeled to her file, which should be placed in a closed status." There is no explanation for this recommendation because nothing was closed, her case until the deportation order continued.

On March 1, 1949, the SAC, San Diego, F.M. McIntire, by form letter response to Director Hoover informs him that the Security Index card data has been updated on Rose Rodriguez Bemis that was Security Matter-C and lists her new address as 6426 Medio Drive, San Diego, California. Within days, March 3, 1949, the SAC, San Diego receives a one-page letter from the Officer in Charge of an unidentified agency, U.L. Press, that they have a warrant of arrest for Rose Rodriguez de Shaffer and Robert Norbert Galvan. Press wanted to know if the FBI can send an agent to accompany them for service of the arrest warrant at their respective homes instead of waiting for them to come into their office to be served and each post bond of $1,000. Galvan was to report on March 10 at 9:30 a.m. and "Rosa Rodriguez-Lopez Shaffer" on "March 14, 1949 at the same time and place for the same purpose."

The San Diego Police Department had a Confidential Informant, Sergeant Al Gayton, at the hearing and identified as T-1. He corroborated the accuracy of the report just cited above to the FBI office in San Diego. Of course he would; he was the informant. The first page of three of this report dated May 5, 1949, is hard to read, blurry, but his identity is disclosed on last page (p.3). The next one-page report dated October 21, 1949, has blurry word images also; it is not readable. The next page accompanying this report which may be part of it or separate documentation is a newspaper article titled "Guatemalans join in Moreno defense," from *The Daily Peoples' World*

dated by the FBI as from October 31, 1949, and stamped as filed on bottom
right corner with date of "Nov.3 1949." The article refers to a three-part series
run in the Guatemalan newspaper, *Diario de la Mañana* as of September 26
through October 12 about her case and those in support of her defense. The
article called the Organizational Secretary of the National Revolutionary
Action Party in power in Guatemala, Augusto Charnaud MacDonald, to aid
in her defense. Another article titled "The Search for Freedom in America,"
follows this one also without citation but for the FBI's own entry of "Daily
People's World, Nov. 3, 1949." This article's author is Luisa Moreno Bemis.
She reveals a tragic upbringing not reported elsewhere in her biographical
sources. She writes:

> For I was born in a tragic land, a land in bondage, although the people had so
> loved liberty that the national symbol was a bird that immediately dies in cap-
> tivity. That is the bird called Quetzal. . . . The sad people of Guatemala slaved,
> suffered and hardly dared to think for 22 long years. Fear was everybody's
> byword. Even the children were afraid. They were cautioned that the walls had
> ears—that the tragedies they saw must be hushed . . . The children carrying
> flowers had to pay homage to the tyrant, a servant of foreign interests. So, when
> my sister and I were questioned by our teachers for not attending the ceremony,
> our parents thought it best to bring us here, to a Catholic boarding school. My
> father found it repugnant to pay homage to this tyrant. That was a sad land and
> a sad people. When we returned in 1921, a physical earthquake had destroyed
> our city; it was being rebuilt. The political earthquake had done away with the
> tyrant—for a brief spell—for soon, there was another pseudo Hitler, a 13-year
> scourge, this time.[30]
>
> You cannot realize how difficult it is for a Latin American country to be truly
> democratic. Foreign intrigue plays too big a part in the affairs of Latin America.
> In most cases, the people do not have a chance.
>
> From New York to Florida, from Florida to Texas and California, in several
> states in many cities and towns, I became a part of a struggle . . . for better work-
> ing conditions, for more pay, for improvements in the deplorable conditions of
> women workers, Negro workers, Mexican workers. Many times, we tried and
> failed partially; but most of the times we were successful.
>
> Then in my case, after investing the best years of my life, seeking no post of
> honor nor financial wealth but simple peace—after this investment, the dividend
> is paid in a most un-American manner; with a deportation warrant!
>
> [The following five pages past this article were entirely redacted, blank.]

Another three-page article follows the redacted pages, "A Question of
Deportment." by Steve Murdock. Handwritten on the right side of her full-
face photo is "Peoples World Sept. 9, 1949" and file stamped at bottom right is

"FBI-San Diego Sep 23 1949." The first part of the article repeats the scenario at the San Diego hearing between her and the questioner, Richard E. Coombs, chief counsel for the Committee on Un-American Activities. This article adds another quote not mentioned elsewhere of her response to the question on placing her citizenship application in jeopardy: "I told Combs that I had taken an oath to uphold the U.S. Constitution when applying for naturalization and that was what I intended to do at the hearing" (p.2). Murdock also wrote that the name Luisa Moreno was a respected one in worker circles:

> Cigar workers in Florida remember her. Cotton pickers in the lower Rio Grande Valley know her. Pecan workers in San Antonio recall her. Beet workers in Colorado, fish cannery workers in San Diego, fresh fruit and vegetable packing shed workers in California and Arizona all know and respect her. (p.2)

The Murdock article also describes her confrontations with the Ku Klux Klan in Florida; her protests against the $3.50-a-week wage for the women shelling pecans in San Antonio; her physical assault by police during the Zelgreen's cafeteria strike in New York; and the "No Mexicans allowed" in restaurants and bars in Colorado. "She remembers towns where workers of Mexican origin couldn't get a haircut and wouldn't let them have their own barber shops," Murdock writes (p.2). This writer also lists the number of influential persons protesting the deportation warrant served on Luisa Moreno such as Carey McWilliams, Robert W. Kenny, former California Attorney General, Ignacio Lopez, publisher of a Spanish language newspaper, Jaime Gonzalez, a YMCA official, Richard Ibanez and Joseph W. Aidlin, both attorneys, and, Beatrice Griffith, an author, as well as scores of union locals affiliated with the CIO and AFL. He quotes her at the end of the article as saying, "They can talk about deporting me but they can never deport the people that I've worked with and with whom things were accomplished for the benefit of hundreds of thousands of workers—things that cannot be deported" (p.3). Protests against her deportation even came from the Guatemalan press and leaders of the Guatemala government, according to Milton K. Wells, Chargé d' Affaires ad interim, US Embassy in Guatemala. He listed those protesting and the role of a political party in his two-page letter addressed to the secretary of state dated October 6, 1949.

There is not much new information in the remaining pages of 1949. A piece has to do with her speech given at the 12th Annual Convention of the California CIO on October 15, 1949, which is almost a verbatim copy of the article she penned and quoted extensively above. There is one entirely redacted page and three that are unintelligible due to blurriness. Several reports are on meetings held at which the FBI had informants and a topic of discussion was the deportation warrant on Luisa Moreno and Roberto

Galvan. Luisa Moreno attended one such meeting, according to the report dated December 12, 1949, from Special Agent W. Albert Stewart, Jr. to the SAC, San Diego. The meeting was held at 5059 Randlett Drive, La Mesa, California on December 5. She spoke to those gathered there on the history of the Palmer Raids of 1917, 1918, and 1919 and how parallels can be drawn with today's war on labor and immigrants.

Sometime between those meetings at the end of the year and January 23, 1950, the bail on Luisa Moreno Bemis was increased from $1,000 to $4,000 without reason, according to a news item in the *Peoples World* of that date in the file with no page number. Luisa's case was also the subject of a meeting held by the American Committee for the Protection of the Foreign Born (ACFPFB). This group and individual members, nationwide, were also under FBI surveillance, according to the report from Special Agent Miles L. Johnsen to this SAC, San Diego dated January 5, 1950. The San Diego FBI file numbers on each attendee (12) of the San Diego meeting are listed at left bottom including the file number "100-6619 (BEMIS)" and "100-1388 (USQUIANO)." By the end of the first month of 1950, a mail cover was also placed on the "Subject's husband, GRAY BEMIS," states the one-page memo from Special Agent William Dettweiler to the SAC, San Diego dated the 31st. There are only three such Mail Cover postcards, dated May 1, May 15, and July 5 in the released files for this year.

In 1950, the deportation hearings began for Luisa Moreno Bemis in Los Angeles, California. There is no report or communication on these hearings in the released files except for copies of articles taken from an open source, *Peoples World*, as indicated by handwriting and FBI stamp at bottom right on solo page. The January 31st clipping severely criticizes the INS witness against Mrs. Bemis as being incompetent and ignorant about personalities and history. A witness for the prosecution, Nat Honig, upon cross-examination confused John Foster Dulles, a US State Department official, with Vladimir Lenin as the author of "communist writings." He was presented on the witness stand by Luisa's attorney, Robert W. Kenny, some wording in articles written by Dulles and others by Lenin. Kenney read the passages out loud to try and show how incompetent and ignorant Honig was about what constitutes communism and communist writings. Honig at the time was a writer for the *Los Angeles Examiner*, a Hearst newspaper. Another two hearings were held on February 5 and 17, according to another open source clipping from the *Peoples World* of the 6th. A newsletter from the Committee for Luisa Moreno Bemis in San Diego dated February 1 states "a three hour hearing on January 24 in Los Angeles was the fourth in the Immigration Service's attempt to exile Luisa Moreno Bemis, former FTA-CIO vice president and vice president of the California CIO Council to her native Guatemala." Obviously, the deportation proceedings took months to reach a final determination. On March 31, 1950, the "Security Index Card on Louisa Moreno Bemis, was Security Matter-C" and was verified as correct one more time by Special Agent Richard T. Winterman. On the March 30, a five-page report from Los Angeles FBI Special Agent W. Nathan Provinse to the FBI director, covering January through March 16, 1950, reported on Guatemalan press covering the Moreno Bemis deportation proceedings. Provinse writes "These proceedings are in a pending status and ultimate disposition will not be known in immediate future." The information contained in this report is from three informants and many references to the *Daily Peoples World*, which is a new name or a misleading typographical error combining the *Daily Worker* and the *Peoples World*, not sure. To be sure, Agent Provinse does not know that Guatemala is in Central America because he attributes the articles he cites as "been published in Guatemala, South America" (p.1). He also reports that informant T-2 does not know if the case against her will be decided in a year. The US Supreme Court recently ruled that deportation hearings had to follow the rules as outlined in the Administrative Procedures Act and perhaps, her case may have to be re-tried (p.3). Another source not identified, and name redacted advised another FBI agent, George M. Gibson, that the editor of *El Espectador* in Pomona, Ignacio Lopez had brought Luisa Moreno Bemis to radio station KOCS in Ontario, California, and made a bilingual recording, "first in Spanish with an English translation." The informant provided a copy of the recording and "a mimeograph copy of the speech" she planned to deliver at the 13th Annual California CIO Council Convention. The informant asked "his name be kept confidential as he does not want any KOCS employees to know the tape was made available" (p.4). The last page provided one name of informant T-2 as Mr. A. E. Edgar of the INS (p.5). The tape recording was sent to Los Angeles and on to the FBI Director's office in Washington, DC.

FBI in New York sent a copy of the folded leaflet and a mimeographed copy of a newsletter from a Bemis-support committee dated 2/1/50 to the SAC, San Diego on April 25, 1950. The Labor Committee for Luisa Moreno Bemis with Richard Lynden, Chairman, at 150 Golden Gate Ave. in San Francisco, California, had published a four-fold leaflet with her photo in the front fold above the bold print: "BECAUSE she was a militant UNION LEADER this woman is threatened with E X I L E." Inside the story is stated under the heading "The Case of LUISA MORENO BEMIS." It begins, "Luisa Moreno Bemis, a U.S. resident for 27 years, is threaten with exile. Mrs. Bemis, who is married to a U.S. born citizen, a combat veteran of World War II, and who has a daughter and a granddaughter born in this country, faces deportation because she has been a militant labor leader." The story details the extortion scheme to let her stay if she testified against her union, against Harry Bridges, against the CPUSA; she refused all deals with the words "I'd rather not be a free woman with a mortgaged soul." The article goes on to list her union work and offices held within labor organizations and her applications for naturalization dating back to 1937 and final papers in 1944 without resolution (fold page 2). On the third fold, the story continues under the bold print title of "deportation affects EVERYONE this is how the PATTERN WORKS." Briefly the pattern is traced to the Palmer Raids and the too frequent violations of the law by INS that the US Supreme Court ruled they must follow procedure. It states that "thirty-five union leaders through-out the nation are under deportation threat right now" (fold page 3). On the back-fold page under "WHAT TO DO" are listed three actions: "1 Write or wire the INS Commissioner and protest. Ask her case be dropped. 2 Send a contribution to the Labor Committee for Luisa Moreno Bemis . . .. 3 Circulate copies of this folder. Get your union to go on record in this case and to send a protest." The folded leaflet was forwarded from FBI San Diego to FBI Los Angeles on May 10, 1950 and informant [name redacted] is credited with first making it available to FBI Special Agent Vernon D. Jensen, according to this one-page memo.

Another article with a handwritten entry on right side middle of page next to the photo of Luisa Moreno Bemis, "the Peoples World dated 5-26-50, p9" and FBI file stamp at bottom right with "May 29 1950" as the date, states the process of the deportation hearing with dates and locations. It then details the case of Peter Harislades who joined the CPUSA in 1935 and then was dropped from membership in 1939 "because the Party dropped non-citizens from the rolls." Given this is an official CPUSA publication, the official pol-icy of dropping non-citizens from membership after 1939 were legal grounds to defeat prosecutions based on CPUSA membership; but not deportations of non-citizens. This same day, May 29, 1950, SAC, San Diego received a two-page notice from SAC, Los Angeles that informants [names redacted] advised that "Luisa Morena" would go to San Diego to establish this branch of ANMA, acronym for American National Mexican Association (p.1). Nothing further is provided on the aims and purposes of ANMA, however, an informant and former CPUSA member, "Dr. Paul Crouch from Alameda County, California claimed that Luisa Morena was a member of District 13 Central Committee of the Communist Party at the time he was also"(p.2). So which truth do we rely on in retrospect as to the FBI criminalizing CPUSA membership particularly for non-citizens?

Fundraising for the defense costs incurred by Luisa Moreno Bemis con-tinued in many places of the country. The SAC, San Diego regularly sent information to FBI Director Hoover as to these types of events. June 6, 1950, is the date on one memo from Special Agent W. Albert Stewart, Jr. selecting a portion of a letter obtained by an informant and made available to another Special Agent, Norman S. Higson. The portion re-typed simply thanked everyone for contributing and referred to the foldout flyer previously mentioned above. It also reiterated the plea to help stop the deportations. On June 8, Special Agent Miles J. Johnsen, sent a solo page memo to his SAC that indicated a participant, "Phil Ougensky (phonetic)" in an earlier memo on the "American National Mexican Association, Internal Security-C" was in all probability Phil Usquiano, a "leading CP member" and also the "Director of the San Diego Civil Rights Congress." The night of June 18, Friday, a membership meeting of the Food Tobacco and Agricultural (FTA) Workers was held and the membership voted to have "each member pay $10 for financial support to Luisa Bemis in her fight against deportation," according to Special Agent Dettweiler who received the information from an informant [name redacted] who in turn advised "he did not attend the above meeting, but received the above information second hand." Is it comforting to know that much of the FBI information is based on informants compounded by the fact that it also is hearsay? At another meeting held on June 2, the same or another informant [name redacted] who was present indicated "$25 had been given to the San Diego branch of the Civil Rights Congress as a contribution." The entire last paragraph of this transmission is redacted. At the end of the month of June on the 27th an article appeared in the *San Diego Tribune-Sun* (no page date or byline) entitled "Deportation Sought for Labor Leader." In this article, the problems of INS not following the rules of procedure in the process of deportation of a person are repeated as is the labor-organizing history of Luisa Moreno Bemis. It does contain the charges she is faced with in the deportation proceedings, which are two-fold: "being unlawfully in the U.S." and "being a member of an organization which believes in advocates and teaches the overthrow of our forces, and violence to the Government of the U.S."

On June 26, 1950, the SAC, Newark sent to the FBI director a five-page memo of which four pages were a list of named captioned "List of Deportees." The name of Luisa Moreno Bemis appeared on the last page. The remarkable note to this memo is that the list (126 names) was obtained from an informant [name redacted] in Newark who had obtained it from the New Jersey State CP Headquarters. The first paragraph concludes: "It is believed that this list is a list of CP members either scheduled for deportations or possible deportation from the US." Special Agent William E. Dettweiller at the FBI San Diego office prepared a one-page memo his SAC on July 1, 1950, advising that an informant [name redacted] who had talked with Luisa Moreno and asked her if she "had ever been a member of the Communist Party." Luisa is purported to have replied, "she had been a member in 1930. She did not state she was a member now, nor did she deny it, making no statement regarding her membership." The informant also advised that the FTA now is collecting $2 more from each member for Luisa's defense. At the end of July, Luisa's Security Index card is reviewed once again for any updates. The form letter does not reveal anything not known before except for a provocative line under "Method of Verification": The handwriting states, "W.G. McGee, Encanto Post office-employment. Surveillance-Residence." From this I conclude that the FBI was not just continuing with the Mail Cover and checking every piece of correspondence coming to the Bemis residence at their home address but also actually physically watching her movements, perhaps that of her husband as well.

No documents were released to show FBI or INS activity during the remainder of the summer. On September 2, 1950, Special Agent William R. Dettweiller sent a memo to his SAC correcting a gender issue of Dixie Tiller, who "is a man and the reference to DIXIE TILLER as 'her' is erroneous and is being called to the attention of the Bureau and Newark Office." The physical surveillance may have caused a problem in that 6426 Medio Drive may have been hard to find. Special Agent William G. Mashaw in a solo page to the SAC, San Diego listed in itemized number steps from 1 to 7 the instruction on how to arrive at that destination. And, he also reported that a post office box, 917, at the Encanto Post Office "was taken out in the name of Gray D. Bemis and Luisa "calls daily for the mail at about 5:00 P.M. or shortly thereafter."

## ARREST AND DEPORTATION

The morning of October 24, 1950, INS officers led by Officer in Charge U.L. Press, knocked on the door at 6426 Medio Drive in Encanto, California. They announced the purpose of their visit to the woman answering the door; she was under arrest for violating the new anti-subversive act.[31] According to the news story, "Alien Anti-Red Law Jails S.D. Laborite," in the *San Diego Evening Tribune*, she was to be held without bail at Terminal Island penitentiary in San Pedro, California.[32] In a subsequent newspaper article, Federal Judge Ben Harrison is quoted as demanding those held without bail be brought to court and state whether or not they are members of the Communist Party.[33] Gray Bemis, her husband, in another newspaper article complained and protested the holding of his wife in virtual solitary confinement without bail when they had already posted a $1,000 bond then a $4,000 bond. He also said, his wife admitted being a member of the CPUSA, but in 1930, not in recent years. Lastly, he told the press his wife was ready to leave the United States as soon as permission was granted. She had a valid Guatemala passport.[34]

An informant [name redacted] told Special Agent William E. Dettweiller, according to his one-page report to his SAC dated November 15, 1950, that at a farewell party for Luisa Moreno Bemis, funds were collected as a going away gift and their plans for departure were discussed. Allegedly, the couple was going to drive to Mexico City by auto and leave the car there for possible re-sale if she needed money. Meanwhile, Gray Bemis would return to work in the United States to earn better wages and help support her in Mexico or Guatemala. The SAC Los Angeles reporting to the SAC San Diego on November 24 that by telephone INS Agent Inspector, Henry Grattan, talked with Gray Bemis, who said they would leave San Diego on the 25th to El Paso and leave the United States by November 30. As soon as this would be verified, the Los Angeles FBI office would be notified. SAC San Diego notified the director of FBI on November 20 that the vehicles owned by the Bemis's were two Studebaker-6 cars, a 1949 and a 1950, and provided the license plate numbers. The closing line indicates the relationship with Mexican security authorities: "the Bureau may desire to advise appropriate sources in Mexico City of the possible visit to Mexico City by the subject." On December 9, SAC San Diego reported to FBI director that Luisa and husband Gray Bemis had in fact been issued a thirty-day transmigrant visa by Mexican authorities. The car they were driving was one of the Studebaker-6's, the 1950 model. The one-page report concludes with the suggestion that the Security Index card be cancelled.

## SURVEILLANCE NOT OVER YET!

On January 25, 1951, the Los Angeles and San Diego FBI offices were exchanging photos and pamphlets on Luisa Moreno Bemis, perhaps for their records of the case. The Mail Cover was still in place. There are two reports from the postal authorities dated January 26 and April 20, 1950, in the released documents for this year. On March 30, SAC, San Diego requested again of the FBI director to cancel the Security Index card and by return memo dated April 13: the "Bureau authority is granted for you to cancel the Subject's SI card in view of her recent deportation to Guatemala." The question remains if she was in fact deported or did she self-repatriate? There is no record or memo or correspondence that she had in fact left Mexico City and arrived at Guatemala City, Guatemala. There is a one-page memo from Frank V. Sullivan, special agent at some unidentified FBI office to his SAC that INS Agent Inspector James S. Bower on September 9, 1952, had:

> advised that Louisa _____, who was deported to Guatemala some time ago, is presently attempting to re-enter the United States through New York City. He related that he has received advice from the Central Office of INS that she will not be re-admitted.

On same date, Mr. B. H. Kirk, Encanto, California, Post Office, advised
that mail is being forwarded to LOUISA BEMIS in care of General Delivery,
Guatemala City, Guatemala.

On November 24, 1952, the SAC, Los Angeles sent a two-page memo to the
FBI director on Luisa Moreno Bemis following up on an earlier request from
Hoover a letter dated January 18, 1952, in which he asked that their office
review "the transcripts of testimony taken before the HCUA." And, in the case
of "a person identified has deported from the Los Angeles area, the office now
covering the residence of the subject should be advised of the nature of the
testimony and of the Bureau's instructions." SAC, Los Angeles complies to
this November letter by providing information on the testimony by Max Silver
before HCUA on January 24 that same year. "Silver testified that LOUISA
MORENO (An alias of the subject) was originally from a small South American
Republic." If we only think in terms of North and South America as the two
continents, then the SAC was in need of more geography lessons. Silver, he
wrote, went on to say she was an important worker among the Mexicans; an
effective labor organizer; and, "was an Organizational Secretary for the CP
in Texas"; then later returned to Los Angeles where she played a role in the
organization of the Mexican-American Congress" (p.1). Again, SAC Los
Angeles needs more accurate information than that being relied on from Silver.
Luisa had never been to California before Texas. She came from Guatemala
to Mexico to New York to Florida to Louisiana to Texas, then California.
There is no information from any source that she was a CP officer in Texas or
anywhere else. She did admit to being a CP member in New York in the early
1930s until 1935. In February 28, 1953, the SAC, San Diego informs the FBI
director that the file on Louisa Moreno Bemis is being closed. This solo-page
memo has an entire paragraph of some sixteen lines completely redacted. In
June 17, 1953, a source [name and title redacted] in Mexico "furnished to
the reporting agent, [Special Agent Arnold D. Orrantia] a copy of the letter"
sent by a professor Seszekeley to Mr. and Mrs. Gray Bemis in Guatemala
City, Guatemala. Inside the letter to Seszekeley was another letter address to
Enrique Albañil, an alias used by Harry Steinmetz. Steinmetz was a person of
interest as was Luisa Moreno as a "Security Matter-C file number 100-906."
San Diego FBI office notified the FBI director of this mail exchange, enclosed
a copy of the Steinmetz two-page letter to the Bemis's, on July 7, 1953. The
letter was a cordial refresher on what Steinmetz had been doing in the United
States and asking about business and job opportunities in Guatemala. He asked
pointedly if they could meet in Mexico City (p.1). If they were to reply to
him, he asked they address it to Dr. Eduard Bordeaux Szekely in *Tecate, Baja
California* but to write on the top of the letter "*Por Enrique Albanil*." Director
Hoover responded to unidentified and redacted persons in a three-page letter

dated December 3, 1953. The first two pages are unreadable due to blurriness but the last page has instructions to "follow the Steinmetz case closely so that appropriate action can be taken in the event Steinmetz leaves the country." The last paragraph is more ominous for the Bemis's. Hoover wrote: "You should also open the case on Gray Dayton Bemis and conduct an appropriate investigation to determine whether he has departed from this country permanently and whether he should be placed on the Security Index." But for the FBI file stamp of March 22, 1954, on the next six pages, two of which are Routing Slips without dates, I would not know they were processed by Hoover. His stamp signature appears on both of the undated Routing Slips and the attached page to each is entirely redacted and blank. The first Routing Slip has "RE: Luisa Moreno De Bemis," while the next one has her name and that of "Gray Dayton Bemis Security Matter-C Bufile #100-147607" and handwritten on this one is "To Sullivan info" Whatever the redacted material on these pages was, another handwritten notation is seen: "I think this is most interesting also" and to the side another handwritten word: "Agree." Apparently, by early 1954 or possibly late 1953, the FBI had already made the determination to include Bemis as a target and classify him as a Security Matter-C for Communist and open a file by the number of 100-50025 on him. Hoover was adamant in wanting to know the whereabouts of Gray Bemis, we can infer from his September 2, 1954, two-page letter to [redacted names] (p.1). On the last page, Hoover makes mention to SAC, San Diego [perhaps it was one of the redacted names, but that was not the usual practice]:

> it is further suggested that since a review of the Bemis file fails to reflect that you have requested WFO to review the passport file of Gray Dayton Bemis at the State Department, you should consider setting out such a lead to WFO in an effort to determine whether or not it can be determined from those records whether Bemis is presently in or out of the United States.

The FBI attention now aimed at Gray Bemis but they did not take their eyes off Luisa, however, given a Routing Slip file stamp dated December 11, 1954, signed by [William] Sullivan "RE: Louisa Moreno Bemis." A total of eight completely redacted and blank pages followed or were part of the information attached to the Routing Slip. Lots of material on Luisa Moreno was withheld under FOIA exemption (b) (1) which is "specifically authorized under criteria established by an Executive order to be kept secret in the interest of national defense or foreign policy."[35] Word reached the SAC San Diego via solo page transmission dated January 4, 1955, that Gray Dayton Bemis "planned to enter the US through INS at Tijuana. O.C. Palmer, Inspector, INS, advised today that to date, there has been no indication Subject entered the US . . . any information indicating Subject's presence in

US, this office will be notified immediately." Three months later on March 25, 1955, the FBI man inside the US Embassy in Mexico City named the "Legat, Mexico" informed Hoover in a three-page report that two confidential informants [names redacted] had attended a cocktail party at a residence on *Calle Michelet No. 37*, Apartment 9, *Colonia Nueva Anzures, Mexico, D.F.* on January 3. The occasion was for Asa Zatz to introduce his new bride to his guests. The bride was Alba Diaz de Zatz, sister to Jaime Diaz, who was the personal secretary of former President of Guatemala, Jacobo Arbenz. "The informants have reported that both Alva and her brother, Jaime, are outspokenly pro-Communist, pro-Soviet, and anti-United States." Present at the party were "Mr. and Mrs. Don Bemis" (p.1). The Legat reported a story that Mr. Bemis told others about his line of "insurance business" in San Francisco, California, and how he met his wife in Guatemala. Supposedly, Mr. Bemis told all that "when the revolution broke out against Arbenz, he was at the Guatemala-Mexico border and thereafter immediately crossed over into Mexico. His wife took refuge in the Mexican Embassy and subsequently joined him in Mexico City in October, 1954" (p.2). The Legat reported that another source confirmed "that one Rosa Rodriguez de Bemis, a.k.a. Luisa Moreno Bemis, had arrived in Mexico City around October 7, 1954." Another informant or the same on, since the names are all redacted, reported that

> Rosa Rodriguez de Bemis was formerly the mistress of GEORGE MINK, the notorious Soviet agent. In approximately 1938 or 1939 MINK was reported to have been active in some type of labor trouble in Florida. Rosa Rodriguez de Bemis was reportedly with MINK on this occasion and traveled with him from Florida to New York City.

The Legat also provided a "1954 Guatemalan license plate number as P-9-196" that she has been driving in Mexico City (p.2). The Legat's informants promised to get him the exact address of residence in Mexico City for the Bemis couple (p.3). In July 1955, the Legat, Mexico City reported that the Bemis couple were still in Mexico City and "associating almost exclusively with Guatemalan Communist refugees."

In September 1955, SAC, San Diego prepared for SAC, Los Angeles a four-page summary report listing all the reports available on Louisa Moreno Bemis. This report was disseminated to four other FBI offices: San Antonio, San Francisco, New York, and Philadelphia. These four FBI field offices communicated back and forth between October 26 and November 21, 1955, adding and amending the content of the earlier summary report. The Legat, Mexico City toward the end of the year wrote to Director Hoover on December 30th that the Bemis's had been living in Cuernavaca, Morelos,

Mexico, the past few months but now were back in Mexico City and he was working for "Samuel J. Novick (Bureau file 100-338889)" at his factory, "Bond Electric Corporation of Mexico, S.A. located at *Kilometro 12 ½* on the Mexico-Puebla highway."

The beginning of 1956 had more summary reports prepared on Luisa and Gray Bemis with the FBI SAC Miami adding information. These reports circulated between all the prior offices, including Miami from January 31 to February 23. The Legat, Mexico City reported on February 21 that Gray Bemis had suffered a heart attack and was in poor health. The Mail Cover put in place by the FBI on both Luisa and Gray in California was still in place as of late 1949 and July 10, 1950, because there is a single sheet with FBI file stamp date of February 3, 1956, listed six pieces of correspondence examined as to content. George F. Munro of the FBI's Mexico City office, not identified as the Legat, dated March 28, 1956, reported in eight pages plus the cover sheet on the activities of "Rosa Rodriguez De Bemis, a.k.a., Luisa Moreno Bemis, Mrs. Gray Dayton Bemis" between January 3, 1955, through March 13, 1955. He provided the Mexico City address for the Bemis couple as being *"Calle Ruatusco #17*, Interior Apartment #23, Zone 7" and verified the employment as previously mentioned as well as the heart attack "during summer 1955" and adds "Prior to his heart attack BEMIS and wife reported in association with Guatemalan Communists refugees and American Communist Group in Mexico City" (cover sheet). This report gives the US passport number for Gray Bemis acquired September 9, 1953. Gray was earning 120 US dollars at month at the Bond Electric Company. Bemis did change his entry tourist card visa for an *Inmigrante* visa which was granted on April 26, 1955, "renewable each year for five years" (p.1). The next two pages describe the "American Communist Group" and their loose affilia-tion with the Mexican CP. It also introduces the lawyer for this group as "Carmen Otero y Gama who is the sister-in-law of VICENTE LOMBARDO TOLEDANO, the well-known Mexican Marxist labor leader." This report was based on information provided by five informants, T-1 through T-5, but T-5 contradicted prior information as to the Bemis couple's activities with Guatemalan refugees labeled Communists. T-5 stated, according to the report, "the BEMIS's were living very quietly in Mexico City and were not in frequent contact with the Guatemalan exiles in Mexico City" (p.4).

The last records released to this author on Luisa Moreno are two dispatches on another subject from the SAC and Special Agent, John Christensen, both of the New York FBI office dated March 2, a two-page memo and April 25, 1956, solo page. Both FBI agents also report that the name "Luisa Moreno De Bemis (wife) appeared in an address book examined by U.S. Customs officials along with his passport belonging to Nathan Buchwald, a staff mem-ber of the Yiddish newspaper *Morgen Freiheit* published in New York City during a recent trip to Israel." A copy of this entry is on file at the FBI New York office under file number 100-7801-1A14 and an alias is used by Nathan in lieu of his real birth name of Naftula Buchwald.

As late as April 25, 1956, the FBI was still monitoring any news or items of interest pertaining to Luisa Moreno. There may well be more files on her but not released to this author.

The Larralde interview of 1995 reveals that Gray died on February 1, 1960. As part of her mourning she traveled to Cuba and volunteered to teach on the island. Some years later she returned to Mexico and settled in Tijuana, hoping to re-enter the United States which was not to be. Short on money in 1977, she took a job managing apartments in Guadalajara, Jalisco, Mexico until she had a stroke and hit her head while waiting on a bus. Her brother, Ernesto, took her in back home in Guatemala. She died many years later, November 4, 1992, at age eighty-five. While she never hid her Guatemalan nationality, everyone else saw her as another Mexican. Her political and trade union work primarily in California was with and for other Mexicans in the United States.

## NOTES

1.  Both quotes are taken from Jeff Smith, "The California Whirlwind, Part Oee," *The San Diego Reader*, June 22, 2011, www.sandiegoreader.com/news/2011/jun/22/ unforgettable-calkifornia-whirlwind-part-one/#/. Accessed July 28, 2019. Part Two is found at www.sandiegoreader.com/news/2011/jul/13/unforgettable-rosa/luisa-calif ornia-whirlwind-part-2/ under title of "Rosa/Luisa: The California Whirlwind, Part Two," July 13, 2011.

2.  Carlos Larralde interviewed Luisa Moreno and daughter, Mytyl Glomboske, on several occasions and these dates are listed in various endnotes of the article by him and Richard Griswold del Castillo, "Luisa Moreno and the Beginnings of the Mexican American Civil Rights Movement in San Diego," *Journal of San Diego History*, San Diego Historical Society, (summer 1997), 43 (3), www.sandiegohistory. org/journal/1997/july/moreno-2/. Accessed July 27, 2019. An earlier article by the same authors on the same subject is "Luisa Moreno," *Journal of San Diego History*, San Diego Historical Society, (fall 1995), 41 (4), www.sandiegohistory.org/journal /1995/october/moreno/. Accessed July 27, 2019.

3.  Several sites provide information on this person such as https://thebiography.us /en/mistral-gabriela/; www.britannica.com/biography/Gabriela-Mistral/; and, www.p oetryfoundation.org/poets/gabriela-mistral/.

4.  See www.poetryfoundation.org cited above.

5.  The Jeff Smith series and the Larralde/Griswold del Castillo have different versions of this name change. The point being that Blanca Rosa Rodriguez Lopez became Blanca Rosa Rodriguez Lopez de Leon from her first marriage then Blanca Rosa Rodriguez Lopez Bemis on the second marriage, and always was Luisa Moreno in her public life.

6. Jeff Smith, Part One.

7. *Ibid.*

8. See his memoir, *Songs My Mother Taught Me* (New York: Random House, 1994), 193.

9. Larralde/Griswold article, 1995, and Jeff Smith, Part II.

10. Victor G. Devinatz, "Communist Party of the United States, Political Party, United States, www.britannica.com/topic/Communist-Party-of-the-United-States-of-America/ Accessed August 1, 2019.

11. History.com, This Day in History, "Bonus Marchers evicted by U.S. Army," www.history.com/the-day-in-history/bonus-marchers-ousted-by-u-s-army/. Accessed July 28, 2019.

12. Joan Hoff Wilson, *Herbert Hoover, Forgotten Progressive* (Prospect Heights, IL: Waveland Press, Inc. 1992), 161–162.

13. *Ibid.*, 142.

14. *Ibid.*, 162.

15. Larralde and Griswold del Castillo in their first article, "Luisa Moreno," claim she met Gray Bemis during one of her organizing trips to San Diego during the period of the Zoot Suit riots, June 1943, whereas Jeff Smith in Part One on his series of articles on her states he was a cab driver in New York.

16. *Rosa Rodriguez L. de Leon v. Miguel de Leon*, Index No. 11730, June 25, 1937, Supreme Court, New York City and cited as f6 in https://sandiegohistory.org/jo urnal/1995/october/moreno/ and in George J. Sanchez, *Becoming Mexican American: Ethnicity, Culture, and Identity in Chicano Los Angeles, 1900–1945* (New York: Oxford University Press, 1995), 244.

17. Peter Afasiabi, *Burning Bridges: America's 20-Year Crusade to Deport Labor Leader Harry Bridges* (Brooklyn: Thirlwere Books, 2016) covers his prolonged official and often illegal harassment; as do two other works, Charles P. Larrowe, *Harry Bridges, the Rise and Fall of Radical Labor in the US* (Rochester, MN: L. Hill Publisher, 1972) and Estolv Ethan Ward, *Harry Bridges on Trial* (New York: Modern Age Books, 1940) its newer edition by London's publisher, Forgotten Books, 2009.

18. Ryan P. Smith, "Guatemalan Immigrant Luisa Moreno Was Expelled from the U.S. for her Ground Breaking Labor Activism," July 15, 2018, www.smithsonian mag.com/smithsonian-institution/guatemalan-immigrant-luisa-moreno-expelled-us -groundbreaking-labor-activism/180969750/. Accessed July 29, 2019.

19. Carlos Larralde, "Roberto Galvan: A Latino Leader of the 1940s," *San Diego Journal of History*, San Diego Historical Society (2006) 52 (3), 151–177.

20. Jeff Smith, Part Two.

21. Larralde and Griswold del Castillo, "Luisa Moreno," 1995.

22. Peter Richardson, "Carey McWilliams," (2011) at www.historyaccess.com/car ey-mcwilliams-html/. Accessed August 1, 2019. For the major work on McWilliams, see Richardson's book, *American Prophet: The Life and Work of Carey McWilliams* (Oakland: University of California Press, 2019). Carey McWilliams, while editor of *The Nation* also had published *The Mexicans in America; A Student's Guide to Localized History* (New York: Teachers College Press, 1968).

23. James Kirkpatrick Davis, *Spying on America: the FBI's Domestic Counter-Intelligence Program* (Westport: Praeger Publishers, 1992), 25–26.

24. *Ibid.*, 27.

25. *Ibid.*, 29.

26. The history of Chambers and Hiss as members of the CPUSA and spies for the Soviet Union and this case is detailed under the title of "The Alger Hiss Case," www.cia.gov/center-for-the-study-of-intelligence/Kent-csi/vol44no5/html/v44i5a01 p.htm/ and at www.history.com/this-day-in-history/chambers-accusses-hiss-of-being -a-communist-spy/ both accessed on August 1, 2019.

27. Kelly Lytle Hernandez, *City of Inmates: Conquest, Rebellion, and the Rise of Human Caging in Los Angeles, 1771–1965* (Chapel Hill: University of North Carolina Press, 2017), 150–157. See also Sanchez, *Becoming Mexican American*, 184 and the 1988 commercial documentary, "Break of Dawn" on this life story now available as of 2000 at www.imdb/com/title/tt0290594/. Accessed August 4, 2019. Pedro and his wife upon deportation settled in Tijuana and he renewed his broadcasting and musical career. In 1973, they returned to the United States to rejoin their grown children and meet the new grown grandchildren. Pedro died at age ninety-nine in Lodi, California, in 1995.

28. See legislation also called the Alien Anarchist Exclusion Act passed during the 65th Congress on October 16, 1918, Public Law 65-221 and codified as 40 Stat. 1012 and known as the Dillingham-Hardwick Act.

29. Source cited at left side of each the two pages just below her photo in handwriting is the best possible and taken from two pages of the article found in the set of files released to this author and stamped at bottom right "100-6619-29 FBI-San Diego Nov 2 1948."

30. Guatemala has been under a military dictatorship longer than any other country in the Americas. Luisa Moreno is referring to two dictators during her time in Guatemala: Manuel Estrada Cabrera, who was in power until 1920; then a military junta until 1931. The most brutal of all dictators took power, Jorge Ubico Castañeda, until 1944. A popularly elected president was Jacobo Arbenz Guzman, who served from 1951 until he was deposed by the CIA-led coup by US Ambassador to Guatemala, John Peurifoy. Guatemala was in civil war from 1960 to 1996. For some reading into this history see Kenneth J. Grieb, *Gentleman Caudillo: The Regime of Jorge Ubico, Guatemala—1933–1944* (Athens: Ohio University Press, 1979); Richard B. Immerman, *The CIA in Guatemala: The Foreign Policy of Intervention* (Austin: University of Texas Press, 1983); Paul J. Dosal, *Doing Business with Dictators: A Political History of the United Fruit in Guatemala* (Wilmington: Scholarly Resources, 1993); and, Nick Cullather, *Secret History: The CIA's Classified Account of Its Operations in Guatemala* (Palo Alto: Stanford University Press, 1999).

31. Internal Security Act of 1950, 64 Stat. 987, Public Law 81-831; also known as McCarran-Wood Act; Subversive Control Act of 1950; and, just McCarran Act. President Harry Truman vetoed the bill only to have it overridden the same day by Congress, September 22, 1950.

32. Page 2. See also "Raiders Grab 2 More Women," *Los Angeles Times*, October 25, 1950,1,10.

33. "Local Woman Must Say if Communist," *San Diego Union*, October 31, 1950, A7.

34. "Mrs. Bemis Asks Right to Return to Guatemala," *The San Diego Union*, November 1, 1950, B14.

35. Listed as the first item on a page sent with response to every FOIPA request made of the FBI and found in subsections of Title 5, USC, Section 552.

*Chapter 2*

# Ernesto Galarza, the First Chicano Activist Scholar

A major omission by those interested in the history of the civil rights struggles of persons of Mexican origin and their progeny, Chicanos, in the United States is an authoritative biography of Ernesto Galarza, particularly his labor organizing, scholarship, and community activism.[1] His own age-limited autobiography does not tell us more than aspects of his early childhood up to a week before entering high school in Sacramento, California.[2] Yet, all the literature on migrant farm workers, especially those of Mexican ancestry, published since the 1940s makes mention of the central role played by Ernesto Galarza in many such efforts. Almost every book credits Galarza not only with reforming the National Farm Labor Union (NFLU), laying the ground work for the ultimate success in the ending of the Bracero Program dating to the late 1940s but also getting the first documentary produced exposing the conditions of farm labor in California, *Poverty in the Land of Plenty*.[3] As member of the Agricultural Workers Organizing Committee (AWOC), which he joined after a brief stay with the National Agricultural Workers Union (NAWU), he helped in the victory by Filipino farmworkers and Cesar Chavez over the Di Giorgio Corporation of California and the rise of the United Farm Workers of America union.[4]

## ERNESTO GALARZA: A SHORT STORY

He was born in a rural village near the outskirts of *Jolocotan, Nayarit, Mexico*, by the *Sierra Madre de Nayarit* on August 15, 1905, to a family of *Magonista* supporters, the early revolutionaries rising against the Porfirio Diaz dictatorship in Mexico. The residents of that area referred to the big town as *Jalco*. By 1913 with the outbreak of full-scale war across Mexico, including the neighboring town to Jalco known as *Iytlan del Rio*, where walls were plastered with "Viva Madero" posters and hand-painted graffiti, revolutionaries took that town from the hated *federales*, the Diaz loyalist army.[5] The Galarza family left Jalco heading toward *Mazatlan* further north, "*Ernesto*, his mother, aunt *Ester*, and uncles, *Gustavo* and *José*." His father, Don Ernesto, senior, was not in the small caravan. He stayed behind. Actually, his parents divorced just prior to the migration north.[6] Working for periods of time where the uncles and Ernesto found work and walking when they had to, the family caravan continued to Nogales at the border, then ultimately into the United States, settling in Sacramento, California. He was eight years of age.[7] "Ernesto assisted his family during the harvest season as a farmworker while he attended school in Elementary and Sacramento high school." It was during these early formative years that Ernesto learned firsthand the inhumanly terrible conditions that he and all other farm laborers endured. "Because he had gone to school to learn English, the Mexican workers asked him to protest over polluted drinking water that had taken the life of one baby in the camp and was making others sick."[8]

The formative years of Galarza as a child and teen seared in his brain a worldview of the rich and the poor, the owners and the workers, and foreign interests in Mexico's economy and social life. He saw the role played by corporations from the United States, England, Germany, France, and Spain that owned and controlled the people working in "haciendas, the railroads, the ships, the big stores, the breweries" all because "President Porfirio Diaz had let them steal it. They owned Mexico."[9] In addition, not only did he see the world this way, he also lived it as a worker. He explains his experience with work in these words,

> Whatever the surprising differences between Mazatlan and the *barrio* in Sacramento, in one thing they were powerfully the same—*trabajo*. If you didn't have it, you spend days looking for it. If you had it, you worried about how long it would last.[10]

In high school, he was a good student who managed to be among the few Mexican kids to graduate from high school and go to college. He learned of a scholarship opportunity at Occidental College, applied and got it. In his senior year at Occidental, he applied and received financial help to participate in a travel abroad program of study; it was in Mexico City. While there he researched and wrote a paper on the Roman Catholic Church and the history of Mexico. He continued to help his family and earn for his expenses by continuing to work in the fields. He graduated from Occidental College and went on to obtain a master's degree in history and political science from Stanford

University in 1929. He married a single mother, Mae Taylor, that same year. She had a three-year-old daughter from a prior marriage named Karla.

Ernesto wanted to pursue a doctorate and Columbia University in New York accepted him; provided some financial support but not enough. He took a job as a research associate with the Foreign Policy Association. His wife started teaching at the private Gardner School in Jamaica, Long Island, New York. Between 1932 and 1936, both took jobs at the school and eventually bought into the business. They were the co-principals of the school. Galarza began work at his job and dug into a topic that would also serve him as his doctoral dissertation, the development of electricity and the modernizing of Mexico, later published in Mexico.[11]

## THE FEDERAL BUREAU OF INVESTIGATION FILE

The Federal Bureau of Investigation (FBI) file on Ernesto Galarza is number 65-HQ-7286 and consists of 118 pages released to this author under a Freedom of Information Act (FOIA) request filed on November 19, 2014, and was assigned FOIA case number 44704. On September 23, 2018, I was notified that the National Archives and Records Administration (NARA) had located the 118 pages mentioned above and charge $0.80 per page for copying or I could travel to College Park, Maryland, and look with one-week advance notice at the documents without charge.[12] The file begins with a letter from D.F. Bryant, Commander, US Navy, at Chevy Chase, Maryland, dated November 13, 1939, to J. Edgar Hoover, Director of the FBI about Ernesto Galarza. It is a short paragraph worth quoting because it contained the bait J. Edgar Hoover loved to bite:

> Subject resides at 1620 South Highland Ave., Arlington, Va., telephone Chestnut 5316. He is a Mexican, well educated, former instructor in Spanish at Harvard U., is a communist, (may not belong to the party); has made inflammatory speeches to negroes in Washington; close friend of Don Luis Quintanilla, Charge d'Affaires of Mexican Embassy and of Ambassador Najera, through whose influence he is expected to be made Chief, Division of Labor, Pan American Union (in process of formation)/ Subject is anti-American, anticapitalist, thoroughly communistic. Has been with Pan-American Union several years [Copy has several lines underscored as indicated above but I suspect these were not the original writer's intent].

Much like a lioness in the wild at prey stalks and readily pounces on its next meal, Hoover jumped at the chance to add one more target to his list of Communists. The FBI surveillance of Ernesto Galarza and his spouse continued until 1967, if we accept the total documents released to me as the complete file. I doubt it. For example, Galarza was most instrumental in organizing the protest against the White House Cabinet Committee Hearings held in El Paso, Texas, during October 1967 for not inviting grassroots leaders of various Mexican American organizations and social movements. President L.B. Johnson had promised to hold a White House Conference on Mexican American Affairs to leaders of mainstream organizations, many of whom had walked out on his Equal Employment Opportunity Commission (EEOC) hearings held in Albuquerque the previous year in March 1966. Only one commissioner of the EEOC showed up in Albuquerque; the rest were staffers without any power to affect any domestic policy change much less social change. The 1967 El Paso protest became known as the La Raza Unida Rump Conference promoted by local student groups from El Paso and the Mexican American Youth Organization (MAYO).[13] Surely, the FBI was watching this gathering and Galarza, one of the main organizers and speakers along with Reies Lopez Tijerina and Rodolfo "Corky" Gonzales, both FBI targets for some time.[14] Yet, these files on Galarza's role with the La Raza Unida Rump Conference are not included in the packet of documents released. "The El Paso Declaration," mainly the intellectual product of Ernesto Galarza boldly proclaimed a new political posture of "La Raza." Here is the statement in its entirety as written on a flyer:

On this historic day, October 28, 1967, La Raza Unida organized in El Paso, Texas, proclaims the time of subjugation, exploitation and abuse of human rights of La Raza in the United States is hereby ended forever.

La Raza Unida affirms the magnificence of La Raza, the greatness of our heritage, our history, our language, our traditions, our contributions to humanity, and our culture. We have demonstrated, proved and again affirm our loyalty to the Constitutional Democracy of the United States of America and to the religious and cultural traditions we all share.

We accept the framework of Constitutional Democracy and freedom within which to establish our own independent organizations among our own people in pursuit of justice, equality and redress of grievances. La Raza Unida pledges to join with all our courageous people organizing in the fields and in the barrios. We commit ourselves to La Raza, at whatever cost.

WITH THIS COMMITMENT WE PLEDGE OUR SUPPORT IN:

The right to organize community and labor groups in our style.

The guarantee of training and placement in employment in all levels.

The guarantee of special emphasis on education at all levels geared to our people with strong financial grants to individuals.

The guarantee of decent, safe and sanitary housing without relocation from one's community.

We demand equal representation at all levels of appointive boards and agencies, and the end to exploitive gerrymandering.

We demand the strong enforcement of all sections of the Treaty of Guadalupe-Hidalgo, particularly the sections dealing with the land grants and bilingual guarantees.

We are outraged by and demand and end to police harassment, discrimination and brutality inflicted on La Raza, and an end to the kangaroo court system known as juvenile hall. We demand constitutional protection and guarantees in all courts of the United States.

We affirm a dedication to our heritage, a bilingual culture, and assert our right to be members of La Raza Unida, anywhere, anytime, and in any job.[15]

Neither are there the files from the FBI's Legat, Mexico City on Galarza's last-minute trip to Mexico City to advise President Luis Echevarria Alvarez against signing an extension of the Bracero Program as proposed by President Gerald Ford in 1973. Galarza was successful; Echevarria did not accept the accord. I know because I was there as was Mexican advisor and former graduate student of Galarza's, Dr. Jorge Bustamante.

## SPY OR COMMUNIST OR BOTH?

In the case of Ernesto Galarza, he was not only suspected of being a communist but also was working for the Congressional Committee on Education and Labor as the Chief Counsel on Labor. This committee was chaired by none other than the Rev. Adam Clayton Powell, the black representative from Harlem.[16] Hoover quickly sent a note to his SAC in Richmond, Virginia, asking him to investigate Galarza and designated his field division as the office of origin for this task. He warned the SAC, Richmond to conduct the investigation "along very discreet and guarded lines and in no way should the office or persons of foreign Government officials be approached in connection with this inquiry." The letter was dated November 22, 1939, the same day Hoover also responded to the Navy Commander Bryant. He thanked him for the "information concerning Ernesto Galanzo [*sic*]." He also promised that the matter would "be given appropriate consideration and attention." Several months later, on March 1, 1940, the Richmond FBI submitted a three-page report conducted by Robert F. Ryan on "ERNEST GALARZA, with aliases ERNESTO GALANZA, E. GALARSA" responding to the Hoover letter of the prior November 1939. The character of the case was designated as "ESPIONAGE."

The first page of this 1939 report repeats word for word the language of Commander Bryant's allegations. Richmond FBI interviewed Galarza's neighbor, George W. Crump, who provided information about the wife, children, on the "grey Plymouth Sedan of year 1939." The local FBI also interviewed William H. Bacon, Galarza's landlord for the past year and a month; he paid his rent promptly. Bacon also informed the agent that his stepdaughter was fourteen years old and the baby was Galarza's. Bacon made it a point to say "that Mrs. GALARZA is not a Mexican." Bacon did speak highly of Galarza and commented that they had recently vacationed in New York and the prior year driven to Mexico. He described Galarza as being "38" years old, "5′9" with "Black" hair and weighing about "155" lbs. "Very sociable, scholarly type" (p.2). The next person interviewed was Herbert S. Mills, "the Assistant to the Chief Clerk of the Pan American Union." Mills reported that Galarza had been employed by the Pan American Union (PAU) for the past three years and was now the Chief of the Division of Labor and Social Information for the PAU. He believed "GALARZA is a citizen of Mexico and has heard rumors that GALARZA was Socialistic in his political beliefs." He verified the license plate of the Galarza's car and the FBI agent checked with the Arlington Police Department and "found to be registered in the name of E. GALARSA" (*sic*) (p.2). Richmond FBI closed the report with promises to contact the Galarza superiors at the PAU "regarding subject connection with subversive groups, or activities indicating acts of Espionage" (p.3).

Just imagine the difference in attitudes and feelings toward Galarza and his family generated by the FBI questioning their neighbors, landlord, and employer about him from that day forward. How would our superiors at any college or university react to such inquiries and pointed questions about any of us? How would they answer the questions of any "connection with subversive groups, or activities indicating acts of Espionage" they thought you or I have had or having? These early defamatory allegations stem from his work with the PAU. The PAU began in the 1900s as an organization "which would promote unity, peace, and economic trade among the other American nations." In 1940, the PAU "created a Division of Labor and Social Information and appointed Galarza as its chief."[17]

SAC, Richmond J.E. Lawler wrote Hoover a letter the following month, April 10, 1940, asking that he consider changing the "Office of Origin from the Richmond to the Washington Field Division." This was a smart move on Lawler's part given most of the Galarza work was out of Washington, DC with the PAU and this transfer would reduce his workload having been increased by this case. Hoover approved the transfer on April 20 by letter to SAC Lawler. By May 1, 1940, FBI SA G.A. Nicholson of the Washington FBI field office reported to Hoover, a two-page report, but still characterized the case as "ESPIONAGE." Agent Nicholson put in the synopsis of the case that Galarza's activities were normal and "reported less radical than average labor worker." He had interviewed Dr. L. S. Rowe, the director general of the PAU and the Chief Clerk, William Griffin. Dr. Rowe described Galarza as "very able and capable individual, whose integrity, in his opinion, is above reproach." "He works long and hard and his record is excellent" were more accolades stated by Rowe, and quoted in the Nicholson report. Moreover, Dr. Rowe said, "he is quite certain that GALARZA, although loyal to his home country, would not engage in any subversive activities or act as an espionage agent in any way" (p.1). Chief Clerk Griffin similarly was complimentary of Galarza. He had known and worked with him for over four years. Galarza, according to Griffin, was "reliable and dependable, and "apparently holds the United States in the highest esteem." Galarza lives an exemplary life, spending the major portion of his time working at the office. The only criticism of the United States Griffin heard Galarza make was "that he feels that the Negro should be given greater privileges and more rights and that educational facilities in greater number should be made available to that race in order that eventually racial equality in the United States be more than just theory" (p.2).

Investigation of Galarza by the FBI did not quiet down for long because on February 13, 1941, SAC, McLean, Virginia, Guy Hottel, wrote to Hoover. Hottel, however, characterized this case as "Internal Security (C)." He informed Hoover that a PAU employee, Helen Waters, had become alarmed about "a number of persons employed at the Union . . . not favorably disposed to the United States form of government." She had complained to their office about "CONCHA ROMERO JAMES" and "one GALARZA." Mrs. Waters alleged "Miss JAMES is an avowed Communist . . . who has arranged for numerous other Mexicans of Communistic tendencies to be employed in the Intellectual Cooperation Bureau of the Union." The home address for Mrs. James was provided as was Dr. Galarza's. Mrs. Waters said that Galarza was "the worse offender of these Mexican brought in by Miss James." She made more allegations against Dr. Galarza such as his organizing "in the colored section of Washington, where he has been spreading propaganda and holding negro Communistic meetings." She also recalled a speech given by Galarza in the winter of 1938, which was "particularly bitter speech against the United States." Hoover wasted no time in writing a solo-page memo on April 17, 1941, to L.M.C. Smith, Chief; Special Defense Unit, recommending that "Ernesto Galanza [*sic*] whose address is 1620 South Highland, Arlington, Virginia" be "considered for custodial detention." "Galanza, [*sic*] Ernesto" was placed on the Custodial Detention Index (CDI) as of April 30, 1941. On the CDI card he is described as: "Known miscellaneous dangerous suspect. Educated Mexican who is anti-American and anti-capitalist." Two weeks later, May 19, 1941, the SAC, Richmond notified Hoover that a mail cover on "ERNESTO GALARZA with aliases: Ernesto Galanso, E. Galarsa. ESPIONAGE" has been placed on him at the South Highland address "for thirty days." In a five-page report dated June 24, 1941, from Special Agent

C.A. Evans of the Richmond FBI office to Hoover, he stated various find-
ings. They also ran a credit check and obtained list of former residences
for Galarza which they listed (p.1–2). His salary and that of his wife were
verified as amounting to approximately $5,275 per annum plus another $400
from honoraria and an unspecified figure earned from a summer project, The
Yearling School, his wife and he operated at Jamaica, Long Island, New
York. The police department at Arlington, Virginia, had no record on him.
Results from the mail cover were reported and names of sender and addres-
sor with postmarks and dates were provided to the FBI by C. F. Simpson,
Assistant Postmaster in Arlington, Virginia (p.2–3). Agent Evans closed with
this conclusion: "subject is purported to be a Mexican and to be anti-Amer-
ican and anti-capitalist. There has also been some indication that subject is
connected with the Communist movement. Previous neighborhood investigations and contact with his employer, however, fail to substantiate this" (p.3).
Because the credit bureau had provided prior addresses for Galarza, Agent
Evans listed five of the FBI filed offices he asked to obtain information on
Galarza (p.4). The last page quotes Commander Bryant's original allegation
about Galarza.

Summer 1941 must have been slow because the next three-page report
from SA R. Howard Calhoun with the Washington, DC, FBI office dated
September 18 had changed his name correctly to "ERNEST GALARZA"
but sill used "alias ERNESTO GALANZA," an obvious typographical error
by someone not familiar with Spanish surnames. The character of the case is
"INTERNAL SECURITY (C)," which suggests the "Espionage" angle has
been discarded and only the Communist label is relevant. The report begins
by providing the Subjects Certificate of Citizenship no. 4549224 issued in
Norfolk, Virginia, on January 27, 1939, to "ERNEST GALARZA" (p.1).
His physical description is included as White male, age thirty-three, medium
complexion, black hair, brown eyes, 5'7" tall, weighing 148 pounds, Mexican
for the prior nationality. He is married and has no distinctive marks. The
search for a citizenship file by Mrs. Geraldine McQuay on the subject uncov-
ered a duplicate copy. FBI, DC was going to keep looking for "rest of the file"
in "the New York office of the Service" (p.3). A copy of the CDI card was
sent by Hoover to the Richmond FBI office on December 19, 1941. The card,
however, was still under the name of "GALANZA, ERNESTO" and only
was updated to reflect he taught Spanish at Harvard University and the latest
allegations: "He is a Communist, but may not belong to the party; has made
inflammatory speeches to negroes in Washington, D.C. He is anti-American,
anti-Capitalist, and thoroughly communistic. He has been with Pan-American
Union for several years." SAC, Richmond H.I. Bobbitt on December 29,
1941, wrote to Hoover recommending cancellation of the custodial detention
card on Galarza because none of the allegations from the past have proven to

be true. But on February 9, 1942, Hoover advised the SAC Richmond against cancelling the custodial detention card on Galarza until they have heard from the Special Defense Unit on the matter.

The New Year, 1942, arrived with a two-page report from Special Agent R.C. Kopriva of the Washington, DC office to Hoover dated the 3rd. It reported to have received the entire file on naturalization records of Galarza. It seems from that investigation of documents that the subject came from *Mazatlan Mexico* "on foot" and arrived in Nogales, Arizona on May 17, 1927. In the details section of the page, the birthplace and date of Galarza as August 15, 1905, in *Tepic, Mexico.* He is married to MAE ROSEL GALANZA as of December 24, 1928, in Sacramento, California. She was born in Florin, California, on January 3, 1902. The couple "have one child, ELIE LOU, who was born on August 6, 1937, at Washington D. C., and, at time of filing the petition, subject resided at 624 North Tazewell Street, Arlington, Virginia" (p.2).[18] Perhaps, this January 3 letter from the local FBI office jolted Hoover's memory and he fired off a short, curt, memo that same day to the SAC, Richmond stating "your office has not submitted a report since June 24, 1941" on the subject. "This matter is extremely delinquent and should be given immediate attention." Hoover reminded SAC, Richmond again on January 13 of no report being submitted on the matter.

Special Agent B.E. Primm from FBI Baltimore reported to Hoover in a three-page report, dated January 6, 1942, that "Mrs. MAE GALARZA was not successful as teacher and not re-appointed for current year. Suspected of being Communist by one principal. Nothing definite as basis for this suspicion. Parent of one of her pupils, who entertained her and subject, believe their attitudes or beliefs not un-American" (p.1) On the next two pages were interviews by the FBI agents with Dorothy Nichols her teaching supervisor, and Kathryn Briker, fellow sixth grade teacher with Mrs. Galarza; both commented on their beliefs and attitudes toward both Dr. Galarza and the wife, Mae. It seems the Galarza's were perceived as frugal and critical of middle-class life "for begin too generous with their children." Supposedly, proof of how spartan a life the Galarza's led was the treatment of the fourteen-year-old stepdaughter who was made to work in the home for $10 a week and then objection to her spending this money on clothes" (p.2). Mrs. Briker suspected them of being Communists or having Communist leanings. "She described Mrs. Galarza as being a woman of a very glib tongue, one who knows all the answers and one who, on account of the influence of her husband, led a very frugal existence. She stated Mrs. Galarza never wore make-up and wore cotton stockings" (p.3). Mrs. Marquise M. Childs, an acquaintance of the Galarza's related how they entertained them in their home. Her husband knew and liked Dr. Galarza very much. They did not think the Galarza's were un-American. They agreed with their criticism "concerning the American middle-class child" (p.3).

On January 22, 1942, upon form memo from Hoover to the SAC, Richmond the CDI card on "ERNESTO GALANZO" was ordered to be changed downward from "Group A: Individuals believed to be the most dangerous and who in all probability should be interned in event of War" to "Group B: Individuals believed to be somewhat less dangerous but whose activities should be restricted."

Spring 1942, March 12, SA R.W. Meadows from the New York FBI office sent Hoover a three-page report on "ERNESTO GALANZA, with aliases." The character of the case was changed to "INTERNAL SECURITY-R." The synopsis of facts which open every FBI report before details are stated, informs that the "NYC PD," the Police Department reflects that subject operated the Gardiner [*sic*] School" in "Jamaica, LI, NY, for about five years prior to 1936, at which time he gave up the school to accept a position with the Pan American Union., Washington, D.C." According to Agent Meadows, the NYCPD's detective that interviewed persons with knowledge of the Galarza couple was "Edward J. Murtagh, Shield # 1923, Special Squad #1." He interviewed Evelyn Wheaton (p.1) and "Mrs. John Adikes" (p.2). Both of them had children enrolled in the "Gardiner School" and had Mrs. Galarza as their teacher, sometimes Mr. Galarza. The two interviewees stated they "and several other mothers" removed their children because of the content of their teaching. Supposedly, both of the Galarza's expressed dissatisfaction with "the manner in which the world was being run and was continually sympathizing with the 'underprivileged.'" The interviewees believed these were Communistic leanings as he often spoke of the "deplorable conditions which had been caused by the enslaving of labor in California." Another reason stated those interviewed but not clearly tied to the removal of their children was this statement: "the subject accepted a colored boy as a student. Mrs. Wheaton could not recall the boy's name. It had been rumored, however, that his mother, a New York City school teacher, was an active worker in the Communist Party" (p.2) Attached to this report was a speech delivered by Ernesto Galarza at a conference of Inter-American Affairs and provided to Mrs. Wheaton by US Representative Jerry Voorhis of California. The Galarza speech was actually a lecture about the "Study of Latin America" delivered in his capacity as "Chief of the Division of Labor and Social Information of the Pan American Union." (p.3).

March 11, 1942, SAC, Richmond despite case on Galarza being closed there, wrote to Hoover a two-page letter informing him of an imminent reclassification by the Selective Service Local Board #2 in Arlington, Virginia, of the status for drafting him into military service. FBI Richmond sent this notice and the CDI card on Galarza plus seven reports and four letters about him to the Baltimore Field Division "for any action it may desire to take concerning the subject" (p.2). On June 8, 1942, SAC, Richmond H. L. Bobbitt, wrote to Hoover asking to close the Galarza investigation because "this file fails to reflect any definite information concerning the nationalistic tendencies of this individual." He also asked to have the Newark Office "discontinue the investigation requested."

SAC, Richmond informed Hoover by two-page report that Ernesto Galarza would probably be reclassified by the Selective Service Board from 3-A to "1-A in the near future." This meant Galarza could be drafted into military service at a day's notice. This report prepared by Agent D.E. Irwin was dated July 9, 1942, and it also included information on the voting behavior of Ernesto Galarza. He "had voted in 1938 and had paid his poll tax for that year but since that time had not voted nor did they have any record concerning him." Galarza had notified his draft board, the Selective Service Boar Local #2 that he was going to Latin America. And, he reported by letter dated April 15, 1942, that "he had returned and that his address would be the Pan American Union, Washington, D.C." (p.1).

## THE PAN AMERICAN UNION

Ernesto Galarza began employment at the PAU in 1936. There were two major upheavals at the PAU and Galarza's Division that ended his relationship with the organization after almost a decade of service. The first confrontation between him and his employer, the PAU, was over the tin strike in Bolivia by those mine workers. In 1942, the Bolivian government passed "fair labor legislation" that protected workers in all sectors much more so than ever. The US Department of State through its ambassador in Quito, Bolivia, denounced the measure and pressured the Bolivian government to reject such reform. The miners went on strike. The State Department's oppositional position was based on the negative impact that higher costs for tin would have on the Allies fighting World War II. Galarza argued this was a transparent ploy to protect US mining interests in Bolivia. Later in life, Bolivia would honor Ernesto Galarza with its highest national honor as the recipient of The Order of the Condor of the Andes in 1956. The second confrontation finally upset the PAU applecart. In 1947, Galarza wrote and publically campaigned against the new bilateral agreement between the United States and Mexico on the importation of Mexican labor. Popularly known as the Bracero Program, Public Law 45 passed by Congress in 1943, became like the intervention by the US State Department that led to the tin strike as far as Galarza was concerned.[19] He saw the Bracero Program as another US agribusiness ploy that was clearly unfair, inhumane, and exploitative of labor on both sides of the border. Those working in agriculture in the United States would lose their jobs to these young, healthy, robust, men from Mexico. He said it as nothing more than a rent-a-slave program and resigned from the PAU.[20] The State Department was pressuring Mexico to send these men to harvest their crops and in so doing, support the war effort. The US men were fighting World War II in Europe's battlefields. Galarza's report opposing the Bracero Program was contracted for publication by Harper & Row, but they ultimately decided against publishing it for being "too explosive."[21]

Behind the scenes and unbeknownst to Galarza was the communication between the FBI in DC and the FBI's contact at the US Embassy with Pierre de L. Boal as US ambassador to Bolivia. They were both trying to figure out how Ernesto Galarza was getting the information on the mining industry in Bolivia and its source. A confidential one-page memo, undated and unsigned by either sender or recipient but about "ERNEST GALARZA" states he traveled for four months around South American countries, "visited Brazil, Uruguay, Argentina, Chile, and Peru, prior to visiting Ecuador." He was "in Quito, Ecuador from March 19 to March 21, 1942." During this tour, he "contacted labor unions throughout South America." The source providing this information to the reporter of this memo also stated that "subject was a Communist, but, as previously noted, investigation has failed to substantiate this allegation" (p.1). Sometime after Hoover decided that his headquarters needed more space and its own privacy from the daily hub bub of agents coming and going. He authorized opening a Washington, DC, office as an FBI Field division; thereafter differentiate between his office and the DC office he began to add to his signature line on some transmissions, Seat of Government (SOG).[22] The next transmission is dated January 2, 1943, a three-page memorandum sent from La Paz, Bolivia to [name redacted] and marked as "Item no. 101." It makes references to seven cables and memos all dated during the month of December [redacted as to names sending and receiving such communication and just a one-line on subject matter]. Apparently, Hoover wanted to know if there "was any connection between the labor trouble in the mines and the plant survey program." [The plant program actually was the Plant Protection Commission]. The La Paz source had already informed him of there being none as of January 1, 1943. However, this memo referred to "relationship between the managements of various mining properties and labor have not been entirely harmonious at any time." The memo then related a brief history of labor strife since September 1941 which was quelled "with soldiers of the Bolivian Army to protect these properties and prevent similar destruction." This memo also identified "JAMES PATTON, president of the National Farmers Union" as who may have given the information about the mining strikes in Bolivia to US newspapers who reported Ambassador Boal as having "interfered in the internal politics of the country and the labor troubles at Catavi" (p.2). Admittedly, US Embassy staff were present at the Catavi mine location because, according to the memo, an American engineer had been abducted and held incommunicado by striking miners for "forty-five minutes." At bottom of this last page, in "Ad addendum: On December 30, 1942, the ambassador advised the writer [name redacted under the signature line] that ERNESTO GALARZA . . gave the information to PATTON which resulted in the newspaper publicity regarding the Ambassador's interference in the internal affairs of this Government." This writer closes with this last line in the addendum: "It is requested that the Bureau submit any information that it may have on GALARZA to this office" (p.3). No other document was released on this specific incident.

The next month on April 16, 1943, Hoover via diplomatic air pouch sent a personal and confidential one-page letter to [name redacted] but it must be his contact at the US Embassy in Bolivia. Hoover sent "all pertinent information contained in the Bureau files relative to subject." The FBI contact is advised to give the ambassador "the information contained in the enclosed memo-randum, but you are not to inform the ambassador that the subject has been investigated by the Bureau in connection with alleged Communist activities. It is not deemed advisable to conduct an investigation in the United States at this time to determine whether subject is in correspondence with anyone in Bolivia" (p.1).

## THE AG'S BOMB TO HOOVER

The CDI program developed and relied on by Hoover since the Red Scare Days and perhaps in an earlier version since the Palmer Raids came to an end on July 16, 1943. Acting Labor Secretary Louis Post disagreed with these raids and reversed over 70 percent of the 1,600 deportation warrants issued to immigrants suspected of wanting "to overthrow the U.S. government."[23] Better stated, CDI should have ended that day, but Hoover found another way to skirt the direct order and not comply fully. Attorney General Frances Biddle via Hugh B. Cox, the assistant attorney general, wrote Hoover a direct order to end the program. The two-page letter is most critical of the utility of this Index. Cox wrote these lines, for example, "individual danger classifica-tions, I am satisfied that they serve no useful purpose"; "there is no statutory authorization or other present justification for keeping a 'custodial detention' list of citizens"; "this classification system is inherently unreliable"; "it is impractical, unwise, and dangerous"; "this classification system was a mis-take that should be rectified for the future"; and, finally, "each card . . should be stamped with the following language":

THIS CLASSIFICATION IS UNRELIABLE. IT IS HEREBY CANCELLED AND SHOULD NOT BE USED AS A DETERMINATINO OF DANGEROUSNESS OR OF ANY OTHER FACT. (SEE MEMORANDUM OF JULY 16, 1943 FROM THE ATTORNEY GENERAL TO HUGH B. COX AND J. EDGAR HOOVER). (p.2)

Hoover did not obey completely. He merged the data of the CDI into the Security Index. He wrote a short one-paragraph note to SAC, Baltimore, on August 26, 1943, on Ernesto Galarza and instructed them to "remove the Security Index card furnished you by the Bureau from your confidential file and place it in the investigative file."

## TURNING TO LABOR ORGANIZING

Moving back to San Jose, California, Galarza took a job as director of Research and Education for the NFLU. But he did not stay home; he traveled and became more a union organizer than a researcher/educator. During the filming of *Poverty in the Land of Plenty*, he began organizing for the NFLU in California, Texas, Louisiana, Florida, and Arizona. His first assignment was to assist in the strike in Arvin, California, against Di Giorgio Fruit Corporation, which they lost.[24] In 1950, he led the tomato workers into a strike at Tracey, California. In 1951, he was organizing cantaloupe pickers in the Imperial Valley and between 1953 and 1954 he was organizing sugarcane workers in Louisiana. While engaged in these organizing efforts, the spate of "Right to Work" laws were being passed by Southern states and ultimately the US Congress. "Galarza became a familiar face in Congressional hearings." The legislation underwent various revision but eventually obtained the support of major unions because the new law not allowing a right to unionize or join a union was limited to agricultural workers. Disappointed and disenchanted with his labor counterparts, he quit the NFLU. He began writing a grant to the Fund for the Republic, which was funded for $25,000. This work became the book, *Strangers in the Field* (1955). He was becoming known as the "migrant academic."

### The Strange 1950s Files

The FBI document trail on Ernesto Galarza takes a huge leap in omission from 1943 when his CDI card was switched to the Security Index file and finally into an investigative file to 1951. The Security Index had been started by Hoover since the days of President Roosevelt and in the 1950s began to include those Hoover regarded as dissidents—some 15,000 individuals.[25] No other document was released to this author until one dated May 10, 1951, after a gap of seven years and three months. And, this one memo is most bizarre and out of character and personality for Ernesto Galarza. Allegedly, Galarza agreed to help the FBI in its investigation of Leon Freeman (FBI file no. 100-11820). This is the substance of a four-page memo from Hoover to the SAC, San Francisco sent on the above date. Hoover is asking San Francisco FBI to seek to interview Galarza residing at 2174 Bridgeway Street in San Jose, California. Hoover enclosed nine reports on Galarza prepared by various FBI agents from 1940 to July 1942. Hoover adds, "The Bureau's investigation of Galarza was terminated during 1943." He also added that a prominent New York attorney, Morris L. Ernst, gave a lot of information to a Bureau agent on the activities of three men: Vicente Lombardo Toledano of Mexico, William Rhodes Davis, and John L. Lewis; and, another person named Jacob Landau. All of these men had insight into the Mexican expropriation of oil away from US companies. The Landau meeting with Ernesto Galarza on this topic convinced him that Galarza knew more about this "Mexican oil deal." Attorney Ernest was equally convinced that another FBI target, Lee Pressman, was behind the Davis-Lewis-Toledano oil deal. Lee was named Leon in the opening regarding line of this memo. Apparently, "Ernesto Galarza was interviewed by a Bureau representative on May 18, 1942." Galarza had a lot of information on this matter as Landau had suspected and shared it with the FBI representative. He told the FBI persons that Lee Pressman was the one who arranged for a Mexican Supreme Court Justice, Xavier Icaza to come to New York and try to meet with John Lewis. That same justice had asked Galarza to arrange such a meeting; "this Galarza was unable to do" (p.2). "On May 23, 1942, Galarza furnished the Bureau with photostatic copies of documents from his files," three of them germane to the Mexican oil deal (p.3). SAC, San Francisco reported to Hoover on July 10, 1951, in a two-page memo on the "Mexican oil deal" as these documents referred to the Mexican expropriation which had been carried out by President Lazaro Cardenas in 1936. In this report, a second interview with Galarza was had on June 30. It was Galarza's opinion that "the Communists were making inroads into the laboring class in South America. He said he took steps to have the "American labor movement to prevent this ... and was referred to Leon Freeman, as legal counselor for the CIO." But Galarza readily saw "Freeman was adhering to the Communist Party line." He did not know if Freeman was a card carrying Communist. Galarza complained that as he presented reforms while working for the PAU to improve working conditions of labor in South America he was opposed by Freeman who "wanted to keep things as they were." As a result of this, he and Freeman were openly hostile. Galarza stated that it was Toledano who claimed credit for being responsible for the Mexican Expropriation Decree of September 1936; "Toledano's name became synonymous with oil in Mexico" (p.1). The issue of the Mexican oil deal is explained this way in the second page of this memo. The expropriation brought US sanctions including a boycott of Mexican oil; the oil workers were out of jobs and the unions on both sides of the border were concerned. The talks between Freeman of the CIO and Toledano of the Mexican union, *Confederacion de Trabajadores Mexicanos* (CTM) were to try to get the United States to buy Mexican oil and Mexico to stop selling it to Nazi Germany. The report documents dates of travel by those named above to Mexico during the years of 1937 and 1939 (p.2). Hoover contacted the FBI's Legal Attache in Mexico City on August 2, 1951, by way of three-page letter sent by Air Pouch and sent him the abovementioned memo on Pressman. Leon Pressman had been called to testify before the House Committee on Un-American Affairs (HCUA) on August 28, 1950. The FBI was trying to establish "or refuting the reliability of the testimony of Pressman before the HCUA." In plain language, the FBI was trying to make a case for perjury, a felony with which to jail Freeman. Hoover finally used the word "perjury" in the second page in this context: "The Bureau is endeavoring to develop the perjury aspects, if any, with regard to Pressman's UCUA testimony." Freeman had testified before HCUA that he only traveled to Mexico once in 1936 in the company of Joseph Eckhart. Yet, others reporting to the FBI, including Galarza, provide more dates of Freeman's travel to Mexico. Hoover was asking the Legal Attache to look into "whether Freeman made any trips to Mexico other than the one with Eckhart in 1936" (p.2). The substance of the Galarza interview with the FBI representative is the subject matter of the May 22, 1952, two-page memo from the FBI director to the SAC, San Diego. In that interview and in his FBI file, it was recorded and reviewed time and again, that Galarza was born in Mexico. Yet, a Sheriff, R. W. Ware, of Imperial County, El Centro, California, had information he obtained from a friend, Ismael C. Falcon, in Mexico City who "can supply information showing the subject is a Spanish citizen and that if this is so, Galarza is in the United States on a false visa." Given that "Galarza is an organizer of the NFLU and in 1951 and 1952 has been actively engaged in organizing members for that union in the El Centro area," the sheriff advised that his experience with the subject "shows that he is one of the more radically inclined organizers of the union although he is not known to be a Communist." Hoover alerted San Diego FBI that they were asking the Mexico City Legat to begin an investigation into this new item that Galarza was a Spaniard. INS was also asked to look into this matter (p.2). The letter sent by Hoover to the Commissioner of the INS is dated May 22, 1952.

On June 2, 1952, SAC, San Diego reported to Hoover and enclosed an article from a farm magazine, the May–June 1952 issue. The article was supplied to them by Sheriff Ware. The article stated C. Ismael Falcon was touring the

West, parts of Texas, New Mexico, Arizona and California. He was being paid for some of his presentations by local groups wanting to hear his comments in which he "claimed that Communists in Mexico were distributing propaganda literature detrimental to Mexican-American relations and to the program of recruiting and hiring Mexican Nationals for work on American farms." Hoover was "especially interested in obtaining his photograph" (p.2). By October 10, Hoover had a response from Raymond F. Farrell, Assistant Commissioner of Investigations Division for INS. They wanted the FBI to "furnish this office the identity and availability of the informant mentioned in paragraph 1 of your memorandum, who advised that the subject has title of Southwestern Organizer for the National Farm Labor Union, and was a citizen of Spain, and was not born in Mexico as claimed." There was no way Hoover was going to get Sheriff Ware to produce Ismael Falcon from Mexico City with such proof. Hoover did try. He wrote to SAC, San Diego on October 28 to "contact Sheriff R.W. Ware . . . and determine if he has any objection to being interviewed by a representative of the Immigration and Naturalization Service." SAC, San Diego on December 2, 1952, in a single-page memo to Hoover informs him that Sheriff Ware now states that Bernard A. Harrison, the secretary/treasurer of the Imperial Valley Farmer's Association and the County Agricultural commissioner was the source of the information on Galarza that he obtained from Falcon. According to Harrison, they paid Falcon some money for coming to El Centro and he was to return soon. Harrison would alert the FBI when that visit would take place. "It is believed that FALCON would be receptive to an interview by a Bureau Agent at the time of his next visit with HARRIGAN, who agreed to advise SA DOYLE of FALCON's presence in El Centro, California."

Hoover had graduated from law school years back and apparently had forgotten the Hearsay Rule. Sheriff Ware was just repeating to the FBI what he heard Falcon said to Harrison who said it to him. Sheriff Ware did not have such proof of Galarza citizenship or birthplace alleged to be in Spain. Hoover had no choice but to punt. He wrote back to the INS "Attention: Mr. Raymond F. Farrell" on January 6, 1953, about this matter and stated: "It is suggested that a representative of your Service contact Sheriff Ware in this matter."

On April 12, 1954, the executive assistant to the attorney general wrote to Hoover a short memo with a request: "May I have whatever information you have in your files regarding Ernesto Galarza." Hoover responded a few days later with a four-page letter. He does not send any reports, letters, articles, nothing but his own narrative to the AG's office, technically his boss. Instead Hoover details some of the more salacious allegations against Galarza that his Bureau investigated. He related this work history from graduate school at Columbia University, with the Gardiner School, the PAU, and the NFLU. He included more salacious remarks attributed to Galarza by others such as criticizing the US government for its treatment of Negroes (p.1). Some of Galarza's public presentations such as the one before the Lawyer's Committee on American Relations with Spain in 1933 were cited. Hoover pointed out that this group was identified by HCUA as a Communist front organization.[26] And, he pointed out the tin strike event that triggered Galarza's resignation from PAU because he alleged the US ambassador had a hand in the internal affairs of Bolivia. To underscore the Communist charge but never substantiated by the FBI against Galarza, Hoover cited "an article in *The People's World*, a west coast Communist newspaper, for July 7, 1944" that "stated Galarza spoke at the University of Southern California." He "criticized the treatment of Mexicans who are in the United States." On a personal note, Hoover made mention that Galarza's step-daughter, Karlan [previously identified as Karla] Rosel Galarza, "was ousted from a Negro school in Washington, known as the Murray Washington Vocational School (p.2). It was reported that when learned that Kiss Galarza was Mexican, which nationality was classified as white by the United States Census Bureau, she was expelled" (p.3). Hoover provided more quotes from Galarza such as before President Truman's Commission on Migratory Labor which he said, "the major objective of the contracting of Mexican nationals and hiring of illegals is to freeze and further depress, if possible, the starvation level of farm wages." The interview Galarza had with the FBI over Lee Freeman was detailed (p.3) along with the assertion by Sheriff Ware of El Centro that Galarza was really a Spaniard and not Mexican as he claimed and stated on government forms (p.4).

The following year, 1955, had little disclosed activity; only one document was released. It was a two-page memo from the SAC, WFO dated the January 20 to the director, FBI on another bizarre volunteer spy caper by a member of the American Legion who was a cab driver in DC. The taxi driver got a note from a drunk passenger claiming to be LINN GALE. The taxi man gave the note to Walter S. Steele who in turn passed it on to FBI agent Albert C. Hayden, Jr. Apparently, the local news media printed that the US attorney had brought a case against someone named BENNETT and Galarza had been mentioned as a witness. The note the taxi man obtained had the name of Galarza on it. Steele thought the FBI "might find valuable in attacking GALARZA's credibility as a witness." SAC, WFO also pointed out in this memo that a Linn Gale was in Mexico and "formerly Mexican editor of *The Daily Worker* newspaper." He was deported from Mexico in 1928 or so. "Gale also started a Communist school on 10th St. N.W. between G and H Sts. and had a bookshop above the school" (p.1). The pilfered note read:

Dear Linn—Please excuse delay in replying-I just sent the copy for our Union paper to the printer today. I suggest that you go to see ERNESTO GALARZA of Pan Amer. Union. He is a real fellow and will do all he can to help you get that information. Is well placed to know where to go for it. He saw the "piece" by Denny—tonight's News, of course. Yours, Fred Blossom.

The FBI paper trail gets sketchy again for almost nine years until November 6, 1963. In a three-page memo to someone from someone [names all redacted as to sender and recipient] about Ernesto Galarza and MAE ELENCHINA TAYLOR GALARZA [assume it is the wife]. The memo begins with reference to ten reports enclosed on Galarza from 1940 to 1942 and the news that "no investigations pertinent to your inquiry has been conducted by the FBI concerning his spouse, Mae Elenchina Taylor Galarza." What follows are repeat information, primarily from the 1954 response to the assistant AG (p.1–3). The new additional information on the last page is about Mrs. Galarza being fired by West Coast School Board from teaching at Los Gatos Union Elementary School. The charges were she "planned to slip Union propaganda into the classroom." The other charges were "secret" (p.3). Finally, the Spanish citizen charge is alluded to but the writer states: "You may desire to consult the files of Immigration and Naturalization Service for additional information concerning Ernesto Galarza" (p.3). There is a news clipping made part of this correspondence. It is purported to be from page 7 of the *Daily Worker*, according to the FBI file stamp at right bottom and dated as "Aug 5 1955." The title is "AFL Official's Wife Fired By West Coast School Board." Nothing more is had on this case.

Another paper trail jump from 1955 to May 18, 1966, almost eleven years this time. Mrs. Mildred Steagall, who worked for Marvin Watson as special assistant to the president at the White House, requested information, a names check, on Ernesto Galarza, "who resides at 1801 Crest Vista, Monterey Park, California. Hoover responded with a four-page memo to Watson on Galarza. He repeated most of the same information he had submitted to the AG previously and now included the firing of Mrs. Galarza as a teacher (p.1–3). The last items related were that Dr. Galarza spoke at the Southwest Conference on Interstate-Intergroup Affairs in Phoenix, Arizona in April 1964. This information was obtained from an open source, the April 18, 1964, edition of *People's World*, a Communist Party newspaper. And, that a check of the fingerprint files held by the FBI "contain no arrest data identifiable with Mr. Galarza" (p.4). An almost identical request dated March 1, 1967, about Ernesto Galarza with all names redacted is the last file in the packet of documents released to me. This three-page memo is almost word-for-word identical to the response sent the White House on May 18 the year prior but for one item. There is a newspaper clipping attached to the letter titled

"'Brown Power' Conferees Deplore Absence of White House Aides" penned by Sidney Kossen. This was obtained by the FBI from an open source, *The Washington Post Times Herald* of March 30, 1967. Chicanos, 600 of them, had gathered for two days in Sacramento, the state capital for California, under the call for a Brown Power Conference and had requested the White House send a representative, and also the vice president. Some federal agencies such as Labor Housing and Urban Development, Agriculture, and the Office of Economic Opportunity did send observers. Galarza was a speaker and reported to have said, "We must imitate and beat the Anglo politician at his own game. Far too much American wealth is spent making war and, in the case of Latin American, suppressing revolution." Galarza also criticized the California governor, Ronald Reagan, for reducing subsidies for welfare and if that is the way, all subsidies should be reduced across the board. He singled out the water supply diverted to farms, "millions of dollars to large wealthy farms."

## Price of Leadership

Undoubtedly, Galarza was a pioneer in many historical respects. He was the first in many categories of contributions made to US society by persons of Mexican origin including being nominated for the Nobel Peace Prize in 1979. One of those categories of contribution seldom noted is the personal price he and his family paid for his leadership and determination. Time and again he put principles ahead of comfort; ideals ahead of economic gain; worker's rights over his own privileges; and, he battled between being a full-time scholar or community organizer. The FBI, relentlessly, monitored his every move, trying to find evidence of his subversive activities and Communist Party membership for years. There was none to be found. He was neither. The FBI knew it and so stated in many documents cited above. Yet, they continued the *ultra vires* fraud of investigating him and his spouse for decades. I wonder what is in documents not released from those huge gaps in the chronology of the surveillance. Clearly, the fact that Galarza worked for the PAU, as the name implies, an aggrupation of sovereign states in the Western Hemisphere of the Americas, North, South, and Central, his public presentations were made for that audience, not just the United States of America. His posture and stance on many issues reflected his work toward that union of nation states not that of the hegemonic United States exclusively. Hoover chose not to understand that it seems reviewing these documents. He never stopped the surveillance.

The last ridiculous allegation was that Galarza had lied on his applications for naturalization claiming he was of Mexican nationality when he really was a Spaniard. Hoover should have known, probably did, that this ruse was based on hearsay on top of hearsay put out by agricultural interests in El Centro, California.

Ernesto Galarza and Mae, his wife, and children must have suffered greatly from all the rumors, innuendo, actual confrontations, and charges leveled at them over the years. All stemming from an illegal abusive use of power by Hoover and his FBI minions across the country. But he and Mae never quit or backed down from any of this. We do not know what other harm came to the children now grown into senior adults.

## NOTES

1. Frank Bardacke, in his work, *Trampling Out the Vintage: Cesar Chavez and the Two Souls of the United Farm Workers* (London: Verso, 2012), 92 states Ernesto Galarza "Was the First Mexican American to Earn a Doctorate in Political Science." *Hispanic Journal of Behavioral Science*, 7 (2) (1985): 135–152, however, in an unnamed author article, "Activism and Intellectual Struggle in the Life of Ernesto Galarza (1905–1984)" to be found at https://libraries.ucsd.edu/farmworkermovement/wp-content/uploads/2012/04/032-Ernesto-Galarza-nan-on-fire.pdf/ accessed August 17, 2019. This article states Ernesto Galarza "was awarded his PhD in Economies in 1947."

2. Ernesto Galarza, *Barrio Boy* (Notre Dame: University of Notre Dame Press, 1971). This iconic book was in its 40th edition as of 2011.

3. Galarza was sued by DiGiorgio Fruit Corporation, its name then, for libel and sought $2 million in damages from him and the Hollywood Film Council. The case was settled for $1 if the NFLU would cease its agitation against DiGiorgio. After the settlement, the NFLU basically died. See Acuña cited in next endnote, 255, for a brief history of this production.

4. Bardacke, *Trampling Out the Vintage*, 92; and these others, as an example, Acuña, *Occupied America*, 225–226, 255; Matt Garcia, *From the Jaws of Victory: The Triumph and Tragedy of Cesar Chavez and the Farm Worker Movement* (Berkeley: University of California Press, 2012), 14, 23, 30; and, Susan Ferris and Ricardo Sandoval, *The Fight in the Fields: Cesar Chavez and the Farmworkers Movement* (San Diego: Harvest Book/Harcourt Brace, 1997), 21, 54, 80.

5. Ernesto Galarza, *Barrio Boy: The Story of a Boy's Acculturation* (Notre Dame: University of Notre Dame Press, 1971), 3, 98.

6. *Ibid.*, 15–16.

7. *Ibid.*, 97, 99, 118–119, 129, 181, 196. See also *Hispanic Journal*, "Activism."

8. *Ibid.*, citing *The Arizona Republic*, June 24, 1973.

9. Galarza, *Barrio Boy*, 238–239.

10. Galarza, *Barrio Boy*, 228.

11. Published under the title of *La industria electrica en Mexico* (Mexico, DF: Fondo de Cultural Economica, 1941). For a more complete listing of all his

scholarship and publications see https://wwwoasys.lib.edu/record=b1210886~SO/. Accessed August 29, 2019.

12. Letter to author from, Archivist, Special Access and FOIA Staff with NARA, two pages. On October 10, 2016, I emailed accepting to pay the amount of $94.40 for these files and to process and send them. On July 12, 2017, I received a letter from the Section Chief, Record/Information Dissemination Section, Records Management Division informing me that the process was underway. It was still more months into 2018 that I finally received these pages. I write this to chronicle the time expended in doing FOIA requests and receiving material.

13. Acuña, *Occupied America*, 297. See also Armando Navarro, *The Mexican American Youth Organization: Avant-Garde of the Chicano Movement in Texas* (Austin: University of Texas Press, 1995) for a political biography of this organization.

14. See Ernesto Vigil, *The Crusade for Justice: Chicano Militancy and the Government's War on Dissent* (Madison: University of Wisconsin Press, 1999) and my *Tracking King Tiger: The FBI File on Reies Lopez Tijerina* (E. Lansing: Michigan State University Press, 2019) for the only two recent books utilizing FBI documents to analyze these two leaders and organizations.

15. In author's personal files from days as cofounder of MAYO in Texas.

16. See https://libraries.ucsd.edu/farmworkermovement/wp-content/uploads/2012/04/032-ERNESTO-GALARZA-MAN-OF-FIRE.pdf/ accessed August 17, 2019.

17. *Hispanic Journal*, "Activism."

18. For some more biographical data on Ernesto Galarza see https://egare.ucr.edu/about.html/ and in *The Hispanic Journal*, article "Activism" fully cited above in endnote 1.

19. The first importation of Mexican labor during this time occurred earlier in 1942 as an emergency labor measure. See a quick historical summary of this legislation and program in Acuña, *Occupied America*, 255–257.

20. A subsequent transmission from the FBI to field offices contained two editorials undated and without source indicated both written by James A. Wechsler and may have been published in the *New York Times* but the FBI redacted all that information. The two editorials are entitled: "Boal Expose Costs Galarza His Pan-American Job," and "On the Resignation of Ernesto Galarza." A most interesting note at right bottom of his latter editorial clipping copy is "Clipped at the Seat of Government." Hoover apparently self-anointed his FBI headquarters, not the White House, as the seat of government for the United States.

21. *Hispanic Journal*, "Activism," cited in parenthesis "(M. Galarza, personal communication, December 1984)."

22. William Sullivan, *The Bureau: My Thirty Years in Hoover's FBI* (New York: W.W. Norton and Company, 1979), 28, 122. Sullivan also claims that Hoover had FBI agents write his books on Communism and promote their sale: 88–92, 268.

23. See www.britannica.com/topic/Palmer-Raids/. Accessed August 29, 2019.

24. For a brief history of the Di Giorgio dynasty built by Joseph and son, Robert, this strike, and the fight for survival of the NFLU, see Bardacke, *Trampling Out the Vintage*, 240–243.

25. See Davis, *Spying on America*, 98.

26. Galarza was never subpoenaed to appear before HUAC. It would have made for an exciting exchange between him and his inquisitioners. See James Cross Giblin, *The Rise and Fall of Senator Joe McCarthy* (Boston/New York: Clarion Books, 2009) for a biographical narrative on this person, the linchpin of HUAC and the Red Scare era.

## Chapter 3

# Ramón "Raymond" Telles, First Chicano Ambassador of the United States, and His Wife, Delfina Navarro

My research during my years at the University of Texas-Arlington included conducting oral history interviews with dozens and dozens of public figures, mostly all of Mexican origin.[1] This work led me to interview Richard Lopez Telles, brother to Ramón "Raymond" Telles, who became the first Chicano ambassador of the United States to Costa Rica. The actual title for this position a mouthful: Ambassador Extraordinary and Plenipotentiary.[2]

### THE RAMÓN TELLES AND ANGELA LOPEZ FAMILY

Historian Mario T. Garcia researched and published the first and only political biography of Raymond L. Telles.[3] The biographical narrative that follows is primarily based on my interview with his brother and that of Mario T. Garcia.

Patriarch Ramón Telles was an heir and descendent of a land grant family with roots long established in the area known today as *Ysleta*, south of *El Paso* proper. Mario Garcia writes, "Rather than remaining in predominantly rural environment of Ysleta, where his father had inherited a Spanish land grant which he eventually lost, Ramón moved to El Paso . . ."[4] Nothing more is revealed about how, why, when, to whom, and consequences of this land grant loss other than his becoming a bricklayer in El Paso. While he was a manual laborer of sorts, he met Angela "Angelita" Lopez, who was from *Chihuahua, Mexico*. The Mexican Revolution was in full throttle at this time and one of its principals, Francisco "Pancho" Villa was based in *Chihuahua:* the Mexican state across from El Paso, Texas. Many Mexicans sought to evade the perils of this revolution by crossing the border into El Paso. The US border town across from El Paso is *Juarez, Chihuahua, Mexico*.

In 1913, the young couple married, built their own *adobe* and brick home at 918 South St. Vrain, and began a family. The first-born son died in infancy. They had named him Ramón, in honor of his father and grandfather. There were three more sons born, Jose Ignacio, Ricardo, and another also named Ramón. This second Ramon is the son who became the US ambassador. He was born on September 5, 1915. Once enrolled in the parochial Catholic school, St. Mary's, Ramón became Raymond and also Ray among his friends; Ricardo became Richard. Like his brother Ramon, Ricardo was named after another child by that name who also died in infancy.[5] The parochial school was predominantly Anglo and under the direction of the Sisters of Loretto. The Catholic high school was run by the Christian Brothers. The predominantly Mexican public schools because of segregation were closer but not good enough for the Telles boys, according to Mario Garcia.[6]

Young Telles was not big or strong enough to compete in high school sports, nor was he very talented intellectually. He turned to math and typing as his favorite subjects and to school plays which proved to be invaluable once he graduated. His first job was as a clerk with the Works Progress Administration (WPA) and then at the Federal Penitentiary, *La Tuna*. Later, when he was drafted into the US Army in February 1941, he was stationed in Brownwood, Texas with the 132nd Field Artillery of the 36th Infantry Division. His mother, Angelita, had died the year before. It was during these years that he met his future wife, Delfina Navarro, also from a family of Mexican refugees, but well-to-do financially. Shortly after Pearl Harbor, Raymond came home to marry Delfina on February 15, 1942. He had made the rank of Sergeant and applied for a slot in the Officer Candidate School. He passed the exam and was relocated to Florida. Delfina had to return to El Paso for lack of family housing at that base until he was reassigned to Kelly Air Force base with the newly created Latin American Division whose mission was to provide airplanes to Latin American countries. Now a Lieutenant, Raymond traveled to Mexico, Brazil, Peru, Paraguay, and other countries in South America. He was promoted in rank to Captain and named the liaison officer of the US Air Force to the Mexican Air Force.[7]

## From Military Man to Politician to Ambassador

Telles returned to civilian life in 1947 with the rank of Major, but re-enlisted in the Air Force Reserve for years and reached the rank of Colonel. Meanwhile, he also returned to this former employment at the La Tuna Correctional facility. He and Delfina built their own home, a duplex, on Nevada Street, corner with Virginia Street. He organized a Mexican American veterans' organization. The marriage produced two daughters, Cynthia and Patricia. In 1948, elder Ramón asked his son, the military veteran, to run for County Clerk on the Democratic Party. Elder Ramón himself had run in the 1930s and been elected Constable for Precinct One; a position he held for a long time.[8] Constable Ramón Telles and wife, Angelita, had developed several business ventures that served him well in local politics. They owned a neighborhood grocery store, a taxi service, his rental properties, and with son Richard, started a juke box, *pianola* in Spanish, network of machines in every Mexican bar and restaurant. These were operated and managed by Richard, the younger brother. The campaign for county clerk relied on the Mexican voters in Constable Telles Precinct One; the veterans organized by Raymond and others; and, the many clients of Mexican bars and restaurants where Richard's juke boxes played their favorite music. As Richard put it, Raymond was the brains and he was the muscle in registering voters and getting them to the polls. This was the era of the poll tax where an eligible voter had to pay $1.75 for the privilege of registering to vote, then came the actual voting. Richard's operation drew out 92 percent of the eligible Mexican voters.[9] Raymond did not finish his term because he was called back into military service during the Korean War in 1951; his father died the following year. Upon return, he ran for mayor of El Paso and won. During his second term in the Mayor's office, which he won handily being unopposed, he was picked by President John F. Kennedy to be his ambassador to Costa Rica. "It was rumored from time to time that he would next be named ambassador to Mexico," writes Mario T. Garcia. "Raymond Telles served in Costa Rica for six years (1961–1967) . . . an unusually long tenure for an ambassador in any one country."[10]

### President-elect Transition Teams

John F. Kennedy as presidential candidate among others from the Democratic Party faced tough opposition from inside this own party, not to mention the Republicans with the sitting vice president, Richard M. Nixon as their candidate. The 1960 General Election was a close electoral contest with Nixon carrying the Southwestern states of California, Arizona, and Colorado while Kennedy and his running mate Lyndon B. Johnson barely eked out a victory in Texas and New Mexico. The only Mexican American member of Congress in 1960 was the US Senator from New Mexico, Dennis Chavez, who passed away within two years on November 18, 1962.[11] While Senator Chavez was the titular head of the Viva Kennedy Clubs, the Mexican American component of the JFK/LBJ campaign, it was the grassroots work of others such as Albert A. Peña of San Antonio, Texas and Vicente Ximenes of Floresville, Texas, as but two examples, that got the Democratic ticket the electoral victory in Texas. The Democrats carried Texas by the slimmest of margins, 46,257 votes out of 2,311,084 cast and the national election by the narrowest of margins in the twentieth century.[12] The Viva Kennedy Clubs leadership claimed the Kennedy/Johnson victory was the result of their work. Kennedy and Johnson both felt this group among many other groups in other states could have been the victory tip of the electoral scale; but both publicly acknowledged the debt to many groups, including the Viva Kennedy Clubs.

In 1952, President Eisenhower began compiling a list of government positions he as president had to fill and this list was first published in 1960. It became known as *The Plum Book* and is published every four years just after each presidential election.[13] President-elect John Kennedy had Clark Clifford, and his brother, Robert Kennedy the national campaign manager, recruit and organize a transition team to help him select the best people to run the nation's affairs. Obviously, the Republicans having lost the election had no candidates to consider for the thousands of governmental appointments each president gets to make from day 1 of their administration. The Democrats had to create a list of potential nominees. Sargent Shriver, President-elect Kennedy's brother-in-law, was named the committee head of immediate appointments for the transition team. Shriver had to come up with 1,200 names quickly for the most important positions, ambassadors included.[14] President Kennedy deferred to his vice president on most policy and political matters regarding the Southern states, Texas in particular, since it was Johnson's home state. Vice President Johnson had his own crew of Mexican American loyalists since his first federal elections in 1948 and certainly at the Democratic National Conventions of 1956 and 1960. The latter one was when he had challenged Kennedy for the nomination. Kennedy knew no one in Texas or the other Southwestern states. Bexar County, Texas County Commissioner Albert A. Peña, Jr. was a self-anointed Kennedy man. Medical doctor Hector P. Garcia, founder of the American G.I. Forum, was a Johnson man, both were from Texas and both had worked on the Viva Kennedy Club campaigns.[15] Dr. Garcia's access to Vice President Johnson prevailed in seeking appointees from Texas for federal service; only two, Reynaldo Garza was the first one in March 1961 and, Raymond Telles the second in April 1961.[16] Not much patronage trickled down to those of Mexican origin despite the voter data showing this ethnic group voted almost 90 percent for the Kennedy/Johnson ticket.

## The Role of a US Ambassador

An ambassador has a personality and character that must be held in check as best possible because the person does not represent himself; in fact, he personifies the United States. They are heard as the voice and seen as the *persona* of US foreign policy in the host country. They interact with the highest-ranking officials of the host country and other diplomats representing the interests of the United States and the business interests of major business sector influentials. The ambassador and family live in a fishbowl. US ambassadors also live a socialist life; as do members of Congress, the president and vice president, federal judges, and many senior government officials. For example, members of congress received, in 2019, a salary of $174,000 plus many other perks of staff, travel, parking, unlimited mailing privileges, health, and retirement with full vesting within five years.[17] All senators qualify under this rule. More importantly, they only work about half of the year. In 2018, Congress was in session only 141 days. The congressional leadership gets more. The Speaker of the House earns $223,500 whereas the majority and minority leaders in both houses earns $193,000.

Some 70 percent of ambassadors are chosen by the president and approved by the US Senate; they come from the ranks of career foreign service diplomats, but 30 percent are political figures rewarded for partisan political service usually to the president and or his political party. Raymond Telles was picked from the latter category. The US government, rather better said, the tax payers, pay for everything like in a socialist and communist country to a large extent—health and life insurance, housing, driver, transportation including transportation to vacation destinations, food, expense account, five weeks paid vacation annually, domestic and office personnel, security, generous education stipend for children—and a comfortable salary with benefits. They want for little in terms of personal needs and the necessaries of life.

The salary in 2018 for an ambassador was in the range of $124,406–$187,000 plus a cost of living increase for service and extra stipends for how dangerous the post location is and a hardship on the ambassador and his or her family. There is a 35 percent bump for each of those categories. An ambassador in Iraq or Afghanistan not only gets the high salary but also 70 percent increase for both hardship and danger.[18] Granted that Ambassador Telles served from April 6, 1961 to February 19, 1967 and the wage scale and money benefits were much lower then but, so was the exchange rate from dollars to *colon*, the national currency of Costa Rica.

The current US ambassador in Costa Rica as of August 2017 has been Sharon Day, another political appointee for his service as the Co-Chair of the Republican National Committee. He was born in Texas, but his adult life was spent in Florida.[19]

US ambassadors receive daily instructions from the State Department and must implement those instructions. They are also under internal scrutiny from staff, including the domestic staff usually comprised on host country nationals who tell friends, neighbors, relatives and other interested parties basically all that goes on inside the private quarters of the embassy, the ambassador's home, and the office.[20] While the ambassador in any given country has no control on what the agents of the Central Intelligence Agency (CIA) do or do not do, the CIA does monitor the ambassador from outside the embassy or by the use of informants inside the embassy. The Federal Bureau of

Investigation (FBI), however, has a position of privilege, the Legal Attaché is the official name of the FBI agent stationed in every embassy, at least 60 of them in 2007 staffed by 165 FBI agents plus their support staff.[21] Mexico was the first station of the first FBI man outside the United States beginning in 1939.[22]

## The State Department and FBI Records Have a Hidden Story

The file I have starts with an undated document from the State Department Bureau of Security and Consular Affairs to FBI Director Hoover asking for "an investigation on Mr. Raymond Telles under the procedures established for a Presidential appointee." A brief biographical sketch on him was attached and file stamped by either the FBI or State Department on "FEB 16 1961." This letter is signed by Harris H. Huston, acting administrator of the department named above and ends with one dated July 28, 1976 from FBI Director Clarence M. Kelley.

As ambassador, Telles did an outstanding job particularly when President Kennedy decided to hold his summit meeting with Central American heads of state in San Jose, Costa Rica in March 1963. Earlier the president had been in Mexico to promote the Alliance for Progress, and he had Ambassador Telles at his side. While in San José, President Kennedy stayed in the Ambassador's home. The two got to know each other better. Ambassador Telles convinced a reluctant president to make personal visits to the national, Catholic Cathedral and the University, both in San José. Despite strong objections by the various security and intelligence advisors around the president, Telles prevailed. Both events turned out exceedingly well; those attending to catch a glimpse of the US president were both loud and joyful. President Kennedy was so taken aback and pleased "he got out of the car and walked into the crowd. Thousands of Costa Ricans showed up and were visibly moved when the American Catholic president knelt to pray."[23]

On December 30, 2015, I submitted my Freedom of Information/Privacy Act (FOIPA) request (No. 1323642-000) to the FBI on Raymond Telles. He had passed away in March 2013.[24] Not receiving any documents from the FBI, I appealed the decision and on May 12, 2016, I was given some hope of getting documents if the State Department agreed to release them. I was also informed that the Internal Revenue Service (IRS) also had documents subject to review. On December 7, 2016, I received notice that the FBI had twenty-two pages available but were releasing only eleven pages in full with the remainder being withheld under exemptions (b)(6) and (b) (7)(C) of 5 USC 552. Finally, after years of persistence, I obtained a substantial number of pages from the State Department and more from the FBI.

**The Name Check Program**

The initial request by the White House is to the FBI as the usual procedure in place in 1961 for all presidential appointees and military personnel being considered.[25] Handwritten at bottom left of this first letter are the words, "Teletype to El Paso Bu, WFO 2/20/61 GTS/." This disclosure is followed by a three-page series of notes indicating files and sources consulted, I assume to be part of the investigation. A teletype went out dated "2-20-61" and headlined "URGENT" was sent from the Director's office, to the SAC's in El Paso, Baltimore, St. Louis, and WFO (BSM). It informs that the "State Department has requested an investigation on Telles, position for which considered not stated." It proceeds to describe Telles the same as the description provided in the first document from the State Department. Hoover asks the investigation to be done by February 27, 1961 and "met without fail."[26]

The return two-page teletype from SAC, El Paso to Director Hoover dated "2-21-61 3-58 PM" reviewed most of the biographical data and career steps taken by Raymond Telles described above in the first pages of this chapter and are consistent. The most important additional note is that Raymond was previously investigated for a "top security clearance" requested by the US Air Force. A second bit of new information was the middle name of "Lorenzo" for Telles which soon became Lawrence. The next teletype, a short blunt note, also dated "FEB 21 1961" from the SAC, St. Louis to the Director and SAC, Washington stated, "Army service records for Telles not located, military personnel records center, St. Louis, Mo. Washington Field Office handle. RUC."

SAC, El Paso teletyped SAC, New York a two-page note dated February 21, informing him that the military files including personnel records on "Lieutenant Colonel Telles, USAF serial number" and a member of the Air Force Reserve are at 2623 Air Reserve Center, CONAC Headquarters, Mitchell IAR (sic) Force Base, New York. He asked the records to be reviewed and teletyped to El Paso. The same follow-up was done to investigate his record as employee at La Tuna Correctional facility. The direct supervisor when Telles was employed there now resided in Safford, Arizona. The teletype asking for this review as the SAC, Phoenix dated "2-22-61" and also headlined "URGENT." Special Agent James E. Barrett from the Baltimore FBI office responded in written form dated "2/23/61" about his investigation. He wrote that no records were found, at the "U.S. Army Counterintelligence Records Facility, Fort Holabird, Baltimore on February 21, 1961." On February 24, the SA at El Paso, Willard D. Wharton, reported on the cover sheet changed name and aliases of the Subject; "Raymond L. Telles, Jr., aka. Ramon Telles, Raymond Lawrence Telles, Raymond Lawrence Tellez, Ramon Lorenzo Telles" and added a thirty-seven-page detailed report. SA Wharton detailed which alias was used during which time in Raymond's life, for example, "High school records reflect applicant's name as Raymond Lawrence Tellez and Credit Bureau records show name as Ramon Lorenzo Telles. Military records reflect his name to be Raymond Lawrence Telles." The thirty-seven pages that follow begin with a two-page summary that includes mention of his brother Richard's arrest record, with more detail in subsequent pages covering his "Birth Record" that mention Ramón senior in 1951 changing the original name of his namesake son on birth records to "Raymond L. Telles, Jr." (p.3). Under the section on "Marriage Record" which were found by SA Wharton in "Marriage Record Volume 44 on page 370" that Telles married Delfina Navarro on February 14, 1942. He was twenty-six years old and she was twenty-four "when the license was issued" (p.4). His "Education" information was furnished by the office manager and secretary to the principal [name redacted] at Cathedral High School previously named St. Patrick's High School. SA Whatton also spoke with former teachers there and at the International Business College where Telles took "stenotype, typing, and bookkeeping" (p.6). Delfina Navarro also attended this business school. Mrs. Maude E. Roll, owner of the school claims her school is where the Telles couple met and got engaged (p.7). His "Military Record" traced only his career in the US Air Force and Reserves, not the US Army. In this section are found two entirely redacted sections of some length and of course, all the names reporting the information (p.9–11). Next came the details of his "Employment" beginning with his job at La Tuna, the federal penitentiary near El Paso, Texas. He was hired there on November 2, 1942 and worked under Warden Thomas B. White, Sr. until drafted and returned in 1946; then resigned to run for County Clerk "in 1947 or 1948" (p.12–14). His job performance as County Clerk is detailed in several pages relying on information from a county commissioner and some former county clerk employees (p.15–17). The last section is titled "Acquaintances" and runs from page 18 to 28 reporting what many persons, former elected officials of both city and county, businessmen, newspaper reporters, and other known associates said about Telles and their assessment of his character. Consistently in this report Telles was reputed to be an honest, patriotic, good family man, religious, nonsmoker, non-alcohol drinker, trustworthy, dependable, dedicated, patient with the public, and all of those interviewed recommend him for any federal position. A "Review of Newspaper Morgue File" by another special agent, William H. Nimmins, had many articles on the numerous awards Telles had received during his military career, for example, the Legion of Merit of Mexico, Medal of Merit of Aeronautics of Mexico, National Order of the Southern Cross of Brazil, Honorary Pilot Wings of Mexico, Columbia, and Brazil, and letters of commendation from presidents of Paraguay and Nicaragua. Telles also earned the Bronze Star for his service in Korea in 1952. The newspaper articles also reported on his public service roles as county clerk and mayor, and his civic, service, and church memberships (p.29–32). The last two sections, "Credit Record" and "Arrest Records:" have information about his loans no doubt for home purchases and his employment and found to be "very satisfactory" (p.31–35). Disturbing to me was the inclusion of information on his brother "Ricardo Telles, Sr." aka Richard Telles which had no bearing on Ramón's qualifications for a federal position (p.34–35). The last section on arrests is entirely about Richard Telles. "El Paso Police Department, advised SA [redacted name] that their indices were negative concerning RAYMOND L. TELLES or TELLEZ and all members of his immediate family, which included his wife, brother JOSE and wife, and wife of brother, RICARDO (p.36). The El Paso Sheriff's Office also could locate "no record identifiable with RAYMOND L. TELLES, Jr. The eighteen names searched were listed at the end of the report with four to five more names and kinship redacted (p.37). The SAC, El Paso sent the director, FBI a teletype with some of this information on February 24, 1961. The SAC, St. Louis also by tele-type dated "2-24-61" at "9-22PM RCW" notified the director, FBI and the SAC's at Baltimore, New York, El Paso, San Antonio and Washington Field office, that the file on Telles should have a name change to "RAYMOND LAWRENCE TELLES." SAC, San Antonio on same day teletyped his report on information obtained in that city on Telles to the director, FBI. In this transmission, social security number was entered and the suggestion that Miami FBI be asked to check records there as Telles attended Officer Training School there. The wife of Telles is renamed DELPHINE in this record. SAC's from Miami, Denver, and Phoenix all reported the same day, February 24, to the director, FBI checking records in their respective field offices and found no derogatory information on Telles. Hoover's eye caught something on March 9th. Apparently, SA Willard D. Wharton in his report of 2-21-61 quoting another SA [name redacted] "captioned quote et al, com-munistic activities unquote which lists one Ramon Telles among others as being actually or allegedly engaged in communist activities. Rerep does not resolve this. "Conduct necessary investigation to determine if identical with appointee or appointee-s father." SAC, El Paso cleared this up the next day by "URGENT" two-page teletype. SA Wharton re-interviewed the former Sheriff and now a banker who had first mentioned this connection. Banker "Chris P. Fox recalled that" he attempted to obtain such information. And, that in 1940 "long list of names of such persons was compiled by his office including the name 'Ramon Telles', with no further identifying data" (p.1). He had no further recollection or information "but is certain that his individ-ual is not identical with Mayor Raymond "Ramon" Telles, Jr. or his father, Ramon Telles, Sr. now deceased" (p.2).

Director Hoover transmitted by courier service a summary memorandum on Raymond L. Telles to the Secretary of State on March 28, 1961
with notice that a copy was "being furnished to the Honorable P. Kenneth
O'Donnell, Special Assistant to the President, the White House."

## Ambassador Telles: 1965

Once on the job, Ambassador Telles began meeting his personnel inside the
embassy and accepting the many social invitations that are a big part of any
US Ambassador anywhere in the world. He began getting acclimated to his
routine. The State Department files and those of the FBI jump from 1961
when he underwent the initial investigation to a scandal in 1965. US citizens
operating three companies in Costa Rica filed for bankruptcy proceeding in
federal court for the Southern District in Corpus Christi, Texas on January 25,
1965. The Trustees named by Federal Judge Reynaldo Garza contacted the
US Embassy in Costa Rica asking for help in locating the directors, officers,
and employees of the three companies based in the country.[27] The Second
Secretary of Embassy, Melville E. Blake, Jr. replied with a ten-page report
sent to the State Department on or about February 1, 1965. Apparently, the
trustee and his men together with Joseph P. Equi, representing the SEC visited with the ambassador in San Jose on January 22. The men in charge of the
three companies were located and attended a meeting at the Embassy in San
Jose, Costa Rica on January 27 at 9 am (p.10). The remaining pages detail a
summary of the three enterprises that combined were operating a coffee plantation in or near San Vito de Java in Costa Rica. These men, A.E. Walton for
TICO and C.H. Cravens for Gromaco, S.A. and Gromaco, Inc. had been selling investment contracts under Texas laws but were not registered with the
Securities and Exchange Commission (SEC) for such an investment venture
(p.2,4). Since 1963, the SEC was looking into this business enterprise operating under the name of Texas Independent Coffee Organization, Inc. (TICO).[28]
The TICO representatives were ordered to turn over keys to the Trustee and
they refused on advice of counsel that under Costa Rican law, no US federal
court had jurisdiction (p.6). Nothing was accomplished by the Trustee other
than learning of extensive debts owed by TICO including salaries not paid
of employees (p.6). They returned to the US (p.9). The next day, February 2,
another two-page report was filed with the State Department signed "For the
Ambassador:" by Mr. Blake, the "Second Secretary of the Embassy." This
communication reports of hiring a local attorney to help the ambassador assist
the Trustee and follow a U.S. court order. "Mr. Harry Zurcher was selected"
as of January 26 (p.1). Mr. Zurcher, according to this report presented some
serious allegations against TICO, namely that they did not pay wages to
employees and that they did not own or even lease the land on which their

operation was based. They held the land under what is called in Costa Rica as "legal squatters" (p 2).[29] The records released do not include much more on the TICO case except for some innuendo aimed at the ambassador. There are two handwritten letters, a two-page one postmarked in Corpus Christi, Texas in 1965 if the envelope is the carrier for the letter is on Hotel Congressional in Washington, DC, letterhead, whose date is unreadable, but addressed to "Dear Mr. Crockett". The other is a four-page letter without carrier envelope and no date but for "SUNDAY—on top right just below the letterhead of Rose Lawn Memorial Gardens of Brownsville, Texas." The handwriting appears to be from the same person. The name is redacted. The two-pager addressed to "Mr. Crockett" discusses the departure from Costa Rica under duress; fear for his and his family's life. He discloses he worked for Gromaco SA in Costa Rica under the direction of Cleve Cravens. The summary report indicates that Cravens owned 03.5 percent of Gromaco stock and owned an airplane he used to fly in and out of Costa Rica (p.5–7). This unknown writer makes serious allegations in this letter against Cravens, that he asked him to shoot people, burn the house of Sonny Applewhite (p.1), gave six hours of testimony before Judge Garza in Corpus Christi about "the farm and Cleve Cravens." He asked that Ambassador Telles be thanked for "helping me get out of the country. Mr. Cravens never intended for me to leave alive—" (p.2). The next and longer letter is more readable and has more serious allegations. In this letter, he discusses a conversation with a State Department official [name redacted] during which he disclosed hearsay, "I told him, Cleve told me, he gave Raymond [the ambassador] $300.00 up every month for political favors. He told me the FBI would call me soon—They haven't yet, but I expect them any time." He alleged that Cleve was out to destroy the farm operation and was going to use an attorney [name redacted] because he had that attorney under his thumb with threats of disbarment (p.2). Cleve's real goal was to take over the coffee plantation and he was going to get $50,000 from another source to finance the takeover. He claims he talked Cleve out of doing this. He also reveals much about Cleve, the racist:

> I only wish I could go to the Costa Rican court and tell them what I know. How Cleve, in his heart, hates all Costa Ricans. He only smiles at them to use them and the minute he is away from them calls them dogs—
> If this fellow [name redacted] who runs the diary, knew how Cleve talked about him and how he tricked him in Radio Club. Said he and [remaining line is cut off bottom of page 3].
> [continues with] that could help him in business. She got to sleeping with in-laws so they got divorce. Wonder how much [name redacted] would think of Cleve if he knew Cleve was telling people (several times to me) that his wife was nothing but a painted prostitute. She gave it away instead of selling it. Cleve

said he slept with her several times and had to finally get people to go with him every time he needed to see [name redacted] so he wouldn't be alone with his wife. [Name redacted] was nephew of the President of Costa Rica—His wife name is [name redacted] (p.4).

In federal court in Corpus Christi, meanwhile, in Civil Action No. 65-C-1 In The Matter of Texas Independent Coffee Organization, Inc. GOMACO company and GOMACO, S.A. a source [redacted name] testified in open court via deposition. There are five pages attached to the court filing cited above numbered 90–94 at top right. On page 93, the witness under deposition stated and it is underline in the copy:

> That was another thing that Cleve [Cravens] told me that before the government cut his money off that he used to go up and leave three hundred dollars every two or three weeks on Raymond Telles's desk for political favors, because he knew he couldn't make it on what Uncle Sam was paying him.

The above declarations in writing and via deposition may be connected to the next four-page document, also without dates and preparer. It is about "SUBJECT: Ambassador RAYMOND A. TELLES" and begins with a date of January 13, 1966 as when Ambassador Robert F. Woodward had received a letter in late November or early December 1965 from Alex A. Cohen, a longtime employee in the US Embassy in San Jose, Costa Rica and his former employee there Woodward was the US ambassador there from 1954 to 1958, appointed by President Dwight Eisenhower. Woodward, a career foreign service officer discussed this matter with Ambassador Charles R. Burrows, Director of the Office of Central American Affairs for the State Department. Burrows arranged to meet with Cohen in Florida on December 18, 1965. At that meeting, Cohen told Burrows he would not share who his source was for the information but felt the State Department should know what "delicate information" he had. He reported that it was about Ambassador Telles' wife. The preparer of this report, perhaps Burrows wrote:

> Cohen said his source told him that Ambassador Telles' wife was referred to as "the big whore of the American embassy" in San Jose. The source, also told Cohen that Mrs. Telles had been seen, either by the source or someone, leaving a house of assignation in San Jose.[30] The source informed Cohen that as a result of the above activities, there are pictures of Mrs. Telles in a compromising position and plans are in existence to use them for blackmail purposes. Mr. Cohen did not state who had the pictures or how it was planned to use them.
>
> In addition to the above Cohen said his source told him that Mrs. Telles drinks to excess. Cohen added that he was personally aware of this fault and

is common knowledge among certain circles in San Jose. Cohen would not divulge his source, but said he felt the information was such that he should pass it to the Department of State. Cohen stated that he felt his source was a man who was reliable. [last lines are redacted but for "Ambassador Burrows" at bottom right] (p.1).

Ambassador Burrows defended Mrs. Telles with his own opinion in this report. He stated he never saw her drink in excess of scotch and water, her favorite while the ambassador only drank cokes. He also said he never heard any such rumors about Mrs. Telles. Burrows stated, "that it was his experience in Central American countries that the Nationals spread personal rumors about anyone and everyone." Burrows also had an alternative opinion about Cohen and his possible motives in disclosing this information. In 1963, Cohen had been transferred from San Jose elsewhere and he did not want to go so he retired. He was married to a Costa Rican woman and was "practically a Costa Rican." He spoke Spanish. Burrows felt Cohen may be using this information to show he was in the know and could be of help once again as part of the foreign service. Burrows pointed out that Cohen mentioned during this discussion how he could help with the negotiations going on between Great Britain and Guatemala over British Honduras. "He said he could use the per diem" (p.2). Burrows did point out that if this was true about Mrs. Telles that could explain why the ambassador had cut back on entertainment for the staff. The possible blackmail may be draining him. But Burrows "reiterated that he had no reason to believe any of the story was true." The report continued with information on investigations conducted, not necessarily as a result of these allegations but routine, such as review of the Security and Personnel file of the ambassador in January 1966; the Medical Division physical examination of Mrs. Telles in 1961, 1964, and 1965 "no questions arose of a psychiatric nature. Her file is entirely clear. Ambassador Telles' Medical file is likewise clear." On the contrary, the review of Cohen's file showed three marriages, two divorces, foreign service assignments in various places until 1942 when he was assigned Costa Rica. He stayed there until January 31, 1963 when he retired from the "Political Officer, FSR-3" rather than be transferred. "Cohen was born in Holland in May 28, 1897 and became a naturalized US citizen in 1918 while in US military service." The report also states that Cohen was a controversial figure in that he had extensive contacts with prominent Costa Ricans, many in the government, his business interests, and his marriage to a Costa Rican woman (p.3). In closing, the report states Cohen received a Superior Service Award prior to his retirement and that he had successfully fought a transfer as early as 1962. Cohen "did not blame Ambassador Telles for the situation" because of which he had to choose retirement over transfer (p.4).

The ugly calumny about Mrs. Telles did not go away. Between the Burrows meeting with Cohen and the report, the Miami Office of Security for the Department of State investigated the matter. Agent William D. McKee out of the Miami office submitted his three-page report dated February 21, 1966, on the ambassador and his wife. He interviewed Alex A. Cohen on February 16 in a motel room in Gainesville, Florida. Cohen is described a reluctant, paranoid, afraid, hesitant, because the room may be "bugged" and "walls have ears." He still refused to name his sources for the information on the Telles's. He did give up "two additional informants that source claims can support information pertaining to Mrs. Raymond A. TELLES" (p.1). Cohen promised McKee that he would ask permission of his main source to reveal its identity (p.2). Cohen did provide the name [redacted] of a retired US Consul who stated: "Mrs. TELLES had 'been (here Mr. Cohen used an obscene term referring to sexual intercourse) everyone around town.'" One more name was given up by Cohen, "Mr. Fernando LARA BUSTAMANTE, former Foreign Minister of Costa Rica, who now has a law office in San Jose" and "who could testify regarding the excessive drinking habits of Mrs. TELLES and her general reputation in San Jose." As to the compromising photographs and being seen in a location known for its ill repute and the various escapades of Mrs. Telles, Cohen was relaying hearsay. McKee recommend someone not connected with the Foreign Service or an Inspector, who spoke Spanish, be assigned to investigate without contact to the Embassy (p.3).

Mr. Glyn T. Brymer out of Los Angeles Office of Security for the Department of State submitted a nine-page report on Ambassador Telles to his headquarters with attachments. The report centered on the character of Cleve Cravens and his nephew, a probation officer named Howard Vaught, and the assistant US attorney, Douglas M. Smith. All those interviewed or providing testimony in the bankruptcy case in Corpus Christi, Texas had negative things to say about Cravens from being a con man, swindler, dangerous, to a potentially violent man. The name [redacted] who saw Cravens give money to Ambassador Telles was provided (p.9). Attachments to this report are extensive pages from another assistant AG, Fred Vinson, and the actual US Attorney Woodrow Seals about Ambassador Telles and the payments made by Cravens. Seals is asking Vinson in his communication if the FBI should not be brought in to investigate the matter.

In a March 14, 1966, supplemental report, two-pages, from William D. McKee from that office that Alex A. Cohen in correspondence with them had refused to name his source. By letter of February 28, 1966, Alex A. Cohen wrote to the Miami Field Office:

Dear Mr. McKee: With regard to your question, nothing doing. My answer is still no. Even though it may be very confidential, I still don't want to be mixed up in such a delicate question as the one exposed. . . . I hope that you and the Department will understand that I have to respect the wishes of my source on the subject (p.2).

Given the Cohen refusal, Agent McKee wrote as the last line of the above report, "no further action is being taken by the Miami Filed Office."

In April 1966, William Crockett, the person the letters were addressed to previously about Cleve Craven signed a "Memorandum for the Record" but without indication as to which record and what agency. It does state that "SY has checked out this matter with CIA and that Agency has received no reports or information that would substantiate such a charge . . . No further action will be taken at this time." The last line reads, "SY has been requested to alert their Regional Security Office to be alert to this situation." No indication as to what SY is or part of what agency is provided.[31]

G. Marvin Gentile, the Deputy Assistant Secretary for Security on July 12, 1966 sent J. Edgar Hoover "material which may be of interest to you." It was a file on Raymond A. [sic] Telles that included most of the documents cited above. To be sure, Hoover had opened a file on Telles at that time if he had not already done so.

### The Last Year as Ambassador: 1966–1967

On July 28, 1966 Denman F. Stanfield sent "The Ambassador" a note in which he related his recollection of a letter he read addressed to [name redacted] which repeated the allegation that Cravens would give the ambassador cash money, "$300 and $500 on two different occasions." Stanfield informs the ambassador that the source of the letter usually stays at the President Hotel and would be returning. "I left word at the hotel for him to get in touch with me when he returns." More fuel is added to the fire with a short one-page note from SY/SAS-Patrick M. Rice to "The File" dated August 5, 1966. It states that a newspaper man, "Leary of the Washington Evening Star [underscore in text] had informed Inspector Joseph Burks, also of IGA, on August 1, 1966, that he was preparing a story concerning questionable financial activities of Ambassador Telles." A clue is found that there is more to this than the documents released show. The last paragraph of this note to the file reads, "On August 2, 1966 Mr. Ederhertz, Attorney for the Department of Justice, who is handling the Telles matter in the absence of Attorney William Ryan, was advised of the above information." Before the month is over, Ryan is writing again to "The File" and documenting the progress of the investigation being conducted on Ambassador Telles now in another position with the federal government. The DOJ was investigating the ambassador. The only disclaimer on Telles being innocent of wrongdoing if not actual criminal activity is the last line: "[Name redacted] He further stated that the Department of Justice had no further information to indicate the Ambassador had taken payoffs in the amount of $25,000." William Ryan was the Deputy Chief of the Fraud Section of the Department of Justice in 1966.

On August 29, 1966 Patrick M. Rice, Agent of the SAS-Washington Office of the State Department, submitted his report on Ambassador Raymond L. Telles, Jr. for the month of July 11 to August 26. This twelve-page report clearly details all the allegations made against the ambassador including the deposition pages of testimony admitted in the federal bankruptcy case of TICO being heard in Corpus Christi, Texas (p.2, 4). Moreover, he was given the names of witnesses by Rice who said they saw the transfer of money from Cravens to Telles (p.1, 2, 3). Ambassador was asked to cooperate with providing copies of his bank accounts, which he listed readily (p. 9). Ambassador Telles from this point forward should have known he was under serious investigation with formidable credible evidence that could end his career. He was made aware that not only his direct employer, the State Department, but also the FBI and the CIA, perhaps the IRS were all looking into these allegations of wrongdoing. Nevertheless, or perhaps because it was true, he proclaimed his innocence throughout the interview with Agent Rice and denounced the accusations as completely false. Agent Rice filed a supplemental six-page report on Telles on September 2, 1966, covering a period from July 14 to August 29. In this report:

> Ambassador Telles emphatically denied allegations that his wife had left a party at the Spanish Embassy in San Jose in August, 1965 in the company of other American women and Costa Rican males; his wife had been intoxicated at San Jose clubs; his wife visited a hotel of poor repute named 'El Francis'; and that there were pictures of her in a compromising position (p.1).

The report goes on to state that the August date was wrong because the Embassy records did not show such an invitation; the correct date found by Agent Rice was September 16, 1965 (p.1). Telles agreed to have his wife be interviewed and she also "emphatically denied the above allegations." She offered more information on her activities to show "she has been too busy with charity work to engage in misconduct" (p.1) Agent Rice worked in the Special Assignments Staff (SAS) of the Office of Security whose chief was David. H. McCabe and the office was under Deputy Assistant Secretary for Security, G. Marvin Gentile.

The next page begins with the heading of "Interview with Ambassador TELLES DETAILS" and states the interview by Agent Rice of Raymond Telles took place in his embassy office on July 29, 1966. Rice presented the allegations made against Mrs. Telles and added "that Mrs. TELLES had been seen intoxicated at the Union Club, the Tennis Club, and the San Jose Country Club. He repeated the allegations of the photographs of her "in a compromising position" and "being seen leaving a hotel of poor repute named 'El Francis'" (p.2).

The ambassador denied each of the allegations and stated: "she takes a social drink but always in moderation and that she has never been intoxicated." He also said he "had never heard of a hotel named 'El Francis' in San Jose; and that "he checked the San Jose phone book and could find no listing for 'El Francis" nor did the Costa Rican Tourist Bureau have a listing for such a hotel. As far as the compromising photos of his wife, the ambassador said, "they would have come to the surface by now." He blamed the Communists as the only ones who give him a hard time and demanded to know the source of this information against his wife (p.2). He was asked if she would accept an interview on the allegations. Ambassador reluctantly agreed citing some health issues his wife was coping with found by personnel at Beaumont General Hospital in El Paso, Texas and he placed three conditions on the interview (p.2). These were, in essence, that she be told the allegations "did not originate with anyone in the State Department or Embassy in San Jose"; he had stated they "were false and untrue, that he had complete confidence and trust in his wife and her conduct"; and, lastly, that "this was a chance to defend herself" and that Rice check with "the Costa Rican people and the Americans living here have for both he and Mrs. TELLES (p.3). Agent Rice did interview of Mrs. Telles on July 29, 1966, at the embassy residence without the presence of the ambassador who was in the residence at the time. She was told of the three conditions the ambassador had placed on the interview. She was told the information about her conduct had not been solicited by the Department of State. She "responded immediately by stating that all the allegations were false and there was no truth to any of these." She repeated the same information the ambassador has provided about wrong dates and the company she kept during the party at the Spanish Ambassador's residence (p.3). As to the excessive drinking at socializing at various clubs, she said they were completely false. "She said that at social functions she takes a social drink, but her drinking is always in moderation and she has not been intoxicated" (p.4). She denied the existence of any photographs of her in a compromising position and "challenged the person making such a statement to produce the pictures." She then detailed her charity work (p.5). Her last remarks had to do with her health which had deteriorated given such activities and "has been too busy to get involved with any misconduct." She admitted to being "hospitalized for a time several years ago." And, she said a scrapbook was being organized to document all these charitable activities to be sent to "Mrs. Lincoln Gordon" in care of "Mrs. Betty Edison" at the Department (p.6).

SY-Henri G. Grignon sent a memorandum to David H. McCabe, Chief of the Office of Security at the State Department on October 12, 1966. The substance of the two-page memo was that their investigation had produced nothing concrete and that the DOJ "had notified the Department of State that no further action appeared to be warranted in his case" and based on this "SY had forwarded to Mr. William J. Crockett and to Ambassador John M. Steeves . . . that no further action bet taken . . . against Ambassador Telles and against his wife" (p.1). Telles wanted a letter, wrote Grignon, and was referred to Ambassador Steeves. He also wanted to know who to contact at DOJ to discuss the source of these allegations. He wanted a letter clearing him and his wife of any wrongdoing. He was only promised the name and contact information of the person at DOJ (p.2). Handwritten note at mid-page 2 on the right is the wording "It was determined from Atty. Wm. Ryan Justice that Amb Telles should see HAROLD REIS Ex asst t the A.G. this info relayed to him from Cooper on Costa Rican Desk 10-12-66."

Ambassador Telles must have known by this time that his days as ambassador in Costa Rica were numbered given the negative environment swirling around him and his wife, Delfina. I also assume that the new president, Lyndon Johnson, being the manipulator of men and women in his service as government employees and political operatives became aware of these rumors as well. Johnson, the Texan, also kept his eye on the growing political clout of Mexican Americans in his state; Telles was a rising star among this important constituency so necessary for his upcoming re-election in 1968. The ambassador post in Mexico City may have been the next career goal for Telles but it should not have come as a surprise to him to be called back to Washington, DC instead.

## New Job in DC

The affairs of state continued to be well promoted by Ambassador Telles post Kennedy assassination, but President Lyndon Johnson declined to move Telles from Costa Rica to Mexico. President Johnson announced the appointment of Ambassador Telles to be the Chairman of the US Section of the newly created Joint US Mexican Commission on Border Area Development headquartered in Washington, DC. Telles served in this capacity from 1967 to 1969.

Clarence A. Boonstra was named the new ambassador to Costa Rica.[32] The FBI's Legat in Mexico City informed Hoover by two-page Airtel dated January 26, 1967, that Telles had resigned as Ambassador to Costa Rica and was to be replaced by "Clarence Boonstra who as the Minister and Deputy Chief of Mission (DCM) in Mexico City." The Legat suggested Hoover send a "letter of congratulations and appreciation to Ambassador TELLES in connection with his new appointment . . . and also . . . to BOONSTRA." He also let Hoover know that Mr. Boonstra would be in D.C. "for a briefing and conference until approximately 2/5/67 . . .." By March 17, 1967, Ambassador Telles was in his new post in Washington, DC. He wrote to FBI Director Hoover on Department of State letterhead as one of his first tasks. Apparently, Hoover had taken his Legat's advice and written him earlier on February 23 to congratulate him on his new position of director of the US-Mexico Joint Commission on Economic and Social Development of the Border Areas. Telles wrote back that March day thanking him and chiding that the commission title was too long and finding some shorter name. He added that he looked forward to working with him and the Bureau, "the splendid relationship that has always existed between your Bureau and any functions I have been associated with will continue."

Despite Ambassador Telles being in a new position, old baggage from San José, Costa Rica kept surfacing. On January 28, 1969, Louis M. Marrano, the Regional Security Officer based in Panama, wrote a two-page report to his superior at the Department of State, G. Marvin Gentile about the last days in office of Raymond Telles and his wife. Marrano stated that he learned while visiting the San Jose embassy in Costa Rica with [name redacted] that the Telles' "had purchased about $400 worth of food-stuff from the Embassy commissary which the Ambassador then resold to his Costa Rican friends." He reported that while en-route to DC. the Telles's stopped in Panama and shopped at the military PX and bought more items, shoes, for example, which they shipped back to the Costa Rican Embassy for pick up by their friends. The ambassador had called the embassy to alert them to these goods coming and who to deliver them to. Mrs. [name redacted] added to the conversation stating there seemed to be a double standard for the ambassador and his wife.

> She remarked that she could not understand why the promiscuous behavior of Mrs. Telles was permitted to continue when it was common knowledge among the Embassy wives that Mrs. Telles was having an affair and sleeping with a U.S. Major of the Defense Attaches office (p.1).
>
> It was reported that Mrs. Telles had "taken with her into the Embassy commissary several Costa Rican friends who would purchase commissary items." This was contrary to Embassy regulation prohibiting the purchase of commissary supplies by other than American personnel.
>
> In accordance with the standing instructions contained in your "Eyes Only" memo dated April 25, 1966, same subject, no action or investigation was undertaken by me, pending your instructions (p.2).

This last set of allegations were swept under the rug by Mr. Gentile. In a short one-page memo from SY/SAS John R. Ellis to SY/E Frederick W. Traband dated February 4, 1969, Ellis informed Traband that the Marrano memo had been discussed with Mr. Gentile and he advised that:

> while it is somewhat obvious that there must be substance to some of the allega-
> tions since they continue to arise, no extensive investigation can be conducted
> without undermining Ambassador Telles' position and his integrity as Chairman
> of the U.S.-Mexico Border Commission.

There are no other records released after February 1969 and during the next years until 1971. In between these years, Telles stayed in Washington, DC, relying on consulting contracts to make a living and afford to stay in the nation's capital area.

## The Republican Administrations

On June 14, 1971, Alexander P. Butterfield in the White House, the deputy assistant to President Richard M. Nixon, began another investigation into Raymond L. Telles.[33] Butterfield wrote to FBI agent Robert H. Haynes requesting an investigation of Telles not for alleged wrong but for a new political appointment and attached his biography. Of course, such a move necessitated an FBI investigation for such appointees and a security clearance. The entire month of June 1971 was spent on this FBI investigation because Nixon was going to name him Chairman of the Equal Employment Opportunity Commission (EEOC).

The FBI Director's office on June 15, 1971 sent out its usual urgent teletype request to various FBI field offices: El Paso, St. Louis, Baltimore, Denver, and the Washington Field Office, separate from the Director's headquarters. The teletype provided scant biographical information on Telles but enough to identify him. The teletype refers to prior investigations, "See urfiles which indicate previous special inquiry of Telles in nineteen sixtyone, at which time he was mayor of El Paso" and a second one, "following investigation he was appointed U.S. Ambassador to Costa Rica." The 1971 teletype requested "complete background data, including present locations of all close relatives, and set out leads at once. . . . It is imperative BUDED be met without fail. No delay will be tolerated." The BUDED was set for June 22. Denver FBI was the first to respond on June 16, 1971 with the news that the military file was not located and a special search for it was underway. St. Louis FBI on June 17th provided information on Telles most of which was already stated in the initial biography sent out by Director Hoover except for one last item. It reads: "This employment [the US-Mexico Border Commission] was terminated on August 11, 1969, as Chairman of above and personal rank of Ambassador by reason of resignation and exercising retirement rights, effective same date. The records indicated he had 22 years and 7 months creditable Federal service and that 8 years and 4 months of which was with the Department of State." SAC, WFO on June 18 by teletype to the FBI director and SAC's at Alexandria, Albany, San Antonio, El Paso, Dallas, Tampa, Springfield, and Baltimore sent a six-page report on the relatives of Raymond Telles, addresses of residences, and who had since died: mother (p.1), wife, wife's brother [name redacted with address], the two daughters [names redacted] who live with Telles in Bethesda, Maryland; and the brothers, Jose and Richard with addresses (p.3). His employment was listed as "self-employed consultant and works out of his home" with the name of one company provided, "Zia Corporation, Dallas Texas." This report also listed several lines, all redacted, of persons who worked for Telles while he was an ambassador in Costa Rica (p.4). Several references are listed but redacted but for: Ewing Thomason, US District Judge in El Paso, Texas and William Farah, of Farah Manufacturing in El Paso, Texas, (p.5). Ernest Guinn, US District Judge in El Paso and Ralph Yarborough, former Senator, now practicing law in Austin, Texas (p.6). The SAC, Alexandria sent SAC, Washington Field, information on June 21 that they had investigated a former staff member who was now employed at the Smithsonian Institute [name with address redacted] but with his office number as "381-6361." The last line indicates the investigation was broadened to include another intelligence agency, "Alexandria will report results of CIA check re appointee and family." SAC, WFO on June 21st also reported another consultant contract by Telles was with Land-Air Enterprises in Dallas, Texas. Springfield FBI reported on June 21, 1971 by teletype that "numerous attempts made up to and including instant date to contact [name redacted] proved negative. Neighbors are unaware of whereabouts." El Paso, Denver, Albany, Oklahoma City, Dallas, Tampa, Chicago FBI offices all reported favorable impressions of Telles by those they contacted. The San Antonio FBI also reported on this same day with little new information. San Antonio did report that former Senator Yarborough thought Telles "is outstanding person of good character, reputation, is unquestionably loyal American citizen whom he would give an unqualified recommendation for position of trust with U.S. Government." And, San Antonio on June 22 reported that Telles had been named a "Director at Large by Signal Life Insurance Company, San Antonio, from December fifteen, sixty-nine to July thirty-one, seventy at eight hundred dollars a month plus two hundred dollars advance bonus" for public relations work." Telles also was a director the National Economic Development Association (NEDA) and chair of two committees: By Laws and Management, reported Chicago FBI on June 22.

The final report, nineteen pages, was prepared by [name redacted] on the 22nd and submitted to [redacted] on Telles which contained mixed comments. For example, "Several associates feel appointee is not intellectually qualified to handle position [written in between handle and position was word "some" and position was made plural by a handwritten s]; and felt being an ambassador was above his ability." On the other hand, the report states: "Texas Senators recommend. Senator Goldwater interposes no objection to appointee" (page P). Most of the persons interviewed expressed favorable recommendations but one, Arturo G. Constantino with the Agency for International Development (AID). Constantino felt Telles was above his pay grade as ambassador (p.4) and "regarded as 'an innocent among the wolves.'" Constantino doubted Telles's intellectual ability and flat out stated: "I would not hire him." He wanted to know for what position specifically Telles was being considered (p.5). Another unnamed person because the name was redacted, expressed similar reservations about Telles's ability to fulfill the duties of a US ambassador. This person who was indirectly supervised by Telles felt he was not a failure at the job, but surely "was a poor ambassador" (p.8). US Senator John Tower, Republican from Texas, recommended him in 1961 and would do so again (p.13). Lloyd Bentsen, the Democratic US Senator from Texas also recommended him (p.14). The neighbors in Bethesda, Maryland [names redacted] spoke well of the ambassador and his family (p.16). Credit checks and police records were searched and all reports were not negative, found to be satisfactory at US Park Police, Montgomery County Sheriff's Office, Credit Bureau, Inc., Metropolitan Police, the House Committee on Internal Security, US Secret Service, and the Department of the Treasury were the agencies contacted (p.17). The money passed to Telles, as alleged by some, was found by the DOJ's FBI and Department of State to be unsubstantiated and took no action on the matter (p.18). El Paso FBI, also on June 22, filed its thirteen-page report. The beginning pages are laudatory until it states, according to Ralph Seitsinger, a member of the City Council when Telles was mayor stated : "Mrs. Telles was a person who displayed some tendency to lack of control of temper" and that Mr. Telles "had had some difficulty in political life because Mrs. Telles (p.4) had sometimes tried to interject herself into Mr. Telles' business" (p.5). The newspaper editor of the *El Paso Herald Post* [name redacted] is quoted as being critical of Mrs. Telles "in that she had a somewhat arrogant, abrasive personality" (p.7). Joe M. Herrera, a vice president of State National Bank, had the same opinion of Mrs. Telles (p. 7, 8). There was criticism of Richard Telles, brother to Raymond, the ambassador (p. 9, 10) and of Telles himself during his campaign for Congress against Richard C. White. Allegedly, Telles had been rude and hot tempered against someone [name redacted] who accused him of being pro-union yet he was supported by William Farah, found guilty by the National Labor Relations Board (NLRB) of unfair labor practices on Mexican American workers in his El Paso and other plants (p. 10, 11). Telles was "calling her a part-time political hack (p.11). Many more persons [names redacted] were contacted including District Judge Edward F. Berliner, District Judge Jack Fant, J. W. Wally Fields, County Sheriff Mike Sullivan, Robert E. Minnie, police chief and city alderman, Sal Berroteran (p.11). The last page details the accidental killing of Rodolfo "Rudy" Carrillo by Richard Telles while at the El Patio Bar sometime in 1952 which case was dismissed and other charges against the brother, Richard (p.13).

Red flags went up at the SAC WFO who reported on June 24, 1971, to the director FBI that former Ambassador Telles had been issued a passport on November 28, 1969 at Washington, DC, for a three-week business and pleasure trip to Costa Rica. This airtel was six-pages in length. The airtel had little to do with the passport or trip to Costa Rica; it was about comments made by others about Telles. The material is reported in other documents mentioned previously, nothing new other than Rep. Henry B. Gonzalez quoted as recommending Telles (p.5). That job did not last long because President Johnson quit the 1968 presidential race. The Democrats lost the election. President-elect Richard M. Nixon dismissed him from this last position at which point Raymond Telles had decided to return to his hometown and challenge the incumbent US Representative Richard White, a three-term Democrat holding the 16th District out of El Paso. Despite brother Richard's barrio connections and voter turnout ability, Telles lost this race almost two to one.[34]

There are no additional records from this date to July 1976.

## Fast Forward to 1976

The Director FBI by teletype on July 7, 1976 once again requested a special inquiry with Buded of July 14 be done on Raymond L. Telles for a presidential appointment. The teletype went out to five FBI field offices: Los Angeles, Denver, Baltimore, El Paso, Alexandria, and the Washington Field one. The same biography of Telles was attached to the form request that was sent to those field offices on July 6. Washington FBI office on July 8 added two more field offices to the request for data to respond time to the Special Inquiry: Boston and Phoenix. The various FBI offices reported within the time frame given of June 14 with no new information on Telles and some update on the daughters, brother Richard, and his retirement from the US Air Force Reserve with the rank of Colonel on September 5, 1975. Phoenix FBI reported to Hoover and the New York FBI office on July 12, 1976, by urgent teletype of two pages that Telles was personally interviewed on July 8 and gave one reference: Gov. Raul Castro of Arizona who was at the Democratic National Convention; New York was asked to go interview him promptly (p.2). The next day, 13th, Secretary of Health and Welfare for the State of California was interviewed about Telles in Sacramento, California by that FBI office who recommended Telles "for a high-level position in government." Also, on the 13th, New York reported that Governor Castro "highly recommended appointee." The CIA, credit bureaus, police departments, and other references all reported favorable opinion of Telles for any appointment. The SAC Alexandria by airtel reported on July 14 that "the files of the Central Intelligence Agency (CIA), Langley, Va, . . . contained no pertinent identifiable information concerning the appointee's wife, DELFINA NAVARRO TELLES." SAC, WFO also on the 14th reported in a lengthy thirteen-page report to the director, FBI that the "appointee was the subject of a Fraud Against the Government case investigated by the FBI instituted in June, 1975" The case did not go forward "for lack of prosecutive merit" (p.1). The salary of Raymond Telles at the EEOC was documented as being $36,000 in October 1971; $38,000 in April 1972 and continued until August 3, 1976 (p.2). Many persons associated in some capacity with the EEOC were interviewed [all names redacted] (p.3). The neighbors, four of them [all names redacted] of the Telles family who lived at 6808 Whittier Blvd. in Bethesda, Maryland were also interviewed. Several more references were contacted including a former FBI Special Agent and former Ambassador to Panama, Joseph Farland and his wife, Virginia C Farland, and a retired judge and wife, James and Cecilia Moran, both retired. All these references gave Telles high marks and recommended him for a high position (p.7–12) with substantial redacted material on page 8. All credit, police, and other law enforcement agencies reported nothing negative and gave Telles and his immediate family good recommendations (p. 13). The only missing piece was a report from the IRS, which was the subject of the SAC, WFO dated July 19.

The final report on the Special Inquiry regarding Raymond L. Telles was submitted to the White House Staff Assistant (Security) [name redacted] on July 21, 1976, "by liaison." The summary five-page report was attached to this cover letter. The new FBI Director Clarence M. Kelley makes reference to prior "Applicant-type investigations" conducted on Telles in 1961 and 1971 and clarifies that the substance of this summary is since June 1971. He adds "the results of the 1975 investigation concerning Ambassador Telles and his wife, which are mentioned on page four of this summary memorandum, have been previously furnished to you." The heading title of the summary report is clear and at the same time, raises more questions:

THE INVESTIGATION OF AMBASSADOR TELLEZ COVERED INQUIRIES AS TO HIS CHARACTER, LOYALTY, ABILITY, AND GENERAL STANDING, BUT NO INQUIRIES WERE MADE AS TO THE SOURCES OF HIS INCOME.

The summary states information gathered from references and sources and proceeds to listing the relatives and the usual credit and police reports. All satisfactory other than the mention of the troubles associated with Mrs. Telles. In July 1975, Mrs. Telles, the ambassador, and one other [name redacted] "were responsible for illegally bringing an alien into the United States to work as a domestic." The FBI investigated and reported its find-ings to the AUSA who declined to prosecute "inasmuch as the documentary evidence obtained during the investigation contradicted the initial allegation" (p.4). The last communication in the released files is from FBI Director Kelley to the White House dated July 28, 1976, in which he refers to his sum-mary report of July 21. He informs the White House Staff Assistant (Security) [name redacted] that IRS has sent in their report and "There is no record of unpaid taxes, liens, criminal tax investigations, or civil penalties for fraud or negligence concerning these returns." The returns examined were those "filed by Ambassador Telles for the years 1973, 1974, and 1975. This concludes the investigation in this matter."

President Nixon had chosen Telles as a bi-partisan gesture and to court the growing Mexican American vote, to chair the EEOC where he stayed for five years until 1976. A scandal hit Telles in the face, however, over the hiring of a domestic worker from Costa Rica that same year. He and his wife had hired and brought to the United States a young woman who was undocumented. The young woman claimed she was a "student" who did some domestic work. For the domestic work she alleged being paid less than the minimum wage. She called the Immigration and Naturalization Service (INS) herself to complain of being exploited as a domestic. The Telles family complained she repeatedly disobeyed the family house rules. The INS and the FBI both inves-tigated the allegations. They found the young woman had entered the United States on a student visa but now was overextended, a deportable offense. The federal agencies dropped the case. Mario T. Garcia wrote, "From the review we have concluded that further action on this matter by the United States Attorney's Office is not warranted."[35] Despite the smear in the press and subsequent federal agency exoneration, President Jimmy Carter named Telles head of the Inter-American Development Bank with headquarters in El Salvador, Central America. The ambassadorship in Mexico, Telles's dream job, went instead to Julian Nava later in 1980.[36] The Inter-American Development Bank job was not a walk in the park for Telles and his family. While in El Salvador, he was under heavy security guard detail most of the time; survived several attempts on his life; and, escaped torture at the hands of guerrillas convinced he was a US spy.[37] Ronald Reagan defeated President Jimmy Carter in 1980 and he was recalled back to DC.

Telles again had no recourse but to seek opportunities back in El Paso. The problem, however, was that the "domestic worker case" which had been dropped in 1976 was resurrected in the early 1980s and the US Attorney's Office in Virginia indicted Raymond and Delfina Telles on these charges. The problem was the Telles's were found to have helped the young girl in their home enter the United States; helped overstay her visa; and, did not pay her the fair wages for work done around the house, not even the minimum wage.

## The Prosecution Began and Continued

For personal reasons of protecting his wife, Raymond agreed to a plea deal in which Delfina would be dropped from the case. He would plea to a misdemeanor crime and pay a fine.[38] Telles agreed to all these terrible conditions and pled guilty. In 1982, unemployed once again, he found himself courted by Maury Page Kemp of El Paso to become the vice president of the First Financial Enterprises. Kemp had founded, owned a controlling interest and had many subsidiaries tied to this business venture. Kemp was looking to expand into international markets in Latin America and Telles had the connections and was held in high regard by many influential persons in many countries. This was Telles' first venture into the private business sector and his job was to seek investors for Kemp's insurance business and banking operations. Within years, he was able to recruit Mexican investors for Kemp's three insurance companies and his bank, First Financial Savings and Loan Association. His efforts resulted in what was estimated to be $30 million dollars from these investors. The bank was badly managed, however, and was declared insolvent in 1988; Telles resigned. While Telles had not asked investors to fund his side of the Kemp operation, he was the face, voice, contact, and interpreter for the Mexican investors putting money into Kemp's insurance companies and bank. For all practical purposes, the person held responsible for the gigantic collapse of the enterprise from the Mexican investor's perspective was Telles. He was the one the Mexicans held responsible; otherwise they would not have invested. There was no protection for these Mexican investors or any other investor; the Federal Deposit Insurance Corporation (FDIC) did not cover an enterprise not incorporated and registered in Texas much less one formed and licensed in the West Indies.

The Mexicans sued in federal court and included Telles as a defendant. Telles claimed he did not know this legal fact. He and others were soon summoned before the Grand Jury, indicted, arraigned, and faced both the local District Attorney on the charges involving the Texas Securities laws and the US Attorney for violations of federal laws. Ultimately in the early 1990s, Kemp was found guilty of some violations and served prison time in Texas. Telles, after spending most of his life savings in his defense, "more than $100,000 and had wiped out his life's savings" and many months of grueling questions under oath widely reported in the national and local press, was found not guilty of any illegality.[39] There is a vocational school in El Paso named in his honor, the Raymond Telles Academy.

## Price of Leadership and Public Service

The price of leadership and public service, as the life story of Ramón and Delfina revealed, was expensive and very painful to them, their family, and those who admired them. It is as if there are two stories of their lives, the one the public knows from secondary sources and mostly laudatory; then the hidden history in the pages of intelligence agency documents based on investigations stemming from calumny, distortions, lies, falsehoods, and rumor. In the end, the happy and long marriage of the Telles couple, was as it began, happy to be together, poor, and without much to enjoy from their life of public service and his leadership. Delfina did her share of public service not as first lady of the embassy in San Jose but as the County Clerk for El Paso County when appointed to fill in for her husband, off to the Korean War, as President Nixon's appointee to the Defense Department Advisory Committee on Women in the Services; and her incredible number of hours spend on charitable work, as reported in her obituary cited below as the last reference.

In the 1990s, the daughters took care of Delfina and Raymond. They relocated to California. Delfina, a year older than Raymond, died on May 6, 2010 at age 93 in Los Angeles, according to the obituary in the *Los Angeles Times* of May 12. They were married for 68 years. Raymond lived three more years with oldest daughter, Cynthia, in Sherman Oaks, California. He passed away March 8, 2013, at 97 years of age. He is buried in El Paso, Texas.[40]

## NOTES

1. The author has conducted over a hundred public history interviews and these can be found at https://library/uta.edu/tejanovoices/gallery.php/ and not all have been digitized and placed at this site but interested persons can go to https:// library.uta.edu /special-collections/collections/ and scroll down to Tejano Voices or visit the library on campus in Arlington, Texas. The interview with Richard Telles was done on June 22, 1996 in El Paso, Texas, 123 pages.

2. See https://history.state.gov/about/faq/ambassadors-and-chief-of-mission/ accessed August 9, 2019.

3. Mario T. Garcia, *The Making of a Mexican American Mayor: Raymond L. Telles of El Paso,* Southwestern Studies No. 105 (El Paso: Texas Western Press, 1998).

4. Ibid., 8.

5. Ibid., 1–8.

6. Ibid., 13–14.

7. Ibid., 20–23, 24 (this last page has photos of these meetings).

8. Gutierrez, *Telles*, 7–8.

9. Garcia, "Chapter Two County Clerk," 29–49 and "Chapter Four Richard Telles and Barrio Politics" in *Telles*, 85–101; see also Gutierrez, *Telles*, 12, 16, 23, and 28.

10. Ibid., 133.

11. See short biographical data on him in Matt S. Meier, *Mexican American Biographies: A Historical Dictionary, 1836–1987* (Westport: Greenwood Press, 1988) and Nicolas Kanellos, *Hispanic American Almanac* (Farmington Hills, Michigan: Gale, 2002).

12. The political biographies of these two men are in my book, *Albert A. Peña Jr. Dean* and Michelle Hall Kells, *Vicente Ximenes, LBJ's Great Society, and Mexican American Civil Rights Rhetoric* (Carbondale: Southern Illinois University Press, 2018); and, an older work by Julie Leininger Pycior, *LBJ & Mexican Americans: The Paradox of Power* (Austin: University of Texas Press, 1997).

13. *The Plum Book* currently is published by the Senate Committee on Homeland Security and Governmental Affairs (https://www.hsgac.senate.gov/) and House Committee on Government Reform (https://oversight.house.gov/). In 2016 it listed 9,000 positions that needed to be filled over the presidential term. In 1960, the figure of positions to be filled probably ranged about 5,000. More importantly, before the Eisenhower victory the Democrats controlled the White House for twenty-two years prior. After Eisenhower, the Democrats had to remove Republican appointees with their own nominees and Ambassadors were high on the list of those to be filled.

14. For some of this history see https://historyinpieces.com/research/video/preside nt-Eisenhower-presidentelect-kennedy-meet-white-house-december-1960/ and www .nationalarchives.com/200-UN/33-9h/ for video and transcript/.

15. See my work, *Albert A. Peña Jr. Dean*, 99–116; and, Ignacio M. Garcia, *Viva Kennedy: Mexican Americans in Search of Camelot* (College Station: Texas A & M University Press, 2000).

16. Gutierrez, *Albert A. Peña Jr.,* 142 and see Kells, *Vicente Ximenes*, 153.

17. There are two sources for this information: www.maciverinstitute.com/2018/ 06/the-perks-of-congress-pensions-free-parking-haircuts-and-so-much-more/ and www.thoughtco.com/salaries-andbenefits-of-congress-members-3322282/; and, there is the government source, the U.S. Office of Personnel Management, that covers it all in difficult language.

18. See www.careertrend.com/benefits-duties-ambassador-39841.html/ accessed August 8, 2019.

19. See www.afsa.org/list-ambassadorial-appointments/ accessed August 8, 2019.

20. See www.careerexplorer.com/careers/ambassador/ for details of the job.

21. FBI Director Hoover began this program in Mexico City in 1939 by naming Gus T. Jones, former Texas Ranger and San Antonio Special Agent, as the first FBI agent posted outside the US and inside the US Embassy. See www.archives.fbi.gov/ archives/news/testimony/the-fbis-legat-attache-program/ for details on this position. The Legat, as he or she are named in FBI documents, reports on the business of the embassy and of the ambassador, an in-house spy to put it bluntly.

22. See Marc Becker, *The FBI in Latin America: The Ecuador Files* (Durham: Duke University Press, 2017): 20.

23. Ibid., 133–136.

24. Under FOIA rules and that of the Privacy Act, if a person is dead anyone can file a request for those records, if any, held by any federal agency provided an obituary or proof of death accompanies the request. If not, the person must provide a notarized affidavit giving the requestor permission to request those records under their name.

25. M.L. Corbett, "What Does an FBI Federal Background Check Consist Of?" (July 25, 2018) at https://work.chron.com/fbi-federal-background-check-consist-of-28722.html/ and for a personal identity summary held by the FBI go to www.fbi.gov/services/cjis/identity-history-summary-checks/ which costs $18 to search and obtain if there is one or not. Another source is www.edo.cjis.gov then the link to "Challenging your identity history summary." As of 2001, the procedures have changed for a security clearance by the FBI; go to www.military.com/veteran-jobs/security-clearance-jobs/ accessed August 10, 2019.

26. The FBI has a Name Check Program where federal agencies may request for a name check for criminal history which is public information on anyone. The practice began under President Eisenhower's Executive Order 10450. In 2014, the FBI handled 3.2 million such requests. In 2016, the number of requests had hit 3.7 million and down by a million in 2017. In 2019, the FBI receives about 65,000 such requests weekly.

27. Trustees were Oscar Spitz for TICO, Charles R. Porter, Jr. as general counsel for Trustee Spitz and Kenneth Bennight, accountant for Trustee Spitz (p.1 of Summary Report dated February 1, 1965 from the embassy in Costa Rica.

28. Coincidentally or intentionally, the use of TICO is culturally relevant because that is the term used by Costa Rican nationals to refer to themselves; they are Ticos.

29. The notion of *terra bullius* (nobody's land) that a person can physically occupy and possess land (squatter) under the assumption that it has no owner is long standing. First, not all cultures have the legal principle of private ownership of land, for example indigenous tribes. Second, physical possession does not mean legal right, for example something stolen. Third, physical taking of lands as in war does not confer legal rights either unless later incorporated in a treaty ending the hostility, for example, the Treaty of Guadalupe Hidalgo giving the United States rights of sovereignty in the Southwest, formally the northern half of Mexico before 1848. Squatter rights stem from the Papal Nuncio's many *Bullia* issued to justify taking of native lands in the Americas from "savages" by the Portuguese and Spanish. These *Bullias* became known in English as the "Doctrine of Discovery" and made US law by the Supreme Court. Britain invoked this right in the taking of the entire continent of Australia. In Central America many US companies in collusion with domestic elites and the military took indigenous lands and built commercial empires that became multinational corporations such as United Brands did in Guatemala, and this example of a coffee plantation in Costa Rica.

30. In old English this means a house or place that rents rooms by the hour.

31. A search for glossary of terms used at the Department of State did not reveal what is meant by SY. There is no such entry at www.travel.state.go/content/travel/en /us-visas/visa-information-resources/glossary.html#S/ accessed August 12, 2019.

32. UPI wire story carried by the Washington Capital News Service with date of January 16, 1967 in the released records.

33. Butterfield served as Nixon's Deputy in the White House from 1969 to 1973 and was the witness at the Watergate hearings that revealed the taping system inside the Oval office. See www.youtube.com/watch?v=MeQXopJ5U-Q/ accessed August 12, 2019.

34. Garcia, *Telles,* 139–147 and Gutierrez, *Telles*, 42–44.

35. Garcia, *Telles*, 150, endnote 21 on 151, 179.

36. See Nava's autobiography, *Julian Nava: My Mexican Journey* (Houston: Arte Publico Press, 2002), 136–165.

37. Garcia, *Telles*, 147–148 and Gutierrez, *Telles*, 52–53.

38. Ibid., 151.

39. Ibid., 152–157.

40. For her obituary see www.legacy.com/obituaries/latimes/obiturary/aspx?pid =142688451 and for his obituary see www.dignitymemorial.com/obituaries/el-paso -tx/raymond-telles-5461078/ Both accessed on August 13, 2019.

## Chapter 4

# Salvador Buruel Castro of the Los Angeles School District Student Walkouts of 1968

In 1943, as a ten-year-old shoeshine boy in downtown Los Angeles, Salvador Castro had never seen a *pachuco* wearing a Zoot Suit or the police and military men beating them up.[1] He shined shoes on weekends to earn a little money. His corner was on Seventh and Broadway, next to the Clifton Cafeteria. The police and military riots were so violent and dangerous that the city officials imposed a curfew of 9 p.m. on the Mexican community, not the sailors. A twelve-year-old from his barrio snuck out past 9 p.m. through an alley and was shot to death by the city police. Nothing was done about this police murder despite the loud protests from the Mexican community.[2] Sal never returned to shine shoes in downtown LA. These events including a veteran's memorial for World War I veterans at a city park his uncle took them to where he and they were ignored and segregated, had a lasting impression on Salvador Castro.

Like many other Chicano kids of that time, his parents were from Mexico who fled the Mexican Revolution and settled in LA after brief stays, first in Nogales then Tucson, Arizona. Sal, as he was called at Rowan Elementary school, was born in the Boyle Heights area of east LA on October 25, 1933. He called himself a "Depression Baby." That era in US history, comparable to the happenings now with Mexican and Central American immigrants without acceptable documents to have lawful residency in the United States, became seared in his mind. Both his parents, when they first crossed into the United States applied and received temporary visas to stay. His mother renewed her visa timely; his father did not. When the Border Patrol began their sweeps of the LA barrios looking for Mexican to deport during those years, his father, also named Salvador, was among those deported in 1935. Sal recalls the semi-annual trips to see his father in *Mazatlan, Mexico*, which coincided with his mother's visa renewal. Sal enjoyed these train rides as did his mother because the transportation cost was free. His father worked for the rail company that operated in Mexico and this was a perk of the job. His first years of schooling took place in Mexico at a private Catholic school where he developed his love for history and his cultural heritage. He fostered and cherished both and ultimately became a history teacher as an adult as well as a vocal advocate for his Mexicaness. Sal called himself, as all others did in east LA, *mexicanos* or Mexican. The 1960s is when he opted for Chicano.

He already knew Spanish, as it was his first language, and had no trouble in the Mexican school. Entering the English-only schools in east LA was another nightmare altogether. He had lots of troubles learning the language and bearing the brunt of discrimination leveled at all Mexican kids. As a kid, he had to face segregated public facilities like the public swimming pool, theaters, parks, and church. Once he saw his first-grade classmate, Juanito, pee in his pants because the teacher insisted on him asking permission to go in English. Juanito did not know how to say it. Many of his peers at the elementary school were immigrants also but from Russia and Germany, mostly Jewish. They pronounced his name as "sourdough." This name pronunciation caused many fist fights for Sal until he resigned himself, with his mother's urging to allow the name change from Sourdough to Sal.

As a result of the regular trips to Mexico, his mother became pregnant and gave birth to a brother, David, but he only lived for six months. There were no other siblings because his parents divorced by 1943. To survive, his mother took Sal to live with her relatives in a crowded small house. The family meals had to be by turns because all of them could not fit at the table at once. Sal was allocated the third shift and ate what was left, if much at all. Life got better for his mother but not Sal. His mother, Carmen, remarried when he was eleven or twelve years old. His stepfather was Antonio Zapata, an ex-Merchant Marine who was as tough and mean as he was abusive toward Sal, sometimes to his mother. The new family moved to east Hollywood and Sal got a new brother, Tony. Sal had to work for his stepfather, a shoemaker, for no wages; that money supposedly was to pay for his tuition and books. He was sent to Catholic school with mostly white ethnic kids whose parents were Irish, Italian, French, and, of course, Mexicans and a few blacks. The students were tracked into two language tracks, Spanish and Latin. Most of the Mexican students were in the Spanish track and the others in the Latin track. Sal met his first wife, Annette, in high school. They went to each other's prom as dates and he graduated from Cathedral High School in 1952. In addition to working at his stepfather's shoe repair shop, Sal also worked at the Swede Blouse Company after graduation. The following year he was drafted and reported for duty at Fort Ord, California. He went for additional military training at various bases in the South and was shocked to see the "White Only" and "Colored Men" signs everywhere. He experienced this type of segregation at a Dallas, Texas restaurant despite being in full dress Army uniform. Sal never left the country during the Korean War and he never made rank past Private First Class due to a disciplinary infraction he committed against a captain. Upon discharge in June 1955, he returned home to marry Annette on August 27. He was twenty-two years old; she was nineteen. They quickly got to making babies, Gilbert within the first year of marriage, then Jim, two years later. During these years while working three part-time jobs, he enrolled in LA City College using his $175 a month G.I. Bill stipend to pay for books and tuition. The first book he found on Mexicans was Carey McWilliams's *North from Mexico*; later he discovered Rodolfo Acuña's *Occupied America: A History of Chicanos*, which became his Bible. The McWilliam's reading experience convinced him to change his major to social science and focus on history. Given the wife's help with the family budget and caring for the babies, he got his Associate Arts degree in 1957 and moved on to California State University at Los Angeles, then called LA State College.

## VIVA KENNEDY CAMPAIGN AND
## BECOMING A TEACHER

His wife and family were not too supportive of Sal's pursuit of a higher degree at the state college.[3] They wanted him to settle down, work all day, and support his growing family. When he got bit by the political bug and decided to volunteer for the John F. Kennedy 1960 presidential campaign, he jumped in head to toe. He made every speech, event, appearance, and street rally that featured Democrats, especially someone for the Kennedy's campaign. When candidate Kennedy showed up to campaign in LA, Sal was part of his student entourage and met the senator face to face. Kennedy won the California primary and the November General Election by the smallest of margins, but he won. Sal graduated that first year of the Kennedy administration with a BA degree but without a teaching credential. He had to undergo two more years of teacher education and training to get into the classroom, which he did. He did not want to teach little kids; he wanted high school or at least junior high level. Sal accomplished his teacher training at Belmont High School, close to downtown area. Most of the students were Mexicans and lots of Japanese with some blacks and whites making up the student body. Sal was nearly thirty years old by then. And soon to be divorced after only seven years of marriage when his wife filed for the termination of their relationship.

Castro's first full-time teaching job was with the Pasadena school district at Washington Junior High. By 1963, he was teaching at Belmont High School, one of three Mexican American teachers for a more than 60 percent Chicano student body. He learned the word "Chicano" from his students. And, he also learned not to challenge the school administration as a rookie teacher. Sal was suspended from teaching at Belmont within his first semester for encouraging some of his students to speak at an assembly in Spanish. Since he was a first-year teacher and technically on probation, he not only could be suspended but fired. He was reassigned to teach at Lincoln High School—a school with "over 90 percent of the student body, which numbered more than 2,000" Mexican kids.[4] Over at Roosevelt High School the percentage of Mexican students was 83 percent and at Wilson High School the percentage of Mexican students was 76 percent.[5] These east Los Angeles high schools were the leftovers from the era of segregation and designation of Mexican schools just a decade or so earlier.

## DESEGREGATING THE MEXICAN SCHOOLS

In Texas like California and other states, Mexican students were segregated from white students in school districts.[6] There were schools designated the Mexican schools. In the 1940s there were in Texas alone, 122 such schools operating in fifty-nine counties. Mexican parents sought financial help from the only civil rights group operating in the state, the League of United Latin American Citizens (LULAC) and filed a lawsuit to end the practice, *Jesus Salvatierra vs Del Rio Independent School District.* In May 1930, Judge Joseph Jones heard the case and ruled in favor of Mr. Salvatierra only to have the school district appeal the case and win reversal on the major point that segregation could continue. The parents and LULAC tried to have the case reheard but were denied relief by the appellate court. Even the US Supreme Court declined to hear the case.[7]

In 1930, businessmen and growers were concerned about the growing numbers of their Mexican laborers who were settling in Orange County, particularly their city, Lemon Grove. Those who belonged to the local Chamber of Commerce pushed the school board to set up a Mexican school to keep these type students away from their white ones. The school board did just that on July 23, 1930, and on January 5, 1931, Lemon Grove Grammar School principal, Jerome T. Green, barred the door to any Mexican student. He referred them to their new school which the Mexican parents and students dubbed *La Caballeriza* (the Horse barn). Parents organized *el comite de vecinos de* Lemon Grove and sued in state court to stop this segregation. The case, *Roberto Alvarez vs. the Board of Trustees of the Lemon Grove School District* was filed on February 13, 1931, and heard. Over in the legislature, Assemblyman George R. Bliss of Carpinteria, California, introduced a bill to make the segregation of Mexican children legal. Judge Claude Chambers of the Superior Court for the County of San Diego, Petition for Writ of Mandate No. 66625 listened to the evidence and argument and ruled against the school district on March 30, 1931. While it was undoubtedly a major victory it was a state case and whose remedy applied only to the Lemon Grove school district.[8]

In 1947, five Mexican families sued in federal court the schools in Orange County, California, over the forced attendance and designation of Mexican schools for their children. They won their case, *Mendez v. Westminster.*[9] The practice of segregation, however, did not end like what happened after the first *Brown v. Board of Education of Topeka, Kansas* case.[10] The difference between the two cases was racial designation. In 1940, the US Census Bureau first applied the racial designation to persons of Mexican origin as Caucasian or White. African Americans remained Negroes, Colored, or Black. The school districts across the nation continued to segregate Mexican kids based on the lack of English language proficiency and later, on migratory labor status, not race. Finally, in 1954, three weeks before the *Brown* decision, the US Supreme Court (SCOTUS) in *Hernandez v. Texas* ruled that being classified white but not treated as white was equally unconstitutional and denial of equal opportunity.[11] The *Hernandez* case is what gave constitutional civil rights to persons of Mexican origin in the United States.

## EMPOWERMENT AT CAMP HESS KRAMER

Seething underneath Castro's psyche was the lack of empowerment among his Chicano students and community generally. Castro could relate to their feelings of being treated as second class persons, the discrimination from Anglo peers, teachers and administrators, the police harassment, poverty, and the lack of self-esteem. The English-only policy and curriculum struck him in his heart and mind. His students, like he once had been, suffocated under that hegemonic language regime. He knew first-hand the difficulties of living in poor housing in bad neighborhoods wrought with gang violence; the low expectations shared by all from Mexicans, including other Mexicans. He knew what it was to dumb down to fit into those low expectations. Nobody wanted to be smart and Anglo-like, better to be just one of the *vatos*. Very few of his students had thoughts of going to college; most wanted to reach the age of sixteen to drop out of the school system and find a job. The school district enrollment of Chicano students topped 130,000 in the LA school. As an example, Garfield High School had a dropout rate of 57.5 percent among Chicano kids; the average class size was forty students and on average there was one counselor to 4,000 students in the district.[12]

What bothered him the most, however, was the ignorance among his students of their Mexican culture and the Spanish language. He could not stomach their self-deprecating posture before Anglo society of not knowing their history and contributions to the United States like the proven valor of the *mexicano* soldier in prior wars. He knew the Chicano kids had a fighting spirit, but they had no idea of what to fight for much less how. If a student did badly in school his parents blamed her or him, not the school. Parents were ignorant and unaware of what went on behind those huge walls and inside the buildings. The prevailing philosophy was to get them out of school and put them to work or marry them off.[13] Being a former military man, he knew what it took to fight an enemy bigger and more powerful than you. Castro set out to correct this pervasive ambiance of powerlessness. His brainchild became the annual retreats he held for interested students just north of LA at Camp Hess Kramer. He wanted to "inspire a new generation of Mexican American leaders out of the high schools" and joined other community leaders as member of the Mexican American Education Committee to begin this work.[14] This committee pressured the school district officials for reform and also the county government which created the LA County Commission no Human Relations. Among those active in this latter group was Tobias Kotzin, his mother's employer, who made possible the funding for a first gathering of Chicano students at Camp Hess Kramer. The chairman of the county commission was Rabbi Alfred Wolf who offered Camp Hess in the Malibu mountains overlooking the Pacific Ocean as the location. Castro joined the group and, more importantly, became a counselor for the first conference held during Palm Sunday weekend in 1963 under the name of Spanish-speaking Youth Leadership Conference. The name was changed the year following to Mexican American Youth Leadership Conference. In 1970, it became the Chicano Youth Leadership Conference (CYLC). The students, all Mexicans, were chosen by the various high schools in LA, mostly public some private, which had large numbers of such students in their populations. The students had to have good grades, some leadership experience with school activities, sports or clubs, and willingness to go to college. The first group of Chicano kids numbered "about 100 to 150 students, almost equally distributed between boys and girls" and the various LA schools.[15] The rest of the forty-six-year story of the CYLC became a history of Chicano student empowerment, enablement, networking, and self-realization of goals until 2009 when it lost funding. Thousands of Chicano students attended this annual conference and not only went on to college and graduate but also became outstanding members of the greater community. One such person among many was the Chicano kid, Montezuma Esparza, a 1965 attendee, who was a leader of the 1968 student walkouts. Professionally, he has become a noted film producer of many movies. He is the man, however, behind the movie of these walkouts and Sal Castro's role in that protest, "WALKOUT!"[16] There were many, many others who found opportunity and professional success such as Carlos R. Moreno, another 1965 attendee, who went on to graduate from Yale University and Stanford Law School. Later in 2001, he became an Associate Justice of the Supreme Court of California; all because of Sal Castro and the CYLC.[17]

Camp Hess Kramer itself has a rich history of empowerment not only for Chicano students but also among the Jewish community. In 1952, Harry S. Mier bought 110 acres of land in Malibu off the Pacific Coast highway just north of LA and donated the land in honor of his lifelong friend and Wilshire Boulevard Temple member Haskel "Hess" Kramer. Receiving the donation were Rabbis Edgar R. Magnin and Alfred Wolf and Temple President George Piness. Together they created the camp on that acreage as a retreat center for Jewish youth and families.[18] In 2018, the infamous Woolsey Fire burned most of Camp Hess Kramer down to ashes and it had to be rebuilt.[19]

## THE LA WALKOUTS OF 1968

From the first day in class as a student seeking a teacher certification, Sal Castro began studying why Mexican kids from Mexico did better academically than Chicano kids in the LA schools. His research led him to conclude that it was the confidence of the Mexican kids in their identity: language, history, culture, and image. The Chicano kids did not have that but stereotypes applied to them were breeding insecurity about who they were. They had no positive identity. Castro, as one of the three Chicano counselors at Camp Hess Kramer began turning his students away from being self-haters to Chicano nationalists.[20] "My classes and the students I could reach became a laboratory for awakening a new identity of pride and self-respect," Castro stated to Mario. T. Garcia, his co-author on his autobiography.[21] According to Mario T. Garcia, professor of history at the University of California at Santa Barbara, Castro had a plan to correct the multitude of injustices leveled at Chicano students: a walkout. He began germinating this plan in his classrooms at Lincoln High School in 1966–1967, then at the CYLC of 1967. From among those interested students in his plan to make a statement, he gathered phone numbers to create a phone bank. There were no internet connections or cell phones then.[22]

In the classroom and out of it, Castro was incessantly encouraging his students to join and run for school positions in clubs and class officers; to get into the senior honors club; to attend public governing board meetings; to get involved with the Chicano Movement. In California that meant supporting Cesar E. Chavez and his efforts to organize farm workers and to oppose the war in Vietnam because Chicano dropouts were being drafted only to be killed in disproportionate numbers in that war zone. Earlier in 1965, the black community had rioted in the adjacent neighborhood of Watts. Castro witnessed the reaction to that rebellion; the black community had made a statement. He pondered how to do his statement without the violence. His father during a rare and infrequent visit, discussed the overall deplorable situation being suffered by Chicano kids in the LA schools. His father told him the story of how when his fellow railroad workers wanted benefits and improved working conditions, they went on a *huelga*, a strike. He reminded Sal that Cesar Chavez was doing the same thing to the growers plus boycotting those who supported the growers. The refresher course on organizing and striking was epiphany for Castro. He had met Chavez earlier at a Mexican American Political Association (MAPA) convention in 1965. Of course, he knew about the grape strike and related boycotts of grapes, wine, and stronger liquor. He reached out to college students who had been at his CYLC gatherings at Camp Hess Kramer to help organize a protest. He brought back to his campus the newly formed Brown Berets. They organized out of the Young Citizens for Community Action shortly after the 1967 CYLC retreat. Vicky Castro, no relation to Sal, and David Sanchez created a coffee house to hang out for the Brown Berets and their recruits. On any given weekend, the Piranya Coffee House on Olympic Boulevard and Atlantic in east LA had a speaker on relevant political events and music. Cesar Chavez, Stokeley Carmichael, Sal, for example were some of the speakers at these weekend gatherings. The crazy thing was the fun place did not serve coffee, despite its name.[23] Then on April 28, 1967, *Time* magazine gave Castro the ammunition to trigger the making of a statement, the school boycott. The article, "Pocho's Progress" in *Time* was about the half a million plus, more like 600,000, Mexican origin population of east LA. The article, according to Garcia and Castro, stated:

> Nowhere is the pocho's plight for potential power more evident than the monotonous sub-scab flatlands of East Los Angeles where 600,000 Mexican Americans live. At the confluence of the swooping freeways the L.A. barrio begins. In tawdry taco joints and rollicking cantinas, the reek of cheap, sweet wine competes with the fumes of frying tortillas. The machine-gun-patter of slang Spanish is counterpointed by the bellow of lurid hot-rods drive by tattooed pachucos.[24]

Sal was furious not just at *Time* magazine for running such an insulting article about him and his people but at the Mexican ancestry politicians in LA, California, and the rest of the nation who said nothing. Not one statement of protest was heard or read in the subsequent issue of *Time*. Sal, on the other hand, used the article to organize those who took offense and wanted to make a statement. He wrote: "If the adults couldn't or wouldn't lead, then the kids would."[25]

For months beginning in January 1967, Castro had been drumming up support for such a school walkout, a general *huelga* of east LA high schools. He names many of the early co-organizers and supporters in his book and how the list of demands from the students was prepared.[26] Sal details the trigger event: the Wilson High School early walkout over a school play. The principal, Donald Skinner, a very conservative man, cancelled the play after weeks of practice and rehearsals because of a line in the script between a man and his wife that alluded to having sex by saying, "Shall we go to work today or go back to bed?" The kids involved with the play walked out of their classes the following Friday. None of the leaders of this impromptu walkout had been coming to the meetings with the other high school kids. What began as a bluff against the administration who heard of a possible walkout in protest to conditions was now an open secret. The students at Garfield High took the lead in following up on Wilson, they walked out of classes the Tuesday after Wilson's Friday walkout. The students at other high schools felt there was no going back. The police ensured there would be no more walkouts, they arrested several of the Garfield students. Wednesday more kids walked out of classes at Belmont High and Lincoln and Roosevelt. It was at Roosevelt that police intervened quickly and beat students and made arrests. The inner circle of Castro's team from the area colleges, parents, community leaders, and walkout leaders met regularly at the Episcopalian Church of the Epiphany; included were some undercover police officers like Bobby Avila, who pretended to be a student at Lincoln High. The walkout fever spread to other high schools beyond east LA to San Fernando, Montebello, and even North Hollywood. Some white students at other high schools from Venice, University Park, and North Hollywood also joined in solidarity and support. Black students at Edison Junior High school walked out in support and to protest their conditions; others staged sit-ins at their schools.

To keep the protesting students together and joined, the walkouts would continue through Friday, March 8 and meet at Hazard Park for a rally after leaving the classrooms. Sal Castro under threat of losing his teaching credential, walked out with his students from Lincoln High. Thousands of students walked the miles to Hazard Park; at times it seemed like a parade. The police behaved and ensured kids were not run over by cars in the streets. An undercover cop in an unmarked police car let Castro sit atop his vehicle so kids could see him and be calmed by his presence.[27] The major media outlets began to show up to film and interview. The prominent politicians of the areas, Congressman Eduardo Roybal and newly elected school board member, Dr. Julian Nava, made appearances but no public comment of support for the students demands and overall issues was forthcoming from them.

Only US Senator Robert Kennedy, in the state to meet with Cesar Chavez, made time to speak and publicly support the walkouts. He posed for photos with some of the student protestors at the Los Angeles International Airport. Sal and his carload of students went to the wrong terminal, but others found the right one and got the public support and photographs. Senator Kennedy even raised his clenched fist and shouted, "Chicano Power." Kennedy followed up with a telegram, which read: "I support fully and wholeheartedly your proposal and efforts to obtain better education for Mexican Americans. *Viva La Raza.*"[28]

The following Monday, March 11 at 3 p.m. the LA school board met with the students and their parents to negotiate their demands. The school board tried to stall the resolution of the demands for weeks on end, meeting after meeting not late spring. Sal during these tumultuous times made time for personal matters, he had fallen in love with a wife-to-be, Carole Lerchenmuller, a teacher colleague. She was to be his date for a student prom both had volunteered to chaperone; he stood her up that May 31. When Sal went to pick up his tuxedo and returned to his apartment to change clothes he was arrested by local police. They handed him a search warrant and proceeded to rifle through his property and belongings in the apartment. They took several items The Grand Jury had returned indictments on thirteen people involved in the walkouts. They became known as the "LA 13." He was booked into the county jail. By arresting him on Friday afternoon, no arraignment or bail could be set until the following Monday. His lawyer, Oscar Zeta Acosta hired by the Educational Issues Coordinating Committee (EICC), the group formed by the parents of boycotting students, came to see him the next morning. Zeta Acosta told him the charges were conspiracy and his bail was set at $12,500. This amount of bail was more than twice the usual amount set for someone charged with assault with a deadly weapon and ten times more than for a burglary. The following Monday he was taken for arraignment and saw one other "conspirator" Carlos Montes. Once inside the county building basement he saw others: David Sanchez, Montezuma Esparza, Gilbert Cruz Olmeda, Ralph Ramirez, Eliezer Risco, Joe Razo, Fred Lopez, Richard Vigil, Henry Gomez, and Pat Sanchez.[29] Zeta Acosta did not make the arraignment but lawyers from the American Civil Liberties Union (ACLU) did and were able to get a bail reduction to a reasonable amount which was promptly posted by those in the audience, $250 each. The two Democratic senators running for President, Robert Kennedy and Eugene McCarthy, had contributed to the bail fund of the LA 13: $10,000 each. He tried to report to his classroom for teaching duty on Tuesday only to be escorted out the building and informed he was suspended. Senator Kennedy was shot and killed that same evening; primary election day in California. Sal and his girlfriend, Carole, were there in the ballroom when it happened. Castro had been invited by both Kennedy and McCarthy to their campaign celebrations at their respective hotels.

The summer of 1968 was difficult for Castro, jobless and income poor, and with no resolution by the school board on the student demands plus his trial. Without money, he was able to hire Herman Sillas as his attorney. Each of the LA 13 was advised to seek separate trial and not give more credence to a conspiracy by appearing in court together. As the new school year was to begin, the students involved in the walkouts devised a new strategy to pressure the school board. They conducted a sit-in at the board meeting held on the last week in September. The sit-in lasted until October 2 when the school board called the police to remove and arrest them. The next day, the school board voted 5 to 1 to re-instate Sal Castro to his teaching position at Lincoln High School. Returning to the classroom also meant retaliation and punishment for his role in the walkouts. One more walkout occurred that fall at Roosevelt High because a teacher had called a student a "Dirty Mexican"; otherwise slowly the educational bureaucracy began to reform itself by hiring more Mexican teachers, counselors, administrators, and cafeteria and custodial help. But Castro was not welcomed at the district in any capacity. He took a leave of absence and tried television production, then returned and was re-assigned to North Hollywood High School, whose student body was predominantly white and Jewish. His trial and that of the other defendants never took place because the lawyers for the LA 13 unsuccessfully challenged the make-up of the Grand Jury. The Superior Court upheld the charges because the exclusion of Mexicans from the Grand Jury was not intentional; therefore, the indictment process was proper. On appeal, however, the Second Appellate Court found the process unconstitutional and dismissed the indictment. After two years, Castro and the other were no longer indicted felons for merely protesting; a civil right guaranteed by the First Amendment of the US Constitution—the right to assembly and the right to present grievances.

## LIFE AFTER THE BLOWOUTS

Sal Castro's life was never the same after the Blowouts, as they called the student walkout of classes. As one of the boycotters of classes, John Ortiz explained to Castro and others that the word "Blowout" was a hip term used in the eastside among jazz enthusiasts. In context of jazz music, a player who "blew it out" was expressive of how well the performance was.[30] The students appropriated John's term to express their frustration with the school system and how well the walkout of classes was going to work as a remedy. The media picked up the term and it became the iconic lingo among those involved and keeping tabs on the dramatic situation which changed education for the better for all. It did not fare well for Sal Castro and his growing family with the second wife. He was *persona non grata* among the school district personnel, even clerks where he was assigned to teach.

Ten years after he was first assigned to Belmont High, in 1973, Castro was transferred there after successfully defending and re-obtaining his teaching credential. He was not well received at all and shunned by most personnel but watched for any "deviant" behavior he exhibited, according to some teachers and clerks who came around to befriend him. The school system, he found was still tracking too many Chicano kids into vocational tracks, punishing the use of Spanish, keeping eligible Chicano kids out of the advance placement courses, and the Chicano Studies class made available as a new course was an elective where all the expected-to-dropout students were placed. It took him years to become the teacher of the Chicano Studies class. The school district had met this demand with this course and made a few other reforms like hiring a few more Chicano and other Latino extraction teachers, lots of new Mexican cafeteria workers, and the drop out phenomenon was not reduced, only delayed. The school district implemented some of the walkout demands like allowing pregnant girls to come back to classes and try to graduate; some did. When Castro openly addressed this issue in his classes and ASP, he was almost fired by John Howard, a new principal, for bringing a doctor and nurse to school to talk about birth control and abortion. Another reform was the "4-4 program," which allowed potential dropouts due to economic reasons to take classes in the morning and go work in the afternoons. It was a move in the right direction but only delayed the ultimate decision to drop out in the last years of high school. The remedy for dropout prevention occurred with the implementation of a program called just that which Castro was able to change its name to Academic Support Program (ASP). Castro found a niche in this program and obtained a reduction in his teaching load to be one of the teachers meeting with students deemed to be on the verge of dropping out. The program met with some success. Another victory was his successful move to establish a Chicano Scholarship Night working with the Association of Mexican-American Educators (AMAE) and the new baseball franchise the Los Angeles Dodgers. He was able to convince the team's owner, Peter O'Malley to give him half price tickets to some games, which he could sell for full price to use as scholarship funds. And, he convinced O'Malley to let him bring live entertainment prior to the game. More importantly, using all his classes and the face-to-face, one-on-one conversations with students in the ASP led to an open door for recruitment into his annual CYLC. Despite some of these changes, Castro's biggest problem over the coming years from late 1970s into the 1980s and well into 2003 was drug dealing in the high school. A lesser problem was the constant pressure from military recruiters and their presence on each high school campus. They targeted Chicano kids to recruit and were very successful.[31]

The other aspect of his personal life that did not change much were the constant death threats he received by letter and telephone; sometime notes left stuffed behind his windshield wipers on his pick-up. Everyone knew his truck; anybody could have put such a note as a prank, a dare, a scare, or a real threat. They, whoever that was, were letting him know they knew where his truck and he were located at any given time. The letters also sent the same message, they knew where he lived and worked. Their content did not bother him; he figured they were cowards to hide behind being such notes and unsigned with no return address. The senders really did not want to have to face him much less attempt to hurt him. His phone with such threats rang in the middle of the night with anonymous voices sounding out the dangerous words such as "Castro, you'll be dead by tomorrow." He never reported "them because I wasn't too concerned about them. I figured they were sick tricks. I also didn't report them because I was pretty certain the FBI was tapping my phone anyway and so they knew I was getting threats. . . . Maybe it was the FBI itself that was threatening me. Who knows?"[32] Castro had good intuition and a healthy, reasonable paranoia about his Chicano activist status drawing all kinds of attention including the police at all levels. He was not wrong as the FBI files below will show.

## OTHER WALKOUTS ACROSS THE COUNTRY

It would seem to many, given the publicity surrounding the LA walkouts that this was the one-shot type of Fourth of July fireworks, full of flash and light then fizzle out. Not. There were hundreds of Chicano student walkouts across the nation. Almost as if coordinated, Chicano students, 3,000, in San Antonio's Edgewood High School walked out of classes beginning on May 16, 1968. They demanded basically the same school reforms as those made by the LA students.[33] On November 14, 1968, deep in the Rio Grande Valley of Texas, 140 Chicano kids walked out of their classes at Edcouch-Elsa High School. These kids suffered greatly for putting their political courage on display. Many of the 140 were suspended, 43 were expelled, and 7 were arrested and jailed. A federal court had to enjoin the school district from refusing to re-admit them, but not until 1969. Many simply did not return. Mari Lozano recalls she was among those suspended, removed from the student council and stripped of her football sweetheart title.[34]

On November 20–23, 2019, Chicanos met in San Antonio, Texas, to celebrate half a century of activism they began with the walkouts across the nation. The conference was called The National Chicano Student Walkouts

Conference and held at the downtown campus of the University of Texas at San Antonio. One of its purposes was to begin a database of all the walkouts that occurred in the late 1960s and early 1970s, giving more impetuous to the Chicano Movement of that era. Not one thesis or dissertation has been written to date that documented all these walkouts.[35]

## NEW CHICANO HISPANICS OR IS IT LATINOS?

In the 1980s, the Ronald Reagan wars in Central America he initiated as president produced thousands of new refugees fleeing the violence in their respective countries, especially El Salvador, Nicaragua, Honduras, Guatemala, and even Cuba. These new immigrants settled in many areas in the United States, but in LA they moved into neighborhoods close to Belmont. The new Chicano kid became the new Latino kid. The English-only criteria reared its ugly head again so English as a second language (ESL) classes had to be implemented. The *Fiestas Patrias*, a Mexican holiday on September 16 and *El Dia de la Raza* on October 12 gave way to Hispanic Heritage month and the celebration of all those Central American countries plus Chile and Brazil, who also celebrate independence movements during that period of September 15 to October 15. While Lyndon B. Johnson, as president had called proclaimed Mexican American Week in 1968, Reagan as president expanded the celebrations to a month and included these new immigrant groups.

The new immigrant Latino kids soon faced the same problems the Chicano kids and newly arrived immigrants from Mexico dealt with daily; they were treated like the Chicano kids were treated. Many of the Latino kids identified with the Chicano Movement instead of their nationalities. In Spanish they remained *Salvadoreños* or *Guatemaltecos* same as those from major cities and regions in Mexico, *Chilangos* (from Mexico City), *Tampiqueños*, *Jalisenses*, or *Sonoreños*. In English, however, they all became Hispanic because of the mandate issued by the Office of Management and Budget in May 1977 not only racial classifications to be used by all but also only one ethnic group in the United States: Hispanic. Many who objected to any identification with Spain given that inglorious history of conquest and genocide in the Americas, north and south, opted as pushback to identify with yet another European monarch, Napoleon III, with a similar history of conquest in the Caribbean and Mexico in 1860: Latino. Diversity among these Spanish-speaking groups created chaos with ethnic identity and Chicano nationalism.

One of the Cuban refugees that made it to LA, Martha Bin, soon became the principal at Belmont High School replacing John Howard who Castro had managed to pin with theft of school monies and was fired. While Principal Bin, a Latina, was convinced Sal Castro somehow was a communist, perhaps because of his last name, she kept him on a tight leach. She even refused him time off during his lunch hour to receive a Teacher of the Year award from *Padres de la Comunidad.* After Bin left that post, all subsequent principals were Latinos of different sorts, some of Mexican ancestry.

California turned right wing starting with Ronald Reagan as governor and only moved further right because of several events such as the Rodney King beating in 1992. The subsequent riots prompted by LA police brutality were the most covered media news story nationwide. Blacks were filmed in action against the police and looting businesses. The Latinos captured on film and arrested by police were mostly from Guatemala and El Salvador. Locally, many of the participants with Castro in CYLC and the walkouts began to move up the elected and appointed official ladders in the city, state, and nation. In 1983, Victoria "Vickie" M. Castro, who was central to organizing the 1968 walkouts, as were other Chicano college students, was hired to be the principal at Belvedere Junior High School. Ten years later, 1993, she was elected to the LA school district Board of Education. She served for eight years, including one as president of the board. She retired from the school system in 2006. The Chicano students of 1968 were becoming the *veteranos* of the Chicano Movement.[36] The school board seat Victoria Castro occupied, District 5, was because of gerrymandering away from at-large elections to single-member districts. This seat is the safe Chicano seat where many such voters are packed. The other Chicano and Latino voters are cracked into smaller numerical units in other districts. This is the one safe district that will elect a Chicano person until 2019 when Jackie Goldberg, a non-Latina of seventy-four years of age, was elected to represent them on the school board. She had previously served on the board in the late 1990s.[37] And, eventually the LA school board even hired as Superintendent of schools some "Latinos" as Castro labeled them: "Bill Anton, who didn't emphasize his Latino roots, was the first, and Ruben Zacarias was the second."[38] In 2005 until 2013 Antonio Ramón Villaraigosa, a CYLC participant in the 1970s, became the first Chicano mayor of Los Angeles since 1848.

In 1994, various propositions' voters were asked to support or oppose at the ballot box caused massive protests. A series of walkouts by Latino students occurred to express their opposition to one, Proposition 187, which would bar public assistance to undocumented immigrants. Castro encouraged the student to protest but did not take an active role in helping organize these walkouts. Castro did put a US flag on his pick-up and led the 400 Belmont High students in their walkout to the larger group marching toward City Hall. On June 2, 1998, Proposition 227 passed.[39] This was the English-only measure aimed at eliminating bilingual education. In 1999, barely two years into the implementation of 187 because it did pass, came Proposition 209 to eliminate affirmative action which also passed. Then came the big protests of the 2000s, in which millions of Mexicans and some Latinos marched in all the major cities of the United States. These protests were the largest ever in the history of the country.

## THE CYLC BECOMES THE LATINO
## YOUTH LEADERSHIP CONFERENCE

Castro informally refers to his program not as the CYLC as he did for decades, but as the Latino Youth Leadership Conference. He made the informal change to align himself with the great changes in demography, ethnic identities, and political consciousness, he wrote. The funding for the CYLC he relied on came from the County of Los Angeles and it dried up early in 1975. He engaged in his own fundraising when he could and found he could not. The CYLC began holding sporadic conferences up to 2003. In some years there was no CYLC gathering. The teacher's union also stopped their financial support and the Camp Hess Kramer alumni continued to do fundraising but not enough. For a while, he held two conferences, with only 100 kids each in the fall and spring with school district funding under the category of after-school programs. That also stopped. The supporters and prior participants valiantly have tried to keep the Camp Hess Kramer annual gatherings alive and going but find it difficult as Sal did. The Sal Castro Foundation is also experiencing some financial difficulties in continuing their program.[40]

## THE CHICANO LATINO YOUTH
## LEADERSHIP PROJECT AND OTHERS

Concomitant with Sal Castro's declining CYLC, another group emerged building on his legacy. Beginning in 1982, the Chicano Latino Youth Leadership Project (CLYLP) with support from the various higher education systems and community college districts started their own leadership training programs across the state, primarily in Sacramento, LA, Bay Area, and the San Joaquin Valley.[41] There are other older programs such as the United States Hispanic Leadership Institute (USHLI; www.ushli.org), which held its 38th annual conference in Chicago, its home base, in February 2020. USHLI not only does voter registration and education as does the oldest, Southwest Voter Registration Education Project (www.svrep.org) but also have specific youth tracks during meetings, gatherings, and conferences to promote leadership among the youth. A Latina-specific, Austin-based program is Las Comadres de las Americas (www.lascomadres.com) with affiliates nationwide. Back in 1970 in Houston, Roman Catholic nuns began Las Hermanas, which grew nationally into a powerful group for Chicanas and later, other Latinas, and has been struggling as of late to remain viable. Newer programs, some state-specific such as the Center for Latino Leadership, operate mostly in Washington State (www.centerforlatinoleaders.org). The Dallas-based Latino Center for Leadership Development (LCLD) is a three-year-old effort with ties to Southern Methodist University's Tower Center, named after former US Senator John Tower (www.latinocld.com). There are many more; missing is an ample body of literature on Chicano/Latino leadership; few books exist mostly on the business and education side and some biographies.[42]

The right-wing sector or US society also has its own youth leadership programs; the most ideologically tied to the ultra-right is that held by the Young America's Foundation (YFA) at the Ronald Reagan ranch in Rancho del Cielo in the Santa Ynez mountains of California. The YFA with $65 million in assets as of 2011 and underwritten by the richest of personalities on the hard right, does not have the financial problems that Castro had, or the more recent Chicano and Latino efforts have. The YFA bought the ranch from the Reagan's in 1988 and began holding 3-day weekend conferences for high school students from across the country. The Reagan's and YFA have a history of political and financial relationship dating back some time before he was ever in the White House.[43]

There is another youth training program on the far-right which is sponsored by the National Rifle Association (NRA) and has at least a twenty-year history. I say at least because the NRA has over dozen programs for gun enthusiast's youth, most of them being the children of NRA adult members. The major NRA youth program for training on the right to bear arms and the NRA's political agenda are the Youth Education Summits (YES) usually held over two-weeks each summer in Washington, DC. The 2020 session was only from July 13 to July 19.[44]

## THE PASSING OF SALVADOR CASTRO
## AND THE CHICANO MOVEMENT

Sal Castro died April 15, 2013, from complications of thyroid cancer. He was seventy-nine years of age.[45] From the perspective of the FBI, Sal Castro's "crime" was not any federal or state offense; it was his major role in the of empowerment of Chicano students in Los Angeles, California over the decades beginning in the mid-1960s. Among his biggest cadre of co-leaders in the walkouts and at CYLC conferences, not to mention his primary supporters, were the members not only of the Brown Berets but student members of the *Movimiento Estudiantil Chicano de Aztlan* (MEChA). In June 2019, a small group of MEChA leaders met and decided to propose the removal of the words "Chicano" and "Aztlan" from the name and suggested MEPA in its stead for Movimiento Estudiantil Progressive Advocacy. The final vote will be taken some time in 2020. To be sure, this proposal has already divided and weakened the organization between those who do not identify with a Mexican origin much less the Chicano term, particularly Chicanas who insist their gender is subsumed in Chicano and want recognition as well as those who opt for a simple X added ass in ChicanX or LatinX to include all genders. Division has been created among those who revere an indigenous root and that excludes others whose lands were also taken like the First Nations and African slaves who built much of early America.[46]

## THE FBI FILE ON SALVADOR CASTRO (105-178715)

The first document released to me on Salvador Castro is indicative of the problems with trying to uncover hidden histories within FBI files. The document is an Airtel sent from SAC, LA to the director, FBI on March 12, 1968. It is a two-page document, the cover page and one numbered "-5*-". No explanation is given for the missing pages, obviously 2–4, and no exemption is claimed for withholding these pages. The subject matter is categorized as "Racial Matters" and reporting on two school protests the FBI labeled as "Youth Disturbances." Racial Matters was the name of a COINTELPRO aimed at Black Americans from the 1960s into the 1970s.[47] The FBI director of all COINTELPRO's was William C. Sullivan, J. Edgar Hoover's head of the Domestic Intelligence Division.[48] This report with the complete set of documents received wide distribution to "local military agencies, the USA, Los Angeles, and the U.S. Secret Service, Los Angeles, have been furnished a copy of the LHM." The local informants and sources on this detail "have been alerted to report any further disturbances of a similar nature to this office."

The actual disturbances took place on March 6, according to the FBI Airtel on page 5. The FBI office in LA first learned about them and Sal Castro not from informants but from the news coverage by the *Los Angeles Times* of these events.[49] The newspaper reported on a three-hour Board of Education meeting at which the student demands were discussed. The School Board agreed to grant amnesty to protesting students but did not budge on removing police from the campuses or releasing students who had been arrested during the protests. Sal Castro, "a teacher at Lincoln High School . . . indicated he walked out with the students." Three days later from the first Airtel on this matter, a second Airtel followed from the SAC, LA to the director, FBI. This was a two-page cover sheet and single page LHM based on information provided by a source [name redacted]. Given that "no reported violence on 3/13, 14, or early 15/68 at any high school in the Los Angeles area" and the local police suggesting none was anticipated, the local FBI office in LA wanted to close the case (p.2). The informants keeping tabs on teacher Sal Castro reported he was going from high school to high school trying to get other students to walk out of classes and speaking at various rallies such as the March 12 one at "Rancho Playground, Motor and Pico Avenue, Los Angeles." Another source labeled Castro "an agitator and the leader in the walkout of 250 Lincoln High School students on March 6, 1968." This same source stated that "In May 1967, Castro was allegedly telling his students that Mexicans should not fight Negroes, but that they should join in fighting the police" (LHM single page). A two-page LHM followed the teletype reporting that Brown Berets members had been arrested May 31, 1968 for "participating and conspiring to disrupt the Los Angeles School System during March, 1968."

The Castro file goes dark for months and on June 3, 1968, he is resurrected in the FBI files maintained on the Young Chicanos for Community Action aka Brown Berets. A three-page teletype went out from LA to the DC FBI headquarters that day. It repeated the March 6–15 history of the student walkouts at two high schools, as stated to the LA office by informants [names redacted] (p.1). Page 2 is heavily redacted but for a couple of lines in the entire page that report "The following persons have been arrested: Salvatore [*sic*] B. Castro, Thirty Four; [rest is redacted] . . . and " set at twelve thousand five hundred dollars for each person." The last page of the teletype also reported on the June 1 demonstration in front of the Parker Center, police department headquarters, "by two hundred persons and on Sunday, June two last, by seven hundred persons protesting arrests of above individuals. No incidents or arrests occurred from the picketing" (p.3). The three-page LHM following the teletype, dated the same June 3, "requested Bureau advise of Bufile by FD-217" (p.1). Two of those sought for arrest could not be found because they were in Washington, DC. The FBI "forwarded to the Metropolitan Police, Washington, D.C." those arrest warrants (p.2). Page 3 is missing. Interestingly, on the left-side margin in handwriting is a notation indicating this Airtel was also forwarded to the Central Intelligence Agency, the State Department, various other intelligence agencies: NIC, ACSI, OSI, and Secret Service in addition to the DOJ's US attorneys.

Again, the FBI files go dark until September 9, 1968, by Airtel from SAC, San Diego to the director on that date. The subject heading is "Mexican American Militancy IS-Spanish-American." The words "Mexican American Militancy" may well be a COINTELPRO operation in place to target Chicanos, but I have not found direct evidence on that point only circumstantial.[50] The cover sheet lists four informants SD T-1 to SD T-4 [names redacted] but one "SD T-3" is further described as "RI-PROB (Ghetto)." The FBI did have such a program name for informants on African American targets called the Ghetto Informant Program (GIP).[51] The LHM accompanying the Airtel was at least four pages. This report coming from San Diego has as its focus the content of Chicano student newspaper, *La Verdad* and the sponsoring organization, Mexican-American Youth Association (MAYA) (p.1). One of these Chicano students in MAYA subscribed to the *People's World*, according to an informant. That person or another MAYA member became the target to get their home address. The help of the San Diego Gas and Electric Company furnished information on the name, address, and dates of service under the name [redacted]. This person or another MAYA member was identified as a college student at San Diego State College. Other MAYA chapters were formed at City College and Mesa College in San Diego. According to informant SD T-3 on July 17, 1968, LA Brown Berets traveled to San Diego to enlist support form MAYA to help Sal Castro (p.2). Page 3 is missing. Informant SD-T-6 on August 16, 1968, reported that fundraising was going on and being planned to help Sal Castro financially with his legal defense. A fund was started, "The Chicano Legal Defense Fund Committee." A future meeting for this purpose was set for "late September, 1968" (p.4).[52] A teletype from Los Angeles to the director on September 28 confirmed that "forty to sixty Mexican Americans are presently carrying out intentions of remaining at least over night and possible all weekend inside doors of Board of Education, as reported in Retels." This information came from the "Los Angeles PD Intelligence Detail." Two days later, the 30th, another teletype from LA reached the director, FBI stating the occupation of the Board of Education meeting area lasted all weekend. There were thirteen protestors still in the board room insisting on staying until the next board meeting. "No attempts made to remove demonstrators from building."

## THE SIT-INS CONTINUE

A teletype from the LA FBI office to the director, FBI was sent on September 30 at 10:42 p.m. to advise that "Approximately twenty to twenty-five in Brown Beret uniforms" were among the eighty-five to ninety protestors. Some six Brown Berets chose to stay overnight in the building and were allowed by Paul Engles with the Security Office of the school board but that they had to leave by the close of business the next day or be removed. Another teletype from LA FBI to the director was sent on October 2 informing that Paul Engles had "granted permission for demonstrators to remain overnight once again." Later that same day, another LA FBI teletype went to the director that some "two hundred in size" demonstrators had showed up at the board room. Engles said to those in the building after the meeting had ended, they would be arrested and thirty-seven of them "submitted peacefully to arrest. Two or three of these arrested were Brown Berets."

The FBI released the next sequential document dated October 3, 1968, a late-night, 10:44 p.m., teletype from FBI LA to the director, FBI reporting that the "noon demonstration scheduled this date did not take place." However, the LA school district security chief, Paul Engles, reported to the local FBI, who in turn passed the information on to J. Edgar Hoover that "approximately two hundred Mexican Americans and supporters of Castro present" at 4 p.m. when the school board convened for a session. An internal three-page memo from George C. Moore, the "dirty tricks man" working for William Sullivan, head of the FBI's Domestic Intelligence Division, dated October 3 followed the teletype.[53] Moore reported to Sullivan that other walk-outs or disturbances were taking place similar to the events in LA. The one he mentioned, not a walkout or sit-in, took place in Zion, Illinois, at Zion-Benton High School. This incident involving black students occurred because of a physical fight between "a Negro and a white youth." Police responded to the call and the police chief "was injured when he was struck on the head with a club by the Negro. Seven youths were arrested." Somehow, Moore made more connections between events occurring in other parts of the country. He wrote, "About 300 Negroes halted traffic in Cleveland, Ohio, yesterday afternoon. [Name redacted] a local extremist black nationalist, berated the police. There was, however, no violence." The Moore memo does not elaborate or explain why blacks stopped traffic. What was the point or issue they were trying to focus attention upon by their tactic? Then came the link to Chicanos in LA, "In Los Angeles, California, 37 individuals who were part of a sit-in demonstration at the Board of Education were arrested last night when they refused to leave the building at 10 p.m." Moore explained that the demonstration was about seeking reinstatement of a teacher [Sal Castro] "who had been suspended after being arrested and indicted for participating in a disturbance in Los Angeles high schools during May of 1968. These demonstrators are Mexican-Americans." He then indicates who else received his information: "Pertinent information with respect to the above is being furnished by teletype to the White House and other agencies and officials" (p.1). So far, in the released documents there is no reference in the section allotted on each file for who else is receiving the information to the White House, unless it is disguised as "Secret Service" or the DOJ's Assistant Attorney General staff who may have forwarded the information themselves.

More explanation for the black related events in Zion and Cleveland is provided that what was previously states as follows: "The Chief of Police was admitted to a local hospital and 51 stiches were required to close the wound. [Name redacted] and six other youths were arrested. Police are searching for [name redacted]" (p.2). Interestingly, the redacted blanks are short in length.

The first one is only six characters long, hardly room for a full name. The second is a bit longer at ten characters for only a short full name. It seems to me that these are only first names and known to the source of the information passed on and used by Moore. The paragraph on the Cleveland street protest was about a group demanding "that the police return the gas masks and other items confiscated by police during a raid on [3-4 characters redacted] headquarters on September 27, 1968." possibly BPP, the Black Panther Party. Salvador Burnel [*sic*] Castro is named as the arrestee and indicted teacher in the next paragraph (p.2). The memo confirmed the trial date as set for October 21, 1968 (p.3). Meanwhile, the LA FBI office had teletyped the director at 11:18 a.m. on the October 4, alerting him that Sal Castro had been reinstated by the school board to his teaching position.

The first page of the LHM titled "Possible Racial Violence Major Urban Areas Racial Matters" and designated "Confidential" was also dated October 4. The first material on Mexican Americans begins on page 5 and reports from a front-page article in the *Herald Examiner* of LA dated September 27, 1968, that "a crowd of folk singing Mexican-American parents, students, and a handful of Brown Berets staged a sit-in at the Los Angeles City Board of Education offices on September 27, 1968, after board members refused to return a teacher under indictment to teaching duties." This is in reference to Sal Castro. "The school board members refused to reinstate Castro until the case is settled." The wording of the last paragraph is stated entirely:

> In addition to demanding that Castro be reinstated the group is attempting to force the school board members to improve education at Mexican-American high schools. (p.5)

The last page of this report singled out the Brown Berets as the organization behind the walkouts and Sal Castro as the teacher who as "student counselor at Lincoln High School led the first walkout of student at that school on March 6, 1968."

The October 4, 1968, cover sheet from SAC, LA to the director, FBI had a six-page LHM, of which only the first, fifth, and sixth pages were released. The dissemination of this transmission like prior ones was widely sent to intelligence and military agencies. The information contained was based on reports from two sources [identities redacted] (cover page).

A very upset Californian from Van Nuys, Mrs. Rhonda Byron, sent the US Attorney General Ramsey Clark an insulting letter protesting the hiring of Sal Castro as a consultant, "presumably specializing in how to avoid demonstrations and riots caused in the education system." Mrs. Byron asked the DOJ "why not hire Eldridge Cleaver as a consultant to deal with how to avoid civil disobedience caused by racial relations while he is awaiting his forthcoming trial?" She accused Sal Castro of "flaunting and violating the law of Los Angeles, and who has exploited minors to achieve his end," and hiring him is "to condone law-breaking, thereby projecting a hypocritical posture for the United States Department of Justice." She sent copies of her letter to several public officials including "Honorable J. Edgar Hoover, Director, FBI." There is no response by any of those copied, nor AG Clark, in the files released.

The next day, October 8, SAC, LA sent the director, FBI, a two-page LHM, based on information from four sources [names redacted] that "Eliezer Risco, one of the 35 individuals arrested at the sit-in, as set forth in the LHM, is currently on the Security Index, Priority II" (p.2). Another person arrested "Guadalupe Saavedra, aka; SM-C: Los Angeles file number 100-71416 . . . be placed on Priority III of the Security Index" (p.2).

The FBI's Security Index came about when AG Francis Biddle prohibited further use of the Custodial Detention Index (CDI) by the FBI. Director Hoover from 1939 to 1941 placed names of persons on the CDI if he determined they were a threat to the national security of the United States. When prohibited this unilateral and capricious practice, Hoover just changed the name to Security Index and continued the nefarious practice. There were other indexes maintained and utilized by Hoover such as the Rabble Rouser, Agitator, and Subversive indexes. Hoover eventually merged all of these into one Administrative Index (ADEX) and later, after 9/11 this all became the Terrorist Screening Database (TSDB), an electronic database.[54]

Special Agent E. Rhead Richards of the LA FBI office submitted a lengthy, eleven-page, report on Salvador Castro as part of the LHM of October 8. SA Richards reviewed the events with the help of Sergeant Justin Dyer, LAPD Intelligence that led up to Castro and others being charged with a felony, "conspiracy to disturb the peace and disrupt the Los Angeles School System" (p.1). The sit-ins at the school board meeting room during September 28 through October 2, 1968, are detailed on pages 2–3. The list of the thirty-four arrested begins on page 4 through 9 including a Nicaraguan national, Ernesto Chamorro who "was released to U.S. Immigration and Naturalization Service (INS) as an illegal entry and presumably subsequently deported" (p.6). Each of those others arrested were "released on $315.00 bail each" (p. 9). Beginning on page 10 under the subtitle: "Characterization of Individual Arrested" are descriptions provided by informants 1 and 2 for Eliezer Risco, Raul Ruiz, Joe Angel Razo, Carl Vasquez, and "Roger Hoffman Wood is a minister who is associated with John Luce and is active in anti-police and anti-Vietnam demonstrations in Los Angeles" (p.10). "He is active as a leader of activities demanding equality and justice for Mexican-Americans in East Los Angeles" (p.11*). Informants 3 and 4 provided information on Charles Daniel Pineda and Fred Diaz Resendez both with the Brown Berets; Monte Elliott Perez, student from California State College Los Angeles (CSCLA)

and head of United Mexican-American Students (UMAS); and Guadalupe de
Saavedra also with the Brown Berets and the newspaper La Raza. Informant
4 specifically provided information on Josefa Sanchez, who was identified
as having "attended a meeting of the Mexican Commission of the Southern
California District Communist Party (SCDCP) on January 1, 1963, and on
April 3, 1963, attended a Board meeting of the SCDCP" (p.11*). Oddly, all
of these names are not redacted only their date of birth and on some also the
place of birth.

On October 11, another irate person like Mrs. Byron from Van Nuys,
Leonard Cory from North Hollywood, California wrote a letter of protest but
to FBI Director Hoover not the AG. It was on the same subject, however,
why would Sal Castro be hired as a consultant by the DOJ. Why he wrote to
the FBI is somewhat answered in his last sentence: "I want to compliment
you on your single handed fight against crime and violence and you also
have to fight the Attorney General of the United States it seems." Director
Hoover responded to Mr. Cory on the 16th thanking him for his interest and
"you may be sure I appreciate your favorable remarks regarding my work."
At bottom of the Hoover letter is "NOTE: See M.A. Jones to Bishop memo,
dated 10-15-68, captioned 'Salvador B. Castro, Los Angeles California.'"
That memo was released to me and made mention of the newspaper article
that Mr. Cory had read and subsequently wrote to the director. In this three-
page memo from Jones to Bishop, several written sections are intriguing.
The first is a reference to a note Hoover added somewhere in these transmissions but on none that I received stating that the director had "noted 'Run
this down and find out just where is he working?' H." Jones made Castro a
member of the Brown Berets and "one of a group of approximately 70 to 80
school teachers invited to a seminar at Washington, D.C., by the Community
Relations Service of the Department of Justice. He was reimbursed for
travel expenses and loss of salary from his teaching position while attending the seminar. He has not been an employee of the Department" (p.1). In
closing, Jones traces the transfer of the Community Relations Service from
the Department of Commerce to DOJ some eighteen months prior. The last
sentence reads: "There is nothing unfavorable in Bufiles regarding Cory and
no prior correspondence with him" (p.3). The FBI Director Hoover himself
wrote a two-page note to the AG on the 17th on the alleged "consulting job"
with the DOJ that some persons were complaining about with copy of the
newspaper article it was first mentioned. Hoover also admitted in writing that
the investigation of Sal Castro by the FBI was part of his COINTELPRO via
the Racial Matters investigation (p.1). And he adds that most people do not
know the Community Relations Service works autonomously from the DOJ
and this type newspaper article of "information could result in embarrassment
to him" (p.2). When "H" made the note on his own memo to "run this down"

mentioned above, the FBI wheels turned quickly and found the page. The copy does not provide a source or date or page.

SAC, San Diego sent an Airtel to the director, FBI on October 17, 1968, about "Mexican American Militancy IS-Spanish-American." This SAC also disseminated widely to other intelligence and military agencies his LHM of what may have been two or more pages; only page 2 was released. The LHM was based on four informant sources [names all redacted]. The informant monitoring the Students for a Democratic Society (SDS) heard at one of their meetings in October that MAYA from the same college was going to hold a teach-in on the 20th to discuss how US students could relate to Mexican students in Mexico City in their revolutionary struggles. They were going to invite members of the BPP to join them in this endeavor. The leaflet announcing this teach-in was being passed out at the office of the Peace and Freedom Party in San Diego, California (p.1). The LHM also described the MAYA group's efforts to raise funds for the legal defense of Sal Castro and why the Brown Berets are called that. The name comes from the group "wearing brown berets and khaki-colored Army fatigues jackets. They are a militant youth group and demanding immediate action to improve the economic standing of the Mexican-American people by city, state, and federal government." Surely, the FBI should not have interpreted this as some revolutionary agenda; but they did.

A month later, November 22, 1968, SAC, LA sent a single-page memo to the director with two newspaper clippings related to Sal Castro. The memo reviews the facts as the protests at the school district offices led to arrests including Castro and his subsequent suspension from teaching. One of the newspaper clippings is from *The Militant* of October 25, 1968, page 9 entitled "L.A. Chicano community wins victory." The second clipping, also from *The Militant* was from the September 20, 1968, issue on page 9 entitled "L.A. Chicanos at Board of Ed."

Closing out the year a long report from the LA FBI office, perhaps nineteen pages long, but only three released is actually on the Brown Berets but because Sal Castro was not only identified as being a member when he was not, but also because the Brown Berets did collaborate in important ways with the walkouts of 1968 and as co-defendants in the charges leveled against them all by the LAPD. The report is based on informants, T-3 and T-4, and explains the background leading to the arrests and charges against Sal Castro and other "conspirators." Quoted verbatim is this paragraph with major portions redacted following these words:

> The source indicated that these indictments resulted from an extensive 12-week investigation by a special task force of Intelligence Officers from the Los Angeles Police Department (LAPD), Los Angeles County Sheriff's (LASO) and the District Attorney's Office. (p.10)

*Chapter 4*

Informant T-4 stated that the Brown Berets were going to leave live rounds of ammunition in their seats as soon as they left the school board meeting but opted instead to use "several rounds of .22 caliber and .32 caliber ammunition" and tossing them "on the desk of one of the board members by one of the BB." Then, according to T-4 on Saturday, September 6, 1968, "eight members of the BB organization went to the San Bernardino mountains for target practice. The individuals along with the weapons they took with them are as follows:" (p.15). This list of names and description of weapons was not released. The names of those indicted who became known as the LA 13 included two persons who were part of the Brown Berets. "Ramirez and Montez were believed to be in Washington, D.C. taking part in the poor peoples' crusades [*sic*]" (p.19).

While dated January 30, 1969, the LA FBI report, perhaps more than seven pages, covered the period from September 13, 1968, to January 6, 1969. Relying on informants, T-1 through T-5, the report provides summaries of activities undertaken by their targets of surveillance; other than Castro all were Brown Berets [names redacted] (p.4, 6, 7). Page 5 is missing.

## THE LEGAL PERSECUTION OF SAL CASTRO

Court proceedings against the LA 13 are the subject of the SAC, LA one-page memo to the director, FBI dated February 25, 1969. The first hearing was on motions presented by the lawyers representing each of the thirteen. It had been advised to have separate lawyers and avoid the appearance of being a group of conspirators, one of the charges. The motions presented by the defense were systematically denied by the trial judge. A new trial date of April 1, 1969, was set by the judge. The trial date became a litigation pin pong ball between the DA and trial judge on the one team and the battery of defense lawyers on the other. The motions denied were appealed by the defense attorneys on various constitutional and procedural grounds. Richard Hecht, the assistant district attorney for the County of LA kept the SAC, LA informed as to the trial date settings. Hecht reported regularly to the LA SAC, who in turn notified Director Hoover in Washington on these developments or postponements is the better statement. The memos from LA's SAC of April 30, June 27, and August 19 indicate how slow the judicial system works. Each of these memos from the LA SAC to Hoover informed of a new trial date. The last memo cited above finally stated, "the California Appellate Court is considering appeal for the thirteen individuals under indictment and no new trial date has been set."

The summer came and went without news on the appeal filed by the LA 13 so the supporters of Castro and the others returned to rallies to show support. The teletype dated October 6 at 8:07 p.m. from the LA SAC to the director, FBI was about that subject. He informed that "three to four hundred individuals, mostly Mexican Americans, assembled at La Placita on Main Street in Los Angeles for a rally supporting reinstatement of captioned individual" [Sal Castro]. The crowd then marched from "La Placita to the school district offices" and about "one hundred individuals remained at Board of Education." Director Hoover raised the ante on Castro with his transmission to the director of the US Secret Service dated October 7. Hoover submitted on Salvador Bernal [*sic*] Castro an FD-376 to the Secret Service. This is a form with blanks to mark off what action is being requested by the FBI from the recipient. In this case, Hoover checked off the box "5. [box to mark] Subversives, ultrarightists, racists, and facists who meet one or more of the following criteria: "(c) [box to mark] Prior acts (including arrests or convictions) or conduct or statements indicating a propensity for violence and antipathy toward good order and government."

By the end of 1969, no word was had on the decision by the appellate court on the Castro and others known as the LA 13. Dutifully SAC, LA reported to director, FBI on January 16, 1970, that Castro as still employed by the school district but not into classroom duties due to the indictment. It also noted that "Prosecution in this matter has still made no progress, due to numerous motions by the defense." As the one-year anniversary of the 1968 walkouts neared, the supporters of the LA 13 renewed their protests and demonstration demanding reinstatement for Castro and dropping of all charges on him and the others. Of course, if by some miracle the charges would be dropped there would be no need for reinstatement it would be automatic. "Castro was present for short time but left and was not involved in any arrest" at one of these protests, the one at Roosevelt High School, according to the SAC, LA memo of March 6 to the director, FBI. A few days later, March 9, SAC, LA reported to Hoover that the demonstrators at Roosevelt had returned to protest. They "lined up on sidewalk and blocked traffic near school." This information came from an informant not identified [name redacted]. Teletypes raced across the country from LA to Washington, DC, keeping the FBI director informed almost day by day of the happenings in the city with protestors for Sal Castro and the others of the LA 13. Daily teletypes from March 10–13 provided a running tally on the number of protesters and numbers of them arrested. An LHM, six pages, more fully described the events taking place in LA. The Brown Berets, it was noted were participants in these anniversary demonstrations but not the leaders of them (p.1). Rock and bottle throwing by the protestors was reported by an informant as having occurred on March 10 at Roosevelt High School (p.2). On March 12, the resistance upgraded to "gasoline-filled bottle was thrown into the parking lot of the Hollenbeck Division of the LAPD. The bottle struck a vehicle occupied by two LAPD officers; however, it did not explode, and no injuries occurred." The police were able to get the license plate number of the car "from which the bottle was thrown." It belonged to David Sanchez, the prime minister of the Brown Berets. No sooner said than done, "he has been arrested and charged with 'Assault with a Deadly Weapon' or 'Assault with Intent to Commit Murder'" (p.3). The remaining pages of this LHM are titled "Appendix" and contain a brief history of the Brown Berets together with a booklet (p.4), and the Brown Berets "Ten Point Program" (p.5–6).

Again like in the late winter, early spring, the LA FBI office reported on the appeal by the LA 13 without any change on April 29, May 26, and July 27. SA E. Rhead Richards, Jr. got into trouble with his writing and was reprimanded by someone up the chain in Washington, DC, whose initials are "LEB." The report Richards, Jr., sent had wrong wording and wrong characterization of subjects, according to the handwritten notes in the center and bottom of the first page initialed "LEB/lmb" on the LHM cover sheet dated September 10, 1970. Ten informants provided information to Richards, Jr. in the making of this report including a three-page cover sheet using letters instead of numbers. From St. Louis the LA FBI wanted the military records on Sal Castro. Informant T-1 reported Castro was "in the U.S. Army from 1953 to 1955" (cover page B). The list with names of informants has all names and locations redacted (cover page C). On September 10, 1970, Hoover renews the FD-376 to the Secret Service on Castro with the same blanks marked and adding under "Photograph [box check] enclosed." That same day SA E. Rhead Richards, Jr., submitted his fifteen-page report to his SAC, LA on Salvador Bernal [*sic*] Castro. After two years of monitoring and writing out his name, the FBI continues to misstate his middle name. It was never Bernal, and has always been Buruel, his mother's maiden name. They also misstated his first name as Salvatore, not correctly as Salvador. The only name they always got right was Sal Castro. Richards, Jr. provided in "I. Background" some information on Sal. His "birth certificate" from the Recorder's Office indicates he was born October 25, 1933, at Montebello, California, to Salvador Castro and Carmen Bernal [*sic*] Castro, according to informant T-1. Sal "married Annette O. Castro in Los Angeles, California, on August 27, 1955 and separated on March 28, 1962 with final decree of divorce entered on September 5, 1963." T-1 also reported that Sal attended and graduated from Cathedral High School in LA from 1949 to 1952. He then pursued an Associate of Arts degree from LA State College (p.2) after attending there from 1957 to 1963. T-I heard that Castro was on sabbatical leave from teaching and studying at Claremont College in preparation for a doctorate degree. This same source further provided information on Castro's military service in the US Army from 1953 to 1955. T-1 provided information on his employment record beginning in 1953. T-3, another informant repeated the known information about Castro's criminal record, the arrest along with the

LA 13 (p.3). T-2, a different informant, clarified that Castro may not be on sabbatical because he could not find an application for that leave (p.4). Together, T-1, 2, and 3 pieced together where Castro had lived over the years and provided those physical addresses. T-4 chimes in with the information on the conspiracy charges (p.5) that Castro was not among those doing the sit-in when arrested and later charged with this offense. T-5 expressed the opinion that court case "would be completely dropped against Castro and the other defendants." T-1 and 3 provided their sightings of Castro to prove he was present at various demonstrations (p.6). Between pages 7 and 9, more entries are made of information provided by these informants and others, T-6, 7, 8, 9, and 10 on Castro being seen at the BPP headquarters, receiving the *People's World*, meeting with others at the Peace and Freedom Party gatherings, and meetings of those affiliated with the Socialist Workers Party (SWP). Page 9 provides a physical description of Castro as being 5'10" tall weighing 185 pounds. with black hair and brown eyes, a Social Security card, a California Driver's license number, and a police number for security purposes at the school district of 728 837 B (p.10). The Appendix that follows this report gives brief descriptions on the BPP (p.10A), the SWP (p.11), the Young Chicanos for Community Action also known as the Brown Berets (p.12–15).

The December 28, 1970, two-page LHM did not report anything new but for the notice that Castro had taken an approved leave of absence from the school district and was working for KNBC television station the summer of 1970. He was "discontinued due to the militancy expressed by Castro in their production." The last page listed three names, not redacted surprisingly, who "could be contacted for further details regarding the subject. More explanation about this new job with television and his termination is provided in the LHM dated April 30, 1971, from SAC, LA to the director, FBI. The substantive part of this two-page record alludes to a change in attitude of the Mexican community toward Castro. It reads as follows:

> Apparently sometime over the summer of 1970, some changes took place in the Mexican-American community in relations to Castro, and Castro apparently lost some of his influence. KNBC does not know what caused this apparently change in attitude of the community toward Castro (p.1). . . . KNBC also felt Castro may have been sensitive to the fact that the number of programs had been reduced to 10 from 20 and may have felt his position and the status of the programs had been downgraded by KNBC. KNBC has no plans to utilize Castro's services in any other area. His contract will lapse in June of 1971 and will not be renewed. (p.2)

On June 28, 1971, the SAC, LA reported in a two-page memo that Castro was active on the lecture circuit, speaking at six different venues between

February 3 at Lincoln High School, March 3 at Garfield High School, March 11 at rally in Elysia Park; April 28 at Cal State Long Beach MEChA program, May 4 at *Semana de la Raza* at Cal State Long Beach, and May 5 at Harbor College in Torrance, California (p.1). The July 8, 1971, report of at least five pages from Henry J. Pratt, Special Agent, to his LA SAC reported that the long-awaited trial would be a longer wait, it was reset for July 20 (p.5). No other pages of this report were released only this one and the cover sheet. The SAC LA continues to pursue any link to crime on Castro's part. He informs the director, FBI on August 23, 1971, that he is requesting Castro's criminal record from the California Bureau of Investigation and Identification. From the Department of Motor Vehicles, he solicited any and all vehicle registrations under the name of Salvador Castro and his driving record along with a copy of his driver license. The ASAC, LA received information from the state agencies he contacted on Castro. He forwarded that information to Hoover on October 13, 1971, and noted that Castro's license to drive would expire on October 23, 1973, and that his fingerprint records exist with the State Department of Education.

Finally, on December 7, 1971, the SAC, LA recommended that "in view of the subject's lack of militant activities during the past several months, this case is being placed in a closed status. In the event, the subject becomes active in militant activities, this case will be reopened." LA SAC followed up with the Secret Service alerting them to their closing of the Castro case and implying they should close their file also. He attached the two FD-376 forms they previously submitted.

The Salvador Castro FBI file ends with the release of a last document dated April 17, 1972. It is a teletype sent by the LA FBI office at 6:05 p.m. attention the Domestic Intelligence Division alerting them to the demonstration held by Mexican Americans in front of the US Courthouse on April 13. They were protesting the arrest of Ricardo Chavez Ortiz, who was charged with hijacking an airliner and demanding a press conference to inform the public about the abuse suffered by Mexicans in the United States. That was his only demand to surrender himself and the unharmed crew and passengers. This teletype claimed the "demonstration was led by Sal Castro, former Los Angeles school teacher." Obviously, Sal Castro remained on the watch list of the LAPD and FBI, among others. The LAPD continues to monitor dissent and activist in 2019 but only associated with what are presumed by the police to be leftist oriented persons and groups. A recent article by the *Los Angeles Times* on the police spying on a group called Refuse Fascism (www.refusefacism.org) whose purpose is to drive Trump from office has led to a change in policy on use of informants.[55] The Seattle-based Anti-Fascist Action group popularly known as Antifa has had similar problems with the local and state police not to mention the FBI.

## NOTES

1. The biographical data in this first section on Castro comes from the work of Mario T. Garcia and Sal Castro, *BLOWOUT! Sal Castro and the Chicano Struggle for Educational Justice* (Chapel Hill: The University of North Carolina Press, 2011), 4, 27–74.

2. I will use the term Mexican to refer to the US population of Mexican origin and alternate between Mexican and Chicano with an occasional use of Mexican-American: terms that were in use in the early 1960s and began to change to Chicano by end of the decade.

3. The biographical data in this section comes from Garcia and Castro, *BLOWOUT!*, 75–110.

4. *Ibid.*, 116.

5. *Ibid.*, 116–117.

6. For a history of this type of litigation by Mexican parents see Richard Valencia, *Chicano Students and the Courts* (New York: New York University Press, 2006).

7. See https://www.tshaonline.org/handbook/online/articles/jrd02/. Accessed September 29, 2019.

8. Robert R. Alvarez, Jr., "The Lemon Grove Incident," *The Journal of San Diego History*, 32(2) (Spring 1986), 17. See a movie adaptation of the history and case in Frank Christopher's "The Lemon Grove Incident," at www.imbd.com/title/tt0940722/.

9. 64 F. Supp 544 (S.D. Cal. 1946) and affirmed en banc, 161 F. 2d. 774 (9th Cir., 1947).

10. 347 U.S. 483 (1954).

11. 347 U.S. 475 (1954).

12. See www.unitedwayla.org/en/news-resources/blog/1968-east-los-angeles-school-conditions/. Accessed September 23, 2019.

13. Garcia and Castro, *BLOWOUT!*, 119.

14. This material on Camp Hess Kramer comes from Garcia and Castro, *BLOWOUT!*, 105, 106–109.

15. *Ibid.*, 107.

16. An HBO Production in 2006 by Esparza/Katz Productions and directed by Edward James Olmos, available commercially.

17. See https://www.chicano.ucla.edu/files/events/castro%20programs%20B%26W_52606.pdf/ for a lengthy twenty-seven-page report on the youth conferences, including some testimonials from participants. "Sal Castro and the Chicano Youth Leadership Conference," UCLA Chicano Studies Research Center, *UCLA*, May 26, 2006.

18. See https://jewishjournal.com/old_stories/9950/. Accessed September 25, 2019.

19. See https://wbtcamps.org/recovery/. Accessed September 25, 2019.

20. See UCLA "Sal Castro Symposium," 23–24.

21. Garcia and Castro, *BLOWOUT!*, 127.

22. See UCLA "Sal Castro Symposium," 25.

23. Garcia and Castro, *BLOWOUT!*, 136–137.

24. *Ibid.*,137.

25. *Ibid.*, 138.

26. For the organizing details and names see *Ibid.*, 142–194.

27. Undercover police date back to the Haymarket Riots of 1886 and became full blown operations with US Attorney General A. Mitchell Palmer's squads of informants, undercover police, and federal agents of the Bureau of Investigation, as it was named before become the Federal Bureau of Investigation (FBI) first used in his Palmer Raids targeting immigrants, labor union organizers and members, anarchists, and other dissidents. Later, when another target for repression was added, communists, they became known as the Red Squads and eventually, local police, city and state began to create their own intelligence gathering capabilities with similar units. These intelligence units to avoid disclosure and transparency formed a private entity called the Law Enforcement Intelligence Unit (LEIU). This entity is not subject to FOIA requests, it is not a government agency or program although initial funding did come from the federal budget under the Law Enforcement Assistance Administration (LEAA). LEIU began with 26 members and at last count had 250, including some from Canada, Australia, and South Africa. The state and local intelligence units share intelligence information among themselves and send their material and data to the LEIU to keep it private and inhouse. See Frank Donner, *Protectors of Privilege: Red Squads and Police Repression in America* (Berkeley: University of California Press, 1990) for this history and more. See also Kristian Williams, *Our Enemies in Blue: Police and Power in America,* 3rd edition (Oakland: AK Press, 2015), 246–247, 255–259.

28. For this information and photos see Garcia and Castro, *BLOWOUT!,* 180–182.

29. The list taken from the Garcia and Castro autobiography does not have Carlos Munoz, Jr. listed. See article on the 50th anniversary of the walkouts by Louis Sahagun of March 8, 2019, at www.latimes.com/nation/la-na-eastside-13-walkouts-20180308-story.html/ Accessed September 25, 2019.

30. Garcia and Castro, *BLOWOUT!,* 142–143.

31. This section is draw from *Ibid.*, 221–279.

32. *Ibid.*, 197.

33. See https://laprensatexas.com/edgewood-hihg-school-walkout-of68/ and view mini-documentary at www.youtube.com/watch?vs=6KncINtZBbVY/. Accessed September 27, 2019.

34. See Scott Hollbrook, "Former Edcouch-Elsa Students remember the walkout of 1968," *The Brownsville Herald*, November 15, 2018: 1,4. And see a video clip at https://walkout.netagrv.com/wp/. Accessed September 27, 2019.

35. See https://www.chicanohistorytx.org/ncmsw-conference/. Accessed September 28, 2019.

36. Thank you, David Sandoval, for getting me in touch by email with Victoria Castro. She responded to my email inquiry about these walkouts and role of certain persons including her with the Brown Berets on April 22, 2018. Email is in my possession and made part of the research file for this chapter.

37. See https://latimes.com/local/lanow/la-me-edu-lausd-board-election-analysis-20190516/. Accessed September 26, 2019.

38. Garcia and Castro, *BLOWOUT!:*,278. The current superintendent as of May 2018 is Austin Beutner.

39. The measure was repealed on November 8, 2016.

40. See https://www.salcastrofoundation.org at 3371 Glendale Blvd, #423, Los Angeles, CA 90039-1825. It was not easily accessed on September 26, 2019, nor by telephone at 626-824-5199.

41. See https://www.clylp.org for links to history, board, mission, and program information. Accessed September 26, 2019.

42. This chapter is based on an autobiographical work as is most of Mario T. Garcia's books on political leaders of the Mexican community. See my own autobiography, *The Making of a Chicano Militant*; on Severita Lara, the Chicano student leaders of the 1969 school walkout in Crystal City, Texas, *We Won't Back Down!* (Houston: Arte Publico Press, 2006); a biographical work on a political leader, *Albert A. Peña, Jr.: Dean* and 1st place winner in category of Best Biography from International Latino Book Awards in 2018); and, my English translation of the Reies Lopez Tijerina autobiography, *They Called Me "King Tiger": My Struggle for the Land and Our Civil Rights* (Houston: Arte Publico Press, 2000). A most recent biography is Lorena Oropeza, *The King of Adobe: Reies Lopez Tijerina, Lost Prophet of the Chicano Movement* (Chapel Hill: The University of North Carolina Press, 2019).

43. See https://www.reaganranch.org/rancho-del-cielo/timeline for the history of the relationship and www.reaganranch.org/the-reagan-ranch-center/reagan-and-yaf/ Accessed September 29, 2019.

44. See https://yes.nra.org/ Accessed September 29, 2019.

45. See https://www.latimes.com/news/obituraries/la-me-sal-castro-20130416 %2C0%2C6720373.story/ and also www.calstatela.edu/univ/ppa/publicat/today/story/archives/fall2013/castro_5.php/ for details on his life and some photos in the latter source. Accessed September 21, 2019.

46. See Dorany Pineda, "'Chicano' and the Fight for Identity," *Los Angeles Times*, June 3, 2019, at https://www.latimes.com/local/california/la-me-mecha-chicano-cont roversy-20190603-story.html/. Accessed September 28, 2019.

47. Kenneth O'Reilly, *Racial Matters: The FBI's Secret War on Black Americans, 1960–1972* (New York: Free Press 1991).

48. William C. Sullivan with Bill Brown, *The Bureau: My Thirty Years in Hoover's FBI* (New York: W.W. Norton & Company, 1979.)

49. March 12, 1968: I-1.

50. For a review of COINTELPRO operations the FBI admitted to conducting before US Senate hearings on the matter in 1976, see Davis, *Spying on America*. An earlier exposé on these COINTELPRO's is Nelson Blackstock, *COINTELPRO: The FBI's Secret War on Political Freedom* (New York: Pathfinder, 1988) and for actual copies of such documents on various COINTELPRO operations see Ward Churchill and Jim Vander Wall, *The COINTELPRO Papers: Documents from the FBI's Secret War Against Dissent in the United States* (Boston: South End Press, 1990).

51. This program was initiated by US Attorney General Ramsey Clark on September 14, 1967, under the administration of Lyndon B. Johnson just prior to

Richard Nixon being elected president. The GIP broadly expanded the scope of domestic intelligence authority and practice by the FBI. See also cited above Davis, *Spying on America*, 101–102.

52. The listing of SD T-6 is a not included in the first cover sheet page, nor is a SD T-5.

53. See Report number 94–755, titled *Intelligence Activities and the Rights of Americans*, Book II, Final Report of the Select Committee to Study Governmental Operations with Respect to Intelligence Activities, by the U.S. Senate (Washington, DC: United States Government Printing Office, 1976): 16 and the footnotes, 90 and 91 for mention of George C. Moore being the FBI man in the Domestic Intelligence Division suggesting the illegal tactics I refer to as "dirty tricks."

54. Curt Gentry, *J. Edgar Hoover: The Man and His Secrets* (New York: Penguin Group, 1992) has the early work on these first indexes which were physical index cards on each name.

55. See https://www.msn.com/en-us/news/us/lapd-to-change-policy-use-of-spies /ar-AAHFDfN?Dcid=spartanhp/. Accessed September 28, 2019. The LAPD was among the first major cities to create an intelligence unit with a necessary network of informants and was also the first police unit to begin to militarize their operation with the creation of a Special Weapons and Tactics team (SWAT). See Radley Balko, *Rise of the Warrior Cop: The Militarization of America's Police Force* (New York: PublicAffairs, 2014), 59–64.

# Chapter 5

# Balde from San Benito, Texas, a.k.a. Freddy Fender

The Federal Bureau of Investigation (FBI) file number on Baldemar Huerta a.k.a. Freddy Fender is 100-HQ-43445.[1] Baldemar in the *barrio* of *San Benito* and other venues where he played his music during the early formative years was also known as Balde. The FBI file analyzed here consists only of sixteen pages released.[2] The FBI relied on several aliases to his name which are listed on these files: Freddy Fender, Valdemar Huerta, Valdemar Huerto, Valdemar Huert, Baldemar Huerta S. Baldemar Huerta, Baldemal Huerta, Baldemar Garcia Huerta, and Balmer Garza Huerta. As any researcher knows, correct information is crucial to getting the correct result. The paltry sixteen pages of FBI records pertain to one event—his anticipated travel to or via Manila in the Philippines in March 1980. While I have submitted an appeal for more records, the process is very slow, months and years slow in other cases involving my Freedom of Information Act requests. Publication deadlines for book contracts do not wait. This will be a short chapter.

## IS THIS ALL?

The sixteen pages are in no way the total of what should exist as files with the FBI in the case of Freddy Fender a.k.a. Baldemar Huerta. There should be more files not because he was involved in more criminal activity much less subversive actions, but because there cannot just be a set of pages on one incident reported out of Manila, Philippines, with no prior record of why there was a file on him to begin with. There is no logic to a tiny sample of records without a preface to the surveillance much less cloture. There is no postscript either or referral to another agency such as IRS, for example. The Manila report is the beginning and the end, we are to believe. Yet, it seems the final destination of this trip or tour was New Zealand where his Gold Record recording, "Wasted Days and Wasted Nights" was rated number 1 for twelve weeks on the pop charts of that country.[3]

Consider this reader, on several occasions, Freddy Fender was made part of the inaugural events involving two presidents, George W. Bush Sr. and William Clinton; and, to play at the White House during the presidential term of Jimmy Carter. These three events should have prompted at least a quick investigation by the FBI and or the Secret Service or both, into the person for the security of the Head of State. There was no request for a Name Check Program query? Where are those files? He was also part of the inaugural event for Texas Governor Ann Richards. Her security detail or the Texas Department of Public Safety must have also done a preliminary security check on him, although they may not have called the FBI, they should have. She was also the Head of State for Texas from 1991 to 1995. Any security check on him by the FBI should show up as a record in the overall FBI file on Freddy Fender a.k.a. Baldemar Huerta.

There are also prison records in existence somewhere in Louisiana. In 1960, he spent three years at Angola State Prison in that state. The local police of Baton Rouge raided his motel room and arrested him and his bass player for possession of two marijuana cigarettes. He was convicted.[4] Previously, he had spent time in the stockade while in the Marines which he joined after turning seventeen years of age in 1953. In the US Marine Corps with the "tank outfit" of Baker Company, 4th Battalion, 3rd Marine Regiment, he began drinking hard and fighting with other Marines or anybody often. "I didn't have no sense. I was a gung-ho type. I wanted to be like John Wayne and all that." Baldemar was not a small guy either, he stood at 5'10" tall.

This lack of control with drugs and alcohol led also to several occasions of confinement and imprisonment for violence and drunkenness. While in the Marines, he was charged and court martialed several times for both, three days for the first offense, three months for the second offense, and finally six months for the third offense plus a dishonorable discharge from the military. This bad mark on his military record kept him from all G.I. Bill benefits associated with being a veteran; no educational benefits, no rights to loans for purchase of real estate by veterans, medical treatment, commissary privileges, and the like.

Upon release from prison, he began re-igniting his musical career in New Orleans for a few years. By 1969, he had returned home to San Benito in the Rio Grande Valley of Texas. None of these records were found by the FBI in their search for records on Baldemar Huerta a.k.a. Freddy Fender and other aliases at my request. Supposedly, the main reason for the files released is that the Legat Manila wanted to know about Freddy Fender for whatever purpose.[5] And, these sixteen pages are the only find in their files. Yet, as it will be shown below, this was the principal issue among others for the Legat, Manila: finding his criminal history.

## BEING MEXICAN IN CAMERON COUNTY, TEXAS

His birth name was Baldemar Huerta and was called Balde as a kid. He was born on June 4, 1937, in San Benito, Texas, in the barrio named *El Jardin*/The Garden, which it wasn't. During the 1930s, San Benito in Cameron County was experiencing segregation; economic problems associated with the Great Depression of that time; and, chronic poverty and unemployment. The farm economy was the only growth areas among all others during this decade. The number of farms started by an influx of Anglo farmers from the Midwest in Cameron County grew to twice their numbers from 1,507 in 1920 to 2,936 in 1930. Employment for most Mexicans was in agriculture given the 120,064 acres under cultivation and production by 1940. The population also grew during 1910, the beginning of the Mexican Revolution, just across the border from Cameron County and all of borderland Texas from Brownsville to El Paso and beyond, from 27,158 to more than double in number to 77,540 by 1930. The influx of immigrants from Mexico in search of safety and work became the primary source of cheap labor for the Anglo farmers and as their domestic help for their families. The county population by 1940 was evenly split between Anglos and Mexican origin peoples; blacks were less than 2 percent of the total. Blacks in the towns across the entire Rio Grande Valley were hardly known as neighbors; they were also segregated into their own neighborhood in Harlingen, Texas, next door to San Benito.[6]

El Jardin was anything but a garden; it was a run-down area of wood structures housing large families of Mexican-origin people, purposely segregated, unpaved streets, no sidewalks, no indoor plumbing, no hot water, poor people, mostly seasonal agricultural workers and Spanish-speaking.[7] Smuggling of liquor and drugs from Mexico in the United States via Cameron County, especially during the Prohibition era was an alternative job and career to being stoop labor in the agricultural fields of South Texas. Balde, "The Bebop Kid," was born into that society plus a *patron* system of politics where the Anglo employer and political bosses of the Rio Grande Valley such as Jim Wells and George Parr paid for the poll taxes of their laborers and domestics, then voted "their Mexicans" on election day. Racism manifested by enforced segregation, rampant discrimination, and police brutality was what he learned to accept as a teenager in San Benito.[8] Like many others, when farm labor in the county and area began to decline, Mexican families went north into the Midwestern states in search of work. Despite those harsh conditions, Balde did see a different lifestyle and social environment from that in San Benito.

And, like too many kids born into poor, migrant worker, Mexican parents, he quit school and sought a way out of South Texas. Mexican American students have the worst record of leaving school without graduating from high school. In 1972, across Texas the "Hispanic" kids drop out of school at a rate of 34 percent of all students.[9] In 2009–2010 students in Cameron County, the "Hispanic" drop out rate was at 55 percent.[10] In 1953, when Balde quit school, I venture to guess it was much, much higher.

Baldemar Huerta a.k.a. Freddy Fender died at age sixty-nine on October 14, 2006, from lung cancer.[11] His biological father had died when he was seven. He did not have a meaningful nor long relationship with his stepfather because he abandoned the family as Balde was becoming a teenager. His mother had to support the family as best she could as migrant farm workers; they had been working in the fields all their lives. They did crops in the Rio Grande Valley, cotton in Arkansas, and beets in Michigan. When Balde was ten years old and called The Bebop Kid, he won a singing contest on a local radio station: his first. He never stopped singing after that.

He dropped out of school at age sixteen and did not return to any type of formal education until he was released from prison and made it back home. He attended Del Mar College in Corpus Christi for a while and learned auto mechanics which he did for money and music gigs on weekends.[12]

## ALCOHOL AND DRUGS

While in his sixties he had many serious medical issues stemming from that early age abuse of alcohol and drugs. In 2000 at age sixty-three, he was given a diagnosis of having Hepatitis C, a type of diabetes. His daughter, Maria Huerta Garcia, the youngest girl, donated one of her kidneys to him so he could live longer. The kidney transplant operation was done in 2002; followed by a liver transplant in 2004. In early 2006, he was too weak to sustain a lung transplant and tumor removals; and, he died shortly thereafter. But not before 2004 when the City of San Benito made him their official "Favorite Son" by placing an image of his face and upper body on a huge water tower at the edge of the Interstate that runs by San Benito. It reads "San Benito Hometown of Freddy Fender" [his name is in signature form].[13] He played his music almost to the end. His last concert was on December 31, 2005.[14]

## THE BEBOP KID BECAME FREDDY FENDER

Baldemar Huerta legally became Freddy Fender in 1959. The name change was deemed necessary to sell his music to Anglos, who might otherwise not buy with a name like his. He said, the name change "helped sell my music better to gringos."[15] Supposedly, Heuy Meaux and he came up with the name combination. Balde picked Fender because that was the name on his favorite guitar made by Leo Fender's company out of Scottsdale, Arizona.[16] Heuy thought Freddy would go well with Fender, the alliteration. When Imperial Records offered him a contract with their label, ABC/Dot, he decided to make the name change a legal fact. Many celebrities of his era, 1915–1945, changed their name and even looks, mainly hair color, to become more Anglo-like. Andy Russell, another famous singer was Andres Rabago from Boyle Heights, eastside Los Angeles.[17] Vikki Carr, another world-famous singer, changed her name away from Florencia Bisenta De Cansillas-Martinez Cordova. She was from El Paso, Texas.[18] Four years younger than Freddy Fender was Ricardo Esteban Valenzuela Reyes born in Pacoima, California, on May 13, 1941. Like Baldemar Huerta, Ricardo Esteban dropped out of school in 1958 just after turning sixteen years of age. The Baby Boomer generation and certainly Rock and Roll *aficionados* know him as Ritchie Valens. His manager and promoter, Bob Keane suggested he change his name away from Ricardo Esteban and just keep the Valenz part of the surname but with an "s" not a "z." Ritchie Valens' famous songs were "*La Bamba*" and "Donna." Tragically he died in an airplane crash while on tour at age seventeen. Ricardo Esteban was inducted as Ritchie Valens into the Rock and Roll Hall of Fame in 2001.[19] Regrettably, Freddy Fender never made it into either the Rock and Roll Hall of Fame or the Country Music Hall of Fame despite his many award-wining recordings in both genres.

Same scenario with name changes happened to upcoming movie stars of Mexican origin and other Latino mixes. Antonio Rudolfo Oaxaca Quinn was born in Chihuahua, Mexico, to Mexican parents who emigrated to Los Angeles. His father found work with a Hollywood studio while Antonio Rudolfo labored with English in school. The school changed his name and became Anthony Quinn. Once he got auditioned in Hollywood he began to get and played roles of the heavy, swarthy, macho guy, occasionally he was that kind of Mexican character also.[20] Other Latinas, not of Mexican origin, but with Spanish names deemed not to help their careers were Rita Hayworth who was Margarita Casino from Brooklyn, New York, and Raquel Welch was born in Chicago, Illinois, as Jo Raquel Tejada.[21] How about the half-Mexican, Linda Jean Cordova Carter who changed her name to stand out among others as Lynda Carter a.k.a. Wonder Woman.[22]

Other half-Mexicans, usually on the mother's side, with an Anglo surname passed for white. Some of these celebrities purposely ignored and often denied their Mexican ancestry such as baseball greatest hitter of all time, Ted Williams of the Boston Red Sox, whose maternal last name was Venzor. "If I had my mother's name, there is no doubt I would have run into problems in those days," he said to his co-writer of one of his books. He was inducted into the Baseball Hall of Fame in 1966.[23] Heard of Jim Plunkett or Joe Kapp, both with mother's who were Mexican Americans? Both are among the greatest NFL football players of all time. Kapp's face and half torso graced the *Sports Illustrated* cover with the title "The Toughest Chicano" on the grid iron. He played mostly for the Minnesota Vikings.[24] The list can go on to continue making the case for how poor the social capital of persons with Spanish surnames is in the United States, then and now.

## BECOMING A MUSICAL ICON

He found great success as Freddy Fender. His first big hit that sold over a million records and went Gold, industry name for million plus records sold, was in 1975 with "Before the Next Tear Drop Falls," a blend of country and pop music. Between 1959 and 1975, Freddy Fender had twenty-one hit records, selling millions and millions of records. In 1975, his other big hit was "Wasted Days and Wasted Nights," a remake of a 1959 song that he could not promote because he went to prison. And, that 1975 year was also when he was featured as one of the artists on a float at the annual Macy's Thanksgiving Parade. Between 1979 and 1999, he had minor roles in eight Hollywood movies, the most noted was Robert Redford's "Milagro Beanfield War" in 1987.[25]

## THE SIXTEEN PAGES

The FBI in the few documents released seldom got his name correct despite checking into or could have checked deeper into readily available to them the passport application, social security records, military records, martial licenses, and criminal records including prison records. If the domestic FBI personnel was not competent in the Spanish language, the FBI's Legats in Manila, Philippines, and Mexico City should have been and caught these flaws in identification.[26] A correct name is essential in getting to the correct information in files, any files, including current day computer generated and stored material. Questions remain as to why the FBI began surveillance of Baldemar Huerta a.k.a. Freddy Fender? What was he doing that caught the interest of the FBI to begin an investigation as to his travels? When did the surveillance begin? He certainly was not part of the Chicano Movement or any kind of flaming Chicano radical at the time. On the contrary, he was a solid mainstream jazz blues and country music kind of guy. In an interview he stated, "I've made it a policy not to get politically involved, there would be people against whatever stand I took."

Let's say I would take the side of Cesar Chavez in the grapes issue. Now, let's say that I have a lot of fans who own farms and grow grapes. They won't buy my records. "Besides," he said, "Nobody helped me when I needed help. There was nobody there except Freddy Fender."

For him, it's not a question of being fair to his people. It's a question of whether he believes in what they're doing, or the way they're doing it. His music, he says, is his most important contribution to his heritage.[27]

At age forty-three in 1980 he was on top of the music world; is that the reason for the surveillance? Freddy's name is under the Gold Star on Hollywood's Walk of Fame; put there in 1999. Freddy's celebrity status continued into the 1990s touring first with Los Super 7 then the Texas Tornados. He did voiceovers for commercials heard and seen for McDonalds, El Chico Mexican Restaurants, Miller Lite beer, and narrated the documentary on Tejano music, *Songs of the Homeland*.[28] We may never know why the FBI insists on claiming this is the entire file on Baldemar Huerta.

## WAS FERDINAND MARCOS BEHIND THIS MANILA CONCERN?

We do know that Ferdinand Marcos was the dictator for almost twenty years in the Philippines. He has an interesting history from the start of his political year with a murder he committed and was exonerated. After serving in the legislature for some years, he was elected president and sworn into office on December 30, 1965. President Lyndon B. Johnson was in office.[29] He was re-elected for a second term under many allegations of massive voter fraud. He declared martial law in 1972. President Richard Nixon was in office.[30] Marcos remained in office as president for life almost until 1986; he died in 1989 at age seventy-two.[31] During this long tenure as absolute ruler of the Philippines, these other US presidents were in office: Gerald Ford, Jimmy Carter, and Ronald Reagan.[32] Marcos, in terms of US foreign policy, was our choice for dictator for all Filipinos. Marcos was in office when this first inquiry was made about Freddy Fender, if we are to believe this is the beginning of the FBI file on him.

A Telex two-page transmission dated April 23, 1980, from the FBI's Legat in Manila to FBI Director reported on "Valdemar Huerta, aka Freddy Fender" [redacted names] advised as follows:

We have been advised by Joe Brown Enterprises LTD, that they are attempting to bring Freddy Fender, American Country Music singer, to New Zealand on 27th May. Apparently, a previous application was blocked by our Immigration department because of Fender's conviction for possessing marijuana, but that since then, Fender has been granted full pardon and restoration of citizenship by the State of Louisiana. Joe Brown Enterprises LTD advise that Freddy Fender's full name is Valdemar Huerto. Request of FBI HQ: Obtain subject's identification division record and Sutel to Manila (p.1). Forward above identification by teletype to New Orleans, apparent location of marijuana possession conviction, and request contact with Louisiana State Authorities to verify pardon and to obtain information, if not clear on identification division records, regarding effect of pardon on conviction. (p.2)

No information is provided on Joe Brown Enterprises LTD as to why that business or agent would report to the FBI Legat Attaché in Manila that they were trying to bring Freddy Fender to New Zealand. Was Joe Brown Enterprises LTD an informant, a snitch, a busybody, an interloper, what? On April 25, 1980, the same identical message was re-sent on three pages but on an FBI form, 0-73, to the Legat Manila and FBI New Orleans. FBI Form 0-73 is used only for incoming teletype messages for routing purposes. A fourth page is entirely redacted but for on top note "NOTE: [redacted] IDENT., TO SA [two blocks of names redacted] DESK, CID, ON 4/25/80."

This busy work of requesting information dating twenty years prior resulted in an exchange of more teletypes between FBI offices. New Orleans sent a two-page message dated May 8, 1980, to the FBI director on this matter of "Valdemar Huerto, aka Freddy Fender: [word or code or initials redacted] RE Bureau Teletype to New Orleans and Legal Attache Manila April 26, 1980," [original teletype has April 23 on it] with this message all in caps:

DUE TO LACK OF DESCRIPTIVE INFORMATION CONCERNING VALDEMAR HUERTO, AKA FREDDY FENDER, INVESTIGATION HAS BEEN NEGATIVE SO FARE CONCERNING HIS CRIMINAL HISTORY IN THE STATE OF LOUISIANA. A CHECK OF THE NEW ORLEANS FBI DIVISION INDICES, THE METROPOLITAN ORLEANS TOTAL INFORMATION ON-LINE NETWORK (MOTION) AND THE CENTRAL INDICES OF THE LOUISIANA STATE POLICE HAVE REVEALED NO INFORMATION CONCERNING HUERTO. A CHECK OF THE PASSPORT OFFICE IN NEW ORLEANS, LOUISIANA, REVEALED THAT HUERTO HAD OBTAINED A PASSPORT FROM THIS OFFICE IN THE PAST, BUT INFORMATION AS TO WHETHER OR NOT HE HAS (p.1) A CURRENT PASSPORT ISSUED BY THE NEW ORLEANS OFFCIE IS UNAVAILABLE DUE TO THE PRIVACY ACT. NEW ORLEANS HAS REFERRED TO THE LEGAL DEPARTMENT OF THE UNITED STATES PASSPORT AGENCY, WASHINGTON, D.C. TELEPHONE NUMBER REGARDING THIS INFORMATION. LAW ENFORCEMENT AGENCIES

IN LOUISIANA REQUIRE INFORMATION ON THE DATE OF BIRTH OF VALDEMAR HUERTO, AKA FREDDY FENDER IN ORDER TO OBTAIN INFORMATION AS TO HIS CRIMINAL HISTORY. BUREAU REQUESTED TO RELAY TO LEGAT MANILA. (p.2)

FBI Director William H. Webster promptly notified Manila in the Philippines by form with attachments all the recent teletype information being requested on Freddy Fender. This form 0-73 was file stamped at bottom right on "May 14, 1980," and also file stamped at mid-right of the page, "10 May 80 0136.'" Who knows when the form was prepared?

On May 13, Legat Manila responded to FBI director in a short teletype on the "Valdemar Huerto, aka Freddy Fender" matter: [Name redacted] advise their records show subject's FBI file number is 5455228. FBI Hq requested to check record and set out appropriate leads and request expeditious handling" [All codes, initials, names, six total, who processed this teletype are redacted]. FBI Director Webster sent a new message to both the SAC, New Orleans and Legat, Manila alerting them to a "Changed" set of names on "Valdemar Huerto, aka Freddy Fender, Huerta S. Baldemar, Baldemar Huerta, Baldemal Huerta, Baldemar Garcia Huerta, Balmer Garza Huerta" [redacted block for initials]. FBI Director Webster proceeded to explain in writing to both offices that previously they used other names that is why he was now ordering a change and providing more aliases. He enclosed to both offices:

one xerox copy each of subject's FBI Identification Record under FBI #545 522 B. Attached For the information of New Orleans, by teletype dated 5/13/80 Legat Manila advised that [name redacted] advised their records reflect subject's FBI number is 545 522 B. New Orleans, based on information contained in the enclosed FBI record, promptly conduct investigation previously requested by Legat, Manila and Sutel results for relay to Legat, Manila. [signature block redacted].

On May 28, the FBI director sent another 0-73 form to FBI New Orleans with the reference to the content of the form [redacted]. The FBI Freddy Fender file ends with a transmission dated May 28 from Manila to the FBI director on "Valdemar Huerto, aka Freddy Fender; Re Man Tel May 13, 1980 [and in handwriting] & by teletype dated 5/28/80 Legal Attache manila advised that [name redacted] ADVISE REQUESTED INFORMATION RECEIVED FROM ANOTHER SOURCE. NO FURTHER ASSISTANCE DESIRED."

Nothing more as to what resulted from the renewed investigation into Freddy Fender nor what the concern was that he was traveling to New Zealand. What is known about him and his song, "Wasted Days and Wasted Nights" is that in New Zealand this hit song stayed on that country's music

charts in the number one spot for twelve weeks. In the United States, charts
he only reached number 8 with that song and did hit number 1 in the country
music charts for a few weeks.[33]

There is no conclusion that can be reached as to why there was the surveillance of Freddy Fender by the Legal Attaché in Manila. While Fender
did have a criminal record in the 1960s, the FBI inquiry being made without
preface or postscript is in April 1980. Fender was not known or even reputed
to be Communist, Left Wing subversive; a Chicano radical; a threat to
national security; a Vietnam era conscientious objector seeking a deferment;
or an international dealer of anything other than exporter of his music. The
FBI, San Francisco office did open a file on Jerry Garcia of The Grateful
Dead band group under SF-25-60572 with copies sent to the Bureau in
Washington, DC. Jerome "Jerry" Garcia claimed to be a conscientious objector in 1964. They kept checking on inconsistencies in his dealings with the
Selective Service Board and their forms such as 100 and 150 for accuracy
and contradictions.

I conclude that the FBI surveils many people for the lamest of reasons or no
reason at all as in this case. We can also conclude that the years of Freedom of
Information Act legislation and amendments have not improved compliance
with the law or its transparency given this paltry set of files on such an iconic
musical figure, as well as Jerry Garcia's four pages.[34] The Grateful Dead was
his first band; then in 1975 he changed over to the Jerry Garcia band and later
began a collection of men's ties. I own a few.

## NOTES

1. Letter from David M. Hardy dated August 20, 2019, to author in response to
FOIA request number 1444774-000 lists the FBI case file number as 100-HQ-43445.

2. Letter with enclosure from David M. Hardy dated August 21, 2019, to author
listing the number of pages being released and the nature of the exemptions utilized
for redacted material.

3. See https://charts.nz/showitem.asp?interpret=Freddy+Fender&titel=Wasted
+Days+Wasted+Nights&cat=s/. This infofact was courtesy of Noreen Rivera,
University of Texas Rio Grande Valley Assistant Professor, Department of Literature
and Cultural Studies on August 28, 2019.

4. See Mike Gose article dated October 16, 2006, at https://www.stripes.com
/news/from-the-s&S-archives-freddy-fender-looking-back-to-see-ahead-1.55429/.
Accessed August 23, 2019.

5. The name Legat Attaché is title for the FBI person inhouse at almost every
US Embassy in the world. See https://www.fbi.gov/news/stories/fbi-celebrate-75th
-anniversary-of-legal-attach-in-mexico-city/ and for audio podcast at https://www.fbi
.gov/audio-repository/news-podcasts-thisweek-marking-a-milestone-in-mexico.mp3/

view/. Despite the news item is about the Mexico city office it contains more history of the position and its origins. Accessed August 26, 2019.

6. For more details on the socio-economic and political conditions in Cameron County, see https://tshaonline.org/handbook/online/articles/hcc04/. Accessed August 28, 2019.

7. See www.freddyfender.com/ for information on awards, music, biography, career, and family.

8. Cameron County, https://tshaonline.org/.

9. See www.childtrends.org/indicators/high-chool-droput-rates/. Accessed August 28. 2019.

10. See www.idra.org/research_statistics/attrrition_dropout_Texas/look-county-high-school-attrition-rates-texas/ and go to Cameron County for these percentages compared to other groups. Accessed August 28, 2019.

11. See Lynn Brezosky obituary in the *Washington Post* of October 15, 2006, at www.washingtonpost.com/wp-dun/content/article/AR2006101400595.html?noredirect=on/. Accessed August 23, 2019.

12. See Gose, https://www,stripes,com/.

13. Google Images of water tower in San Benito with image of Freddy Fender to see this. Accessed August 26, 2019.

14. See www.freddyfender.com for some biographical material and on the Freddy Martinez Museum located in San Benito, Texas. See also www.tshaonline.org/handbook/online/articles/thu96/. Accessed August 23, 2019.

15. See Gose, https:// www.stripes.com/ cited above.

16. Leo Fender from Southern California in developed his first modern-era guitar. He changed the hollow, wood casing, the figure 8 shape and handle with strings. The Telecaster was the first model developed in 1951. He built it as a solid, hard-plastic-type material, with cords whose sound could be amplified electronically without having to stand or sit in front of a microphone to hear the sound. He made Corona, California, his manufacturing base for the first of several instruments to revolutionize music into the rock and roll that generation adopted as their music. Two more models followed: in 1951 the Precision Bass guitar which was Freddy Fender's favorite and the Stratocaster in 1954. The corporate offices are in Scottsdale, Arizona. See www.fender.com for more details and history of the person, the guitar model, and other products he developed.

17. See Steven Loza, *Barrio Rhythm: Mexican American Music in Los Angeles* (Champaign: University of Illinois Press,1993): 146.

18. www.imdb.com/name/nm139888/bio/. Accessed August 25, 2019.

19. See https://www.biography.com/musician/ritchie-valens/. Accessed January 8, 2021.

20. www.biography.com/actor/anthony-quinn/. Accessed August 25, 2019.

21. www.imdb.com/name/nm0000028/ and www.imdb.com/name/nm0000079/bio/, respectively. Accessed August 25, 2019.

22. www.biography.com/actor/lynda-carter/. Accessed August 25, 2019.

23. See his book with John Underwood, *The Science of Fishing* (New York: Simon and Shuster, 1972), 28.

24. July 20, 1070, Vol. 33, no. 3.

25. All of these mentioned in his obituary at this source-www.findagrave.com/memorial/16174412/freddy-fender/. Accessed August 25. 2019.

26. The Legat in Manila is almost as old as the Mexico City office. The first FBI man, Fred Williams, arrived there in March 1, 1935, to aid Gen. Douglas MacArthur, who was in command over the island country. Both left when it was made independent and the FBI did not resume official presence until 1961 with Robert "Bob" Hawley, as the Legat Attaché. See https://www.fbi.gov/news/stories/legal-attach-manila-then-and-now/. Accessed August 26, 2019.

27. Gose, https://www.stripes.com/.

28. www.idbm.com/title/tt0324022/. Accessed August 25, 2019.

29. Athan Theoharis edited a compilation of relevant documents to show the secretive nature and relationships FBI Director Hoover cultivated with important public figures especially presidential candidates and presidents, especially Lyndon Baines Johnson in *From the Secret Files of J. Edgar Hoover* (Chicago: Ivan R. Dee Publisher, 1991): 218–243. LBJ extended by Executive Order the mandatory retirement at age seventy of Hoover allowing him to continue more years even past Johnson's term in office: 218.

30. Nixon was enamored with the FBI since his early years. He applied to become an FBI agent fresh out of law school in 1937. Nixon was deemed not acceptable to Hoover. The FBI did not even bother to notify him of rejection. Later, as vice president he asked Hoover about that application and the Director gave various answers, "Budget Cuts," "Had not passed the bar," "Bar exam schedule conflicted with FBI's hiring plan." See a brief history by Megan Gambino from April 1, 2014, and for a copy of the application at www.smithsonianmag.com/history/document-deep-dive-richard-nixons-application-to-join-fbi-180950329/.

Application is at www.archives.gov/. Accessed August 27, 2019. As president, Nixon kept Hoover on in exchange for political services for him and the White House, according to Theoharis, *Secret Files*, 242.

31. See www.britannica.com/biography/Ferdinand-E-Marcos/ and also www.thoughtco.com/ferdinand-marcos-195676/. Accessed August 26, 2019.

32. Reagan was an FBI informant since 1943, perhaps earlier. As president of the Screen Actors Guild, he testified before the Red Scare days and witch hunt by the House Committee on Unamerican Activities in 1947 naming names of those he and wife at the time Jane Wyman, as willing witnesses, they suspected of being Communists or leaning toward communism. See Steve Palace's article of September 6, 2018, "Ronald Reagan's Early Role as an FBI Informant," at www.thevintagenews.com/2018/09/06/young-ronald-reagan/. Accessed August 27, 2019.

33. For the information on the New Zealand music charts and the Fender hit see https:?/charts.nz/showitem.asp?interpret=Freddy+Fender&title=Wasted+Days+And+Wasted+Nights&cat=s/ provided to me by Dr. Noreen Rivera by email (Noreen.rivera@utrgv.edu. on August 28, 2019. For US charts see www.musicvf.com/song.php?title=wasted+days+and+wasted+nights+by+freddy+fender&=16592/. Accessed October 23, 2019.

34. www.vault.fbi.gov/jerry-garcia/. Accessed October 31, 2019.

## Chapter 6

# Francisco "Pancho" Medrano: The Chicano UAW Union Man

On April 4, 2002, Francisco "Pancho" Medrano of Dallas, Texas, died from cancer at age eighty-one. "He was a longtime political force in Dallas," one of his obituaries stated and continued, "Medrano was best known for decades of union and civil rights work with the United Auto Workers."[1] Both of those categories got him on the target list of J. Edgar Hoover's Federal Bureau of Investigation (FBI). Hoover published or better yet, had published, several books on the evils of Communism.[2] Hoover equated labor organizing, advocacy of worker's rights, civil rights, protest, and dissent as the clues to finding Communists.[3] Furthermore, ethnic and racial groups were a special entity for the Communist Party of the United States of America (CPUSA or just CP in this chapter). Hoover wrote. "Communists adapt their agitation and propaganda to the fears, prejudices, problems, and special grievances or aspirations of the many ethnic, racial, and religious groups to be found in this country." They do this "solely for the purpose of projecting a political and ideological cohesiveness which will align minority groups with the communist movement."[4]

Hoover practically grew up in the FBI since the days it was created in 1908 under the name Bureau of Investigation (BOI). Fresh out of law school he was hired as a clerk in 1918 during the initiation of the infamous "Palmer Raids" aimed at ferreting out anarchists and immigrants. In a few short years, he was named the director of BOI in 1924.[5] A more revealing story on Hoover was written by William C. Sullivan, who spent thirty years as his main man going after Communists, then racial and ethnic groups, anti-war protestors, and finally, the emerging New Left. His first assignment as a newly hired FBI agent was in Milwaukee, Wisconsin and his job were to listen in on the conversations of the local Communist Party cell; he officed next door. He wrote, "I was wearing earphones and recording in longhand what was going on in their meeting. We had a 'bug,' a microphone, planted in their meeting room, but there were no tape recorders back then."[6] Sullivan after he was the supervisor of FBI intelligence operations in Mexico and Central America became Hoover's head of domestic intelligence investigations.

## THE RED SCARE IN TEXAS

The Palmer Raids, mentioned above, were part of the 1920s era dubbed the Red Scare following the suppression of dissent after World War I in the United States. The CPUSA was founded in 1919 from a split between two other groups predating the Russian Revolution of October 1915.[7] In Texas, the CPUSA began around 1933 in Houston, Texas, and some of its members were also members of the Congress of Industrial Unions (CIO).[8] The United Auto Workers (UAW) union was founded in 1935 and joined the CIO, later merging into the AFL-CIO and ultimately splitting from the latter in 1968.[9] As head of the UAW, Walter Reuther began a purge of Communists from its ranks. At the UAW convention held in San Antonio, Texas in October 1947, the regional director, A.R. Hardesty loudly proclaimed the purge, "We have defeated them again and again at their own game and will continue to beat them until they give up their subversive activities in our ranks."[10] One of those UAW members was Francisco "Pancho" Medrano from Dallas, Texas. I was fortunate enough to catch and make him sit for an oral history interview on July 16, 1997; he was forever traveling, advocating labor and civil rights. We talked at length about his life and career, 152 pages of transcript. This biographical portion is based on that public history work.[11]

## FRANCISCO FRANCO MEDRANO: SHORT BIOGRAPHY

His parents, Sabas Medrano, the father was from *Jarral, Guanjuato*, and his mother was Nicolasa Ruiz Franco from *Sabino, Guanjuato*, just across a little river that divides the two villages.[12] Some of his siblings were born in Guanjuato, Mexico, but by 1918 the family fled to the United States, like so many Mexican political refugees. His parents were Zapatistas, followers of Emiliano Zapata, but after he was assassinated his father thought it best, they leave for the United States. They walked from Jarral, Guanajuato to Dallas, Texas, a trek that took over a year and a half. Francisco was born in Dallas on October 2, 1920 (p.9). The reason Sabas brought his family to Dallas was that a brother-in-law, Nicolasa's brother, Bruno Franco and his wife, Anita, had made the journey earlier and settled there (p.1–5). Pancho's father died young at thirty-two or thirty-five. Pancho and other relatives have tried to find out what happened to his father who just disappeared one evening after a confrontation with Dallas Police. He was last seen behind the fire station on Laws and McKinney streets with police. The Maria Luna family saw him in jail and talked with him but when they returned later, he was gone. The family never heard from the police nor were they able to bury him; there was no body to be found (p.8). Pancho said, "There was a lot of discrimination at that time in Dallas. It was still hid, but there was a lot of discrimination here in Dallas" (p.7).

Medrano recalls the discrimination vividly. No Mexican could walk downtown or into a movie house unless it was Mexican night. The businesses had signs, "No Mexicans Allowed" or "No Mexicans Served Here." His mother would take them downtown, buy some food from the back door of restaurants and they would sit on the curb to eat (p.11–13). The Mexicans could not go into Pike's Park, much less the public swimming pool (p.35–36). Over time, his father bought a home next to the land where the old zoo animals were kept until death. "Today, I can still close my eyes and hear the, the roar of the animals at night. Two, three, four o'clock in the, in the morning." The segregated Mexican neighborhood was called Little Mexico. The Mexican kids went to Catholic school, St. Anne's, which was not segregated. The only blacks were nearby on Thomas and Pearl streets and they would play baseball in vacant lots or see them in the theatre for blacks on Elm street (p.15–16). In 1927, he graduated from St. Anne's and the family began to migrate in search of work into Indiana and Michigan.

Pancho was an altar boy for the priest, Cerillo from Spain, who taught young boys the art of boxing. Pancho was about twelve when he began to learn how to jab, the right cross and upper cut, to protect his chin, block punches, hit body punches, and to breathe properly (p.32–34, 37–38). Moreover, Pancho was big, strong and fit from the running and rock busting. He looked phenotypically more African American with kinky hair, thick lips, wide nose, with dark skin, than the dark brown Mexicans.

This newfound sport helped him in his adult life. Pancho tried to enroll at Cozier Tech high school he was singled out by the principal because of his ragged, patch pants, worn shoes, and bad appearance generally. His home for many years did not have any running water, electricity, sewer connection, or gas service (p.25, 27). He was sent to work at a rock quarry with the instructions to come back to school when he had on nice clothes and shoes. The rock quarry was by Love Field and he would bicycle there and worked from sunup to sundown for twenty-five cents an hour. After many months, a young supervisor took him aside and gave him an address to go to for different work. He went and found out it was a war training program. He was to learn how to place rivets on metal for airplanes. After some time learning the riveting, he was to report to North American Aviation in Grand Prairie, Texas, several miles away. At first, he begged for rides and hitchhiked, but then he found a better solution; he ran eleven and a half miles daily to the plant from Little

Mexico (p.26–28). He would get up and start running at four in the morning; later when he started boxing for the company, he would get rides home (p.40).

He married Esperanza Jimenez when he worked at the rock quarry and started a family. The first born was Francisco, Jr., then Roberto followed by Ricardo and a daughter, Pauline. The last child was Rolando (p.49). By then the Medrano's, all of them—mother, new stepfather (pedro Centeno), the stepsister (Lupe), and his own family—had moved into Little Mexico Village, a housing project with all utilities, at 1906 Wichita Street, and paid $3 a month rent. Across the street the Sisters of Charity nuns ran a food kitchen and would regularly give the Medrano's all the leftovers. "And then we would all eat and that is about all we had to eat. Real good stuff. That was the only thing we ate during that time" (p.8, 25–30).

## BOXING

Pancho began boxing at North American Aviation as part of the company's recreation program. As he began to beat everyone in his heavyweight division within the plant, he was sent at company expense to California and Florida representing Texas. Boxing then did not make the amateur or professional fighters wear any protective gear, no head gear, no cup, no bandaging of hands, and the like (p.39–42). His first professional fight was in Hot Springs, Arkansas, for which he was fired at the aircraft plant. He was gone for three days and missed work; without permission (p.42). He started looking for a job at the Ford plant near Fair Park in East Dallas. It was during this time that he first heard about unions and communism. He did not know what either were, but he did like what he heard at the union meetings (p.44). In 1942 or 1943, he joined the UAW local 645 while he worked at North American Aviation but didn't know he had rights, much less benefits, from that membership. Because he was known as the boxing champion, the UAW made him a membership recruiter, an organizer, after he was fired (p.45–49). He started getting involved with politics at the urging of Walter Reuther, their national president who insisted his membership be good citizens. As Pancho said, "And everything in life is, is political" (p.50). There were no advocacy groups among the Mexicans in Little Mexico or in the other Mexican settlement on the outskirts of Dallas by the cement plant on Chalk Hill road. The League of United Latin American Citizens (LULAC) was in existence but not in Dallas. Pancho helped to bring in the American G.I. Forum (AGIF) even though he could not become a member for not having served in the military (p.53). The UAW leaders, local and national, grew to appreciate the skills Pancho developed as an organizer and added political education to his tasks.

He was sent not only to areas like Little Rock during the integration battles but also earlier to the Montgomery bus boycott in Georgia. He was in charge while there for getting gasoline for the private cars used instead of the city buses (p.62). He worked side by side with Rosa Parks and Martin Luther King, Jr. (p.65). He marched in Selma, Alabama, with Walter Reuther and the young SNCC leader, John Lewis, now a member of Congress. He was at the Poor People's Campaign in Washington, DC (p.66). He also traveled at UAW expense to the Dominican Republic, Puerto Rico, Mexico, and other countries (p.60, 69). Walter Reuther instructed Pancho to go to California, Delano, to find out about Cesar E. Chavez. "Well take all the time you want to. A week, a month, a year, whatever and see what, what's happening," were Reuther's instructions to him (p.66). In all of these trips, Walter's brother, Roy, was also involved (p.69). Medrano also traveled to all the places that were in protest mode and organizing themselves civically like forming the Viva Kennedy Clubs, the Political Association of Spanish Speaking Organizations (PASO), the Crystal City elections of *Los Cinco Candidatos* in 1963; Reies Lopez Tijerina after the Court house takeover in Tierra Amarilla, and to the Crusade for Justice in Denver. He spent a whole year as a volunteer in Joseph Montoya's campaign for US senator from New Mexico (p.97). Medrano also participated in many of the Mexican American Youth Organization (MAYO) sponsored school boycotts across Texas and the nation and the farm worker strike in the Rio Grande Valley. He knew Rodolfo "Corky" Gonzales from the days he was a boxer, but Gonzales was a lightweight. They never fought against each other (p.70–74, 80–84).

Medrano met with various Democratic Party leaders and presidential contenders beginning in the 1960s. He was an onlooker when John Kennedy was shot in Dallas; at his side when Robert Kennedy was shot in Los Angeles, and earlier when Lyndon Johnson was running for US senator in Texas (86–94). In short, Pancho Medrano, as political director of the UAW for most of his life, was everywhere bringing resources to support the cause of many leaders and groups, nationally and even internationally. In the oral interview with me, he discussed at length his participation in the Rio Grande Valley farm worker strike and his personal confrontation with Texas Ranger Captain, Alfred. Y. Allee that led to the famous US Supreme Court case bearing his name (p.101–120).[13]

## THE LORDS OF LITTLE MEXICO

The "apple does not fall from the tree" is a popular folk saying but sometimes an apple or two or three that do fall are rotten to the core. The legacy of Pancho Medrano is beyond reproach but not that of all his offspring.[14] The first of his sons, Roberto, did well initially and then something went wrong. He was the first Chicano elected to the Dallas Independent School Board and served for thirteen years. During these years, he met Fonda Vera, in 1976, who gave him two sons, whom he never supported. She sued him for child support and won despite his loud denials of paternity. After weeks of trying to serve him with the paternity order and child support enforcement suit, the court allowed a relative to accept service. His daughter, Patricia, an assistant city attorney for the City of Dallas had to take the notice. A conviction for drunk driving was used in his re-election campaign for the school board effectively by his opponent, Rene Castilla, to defeat him in 1986. He lost his job as center director of the Dallas County Community Action Committee when checks from the program were traced to his sister Pauline's personal bank account. He tried to unseat his nemesis in 1990 to no avail. In the late 1990s, Fonda Vera was finally able to collect some retroactive child support from wages earned by him while employed at Dallas Can Academy. The sons from Vera have never met their father.[15]

In the 2010 Democratic Primary in Dallas County, Dallas, voter fraud charges were filed against several of the Medrano siblings and their children. Daughter Pauline is now the county treasurer for Dallas County.[16] The legacy of Pancho Medrano, however, is still recognized in the city, county, and nation. In 2017, he was honored by the Texas AFL-CIO and mention was made that a Dallas post office and local school bears his name.[17] The FBI records also bear his name.

### The FBI File on Francisco Medrano No. 100-419633

The office of origin for the FBI file on Medrano is Dallas and that case number is 100-9848. It took time for the FBI, both Dallas and at Headquarters to get his name straight. The record from the 1950s to May 28, 1970, named him Frank Medrano, Frank F. Medrano, Francisco Franco Medrano, Francisco Medrano, Francisco Franco Medrano, Jr., with a nickname of "Poncho" and not Pancho, which is the usual one in Spanish for those named Francisco. The character of the case file of the May 1970 memorandum, two pages, from the SAC, Dallas to the SAC, Denver is "SM-C," meaning Security Matter-Communist. This memo refers to an FBI interest and recordkeeping on him since the mid-1950s. For example, the subject of a submission using complaint form FD-71, a mortgage fraud allegation, for "FRANK F. MEDRANO WA FRANCISCO FRANCO MEDRANO" was dated "(9-29-54)" and is heavily redacted in many spaces of the form. Under facts of complaint are found these words, all others are redacted including the action taken and the name of the reporting SA, "MEDRANO WHO IS SUBJECT OF 100-9848 WAS INTERVIEWED BY SAS [name redacted] AND [name redacted]

AT WHICH TIME HE WAS COOPERATIVE. MEDRANO FURNISHED SOME IN IN (sic) FORMATION ON [5-7 words redacted]." There is no mention in his oral history interview with this author of any loan, mortgage, or housing debt. He did not buy his first property until he was in his thirties, in late 1960. Another example is the opening paragraph of the May 1970 memo referred to above which states, "A review of Dallas file 100-9848 entitled 'Frank F. Medrano, aka Francisco Franco Medrano, "Poncho"; SM-C' [*sic*] reveals that Frank F. Medrano has been active in the civil rights movement and the Labor Union in the Dallas-Fort Worth, Texas area since 1955."

The second and third paragraphs of this 1970 memo are full of information that frame the reasons for the surveillance of Francisco "Pancho" Medrano since the 1950s. Here they are in their entirety:

> On 11/22/55, DL T-1, a confidential source, who has furnished reliable infor-
> mation in the past, and who is familiar with some phases of CP activity in the
> Dallas area, advised FRANK F. MEDRANO was active in the Dallas chapter
> of the American GI Forum of Texas, Inc., but was not a member of the CP. He
> described the Dallas GI Forum as dominated and controled [*sic*] by members
> of the CP. (p.1)
>
>    On 1/3/57, DL T-1 advised that MEDRANO was not a CP member and had
> not been approached to become a member because he had failed to show any
> sympathy toward the CP. It was his opinion that MEDRANO was only inter-
> ested in the labor movement and was not connected to the CP in any way.

Obviously, Medrano was of FBI interest for his civil rights and labor union work. Second, despite the acknowledgment that he was not interested or a member of the CP, the character of his case file began as a Security Matter-Communism, as noted above. Third, the FBI relied on informants to keep track of Medrano for them. And lastly, despite informant DL T-1 in November 1955 advising the FBI that Medrano was not a CP member, the American G.I. Forum (AGIF) was dominated and controlled by CP members. If Medrano was responsible for bringing AGIF to Dallas and it was under CP domination and control, why was Francisco not also? In other portions of this memo, Medrano was placed by informants at meetings of the Students for a Democratic Society (SDS) at the University of Texas at Arlington (UTA) in July 1969 and at helping the organizational work by [name redacted] of "a group called the 'Brown Berets' also at UTA." Shortly after the 1957 writing referred to above, another FBI memo was sent from SA [name redacted] to SAC, [office location and name redacted] but dated "March 28, 1957, Dallas, Texas" it states that FRANK MEDRANO had contacted "On 3/13/57, [name redacted] Security Officer, Temco Aircraft Corporation, Dallas, Texas" and had "advised him that he had been interviewed by Bureau Agents regarding some of his acquaintances." Something about this voluntary contact by Medrano was made into a surreptitious contact, "In view of the above information, it is believed that MEDRANO [8-10 words redacted] no further action will be taken in this case." This letter has another ominous closing line about Pancho Medrano that reads, "The Bureau has been advised of this by letter under caption, 'FRANK F. MEDRANO, wa., SM-C,' Dallas file 100-9848." He was still being characterized as a Communist and therefore a Security Matter.

In a letter from SAC, J. Gordon Shanklin in Dallas to [redacted name and address] dated July 11, 1966, he acknowledges receipt of a letter from that person dated July 6 together with the copy attached of another letter from the AGIF. The anonymous letter writer must have inquired about the nature and purpose of AGIF because SAC, Shanklin demurs giving an opinion. Using standard FBI language for such type in queries about groups or individuals, he wrote the FBI, "is strictly an investigative agency and information in our files is confidential . . ." Moreover, he adds, "Our inability to furnish any comment should not be interpreted as implying that we do or do not have information in our files concerning your inquiry." The Dallas FBI did have a file on AGIF, and it is number "100-9734"; and, it is stated as part of the copies of this memo sent to others by Shanklin. I assume that during the 1950s and 1960s possibly later, the AGIF was not only considered a Communist organization or at least under the influence of the CP but also why a file was opened on them.

The SAC, Denver reported on April 30, 1970 to the director, FBI in a two-page memo that Francisco Medrano was in town recruiting volunteers for the Cuban program named the *Vencermos* Brigade (VB). The information on Medrano as VB recruiter came from Captain [name redacted] of the Intelligence Division, Denver Police Department on March 9, 1970. Reportedly, the Captain "indicated that Medrano had been active throughout the southwest in recruiting travelers for the VB." Medrano did not mention this type of work for the VB and Cuba during the oral history interview. On June 4, 1970, the SAC, Dallas sent Director Hoover a name change for Medrano with his photograph with his four-page memo. The old information on his employment at the aircraft plant, UAW Local #848 [which is not the number Medrano recalled during his oral history interview with this author], civil rights work, and as organizer for the UAW is repeated in the first two pages of this transmission. The name used "Francisco Franco Medrano, Jr. 'Poncho'" is entirely wrong (p.3). Medrano did have a son named after him but this report is not about the son. An informant [name redacted along with an entire sentence and a quarter] "advised that the above subject is still employed at LTV [Ling Temco Vought was new name of the same company he worked for in the 1940s], but does not have a security clearance." This informant also kept track of when Medrano was actually at work at the plant as a machinist and when he was on union business. "Medrano has been on leave on union business on the following dates: 2/19 and 20; 2/22 thru 2/27; and 3/5, 10, and 12/70" the SAC, Dallas was told. On the last page of this memo, a photograph was sent for showing it to persons in Denver and other places to ascertain that it was the same Francisco Franco Medrano the FBI was keeping tabs on. It was also reported that Medrano had not been in the Dallas area for over a year; "has been for the past year on extended Leave Without Pay from LTV and has been active in assisting the grape pickers unions throughout 'the Valley'" (p.4).

## NOTES

1. See www.mrt.com/news/article/Dallas-political-leader-Pancho-Medrano-dies -at-81-7809504.php/ accessed August 14, 2019.

2. See Chapter 12, "Extorting Henry Holt & Co.: J. Edgar Hoover and the Publishing Industry" in Claire A. Culleton and Karen Leick, eds., *Modernism on File: Writers, Artists, and the FBI, 1920–1950* (New York: Palgrave Macmillan, 2008), 237–252.

3. One of those books is J. Edgar Hoover, *on Communism* (New York: Random House, 1969); sometimes just cited as *On Communism* and as *Communism.*

4. *Ibid.*, 129.

5. For a short history of the FBI and biography of Hoover, see John F. Fox, Jr., "The Birth of the Federal Bureau of Investigation" written in 2003 at www.fbi .gov/history and www.biography.com/law-figure/j-edgar-hoover/ accessed August 15, 2019.

6. William C. Sullivan, *The Bureau: My Thirty Years in Hoover's FBI* (New York: W.W. Norton & Company, 1979):40.

7. See the history of the socialist party in the United States at www.socialistpa rtyofamerica.us/.

8. For a history of the Red Scare in Texas, see Don E. Carleton, *RED SCARE! Right-wing Hysteria Fifties Fanaticism and Their Legacy in Texas* (Austin: Texas Monthly Press, 1985).

9. For a short history go to www.influencewatch.org/labor.com/united-auto-workers-uaw/ accessed August 15, 2019.

10. Carleton, *RED SCARE!*, 41.

11. Go to https://library.uta.edu/tejanovoices/interview.php?cmasno=037.

12. FBI memo dated May 28, 1970, on the second page has the mother's name listed as "NICOLASA FRANCO CENENTO, Dallas, Texas" [last words redacted].

13. The federal district case, *Medrano v. Allee*, 347 F. Supp 605 (S.D. Tex. 1972) is found at https://law.justia.com/cases/federal/district-courts/FSupp/347/605/140 4229/ while the US Supreme Court case is *Allee v. Medrano*, 416 US 802 (1974) and is at htttps://supreme.justia.com/cases/federal/US/416/802/ and for another oral history project I worked on in collaboration with others from Texas Christian University

and University of North Texas on the experiences of browns and blacks in Texas civil rights struggles and conducted by Moises Acuña-Gurrola, a graduate student, with Roberto Medrano, son of Francisco Medrano, on June 10, 2015, on this case and other topics is at https://crbb.tcu.edu/clips/pancho-medrano-v-a-y-allee/.

14. Rowland Stiteler, "Lords of Little Mexico," *D Magazine*, May 1980 at www .dmagazine.com/publications/d-magazine/190/may/ accessed August 15, 2019, has an exposé on the Medrano siblings as of that date. More currently is the story, "Fortunes of Dallas Political Dynasty," at www.dallasnews.com/news/news/2011/09 /17/ accessed August 15, 2019.

15. Holly Mullen, "My Two Sons?", *The Dallas Observer*, June 12, 1997, at www .dallasobserver.com/content/printView/6402681/ accessed August 14, 2019.

16. See "Fortunes of Dallas Political Dynasty."

17. See www.peoplesworld.org/article/civil-rights-legend-Pancho-Medrano-h onored/ and www.texasaflcio.org/dallas/news/dallas-labor-news-january-13-2017/ accessed August 15, 2019.

*Chapter 7*

# The American G.I. Forum
# and Joe Molina's Case

Like many refugees from Mexico seeking a safe haven in the United States to avoid the violence of the 1910 Revolution, Jose Garcia and Faustina Perez, schoolteachers from *Ciudad Victoria*, fled to the United States in 1917.[1] The Garcia clan were not members of the peonage class in Mexico; quite the contrary. They came from well-to-do family elders and educated parents in the case of Hector P. Garcia and his siblings. Jose's older brother, Antonio, had left for the United States earlier and had settled in Mercedes, Texas, in the Rio Grande Valley. Other Garcia brothers had also left for the United States. Jose and Faustina brought their remaining four children with them to join Antonio in Mercedes, Texas.

## HECTOR P. GARCIA, A MINI-BIOGRAPHY

Hector P. Garcia, one of many children, was born on January 17, 1924, in *Lleras, Tamaulipas, Mexico*. Once in the United States, Faustina gave birth to five more children. Soon thereafter, the Garcia brothers joined Antonio in his business; the Antonio G. Garcia and Brothers Department Store. By the time the League of United Latin American Citizens began organizing itself in the Rio Grande Valley and ultimately in Corpus Christi, Texas by 1929, Hector was about to begin public schooling in the segregated, English-only curriculum prevalent in Texas and the Southwest. His fair, light-complexioned skin helped him pass as "Spanish" and not suffer the stigma directed at dark-skinned Mexican kids and adults.[2] Those looks and good grades ensured by the strong disciplinarian approach taken by both parents, like most other elite Mexican families who sought refuge in the Rio Grande Valley of Texas imposed on their children, got all of the Garcia siblings admitted to the University of Texas in Austin (UTA); the few vanguard minority students of the time. Family finances and the Depression coinciding with Hector's high school graduation had forced him to first attend the local community college in Edinburg, Texas while the two older siblings were at UTA. The family lost the business during the 1930s and all the Garcias had to go not only to school but to work after school, weekends, and nights anywhere for income to keep the family afloat during these terrible years.[3] Hector while still in high school lied about his age and joined the Citizens Military Training Corps (CMTC) and remained active with the CMTC into his years at medical school. All the Garcia children became doctors.[4] He earned money for his service.

On his first trip to Austin to visit his brothers and the campus before transferring to finish college, Hector came face to face with the ubiquitous racist signs at establishments, "No Mexicans, Dogs, Negroes Allowed." The family members traveling with him on that journey had to sleep in the car to avoid those rejections and discrimination.[5] During those years in Austin, Hector made friends with important *personas* who would aid him in his pursuit of justice for returning veterans in later years. These influential people were Gustavo Garcia and Carlos Cadena, and the only Mexican-origin professors on campus, George I. Sanchez and Carlos Castañeda.[6] He did not participate in any of the student activities or organizations; his goal was graduation and medical school in Galveston like his brother Antonio had done. There were fewer Mexican-origin students at the University of Texas Medical School in Galveston than in Austin. When he could make the trip to Denver Harbor, Houston's large Mexican *barrio* that is where Hector P. Garcia could be found on weekends not in classes or clinical duty. He graduated from medical school in 1940 and reluctantly accepted a residency in Omaha, Nebraska, since no Texas location offered him one. He had no money. He hitchhiked to Omaha with a tiny suitcase holding his only dress clothes and undergarments.[7]

The residency in Omaha was interrupted by the attack on Pearl Harbor. Garcia like thousands of others entered military service and became part of World War II. Garcia, however, entered as an officer given his years of training with CMTC but not as a medical doctor. The US Army did not recognize his degree or training. Instead they sent him to Camp Edwards in Cape Cod, Massachusetts as part of an amphibian boat regiment; many months later he finally was transferred to the medical corps.[8] Toward the end of the war, Hector, now Captain Garcia, found himself in Germany, then Italy. There he met his future wife, Wanda Fusillo, married her, and was promoted to the rank of Major.[9] The couple returned to the states but by separate routes. He came with his unit and his Bronze Medal; she by boat many months later.[10] They settled in Corpus Christi, Texas, where his older brother Antonio now lived and began a modest medical practice among the Mexican-origin population.[11]

Once again, he and wife Wanda met the ugly face of chronic racism, poverty, segregation, and economic disparity that he had left behind many years back and she never knew existed. She did not even know he was of Mexican origin; she assumed he was Spanish from Spain.[12] Most of his patients could not pay his fees and didn't. The school kids he saw as patients were malnourished, sickly, and stigmatized. The veterans he saw had no medical benefits available despite the G.I. Bill; those offices and services were far away. They told him horror stories of compensation checks for disabilities being consistently late. Their applications for schooling were not processed timely to enroll or processed at all.[13] Moreover, they often complained of blatant discrimination in bars, restaurants, hotels, bus stations, and employment against them. Tired of hearing this litany of complaints, the doer that he was, Hector P. Garcia made a public call for veterans of Mexican origin to come together. He was a member of the League of United Latin American Citizens (LULAC) but they did not address issues of returning veterans.[14] Those who heard the call did, about 700 men, at the Lamar School auditorium on March 26, 1948. This was the beginning of the American G.I. Forum (AGIF).[15]

The AGIF's incorporation papers were drafted by Gus Garcia in San Antonio, Texas who also became the Registered Agent for Service at 219 International Building, San Antonio, Texas with three incorporators: Hector P. Garcia, Joe Montoya, and Don Contreras. The documents were notarized in Bexar County, Texas, on December 5, 1949. The Board of Directors was limited to ten persons with five being from Corpus Christi, three from the surrounding Corpus area of Robstown, Sinton, and Bishop, and two from some distance away, Taylor and Woodsboro, Texas (p.2 of 6). This information was part of four pages withheld of six. The other released page numbered "-1a-" indicated that this information was also sent to the "ONI, 8th Naval District, New Orleans, Louisiana (RM)."

## THE FELIX LONGORIA INCIDENT

Within months of the organizational formation, AGIF, towns around the Corpus Christi area had also formed local groups under the banner and by end of the year about forty chapters were in existence across Texas.[16] Word spread quickly that there was a group that veterans of Mexican origin in need could call and find help. In January 1949, such a call came from Sara Moreno, sister to Beatriz Longoria, pleading for help in burying her brother-in-law, Felix Longoria. His body was being sent home from the battlefield in the Philippines but the funeral home in Three Rivers, Texas, his hometown was refusing to hold the services in the only funeral home in the city. They were told to hold the wake in their home. Moreover, he had to be buried in the

Mexican cemetery; the practice in all Texas towns at the time. The reason the funeral director, Tom Kennedy, himself a veteran, gave was that the whites in town, "would not like it." Hearing this Dr. Garcia jumped into high gear to protest; he notified a local reporter who in turn, called Kennedy to corroborate the story. Kennedy did not back away from his comments. He added fuel to the fire: "We never have made a practice of letting Mexicans use the chapel and we don't want to start now."[17] The story spread like wildfire into local, statewide, national, and international news. Felix Longoria, killed by sniper fire was a husband, father, and a decorated hero for his valor with a Purple Heart, Bronze Star, and Good Conduct Medal. This case not only became a hot political issue in Texas and the nation but also an embarrassment to Lyndon B. Johnson, the US Senator who had been elected largely by votes in South Texas from the Mexican American community, who had paid their poll tax in effect at the time. The AGIF claimed they had over 100,000 Mexican American voters pay their poll tax to register to vote in 1949.[18] Dr. Garcia had sent him and dozens of other public officials' telegrams asking for help with this case; only Johnson responded. The solution found by Senator Johnson was to bury Longoria in the National Cemetery in Arlington, Virginia, which the family with no other recourse or resources accepted.[19]

The Longoria case brought needed attention to the plight of returning veterans and those of Mexican origin; but for persons in the Southwest they were invisible to the rest of the country. Dr. Hector P. Garcia utilizing the contacts made during his UTA years, both in Austin such as Vicente Ximenes, Gus Garcia, Ed Idar, Cris Alderete, and Professor George I. Sanchez, and in the area of Galveston/Houston, and the thousands of disgruntled and angry Mexican American veterans, was able to organize a national network of AGIF chapters, particularly in the Southwest and Midwest. This network and the relationship built with US Senator Johnson over the Longoria incident raised Dr. Garcia to the level of a national leader without competition.[20] The Mexican community was organized in places such as San Antonio and Los Angeles but had remained regionalized and fragmented into a myriad of groups. LULAC and now AGIF were the two giants known in white political circles. By 1957, AGIF had chapters organized in thirteen states: Texas, New Mexico, Colorado, Utah, Kansas, Nebraska, California, Michigan, Missouri, Arizona, Illinois, Wyoming, and Indiana.[21] LULAC unfortunately, rotated their national leader every year under a one-year presidential rule. The AGIF was somewhat similar except that Dr. Garcia never allowed anyone to challenge him as the founder and national leader regardless of who was president of AGIF at any given time. He attended as many of the state AGIF conventions, all the national conventions, and made sure he was featured prominently on the program of all conventions. When on these trips and not available to his patients, sister Dr. Cleotilde Garcia substituted as the doctor.

She also was his most trusted co-leader in AGIF whether it was helping him lead the Women's Auxiliary at the national level or organizing chapters for the Viva Kennedy Club movements and in 1964 the Viva Johnson movement.[22] She passed away on May 23, 2003.[23]

## 100 PERCENT BACKING OF OPERATION WETBACK

Deportations of Mexican-origin people from the United States have occurred for centuries. One of the largest dragnets akin to ethnic cleansing was Operation Wetback implemented by President Dwight D. Eisenhower in the mid-1950s. The AGIF backed this initiative 100 percent. They wrote letters, they made speeches, they published material, and they encouraged their membership to be in support locally. AGIF's opposition to the importation of Mexican labor, legal or otherwise, began with the Bracero Program in 1947 that lasted until 1964. Ed Idar, the Texas AGIF chairman at one point was the main protagonist against Mexican labor with Dr. Hector P. Garcia, the second. Differences between Mexican-origin people were heightened by this labor agreement and subsequent deportation raids. In 1951, two white professors published a stereotypical monograph on the undocumented Mexican laborers in Texas and used as anonymous racists quotes from other whites in South Texas. In support of this booklet were Dr. Garcia, Ed Idar, and Dr. George I. Sanchez of AGIF and some leaders in LULAC. In opposition were the thousands of Mexican-origin people and their US -born children post-Mexican Revolution diaspora.[24] The turmoil and dissention in the AGIF ranks and with their LULAC allies, especially Alonso Perales, as revered in LULAC as Hector P. Garcia was in AGIF, over this publication and their support prompted the same trio to put out their own pamphlet on the subject.[25] In 1953, AGIF in partnership with an AFL affiliate in Texas published their policy position on Mexican labor; *What Price—Wetback?*[26] The positions on the question of Mexican labor remained fixed, nothing much changed except the intensity of emotion surrounding this question. This conflict continued past the end of the Bracero Program and the banner against Mexican labor was picked up by Cesar E. Chavez and continues with the anti-Mexican legislative initiatives, state and Federal, aimed at Mexicans since to the current Trump administration.

Hector P. Garcia was Mr. AGIF; the main person always. While the AGIF, as was LULAC, a non-partisan organization, neither Democrat nor Republican, the leaders were in close contact with white politicians; there was no other kind. When John F. Kennedy first sought the Democratic presidential nomination in 1958 and 1960, Garcia was drawn to Lyndon B. Johnson, as the favorite son of Texas first, then Kennedy as a second choice, as his candidate. In 1960, however, once Kennedy was nominated and picked Johnson as his running mate, the Viva Kennedy clubs were organized.[27] Dr. Garcia along with County Commissioner Albert A. Peña, Jr. of San Antonio were the real prime movers. From the Viva Kennedy movement sprang two other groups that began to broaden the political horizon and strategies employed in pursuit of justice for Mexican-origin people in the United States. In California, the ex-Viva Kennedy volunteers formed the Mexican American Political Association (MAPA) and in Texas they formed the Political Association of Spanish Speaking Organizations (PASO). While LULAC stressed a pan-ethnic identity and citizenship with the words Latin American and Citizens in their name; AGIF rejected ethnic identity in favor of Americanism and civic pride with their organizational name.[28] According to historian Ignacio M. Garcia, AGIF did not have an ideology or philosophy; Garcia made them opt for Americanism demonstrated by civic pride.[29] The "G.I." was to associate themselves with soldiers who had adopted the term G.I. Joe during World War II to mean anyone in the military service.[30] More importantly, the membership into AGIF required that at least 70 percent of members in any chapter be veterans of military service. For example, Rodolfo "Corky" Gonzalez of Denver, Colorado, and leader in organizing AGIF chapters in that state was not a veteran. He was one among the firsts to leave AGIF in favor of a more militant and ethnic nationalistic strategy to group ascendency. On the other hand, Vicente Ximenes, the AGIF organizer in New Mexico and schoolmate of Hector P. Garcia in Austin, was a veteran and originally from Texas. His father was an elected official in Floresville, Texas, and part of the John Connally political machine. When it came time to place Mexican Americans in high government positions to fulfill promises made by both President John Kennedy and Lyndon Johnson, it was from the ranks of LULAC and AGIF that those nominees were selected and ultimately appointed; not from PASO or MAPA.[31]

## Chicano Movement Stirrings

While the AGIF, LULAC, and those who were to become MAPA and PASO were working to elect John Kennedy as president, others were creating with direct action in the Chicano Movement.[32] Cesar Chavez left the Community Service Organization to begin the United Farm Workers Union in California. In New Mexico, Reies Lopez Tijerina was championing the right to land grant claims which he wanted returned to those descendants and heirs. Rodolfo Gonzales left AGIF and his War on Poverty position to form *Los Voluntarios*, the precursor to the Crusade for Justice in Denver, Colorado. In Texas, County Commissioner Albert A. Peña, Jr., was working for PASO to win electoral victories in Texas towns and did such as Crystal City, Texas, in

1963. These developments caused a rift between AGIF, especially Dr. Garcia, and Commissioner Peña over the Chicano identity, direct action, partisan politics, and disenchantment with the Democratic Party. AGIF under the presidential term of José Cano embraced the Republican Party beginning in the 1970s with Nixon, Ford, and later Reagan.[33]

It was during these early years of the decade of the 1960s and the Kennedy assassination that the Communist label tagged on to the AGIF in its early years by J. Edgar Hoover reared its ugly head again. The rapid growth of AGIF may have been a reason to keep the FBI's eyes on the organization and leadership. By the late 1970s, AGIF had expanded into eighteen more states: Wisconsin, Pennsylvania, Iowa, Oklahoma, Nevada, Minnesota, Idaho, New York, Oregon, West Virginia, Florida, Tennessee, Washington, Arkansas, Connecticut, Maryland, Virginia, and the nation's capital, Washington, DC, AGIF would claim a membership exceeding 150,000 persons.[34]

## FBI File on the American G.I. Forum #62-96541

In 1986, my first article on the FBI surveillance of Chicanos and Mexicans included mention of some files I had acquired by then on the AGIF and other groups.[35] Later, I obtained more documents and can offer, as in this chapter, a more extensive history of this surveillance on AGIF. The FBI file on the AGIF may have begun as early as February 14, 1949, as evidenced by a solo page originating in the San Antonio FBI office under file number #100-7842 and is page numbered as "-2-" at bottom and four other pages seemingly unrelated but in the batch. In this released batch of FBI documents, unrelated and unidentified as to date prepared, recipients, senders, subject matter, and titles are not included. The pages are numbered from 8 to 12 with 11 missing. The first of these pages is half redacted at the top but for the office of origin being HO # 100-8638 for Houston and their file number on AGIF. The bottom half reports that an informant, "In August, 1 950, T-4, of unknown reliability, advised the FBI that the American GI forum was a Texas organization made up wholly of veterans of Latin American descent" It identified Dr. Hector P. Garcia as a "man with political ambitions" and that there is "considerable doubt as to his complete sincerity" (p.8). On the last two pages of this four-page batch, the next one in sequence, at the very bottom is information that suggests the FBI was also monitoring the mail to and from Dr. Garcia. It is also possible that given that Dr. Garcia sent carbon copies of his letter to the US Postmaster General, General Douglas MacArthur, Department of Justice, one of them or all forwarded the letter to the FBI. It reads, "On December 31, 1950, Dr. Hector Garcia addressed a letter to *The National Guardian*, Murray Street, New York City New York as follows": (p.9) and continues on the next page with copy of the actual letter addressed in the salutation to

"Dear. Editor:". Dr. Garcia asked to stop the sending of *The Guardian* to him. And he lauds former President Roosevelt, President Truman, the Civil Rights Section of the Department of Justice, and the Federal Government for trying to better the conditions of Mexican Americans. He expressed "implicit faith that in due time we will have complete justice with all people" (p.10). He signed it: Hector P. Garcia, M.D. Chairman American GI Forum of Texas. There is no page 11 but 12 continues with a listing of two more informants, T-4 and T-6, and these report on information gathered in February 1952; clearly this is out of chronological sequence, but it is what it is in dealing with FBI documents.

## The First Dated Documents

The top seven to ten lines of the February 1949 letter mentioned above are entirely redacted to hide any information as to author, intended recipient, date and, of course, the source of the information elaborated in the content. The matter reported by a redacted source was about Gus Garcia, ex-school mate of Hector P. Garcia during their University of Texas at Austin years, now a San Antonio attorney and the Legal Counsel for AGIF. Gus Garcia was the lead attorney before the US Supreme Court on the *Hernandez v. Texas* (1954) case largely funded by LULAC and AGIF that won civil rights protection under the Fourteenth Amendment for Mexican Americans.[36] Apparently, Claude Williams, the national director of the People's Institute of Applied Religion, was corresponding with Gus Garcia in San Antonio. The People's Institute of Applied Religion had been designated a subversive organization as defined in Executive Order 9835. This Executive Order demanded all federal employees sign a loyalty oath as a requisite of employment.[37] This information was the opening paragraph; the second paragraph, totally unrelated, makes mention of an article dated January 22, 1952, in *The Daily Worker*, an east coast communist newspaper, which described a speech by Gus Garcia at a Laredo, Texas Lions Club luncheon at which Gus Garcia railed against the communist witch hunt aimed at anyone who spoke in defense of civil liberties and the discrimination against Negro people. The next three paragraphs, all about Garcia's speech making, covered his presentations before the National Congress for the United Nations in New York City and reported by the *San Antonio Evening News* of January 29, 1952; and another in *The San Antonio Light* of February 10, 1952, about the job offer to Garcia with the Department of Justice. The third paragraph includes mention of others under monitoring: Dr. George I. Sanchez with the University of Texas at Austin, Edward Idar, the Texas state chairman of AGIF, Dr. Hector P. Garcia, the founder and vice president of the AGIF. This material was taken by the FBI from *The San Antonio Express* dated February 13, 1952. Obviously, many of the top leaders of AGIF were being monitored as to their activities and comments made to others.

During the last year of the Harry S. Truman presidential administration on January 31, 1952, Administrative Assistant to the President David H. Stowe wrote to "Mr. Roach" of the FBI requesting information the Bureau may have regarding "the American G. I. Forum of Texas located at Austin, Texas."[38] He wanted "to know what information the Bureau may have regarding it both subversive and background data." Promptly within days, February 5, 1952, D.M. Ladd responded to the director of the FBI informing him that they searched their records not only on AGIF but also the founder and chairman, Dr. Hector Perez Garcia, and two others: Dr. Carlos Castaneda and Mrs. Adela Elliott. Both had been speakers at the State AGIF Convention held in McAllen, Texas, on August 19 and 20, 1950. A one-page report with half the data redacted was attached to this cover letter. The opening paragraph wrongfully identifies Dr. Garcia as "a dentist in Corpus Christi." It provided information on the incorporation of AGIF in Texas with headquarters listed at "3024 Morgan Avenue, Corpus Christi, Texas." The remainder of the memorandum made mention that AGIF since September and December 1948 had been "critical of the Veterans Administration in its handling of Mexican-American veterans."

## The Early Communist Tie

By March 24 of that same year, the FBI director wrote to the SAC, Houston and sent him "two Photostats of a memorandum dated February 5,1952, summarizing the material in Bureau files concerning the captioned organization" which was AGIF of Texas. Obviously, these copies were of the memorandum just cited above but the redacted material must have been most incriminating because Director Hoover had reached this damming and misinformed conclusion:

> On the basis of the information in this enclosure, it appears that the American GI Forum of Texas may possibly be a Communist or Nationalist influenced or dominated organization. You are hereby instructed to furnish the Bureau with background information concerning the organizational structure, leadership, and activities of that group.

Within three months of the first communication on the AGIF from the White House, Director Hoover had placed AGIF in the category of "Internal Security-C," which means it should be considered a threat to national security because of Communist leanings or influence.

The first report from the SAC, Houston dated June 26, 1952, covered the period of April, May, and to June 24. The maker's name was redacted.

The eleven-page report contains no new material just added information on the Secretary of State charter filed in Austin, Texas, in 1946, and the stated purpose of AGIF. The bold controverting assertion from Houston FBI to the director was that their investigation of AGIF presents "No evidence of subversive activity or infiltration by subversive groups in Corpus Christi." While the last page is numbered 11 there are only six pages released, 3–5, 7, and 11. On page 3, Dr. Garcia's motives as head of the AGIF, are put in question by the reporter. Dr. Garcia is accused of being "a man who was known to have political ambitions" Then the specter of sincerity of his motives is presented: "there was considerable doubt as to his complete sincerity." The second paragraph infers that Communists may be funding the AGIF and that while their activities are well-intentioned and leaders are well educated and capable men; "should the Forum be controlled by subversive leaders, the consequences could result in a problem of very serious proportions and perhaps ultimately have an adverse effect on the United States' relations with Mexico." In parentheses following this statement the American Consulate in *Reynosa, Mexico*, dated August 21, 1950, was the source of the information and conclusion. This State Department file is kept under #100-7254-377. The report continues with a profile on Mrs. Adela Elliott in the last paragraph (p.3) but is redacted (p.4). Dr. Carlos Castaneda was a signer of the call for a First Congress of the Mexican and Spanish-American Peoples of the United States that had met in Albuquerque, New Mexico, on March 24–26, 1939. This listing and name made it into a report of the Special Committee on Un-American Activities, House of Representatives, 78th Congress, Second Session, Appendix, Part II. And, the organization subsequently was cited by the House Un-American Activities Committee "as a Communist front in 1944." The remaining two paragraphs on this page profile another information, all redacted and continued redaction at top of page 5. On this page, the attention is directed at Gus Garcia and citing as the FBI source, *The San Antonio Light* of August 29, 1952, to report that he was resigning from the school board in San Antonio and moving his residence to McAllen, Texas and will practice law in Edinburg, Texas. Two more organizations are mentioned, but redacted, except for the American Council of Spanish Speaking People as being "a Communist front." An informant, name redacted, advised to the contrary as "there is no Communist infiltration in either of these above-mentioned organizations." More redacted material follows about investigative findings in Austin, Texas (p.5). The next page released is 7 and it contains almost a complete redaction of material except to repeat that Dr. Garcia "had been very critical of the Veterans Administration in its handling of Mexican-American affairs concerning veterans." Lastly, this report skips pages as previously mentioned and closes with a page titled "ADMINISTRATIVE PAGE LEADS" and it does list two contacts (names redacted) with information on AGIF in San Antonio, Texas; two more in Austin (also redacted), and contacts in Houston (no names redacted but the use of words "confidential informants" suggest there are more than two. The last portion of this page has approximately thirteen to fifteen lines totally redacted under the subheading of "CONFIDENTIAL INFORMANTS."[39]

## ON INFORMANTS

There are different kinds of informants such as undercover police, military intelligence operatives; spies, paid or unpaid informants, both termed snitches; and, volunteers who offer information such as anonymous callers to hotlines, 911, and in response to public announcements by law enforcement seeking assistance from the public as in the Amber Alerts broadcast nationally and even on freeway electronic monitors. Snitch visas or the S-visa are offered to deportable immigrants in exchange for information other immigrants and or organizations.[40] In the days of Operation Wetback during the mid-1950s, the border crossing card was withheld until the daily crosser returned with valuable information on the targets requested by the US officials at the border crossing. Getting information has always been big business involving large numbers of people, not even counting the law enforcement personnel known as their "handlers." Clarence Kelly, former FBI director in the 1970s, once stated "without informants we're nothing."[41] During the post-Watergate Hearings conducted by Senator Frank Church (D-Idaho), testimony had that at that time the FBI had 1,500 paid informants; growing to 6,000 plus in the 1980s; and over 15,000 post 9/11.[42]

### Closing out 1952

On July 28, Director Hoover sent a terse one-page, two-short-paragraph letter to Assistant Attorney General James M. McInerney of the Criminal Division. Hoover enclosed a report from a Houston FBI Special Agent [name redacted] dated June 26, probably the one just analyzed above. His suggestion was "You may wish to examine this report in detail in connections with the provisions of Executive Order 9823." I assume Director Hoover, despite contrary information on communist influence among AGIF leaders, assumed that their protests over the maltreatment of veterans of Mexican origin constituted disloyalty to the United States. In a separate letter on the same day to the SAC, Houston the director FBI admonished him that provisions of Section 87-D of the FBI's Manual of Instructions, "six copies of future reports in this matter should be designated for the Bureau." But this was not a simple admonishment, Hoover wanted copies to circulate to other intelligence agencies to completely poison the well for AGIF.

San Antonio FBI filed its report on AGIF on October 21, 1952, covering the period from September 16 to October 14 consisting of nine pages released with non-sequential numbering and some withheld pages. The cover page made by [name redacted] begins with four to five lines entirely redacted but leaving information about a speech Dr. Garcia gave at some event and present were Ed Idar, state chair of AGIF at the time and Dr. George Sanchez, was guest at State Convention of Forum in San Antonio 7/52. The words used by Dr. Garcia that were not redacted in this opening "Synopsis of Facts" that probably raised eyebrows at FBI headquarters were "anti-Communist witch-hunt" as a "national malady." The entire section bottom half on San Antonio was redacted (p.1). Redacted as well, after skipping page 2, is the entire page following but for an opening paragraph informing that Gus Garcia, the Chief Counsel for AGIF gave a speech in Del Rio, Texas, about his trip to Washington, DC, and "conference with President Truman regarding minority group problems in the Southwest" (p.3). Another speech by Gus Garcia to a San Antonio group quotes some of his remarks published of all places in St. Louis, Missouri, a publication named "The Appeal," volumes 1 and 8. His comments were taken from page 6 of that publication without identifying which volume or date. Gus Garcia stated the most serious problem of the day was the worst epoch of witch-hunting since the Middle Ages, referring to the Red Scare promoted by Senator Joseph McCarthy (R-Wisconsin). Garcia pointed out that anyone who disagrees with the opinion of the majority or does any original thinking of their own is labeled a subversive or radical. He compared this labeling as that done by Adolph Hitler to cultivate a culture of demagoguery. He also reported that people the world over are tired of war except for the avaricious few, the greedy. The last two paragraphs on this page, as is the top names associated with "The Appeal," are redacted (p.4). Skipping a page, in the subsequent one, two more names are reported on tied to AGIF, Ed Idar and Professor George I. Sanchez. Idar was reported to be associated with another group, American Council of Spanish-Speaking People, seeking to become the "clearinghouse for existing organizations in Texas, Arizona, New Mexico, and California." The reference to Professor Sanchez was that he had resigned from the Texas Council of Human Relations because "lack of support made it unoperative [*sic*]." His letter of resignation was sent to both the Texas Governor, Alan Shivers, and to AGIF (p.6). The next sequential page does mention and list the informants relied upon for this report, but all names are redacted (p.7). The monitoring of the People's Institute of Applied Religion continued about some of their work in Helena, Alabama sometime in December 23, 1949 (p.8). The subsequent pages released as part of this report are numbered neither sequentially nor correctly, raising questions in my mind if they belong here or not. Be it as it may, the content is interesting to the FBI because Dr. Hector P. Garcia and a local realtor from Corpus Christi went before the striking bus drivers in the city to pledge their support and encourage them to continue with the strike. The entire bottom paragraph is redacted ("-P- p.-2-"). The last two pages are on the identity of informants, now expanded to list El Paso and Albuquerque as offices that should be interested in AGIF, and all the matter is redacted. The bottom half of this page deals with informants in San Antonio and Austin, all redacted ("-3-"). The last page is oddly construed. It has on top the list of "STATE OFFICERS" of AGIF of Texas then the salutation to the addressee: Mr. Willard Kelly, assistant commissioner of Immigration, US Immigration and Naturalization Service (INS), Department of Justice, Washington, DC, dated May 15, 1953, which is another reason to suspect the page is placed in the wrong sequence because the report it is supposed to pertain to is from 1952.

It should be apparent by now that the FBI was continuing to monitor and surveil the activities, movements, words and opinions, affiliations, and other associations the top leaders of the AGIF at the time were engaged in. This seems to be a full-court press by FBI informants placed within and with access to the leadership of AGIF.

The FBI reports from Houston on October 23 and December 8, 1952, not only closed out the year but repeated that those previously identified to their office as reliable sources in Houston, Corpus Christi, and El Paso on the AGIF had reported that Dr. Garcia revealed "no evidence of communist infiltration" in Corpus Christi. The commentary on a new AGIF chapter in El Paso found "no evidence of Communist infiltration or influence reported."

The letter that follows the listing of officers is from Ed. Idar, chairman of Texas AGIF, to Hoover and it is an offer to help the FBI identify Communists from Mexico and undocumented persons from Guatemala posing as Mexicans. Explicitly, Idar wrote: "I am engaged in a survey of the Texas border from El Paso to Brownsville in connection with the Wetback problem." He expresses opposition to the idea of an Open Border with Mexico and seeks information.

We have been advised that the Federal Bureau of Investigation recently released a report that shows the total number of aliens in the United States who are members of the Communist Party. We are wondering if your office has information at hand that could break this total down into the major nationality groupings such as Mexican and if such information could be released for us in our survey and eventual publication.

The last paragraph has the request for information on the Guatemalans:

> Finally, in view of the increasing public concern about the infiltration of Com-
> munist elements into the government of Guatemala we would like to know
> if any Guatemalan nationals have been deported in recent months. We know,
> for example, of one instance along the Mexican border recently where a
> carload of Guatemalan nationals traveling with false Mexican papers was
> detained and deportation subsequently effected.
> Sincerely yours
> s/Ed Idar, Jr.
> Chairman

There was a response to this letter, apparently the original was dated May
15, 1953, in the released documents from the FBI director to Idar dated June
3, 1953. Hoover declined to furnish any information because "the recent
statements which you attribute to the FBI was not made by any representative of this Bureau." Hoover circulated this response to four other area FBI
offices in El Paso, Dallas, San Antonio, and Houston. More importantly,
Hoover added to the bottom of his response letter a page and a half of notes.
First, he labeled the AGIF subject matter, as had been the practice for years,
as "Internal Security-C" lest his field agents forget the level of scrutiny he
wanted as follow-up. He also provided the FBI field offices the file numbers
of AGIF-related matter plus some redacted information tied to these files.
On the second full page of Notes, with top paragraph and four more lines
redacted, Hoover points out that the statements Idar mentions were made by
the US attorney general (AG) not the FBI. In closing this portion of the Notes
Hoover referenced the AG's comments to a specific memorandum from him
to all FBI offices and listed the date and identification number but the copy
released makes impossible to read. He provides the data on the incorporation
of AGIF in Texas.

Bending over backwards in courtesy, someone [name redacted] at the
Austin office of AGIF's Chairman, Ed Idar, responded to Director Hoover
acknowledging the letter and informing him that Idar was out of the city until
June 18 or 19 and "his attention will be called to your letter for reply."

Perhaps Idar did reply but for sure Dr. Hector P. Garcia opened another
front in November 1953 on the issue of brutality against Mexicans in
Texas by the INS personnel. Garcia wrote twice to AG Herbert Brownell
complaining of police brutality including one killing in Taylor, Texas,
on several Mexicans and he wanted an investigation into this conduct
unbecoming such personnel. The copy quality of this correspondence is
very bad; not very legible. A copy of the letters to Brownell were sent to
Hoover on what appears to be November 20, 1953, asking he investigate the

murder, shootings, and beatings plus he does congratulate the director for "the fine work that you have done in the protection of our country against Communism . . . and help that your department has given us in our 'Civil Rights Case'." The FBI withheld thirteen pages of material at this point in the packet of files released. There appears to be a two-page response that is file stamped at bottom left with "NOV 27 1963" but the content of this letter to Dr. Garcia is not legible not does it have a letterhead. And there are two other pages, seemingly unrelated, one copying the content of an article from *The Corpus Christi Caller* dated November 19, according to the typed copy, about Ramon Gonzalez, an eighteen year old charged with burglary and received a five-year probated sentence from a Justice of the Peace [name illegible]. The other page is dated October 27, 1954, heavily redacted, and sent from SAC, Dallas to the director, FBI. From what can be read it states the litany from the past years that AGIF is "the target for Communist infiltration at the present time."

A Heads-Up letter was sent from the director to the SAC, Houston on November 16 and to Dallas on 24 of 1954, alerting them to "carefully watch" the AGIF chapters in their respective cities because they got word on October 27, 1954, that it was "reportedly a target for Communist Party infiltration at the present time." Hoover wanted all information to be sent to him and each other. SAC, Dallas responded to the director that they had begun an investigation and sent copies to Houston and San Antonio FBI offices. By January 27, 1955, the FBI Dallas office concluded that their investigation revealed the AGIF "has been infiltrated by the Communist Party in the Dallas area" and they will continue with "an active investigation . . . UACB" (p.1).

## MUCH WITHHELD ABOUT 1955

The following year, February 9, 1955, the director, FBI sent to SAC, Dallas a one-paragraph admonishing him for sending copies of Reurlet and Relet dated January 27, 1955, to the Bureau, whereas they should have been sent to San Antonio and Houston as indicated and not sent. The Director was alerting him he was now sending those copies.

On April 29,1955, the SAC, Dallas sent to the director, FBI the most clear and damaging reaffirming statement on AGIF: "The Dallas Branch of this organization continues to be dominated and controlled by the Communist Party, [redacted two lines] There are said to be at present about 30 members," Next five to six lines entirely redacted. The closing paragraph promised a comprehensive report within the next two weeks. The following May 13, 1955, by Airtel to the director, FBI, the Dallas office reported the comprehensive report to arrive within a week. The thirty-two-page (at least) report did arrive dated May 20 covering the period April 14 through May 3 and was circulated to El Paso, San Antonio, and Houston FBI offices. The reporter's name was redacted as were most of the "Synopsis of Facts" except for a few lines:

> advised this group is composed principally of Mexican-American Veterans who allegedly have banded together to stamp out discrimination against Mexican-Americans, and to seek justice and equality for everyone. This organization said to be non-political [more lines redacted] . . . resent membership is approximately 30 persons [next two lines redacted].

Prior to declassification and release a total of four pages were entirely withheld plus an additional forty-two pages; therefore, the pages on hand number only seven and I will use the page number at bottom of each page to identify, but they are not in numerical sequence. The first page besides the cover letter analyzed above is the Table of Contents which lists as "V. OTHER ACTIVITIES OF COMMUNIST PARTY MEMBERS PERTAINING TO THE DALLAS CHAPTER OF G. I. FORUM (Showing control and domination by Communist Party…………..32" (p.2). The next page has half of it redacted and corrects the AGIF name to show another which is used frequently as well, "GI Forum." It cited Executive Order (EO) 10450 as the source for the US AG designating the Communist Party (CP) USA [remainder of text, about half a page, is redacted] (p.3).[43] The report skips several pages to report on a source who advised an FBI Special Agent that he thinks "this organization may possibly be subversive." His evidence was that a delegation recently visited the County Juvenile Home to protest the "jailing of approximately twenty Mexican juveniles, who were held overnight and [remainder redacted]." Citing a letter dated March 22, 1955, from the Good Neighbor Commission of Austin, Texas, made available to the FBI about getting correspondence from AGIF, local and Austin, complaining of discrimination in restaurants, such as "the Green Hat Restaurant, Lamesa, Texas, and two others refusing to serve U.S. citizens of Mexican descent." The sources of this information were redacted (p.7). Another source, [name redacted as well as about 4-5 lines] also stated the AGIF "is known to be dominated and controlled by the Communist Party in Dallas. Informant advised that the Dallas Chapter is the only Chapter known to be so controlled and dominated by the Communist Party." The remaining two-thirds of this page are redacted (p.8). The next page listed the officers of AGIF; half of this page is also redacted. The officers are listed and not one is from Dallas. "Gilbert C. Garcia, 1st Vice-Chairman" is listed as being from Fort Worth, Texas, the major city west of Dallas (p.9). But, on the next page Mr. Gilbert C. Garcia is credited with organizing the "G.I. Forum in Dallas on September 29, 1954" and that

"Gilbert C. Garcia is the cousin to the State Chairman of AGIF, Mr. Richard M. Casillas, of San Antonio" (p.10). The sequential pages are missing and redaction continues for two-thirds of a page more and only quotes the aims and objectives of the AGIF (p.12). The incomplete report ends with this page.

Hoover sent a copy of this report with letter dated May 23, 1955, to the US AG advising that his FBI had investigated the AGIF and found nothing in 1952. In 1955, however, it seemed the situation as far as the Dallas Chapter went things changed and now it was under control and domination by the CPUSA. The FBI's "security investigation of this organization has been reinstituted, and the results will be promptly forwarded to you upon receipt." On June 8, 1955, the same Dallas FBI report was sent to the Assistant AG William F. Tompkins apparently with the hopes that he would designate AGIF as a subversive organization because he cited EO 10450 and the Internal Security Act of 1950 considering the content of the report. Hoover also sent a one-page-long memo to the SAC, Dallas the next day, June 9, asking that office do a "thumbnail sketch of the AGIF be promptly submitted to the Bureau." And he asked they look into other chapters of AGIF and find leads to this group. Hoover got impatient and sent a reminder note on July 14 to the SAC, Dallas. He gave a deadline of July 25, 1955, for this thumbnail sketch.

The FBI files released do not contain any such thumbnail sketch. As denouement to the building crescendo the files released are two unidentifiable but for the Houston office file number 100-8639. On a page numbered "C" with much material redacted what remains is the history of AGIF founding by Dr. Hector P. Garcia and that as of October 15, 1952 the El Paso chapter had about eighty-six members. More importantly, it stated that the El Paso FBI office had "no information indicating un-American activities by the members or leaders of the American G. I. Forum in the El Paso area." The last page had names of informants redacted.

## Jose Rodriguez Molina a.k.a. Joe Molina
## of the Dallas Chapter, AGIF

In 1946, a returning veteran from military service with the US Navy, Jose Rodriguez Molina a.k.a. Joe Molina got married to Soledad Palomo and shortly thereafter his wife announced the coming of a baby.[44] His plans since graduation from Crozier Technical High School in Dallas, Texas, had been to go to college. Those plans changed with the pregnancy. Instead of a four-year degree partly paid by his G.I. Bill, Molina went to the local business college to quickly learn a trade. He felt obligated to be able to afford the new addition to the family. Part of the curriculum at the business college required he per-form hours of on-the-job-training. He was assigned to the Texas School Book

Depository beginning on February 1947. Over the next sixteen years, he rose slowly in the ranks reaching the position of credit manager. He noticed most of those years that he was the only person of Mexican origin working at the book depository.[45] That seemed to be the case at the book depository; they only hired whites. Among those was Lee Harvey Oswald, whom he saw on occasion but never exchanged words with him.[46]

November 22, 1963, the day of President Kennedy's assassination in Dallas, Texas, was the day Molina's world would come crashing down on him, his family, friends, and the AGIF. This event also gave rise to a new business, that of assassination conspiracy theorists that continued publishing their most recent findings.[47] But for Molina, this day began as any other day except for the front-page news in both daily newspapers of Dallas announcing the visit by President John F. Kennedy to the city for a luncheon at the Trade Mart Center just off the Stemmons Freeway going north from downtown. A motorcade was to carry the president, his wife Jacqueline, and Texas Governor John Connally and his wife, Nellie, in an open top limousine through the streets of downtown. Both newspapers printed the route the motorcade would take from Love Field airport to downtown's Main Street and go west toward the underpass to get onto Stemmons Freeway.[48] Someone changed the route to have the motorcade turn right on Houston Street for a block then left on to Elm Street toward the underpass and enter the on ramp for the freeway which was a quicker and better route to reach the Trade Mart.

Employees at the book depository were informed that the motorcade would pass right in front of the building and they could watch the president's limousine pass by about noon time. Molina and others made plans to be on the front steps of the building to wave at the motorcade and hoped to get a glimpse of President Kennedy and the First Lady. About this exciting day Molina testified under oath as follows:

*Mr. Ball:* Did you go out on the street to see the motorcade?
*Mr. Molina:* Yes, I was standing on the front steps.
*Mr. Ball:* With whom?
*Mr. Molina:* Right next left of me was Mr. Williams and close to there was Mrs. Sanders.
*Mr. Ball:* Pauline Sanders.
*Mr. Molina:* Yes.
*Mr. Ball:* Did you see Roy Truly?
*Mr. Molina:* Yes; he was standing with Mr. Campbell; they were going out to lunch.
*Mr. Ball:* They were in front of you were they?
*Mr. Molina:* Yes.
*Mr. Ball:* You saw the Presidents (sic) car pass?

*Mr. Molina:* Yes.

*Mr. Ball:* Did you see anything after that?

*Mr. Molina:* Well, I heard the shots.

*Mr. Ball:* Where—what was the source of the sound?

*Mr. Molina:* Sort of like it reverberated, sort of kind of came from the west side; that was the first impression I got. Of course, the first shot was fired then there was an interval between the first and second longer than the second and third.

*Mr. Ball:* What did you do after that?

*Mr. Molina:* Well, I just stood there, everybody was running, and I didn't know what to do actually, because what could I do. I was just shocked.

*Mr. Ball:* Did anybody say anything?

*Mr. Molina:* Yes.

*Mr. Ball:* [*sic*] [It should be Molina stating this:] Yes, this fellow come to me—Mr. Williams said, somebody said, somebody was shooting at the President, somebody, I don't know who it was. There was some shooting, you know, and this fellow said "What can anybody gain by that"; he just shook his head and I just stood there and shook my head. I didn't want to think what was happening, you know, but I wanted to find out so I went down to where the grassy slope is, you know, and I was trying to gather pieces of conversation of the people that had been close by there and somebody said, "Well, the President has been shot and I think they shot somebody else," something like that.

Mr. Molina further testified that others saw him on the front steps and lobby of the building, such as Gloria Calvary and that he left the building around 2 p.m. that day and went home. He was asked if he had ever seen Lee Oswald and Molina said he had but never spoken to him. And, he did not see him on the 22nd. Molina testified he arrived at work that day at 7 a.m., had a key, entered the building and went to his office on the second floor where he stayed, ate his lunch, and "went downstairs about 12:15, something like that."[49]

> The next day was even more terrifying for Molina and his family. "Well, on November 23rd following the assassination, I was paid a visit by the local police department at 1:30 in the morning and they sort of wanted to tie me up with this case in some way or another and they thought I was implicated."[50]

The police entered his home, waking his wife and children; "scared my wife half to death." He was not sure if they had a search warrant, but the police did search the house. He did not know what it was they were looking for, but they did ask him many questions.

*Mr. Molina:* Well, they asked me questions whether I knew different persons that belong to the G. I. Forum . . .

*Mr. Ball:* To what?
*Mr. Molina:* G. I. Forum, this club I belonged to here in Dallas.[51]

Mr. Ball continued to ask about the AGIF to understand what type of group it was such as a "Roman Catholic organization" or what? Mr. Molina clarified it was a Veteran's club. He also identified a "Mr. Garroway and a Lieutenant Revill" and the ones doing most of the questioning. His wife, two kids, and he were made to sit in the living room and were subjected to questioning by the police while others searched every room in the house.[52] He was asked to be taken to the police station or would he come on his own by morning. His wife drove him to the police station about 10:30 a.m. and he was met with dozens of reporters and television cameras. While there he was questioned again by "Chief Gannaway" and a "Mr. Fritz" along with an FBI agent and a Secret Service agent. After some four hours at the police station, he was taken home only to have his wife in hysteria over what the major television stations were saying about him being on a list of persons with subversive backgrounds. Soledad, his wife, said she heard the police chief, Curry, say that on television. Molina was furious and called to speak to Chief Curry without success. He did talk to someone named "King" about making a retraction of that statement. The print media, namely the Associated Press, subsequently carried that same accusation across the nation as did the national television networks. He never could get a retraction about being a "person with subversive background."[53]

He was called to account for his role in the assassination by a vice president of the company he worked for, a "Mr. Campbell," the next day after the police station visit. He was fired by December 13, 1963, due to "automation" and finished out the year. He was a credit manager not subject to such technological advances of the time.[54] Over the New Year holidays, he got letters and calls from friends in California and Florida asking him why their newspapers were saying he was a communist and friend of Lee Harvey Oswald.[55] Molina's life and that of his family were never the same since; neither were those associated with the AGIF of Dallas and beyond.

## THE FBI FILE ON JOE MOLINA

The opening pages of the FBI files on Joe Molina are from his file at the Bureau #105-126101. These first pages are from a forty-one-page report dated August 20, 1964, and prepared by W. James Wood with the Dallas FBI office. Interestingly, some informants are identified in this report as follows: DL T-1 was Felix Botello; DL T-2 was Mrs. Margarita Landin; DL T-4 was Mrs. Ruth Lowery; and others were concealed. The remainder of the pages in this chapter are solely from this report so I will only identify them by page number.

## FBI BACKGROUND DATA ON MOLINA

He lived at 4306 Brown Street in Dallas, Texas and was no longer employed at the Texas School Book Depository, instead worked at the Credit Union of Neuhoff Brothers Packers at 2811 Alamo, Dallas, Texas, as a bookkeeper. He was unemployed after sixteen years with the School Book Depository over suspicions he claimed about his loyalty to the United States. He served in the Navy from February 26, 1943, to January 5, 1946. His parents were Pedro Molina from Mexico City, Mexico and Luiz [*sic*] R. Molina from Celaia [*sic*], Mexico. He was born in Dallas on June 18, 1924, the oldest of four more siblings, Faank, Pere, Angelina, and Beatrice. He married Soledad Molina and had three children, Joe, John, and Linda; a fourth child, Sylvia, was adopted (p.2).

Molina joined the AGIF on or about September 29, 1954, when the Dallas Chapter of the organization was formed at the Camelia Room of the Baker Hotel in Dallas. William J. Lowery, Jr. of 4520 Bridlewood Street in Dallas testified before the Subversive Activities Control Board in Washington, DC on September 23, 1963, that he was a member of the AGIF and the CP. The subsequent meetings of the Dallas AGIF were held at the Guadalupe Center and Molina was named in October 25 that same year to head up the Public Relations Committee of AGIF (p.3). The CP, according to Lowery, agreed in November to support Molina to become the Secretary of AGIF-Dallas. Instead, Molina was named sergeant at arms on November 22, 1954. By July 1955, the CP members in Dallas believed Molina could never be recruited into the CP because he opposed the CP faction within AGIF-Dallas (p.4). Beginning in July 1955, however, four of the CP members began to socialize with Molina at his home. Together they agreed to back Frank Martinez for chairman of AGIF. The leader of the CP faction within AGIF was Augustin Estrada. It turned out that Molina was elected chairman at the October 24, 1955, meeting and by December 6, Molina's wife, Nan [this could be an Anglicized nickname for Soledad] was named vice chair of the ladies auxiliary of AGIF-Dallas (p.5). CP members and sympathizers joined in an AGIF-Dallas sponsored picnic at Bachman Lake on April 29, 1956. In 1957, Molina as member of an AGIF-Dallas committee began to protest discrimination in public swimming pool areas such as Vickery Park and to demand free kindergartens for Dallas children. The next year, Molina was part of another committee that demanded the Mayor R.L. Thornton help them end discrimination in Dallas against Latin Americans. But in September 1958 when Molina was elected to a second term as chairman of the AGIF-Dallas chapter, he opposed sending a representative to the convention of the National Association for the Advancement of Colored People. And, by early 1959 Mrs. Molina was elected treasurer of the ladies auxiliary (p.6). In the summer of 1959, the discrimination continued at Vickery Park over the swimming pool as well as meeting of the committee from AGIF-Dallas as to recourse. By August 5, 1962, Joe Molina was the district chairman of District 9 of the Texas AGIF. The following year in November, President Kennedy was assassinated, and Joe Molina was interrogated. Several CP members of the AGIF met to discuss why Molina was interrogated given he was so conservative and anti-communist. The AGIF-Dallas members of the CP were Joe Landin and Felix Botello (p.7).

Joe Molina may have been conservative and anti-communist, he was outspoken advocate for the civil rights of Mexican-origin people. Dallas Police Chief Jesse E. Curry complained about him to SA James S. Weir of the FBI. As an aside when Molina was being interrogated said as much to SA Weir. "Molina had caused the Dallas Police Department considerable trouble in the past demanding such things as listing Mexicans as white persons rather than as Mexicans, and generally protesting alleged discrimination against Mexicans" (p.8a). Molina, after the police searched his home and interrogated him as to his role in the assassination, was asked to face all his accusers at the police station. He came on his own, he said, to clear his name but what happened turned out worse because the questioning centered on how he came to know Lee Harvey Oswald. He admitted to knowing him but not well because Oswald was a new employee and worked a different floor. But the interrogation and his presence at police headquarters for hours prompted the media to label him Mr. X, a suspect among two others (p.9). Molina was re-interviewed on March 25, 1964, and signed a two-page affidavit witnessed by two FBI agents, A. Raymond Switzer and Eugene F. Petrakis, of the Dallas office. In this affidavit, Molina names witnesses that were with him at the time of the shots fired and denied any relationship with Oswald other than seeing him in the School Book Depository building from time to time (p.10–11). Molina recounted the police search of his home on November 23 at about 1:30–2:00 a.m. He repeated that the main line of questioning by Captain William Gannaway and Lieutenant Jack Revill had to do with the AGIF and Oswald (p.12). The police, contrary to what he had just said in this report after they searched his home, gave him an ultimatum: either go with them or show up later at the police station. He arrived at the police station about 9:50 a.m. and waited in the Special Services Bureau office for about forty minutes. While in that room, media persons came in and out of that office to take photographs of him. None ever appeared in the newsprint media or television. Again he was interrogated by Captain Gannaway and Lt. Jack Revill. Later, he was moved to the Homicide Bureau to be interviewed there by Captain Will Fritz. After forty-five minutes and no Capt. Fritz, a detective and another FBI agent interrogated him about Oswald, his work at the School Book Depository, and his whereabouts during the assassination. When they were done, despite being told he could leave, he was not allowed go to by a uniformed policeman at the door. He waited another forty to forty-five minutes in the Homicide Bureau office. Then, Lt. Revill interrogated him again over his role in the AGIF (p.13). He was asked about John Stanford, a state official with the CP. Molina did not know him. He declined to write a statement about the political views of AGIF. Lt. Revill wrote one for him about AGIF and Molina signed it. After being at the police station since 10 a.m. he was allowed to go at 5 p.m. He was never charged, arrested, or detained against his will except for that policeman that did not let him leave. His employment was adversely affected by this experience. His job duties were changed; his letterhead stationery with his name confiscated and ultimately confronted his boss, O.V. Campbell, the company vice president (p.14), who told him the sales of the company were being hurt by the publicity surrounding him; and, then we was fired due to automation, is what he was told. As severance he received three month's pay and his benefits. Thereafter, he had a hard time finding a job and even questioned at the Texas Employment Commission about being a subversive (p.15). The following year he was able to get a part-time job through some contacts with Holy Trinity School in Dallas and eventually it became full-time job as a bookkeeper.

He learned from his wife that Capt. Curry had mentioned his name to the media as a suspect. That new item went viral across the nation. Efforts he made to get Curry to retract that statement did not succeed (p.16). Curry never did. Molina went to an attorney to sue a radio station, WRR, for defamation. Being city owned, the suit had to have been filed within thirty days of the utterance and Molina was many months late (p.17). Later, on July 15, 1964, Molina changed his story about a Secret Service man being part of the interrogation team; there was no such person (p.19). The affidavit Molina signed about AGIF is on pages 20–21 of the report. The narrative from the police perspective of the home search was provided by Detective H.M. Hart, Intelligence Unit, Special Service Bureau, Dallas Police Department (p. 22), and Hart stated that he had no knowledge of any allegations made by police officials to the news media (p.23). Captain Gannaway was also a Lt. Colonel with the US Army Reserve of the 4th Army Intelligence School. He narrated the search warrant of the Molina home explaining that Molina let them in and allowed them to search so the warrant they had issued by a Justice of the Peace was never executed (p.26). Gannaway said the only item taken from the Molina home was an address list of AGIF members. Gannaway also declined to admit he gave Molina's name to the news media or influenced his employment termination in any way (p. 27). Gannaway was questioned by Molina's attorney Otto E. Mullinax on information useful to Molina's suit for defamation but was not helpful (p.28) and he gave a four-page notarized statement to that effect, a copy of which is in the report (p.28a–28d).

Chief Curry is quoted in this report as stating that the Intelligence Unit of the Dallas Police Department had a file on AGIF. In this file were records with dates, times, places of affiliation, and relationships with known Communists such as William and Ruth Lowery, Augustin Estrada, Joe Landin, Dan Yarborough, and Elwood Ross (p.29–30).

## THE TEXAS SCHOOL BOOK DEPOSITORY OFFICIALS

Interviewed for this report were several officials beginning with Roy S. Truly, the Director of the Texas School Book Depository who claimed that early in the fall of 1963 they began looking to automate operations including one slot in accounting. That department had two persons, Otis Williams and Joe Molina, and Williams was the better employee so Molina was let go for that reason not the allegations of being implicated in the Kennedy assassination (p.33). He also commented that Molina after being let go from the School Book Depository was not unemployed for too long, he found a job soon (p.34). O.V. Campbell, Molina's direct supervisor, claimed the same reasons for the termination, not the allegations of being a subversive (p.35). Campbell reviewed the severance package offered and accepted by Molina which included a letter of recommendation (p.36–38). In a subsequent re-interview, O.V. Campbell repeated his testimony almost exactly as before and address the issue of the negative letters coming into the company immediately after Molina's name was disclosed and connected by the media as a suspect employed at the School Book Depository (p.38a–38c). Two other officials with the Texas Employment Commission (TEC) were interviewed about Molina's loss of employment and futile efforts to find employment following the press coverage and job termination. Arthur K. Sayre, the office manager of TEC, provided information furnished by Molina in his interview with TEC (p.39a). There are some notations about Molina refusing some work opportunities by not showing up after being referred to TItche's, a department store, in Dallas on January 17, 1964; a re-interview appointment at TEC for which he did not show or call in set for February 17, 1964; and another referral to the Texas Highway Department, a temporary job (p.39b). Interestingly, the TEC card shown to those preparing this report and quoting it indicated comments made by a job interviewer at TEC, Logan, no first name listed, as follows: "Slightly bald-neat-well dressed, pleasant manner, still has accent, although reared in Dallas." Those preparing this report noted, "No referrals to prospective employers were noted on this card" (p.39c). The woman who allegedly made the remark to Molina during a TEC job interview appointment about being the subversive, Mrs. Bess P. Coville, denied any such comment being made. She did state that Molina during "that interview, he was noncommittal, and she was not impressed with him as an applicant for a full-charge book-keeping job. She did not remember any adverse publicity concerning him, and she did not realize that there had been any adverse publicity against him" (p.39d). Mrs. Thelma Logan, another job interviewer at TEC, recalled visiting with Molina on December 19, 1963, and that he had been requested to resign. When she asked him why, he volunteered of having "been accused of being a member of a subversive group." Molina claimed the police made that accusation and he was looking to sue them over that slander. He denied to her that AGIF was a subversive group or knowing Lee Harvey Oswald. She claimed no opening were available for what he wanted, credit manager, and those were the reasons for no employment (p.39e). R.T. Summer, office manager at TEC, also provided information on Molina's job-seeking ventures and appointments. He discussed the Molina claim for unemployment compensation. Whereas Joe Molina was earning $450 a month at the School Book Depository, his unemployment compensation check was $37 per week (p.39f). The last page of this report released is 41 and it is reporting on Malvin E. Shugart with the US INS, Dallas, Texas. The INS office advised "that his office has no file on Joseph Rodriguez Molina." Why should they, he was a US citizen and a honorably discharged veteran, but then he was at the wrong place, at the wrong time, and belonging to the wrong veteran's organization, the AGIF on November 22, 1963.

## THE AGIF FOUNDER AND A VICTIM PASS

Hector P. Garcia passed away July 26, 1996, at age eighty-four at Corpus Christi, Texas. There is no monument as a tribute to his legacy of contributions to the civil rights of veterans and the Mexican-origin community in general. There is a statute of Selena Quintanilla, the singer, on the oceanfront boulevard, and rightfully so. Dr. Garcia's body was placed in state on July 29 at the auditorium named after Selene. Dozens and dozens of prominent political figures walked past the casket as did thousands who paid their respects.[56] By contrast, the medical offices of Dr. Garcia, where he practiced healing for decades and conducted AGIF business, are left standing but in deplorable condition and eligible for condemnation by the city. There is no historical marker or even a movement among the Forumeers or anyone to designate this site as part of our national heritage. What does continue is the FBI file on the AGIF, Hector P. Garcia, Joe Molina, and many other Forumeers. J. Edgar Hoover, early on the founding of the AGIF, wrongfully concluded they were subversives and probably Communists disguised as American patriots.

Joe Molina passed away on July 8, 2017, in Carrollton, a suburb of Dallas, Texas; he was ninety-three years of age.[57] He had spent the last thirty-three years of his life explaining to anyone who would listen that he was not a communist; had nothing to do with the assassination of President John F. Kennedy; and, did now know why the police and FBI thought he was. According to Jerry Shinley, the infiltration by the FBI of the AGIF began as early as 1948 with its founding by Hector P. Garcia of Corpus Christi, Texas. The first FBI plant within the AGIF was William J. Lowery. He had been an FBI informant within the Texas Communist Party USA since 1945.[58]

## NOTES

1. The biographical information on the Garcia family and Hector P. Garcia comes from three sources. Carl Allsup's *American G. I. Forum: Origins and Evolution* (Austin: University of Texas Press, 1982); Henry A. J. Ramos, *The American G.I. Forum: In Pursuit of the Dream, 1948–1983* (Houston: Arte Publico Press, 1998); and, Ignacio M. Garcia, *Hector P. Garcia: In Relentless Pursuit of Justice* (Houston: Arte Publico Press, 2002). The most comprehensive on the biographical data is the latter work by Garcia.

2. Garcia, *Hector P. Garcia*, 18–19.

3. *Ibid.*, 25–28.

4. *Ibid.*, 29.

5. *Ibid.*, 32.

6. *Ibid.*, 34–35.

7. *Ibid.*, 44.

8. *Ibid.*, 54–55, 59.

9. Ramos, *The American G.I. Forum*, 4.

10. Garcia, *Hector P. Garcia*, 68, 73

11. *Ibid.*, 75.

12. *Ibid.*, 69.

13. Ramos, *The American G.I. Forum*, 3.

14. Garcia, *Hector P. Garcia*, 79.

15. Ramos, *The American G.I. Forum*, 4.

16. *Ibid.*, 8.

17. *Ibid.*, 9, 10–11.

18. Benjamin Márquez, *Democratizing Texas Politics: Race, Identity, and Mexican American Empowerment, 1945–2002* (Austin, University of Texas Press), 36.

19. The Longoria story is well documented and stated by Patrick J. Carroll in his book, *Felix Longoria's Wake: Bereavement, Racism, and the rise of Mexican American Activism* (Austin: University of Texas Press, 2003) and also in the Independent Lens documentary, "The Longoria Affair," produced and directed by John Valadez in 2010; www. pbs.org/independentlens/films/longoria-affair/.

20. See Pycior, *LBJ and the Mexican Americans* for this relationship and its development.

21. Ramos, *The American G.I. Forum*, 30.

22. *Handbook of Texas Online*, R. Matt Abigail and Hugo Martinez, "GARCÍA, CLEOTILDE PÉREZ," accessed October 28, 2019, https://tshaonline.org/handbook/online/articles/fgaay/.

23. Her archival deposits are found at the Mary and Jeff Bell Library at Texas A & M University and at the Nattie Lee Benson Latin American collection at the University of Texas at Austin.

24. Lye Saunders and Olen Leonard, *The Wetback in the Lower Rio Grande Valley of Texas* (Austin: University of Texas Press, 1951).

25. Garcia, *Hector P. Garcia*, 196–198.

26. *Ibid.*, 198–202.

27. Garcia, *Viva Kennedy* has this history.

28. Garcia, *Hector P. Garcia*, 96–97.

29. *Ibid.*, 96.

30. Others claim the G.I. stands for "Government Issue" as all clothing, weaponry, housing, food, training, and the like were supplied to all soldiers upon entry to military service.

31. Pycior, *LBJ and the Mexican Americans*, has much of these political relationships during the Johnson years as does the political biography by Kells, *Vicente Ximenes*. Ximenes was the first Mexican American advisor in the White House. For the narrative on President Kennedy's appointment of the first federal judge of Mexican origin see Louise Ann Fisch, *All Rise: Reynaldo G. Garza, the First Mexican American Federal Judge* (College Station: Texas A & M University Press, 1996).

32. Benjamin Marquez, *Democratizing Texas Politics: Race, Identity, and Mexican Americans* (Austin: University of Texas Press, 2014).

33. Ramos, *The American G.I. Forum*, 123–139.

34. *Ibid.*, 31.

35. See my article, "Chicanos and Mexicanos Under Surveillance: 1940–1980," in *Renato Rosaldo Lecture Series Monograph*, Ignacio M. Garcia, ed., Mexican American Studies and Research Center (Tucson: University of Arizona Press), Spring 1986, 43–44.

36. For this important case decided weeks before *Brown v. Board of Education*, but rarely mentioned much less taught in the public schools see Michael A. Olivas, *Colored Men and Hombres Aquí: Hernandez v. Texas and the Emergence of Mexican American Lawyering*, (Houston: Arte Publico Press, 2006) and for a more thorough discussion see Ignacio M. Garcia, *White But Not Equal: Mexican Americans, Jury Discrimination, and the Supreme Court* (Tucson: University of Arizona Press, 2008).

37. Harry S. Truman Library and Museum, EXECUTIVE ORDER 9835, accessed on October 27, 2019, at www.trumanlibrary.gov/library/executive/orders/9835/executive-order-9835/.

38. The oral history interviews, six in all, with Stowe are at the Harry S. Truman Library and Museum, under David H. Stowe Oral History Interviews, accessed October 28, 2019, www.trumanlibrary.gov/library/oral-histories/stowe1/.

39. The FBI, as all intelligence agencies, utilizes a vast number of informants to collect human intelligence (HUMINT in FBI jargon) on their targets.

40. Alexandra Natapoff, *SNITCHING: Criminal Informants and the Erosion of American Justice* (New York: New York University Press, 2009), 29.

41. Dick Lehr, "The Information Underworld: Police Reliance on Criminal Informants Is a Dangerous Game for Both," *Boston Globe*, October 16, 1988, A27.

42. *The Intercept*, Trevor Aaronson, "The FBI Gives Itself a Lot of Rope to Pull in Informants," January 31, 2017, accessed October 28, 2019, https://theintercept.com /2017/01/31/the fbi-gives-itself-a-lot-of-rope-to-pull-in-informants/.

43. National Archives, *Federal Register*, Executive Orders, Executive Order 10450-Security Requirements for Government Employees, May 27, 1953, accessed October 29, 2019, www.archives.gov/federal-register/codification/executive-order/10 450.html/. This EO revoked the prior one, 9835 known as the Loyalty Oath.

44. I thank Dianne Solis, who first discussed the Joe Molina case with me and gave me copies of the material she had accumulated on this person for her story, including the testimony cited below in endnote 2. She was a journalist for *The Dallas Morning News* at that time, now retired. Her story can be accessed at www.dallasnews.com/n ews/east-dallas/2013/09/13/dallas-mexican-americans-remember-the-jfk-years-surve illance-by-fbi/. Solis first learned of the Molina case from documents at the Mary Ferrell Foundation, Dallas, Texas. Ms. Ferrell passed away in 2004 but her work is available online at www.maryferrell.org/.

45. Jose Rodriguez Molina a.k.a. Joe Molina was interrogated by police shortly after the assassination of President John F. Kennedy in front of his place of employment. He subsequently was called on April 7, 1964, to testify under oath by legal counsel for the President's Commission on the Assassination of President John F. Kennedy, Mr. Joseph A. Ball and Mr. Samuel A. Stern, assistant counsel conducted the questioning at the US Attorney's Office in Dallas, Texas. The seven pages of testimony are not numbered but for the numbers beginning with 368 thru 373 inserted in pages willy-nilly. I numbered the pages at right bottom in black ink 1-7. I will use my numbering in the citations to this narration and reference it as Molina testimony.

46. Molina testimony, 6.

47. Among the most quoted and followed was the District Attorney for New Orleans, Louisiana, James Garrison. He wrote *On the Trail of the Assassins: One Man's Quest to Solve the Murder of President Kennedy* (New York: Sheridan Square Publications, 1998). His entire theory sits on the route map published in the Dallas newspapers that does not show the route to be past the Dallas School Book Depository on Elm Street. Who changed the route is the question and why? The answer leads to the assassins knowing the route and where to shoot from as the motorcade drove by below this building. A more recent book with some new information is James W. Douglas, *JFK and the Unspeakable: Why He Died and Why It Matters* (New York: Touchstone Books, 2008).

48. See front page of both *The Dallas Times Herald* and *The Dallas Morning News* of November 22, 1963, for this route map. It does not have the motorcade going down Elm Street in front of the book depository building.

49. Molina testimony, 6.

50. *Ibid.*, 1.

51. *Ibid.*, 1–2.

52. Jerry P. Shinley, another JFK assassination researcher, states Molina and family were interrogated for "over a period of 6 or 7 hours" and cites the Warren Commission Report at pages 237–238 for that assertion. See his website at www.jfk -online.com/shinley.html and enter Joe Molina at search box on bottom left to find this letter with this information and more.

53. Molina testimony, 2–4.

54. *Ibid.*, 4.

55. *Ibid.*, 4.

56. Ramos, *The American G.I. Forum*, 147,149.

57. See www.dignitymemorial.com/obituairies/Dallas-Tx/joe-molina-7477217/. Accessed October 23, 2019.

58. Shinley's letter posted on his website cited above in endnote 8, which is dated July 17, 1998, on three subjects: Joe Molina, Bill Lowery, and John Stanford.

## Chapter 8

# The Border Coverage Program, the US Intervention in Mexico's Internal Affairs

The Mexican government to this day proudly asserts a major foundational piece of its foreign policy as the dictum once uttered on July 15, 1867, by President Benito Juarez: *Entre los individos, como entre la naciones, el respeto al derecho ajeno es la paz.* Between individuals, like between nations, respect for the rights of others is peace. This Mexican worldview and pledge toward self-governance and self-determination has become their basis of human dignity. During the entire history of relations between the United States and Mexico, the former has repeatedly interfered in Mexican affairs and sovereignty; however, while the latter has not, but for an individual act by Francisco "Pancho" Villa during the course of the Mexican Revolution by raiding Columbus, New Mexico. Even this act, was not taken or sanctioned by the Mexican nation.

Lars Schoultz, noted Latin Americanist scholar, in his book on the history of US policy toward Latin America documents with example after example the hundreds upon hundreds of US interventions in all countries of Latin America plus the Caribbean, including Mexico. The reasons for the interventions, he explains, are "the policies the United States has used to protect its interests in Latin America. It is about the way a powerful nation treats its weaker neighbors."[1] He further describes the "protect its interests" as a threefold strategy: Maintain hegemony over the region; maintain the inhabitants of Latin American in an inferior status and their countries underdeveloped; and impose a bureaucratic structure and laws on these nations that promote US economic interests and US security beginning with the huge disparity in value of those nation's currency and the US dollar.[2]

This chapter details and examines one such interventionist program, illegal and criminal, conducted by the Federal Bureau of Investigation (FBI) in Mexico from the late 1950s to at least 1971, the Border Coverage Program

(BOCOV) by its acronym and code name. I have pursued release of these files since 1983 when I was institutionally linked to Western Oregon State College in Monmouth, Oregon. I filed a Freedom of Information Act (FOIA) requesting such files on BOCOV, number 234,920. I was denied on October 18, 1983 under exemption (b) (1). "Please be advised the material you requested on the BOCOV Program is being withheld in its entirety in order to protect materials which are exempt from disclosure pursuant to that exemption under Title 5, United States Code, Section 552 of the FOIA." I appealed by letter on October 25 that year. That appeal was also denied by letter dated January 20, 1984, by the US Assistant Attorney General at the time, Jonathan C. Rose: "After careful consideration of your appeal, I have decided to affirm the initial action in this case." I was also advised by Mr. Rose that judicial review of this action on the appeal was available "in the United States District Court for the judicial district in which you reside." I lived some seventy miles from Portland, the situs for a federal district court and had no money with which to launch a complex litigation fight with the US government. And, I did not. Instead I contacted others doing similar research and obtained some documents from these colleagues. Many years later, I filed my FOI/PA request again, number 1329195-000, in 2015. This request met with some success and I obtained forty-seven pages of documents from the thousands that must exist.

## COINTELPRO: BOCOV, FBI FILE NUMBER 100-434445-45

The Border Coverage Program or BOCOV allegedly was terminated by the FBI in 1971. But was it? The FBI has undergone several personnel changes from top to bottom and many of the principals involved in the era of admitted BOCOV operations are deceased. The nature and culture of the FBI, however, has not changed much; the FBI still conducts intelligence operations in Mexico and other countries. The FBI maintains a presence in every US Embassy with its Legal Attaché position across the globe. What has also changed is at the cabinet level reorganization from the White House after 9/11 to create the Department of Homeland Security (DHS) and break up the Immigration and Naturalization Service (INS) into three agencies: US Customs and Border Protection (CBP), US Citizenship and Immigration Services (CIS); and US Immigration and Customs Enforcement (ICE). The FBI and INS back in the days of BOCOV collaborated on recruiting informants at crossing points along the US-Mexico border. Perhaps today, the FBI is collaborating with DHS via CBP or ICE and conducting the same type of surveillance and counter-intelligence activity in Mexico. The CBP rolled out a new plan for DHS on May 15, 2009, called the SBI*net* Program with an initial allocation of $100 million in funding to conduct surveillance along the Southwest border; "sensor technology being procured includes mobile and fixed towers, cameras, radars and unattended ground sensors."[3] And, in this modern age of government contracting, most of the hardware, software, and even personnel will be from the private sector. The surveillance methods of the past have given way to dataveillance and invasive techniques that avoid physical contact. Cameras and computers and iPhones all can see, hear, record, capture on video/photograph/and monitor almost all kinds of human activity. Metadata analysis can provide patterns and word searchable data on any electronic transmission from telephone calls, to emails to credit card transactions. Add pilotless drones to the mix and the US-Mexico border is under more surveillance now than during the days of BOCOV.

## Tactics Employed by the FBI in Mexico

As will be seen in the documents by review that follows, the FBI employed these dozen tactics in Mexico:

1. The FBI utilized established sources and hired informants to infiltrate local organizations.
2. The FBI prepared and published articles editorializing against the activities of persons and organizations of which they did not approve.
3. The FBI suppressed Mexican publications favorable to these same targeted persons and groups or which were critical of the United States.
4. The FBI agents send insidious anonymous mailings intended to character assassinate persons and destroy trust and promote factionalism.
5. The FBI in collusion with the INS posed agents as INS agents to fake interviews for border crossing card applications. The withholding of an existing or potential card was used to recruit informants.
6. The FBI printed and disseminated libelous and slanderous leaflets and handbills against individuals and organizations.
7. The FBI surveilled commercial bookstores and magazine stands for the sale of communist literature or any other deemed subversive.
8. The FBI initiated rumors and made innuendos about personal activities of influential individuals whose political views were deemed inimical to US interests.
9. The FBI utilized US consular offices for many of these activities.
10. The FBI promoted an interest in making homemade bombs among groups designed for destruction and neutralization.
11. The FBI made terroristic threats directly against individuals.
12. The FBI lied to the public and other US government officials about the existence of BOCOV and its activities for many years during various presidential administrations.

## BOCOV Begins with Training Conferences

The BOCOV files released do not include the years from 1956 to 1961, those were withheld entirely. The file begins with a five-page document from the director, FBI to the SAC, San Diego dated January 9, 1961, which alludes in the first line to one of those planning conferences for BOCOV that took place, "ReBulet 11-14-60, captioned 'BOCOV,' which set forth action taken on the recommendation made by the 10/24-25/60 Border Coverage Conference which was held at San Diego." Furthermore, it states in this opening and second paragraphs:

> That letter in part advised that there is definitely a place for consideration of some of the tactics currently employed in the Counterintelligence Program on the Border Coverage Program. It was pointed out that the five border offices and the Legal Attaché's Office should be alert for the application of disruptive tactics and in each case should clear with the Bureau in advance any suggestions along those lines.
>
> It is believed that sufficient time has now lapsed for each office to have made an analytical study of the situation faced by it and should be in a position to furnish suggestions to the Bureau regarding means which could be taken to apply counterintelligence tactics where such tactics may be feasible. (p.1)

The more direct instructions on counterintelligence tactics follow:

> In connection with the Counterintelligence-Border Coverage Program, the best method for disorganizing the Communist Party (CP) of related organizations is disruption from within. This can be done through the use of selected informants under proper guidance to raise controversial issues within the organization; to make legitimate criticisms of organizational operations, activities, or lack of activities, or to bring out into the open latent factionalism. In connection with this program, it must be borne in mind that harassment is not to be undertaken merely for the sake of harassment but in each instance the tactics are to be undertaken with a specific purpose in mind of disrupting communist and related activities. (p1)

The next three pages outline in detail the four factors the director, FBI recommended to each of the five field offices implementing this program: El Paso (16), Phoenix (38), San Antonio (45), San Diego (46), and Mexico City (221).[4] First listed is Selection of Informants. The FBI director recommended an analysis of available informants to engage in disruptive tactics. He asked each office to ensure training and briefing on issues and controversial subjects to be raised. Then he listed [six lines redacted] and reminded field officers he had to approve the informants selected before any briefing. Given this was a long-range plan, development of the informants was a necessary goal. The second factor recommended is heavily redacted but the gist seems to be that in the redacted portions the director, FBI actually listed specific illegal activities. It reads as follows in its entirety:

2. Organizational Tactics-Consideration should be given to [redacted 3 lines]. Consideration should be given to the possibility of having [redacted 6 lines]. All border coverage Agents in offices with counterintelligence potential should be alert for any tactics of this type which can be used. (p.2)

Factor 3 recommendation is titled "3. Psychological Tactics-." And, it recommends "anonymous mailings of literature regarding the weaknesses and inhumanitarian aspects of communist either as a party or as individuals." Specifically, it asks the Mexico City office to clip "newspaper or magazine articles" which could be used. This item has about six to seven lines redacted. Item 4. is most alarming given its heading: "4. Neutralization of Individuals-." The recommendation that follows is bland compared to what FBI agents and other intelligence officers understand the word "neutralize" to mean. Ann Mari Buitrago in her book defines to word among the FBI operatives to mean "to render harmless or inactive."[5] The CIA, on the other hand, and the intellectual, conceptual, and applied practitioners of "neutralization" of the Phoenix Program in Southeast Asia, Central America, Mexico, and other countries, according to Douglas Valentine means assassination, murder, cover-up suicide, homicide, induced death, and the like.[6] At this time, Hoover wrote:

Consideration should be given to tactics which would bring individual communist leaders under suspicion of being "imperialist agents," agent provocateur, etc. or generally discrediting them in the eyes of their fellow communists.

The Bureau will consider any well-conceived plan of causing disruption inside the CP or related organizations. In any counterintelligence operation, however, it is imperative that the office submitting the recommendations make sure that it will not jeopardize informant coverage or cause embarrassment to the Bureau. (p.3)

Even though Director Hoover zeroed in on communists as the main targets of BOCOV, the key words or those that follow it, "or related organizations," which in his mind and that of the FBI's culture meant any dissident and perceived left of center organization or leader. In short, it was almost everyone in the Chicano Movement of the time. Hoover knew this, so he added just below factor recommendation 4. That "Albuquerque, through absolute lack of communist activity, is not in a position to implement a counterintelligence

program, however, a copy of this communication is being sent for information of that office." Why? Perhaps, it was suggestions for the future to keep in
mind because at that time, Reies Lopez Tijerina, the Black Berets, and other
Chicano activists on the University of New Mexico and Highlands University
already were under FBI surveillance for suspected "communist," the New
Left COINTELPRO, and the Mexican American Militancy COINTELPRO
investigations.[7] Lorena Oropeza also discusses the same FBI investigations
and use of an informant, Tim Chapa, I interviewed in June 2000 of Tijerina
and others at that time[8] (p.3).

Hoover continued advising all other of the five offices in this lengthy memo
with specific recommendations. He advised the San Antonio office to keep
investigating communist activity "outside of Santa Apolonia." He further
opined that the CP in Juarez was "ineffectual" therefore El Paso should seek
to disrupt the CP Central Committee for the state of Chihuahua and continue
to raise controversial issues and sharpen antagonism among those still holding communist views and sympathies. Hoover went further and suggested to
El Paso and San Antonio to target non-active Communist Party members to
draw out "their communist sympathies and destroy their potential usefulness
as Soviet intelligence agents." In Phoenix, he suggested the FBI office target
"pro-communist groups," for the same reason (p.4). In San Diego and Mexico
City, Hoover wanted the Popular Socialist Party also targeted for BOCOV
counterintelligence activity (p.5).

One by one, the FBI field office began to respond to Hoover's recommendations on tactics to employ to further the goals of BOCOV. San Antonio was
first on January 11 in a two-page memo. But, they prefaced, "As yet, however, no situations have come to mind where we feel that the utilization of the
Counterintelligence Program can be safely undertaken with the possibility of
productive results" (p.1). The memo does have an entire paragraph of about
ten lines redacted which could be about the Santa Apolonia area. I lived in
San Antonio during my years at St. Mary's University and never heard of this
name in relation to a neighborhood, *colonia*, church, barrio, cemetery, or new
development. SAC, El Paso responded next on January 18 with a two-page
memo informing that the State of Chihuahua Communist Party had an estimated membership of fifteen in Juarez. Several names, perhaps informants,
were redacted in the body of this transmission. Like, San Antonio, this SAC
closed his message with "No disruptive tactics possibilities appear to exist
regarding the PCM in Chihuahua City, Mexico since, due to ineffectiveness
in the formal organization there as well as in Juarez there is little to disrupt"
(p.1). San Diego FBI took a month to respond but did on February 7 with a
lengthy seven-page report. This office also reported a small membership in
the Communist Party of *Baja California* (PCMBC). Names are listed but
redacted. It did mention that the PCMBC was divided into two geographical

groups, one over by *Mexcali* and the *Mexicali* Valley area and the other in *Tijuana*. Each had separate governing structures at the municipal level and the names of these persons were also redacted (p.2). In what seems a huge contradiction to the opening paragraph of the report, the SAC, San Diego under the subtitle in capital letters: "TOTAL NUMBER OF COMMUNISTS, FORMER COMMUNISTS, COMMUNIST SYMPATHIZERS, AND OTHER SUBVERSIVES IN THE AREA COVERED BY THE SAN DIEGO OFFICE" provided numbers in each category. The total being 881 but active only 248. The 248 are broken up into the centers of activity noted above, "202 are located in the Mexicali, B.C. area, 26 in Tijuana and 20 in Ensenada, B.C. area" (p.3).

A major problem with analysis of this makeshift table is the lack of definition. What criteria make for a communist sympathizer, for example, and how do you count such persons? The SAC, San Diego provided names of organizations in the last four pages of the report with a brief description of each that the PCM in B.C. had created over the years. Those listed are "STAVE-SINDICATO DE TRABAJADORES AGRICOLAS DEL VALLE DE MEXICALI"; "SINDICATO DE OFICIOS VARIOS (SOV)"; "UGOCM (UNION GENERAL OBREROS Y CAMPESINOS MEXICANOS)" (p.4). "PARTIDO POPULAR SOCIALISTA-POPULAR SOCIALIST PARTY"; and in parentheses "(Formerly the Popular Party)"; "ASI (ASOCIACION DE  SINDICATOS INDEPENDIENTES)" (p.5); "CIRCULO DE ESTUDIOS MEXICANOS (CEM)"; "LIGA AGRARIA ESTATAL-State Agrarian League" (p.6). Each description had some redacted lines and the last one continued into almost all of the content in the last page (p.7).

The "LEGAT, MEXICO (80-10)" on February 9, 1961, notified the director, FBI by three-page memo that [name redacted] of the Monterrey Resident Agency telephonically advised that [redacted name] 1961, edition of the magazine *Cierto-Revista de Monterrey*, in which the Monterrey newspaper, *El Norte* is criticized and tied it to defending FBI activity in Mexico. This edition also attacked President Eisenhower and the President of Mexico. [Name redacted] informed that the "Mexican Ministry of Government" and "the State of Nuevo Leon" are both taking action against the magazine with attempts to suppress the circulation. These entities or their surrogates were going to buy up all the copies printed, some 500 issues which retailed at $2 pesos a copy. Given the suppression, only "20 or 30 copies of the current January issue have actually reached the stands; far from the end of the first print run" (p.1). The content found offensive was translated into English and provided. It does mention the meeting between the US or Mexican presidents. In fact, SAC, San Diego claims the governor of Nuevo Leon personally visited the Legat's office in the US Embassy located in Mexico to apologize for the article (p.3). The governor pledged to "terminate such scandalous articles." What is striking to me about this memo is the disclosure of a "resident agency," in Monterrey as part of BOCOV in the opening paragraph. Apparently, BOCOV operated out of Monterrey as well, not just the other five US offices and Mexico City. And, that a Mexican governor would seek out [redacted name] and pledge to shut down that type of reporting. How? Perhaps, this is the BOCOV way of stating the reverse; that they asked the governor to help shut down the magazine. Is that not disruptive?

The "Legat, Mexico (100-2080)" reported to "Director, FBI (100-434445-221)" again on February 14, responding with more information "ReBuLet 1/9/61 to San Diego" in four-page memorandum. The Legat makes a case why applying BOCOV tactics via his office differs widely from US FBI field offices. Regrettably, the entire discussion is redacted (p.1). The Legat does add his own opinion on program secrecy:

> you should bear in mind the fact that the Bureau's interests in disruptive tactics under the counterintelligence program should be held very tightly within your office on a need-to-know-basis and no indication of the existence of this program should be given to any outside agency. (p.2)

Interestingly, there is a "NOTE ON YELLOW:" subtitle at the very end of this page and the wording is potentially very threatening to either the Bureau or the Legat depending on who wrote it which is not clear:

> The Legal Attaché's analysis of the potential of his office under this program is largely negative in nature although it adds nothing to the information already available to the Bureau relative to the possible difficulties involved. [Redacted second paragraph entirely (p2) and continuing with redacted paragraphs into pages 3 and 4 which ends the memo]. (p.4)

The director, FBI, tersely responds to the legal attaché, Mexico City on March 3, 1961: "Your analysis of the problems faced in Mexico in implementing this project are interesting although they do not include aspects which were not previously known to the Bureau." The remaining three paragraphs to end of the solo page are redacted so no sense can be made of the negatively worded and constructed opening sentence. The director seems to be saying, "Tell me something I do not know." The next week, March 10, the director, FBI sent a one-page memo to SAC, Phoenix asking him to "be alert for any circumstances which develop wherein disruptive tactics could be utilized to widen the rift between [redacted names] and his adherents." And, in the next paragraph, Hoover asked for the SAC to "furnish your comments regarding [more redacted lines]." Special mention is made "to watch for an opportunity . . . to accentuate the difficulties and conflicts which are apparently besetting the Communist Party, the Popular Socialist Party and the Union of Peasants and Farm Laborers (UGOCM) groups in Cananea" (p.1).

## Special Mail Room File for BOCOV

The BOCOV Program was a highly secret counter-intelligence operation aimed at disrupting Mexican political parties and groups, namely the Communist Party and the Socialist Party along with many other groups, Hoover and his G-Men deemed subversive and contrary to US interests. The main BOCOV file, 100-434445, as previously noted, was kept by the Bureau but a second file "due to its confidential nature" was "maintained in the Special Mail Room of the Files Section. This file should be released only with the approval of the Agent supervising the case," so reads the one-page memo from R.O. L'Allier to A.H. Belmont dated April 6, 1961, both high-ranking Hoover assistants. Alan Belmont had been Hoover's number 3 assistant director since 1961 and was the assistant director of the domestic intelligence division since 1951.[9] The Special File Room number for "the BOCOV file (100-356015) . . . should be given restricted circulation since the existence of that project should not become generally known" (p1).[10] Very heavily redacted document files were exchanged between the director, FBI and "Attention: Foreign Liaison Desk" in San Diego, California, FBI field office between March 29, two pages, and May 31, 1962, four pages. Only the latter listing of the 31st has enough legible content to analyze. This document begins with two long paragraphs of redacted material and only three legible lines with minimal redacted material of interest: "While in Los Angeles, she met [redacted name] and they were married in [redacted word containing five characters]. She advised that his date and place of birth were [redacted remainder of sentence]" (p.1). The "she" either was an informant or someone interviewed by someone in the San Diego office. The narrative about the person whose name is redacted from information taken again from the "she" or another informant. The person in question, not the "she" had "previously been identified through other means as identical with [name redacted.] 'About 1935' [4 character word redacted] left Los Angeles to live in Tijuana" (p.2). The narrative continues to discuss more information gleaned from "she" about work location for person in Tijuana and Mexico City, currently and in the past, as well as border crossings. This information may have been obtained from "she" under the extortion and blackmail used by the INS using the border cross cards; more on this special illegal scam to be explained later. But in this report, it is clear she was tricked into the discussion with a possibility of getting back her border crossing card:

When it was apparent to [name redacted] that [redacted word, could not immediately receive [redacted word] Border Crossing card, [redacted word] again
said [redacted words] would be willing to meet with United States representatives at [redacted word] although [redacted word] now conceded that it would
not matter to [redacted two words] whether or not [redacted word] could keep
[redacted word] card. (p.3)

The San Diego Foreign Liaison desk person making this report ended with,
"Under separate caption a letter will set out leads for Los Angeles, Phoenix,
and Legat to check relatives" (p.4).

The June 16, 1961, two-page transmission from the director, FBI to the SAC,
San Diego continues the narrative I assume about "she." Opening line begins,
"Reurlet 5/31/61 concerning the interview held with [redacted rest of sentence],
a member of the Communist Party in Tijuana." At bottom of this first page is
the most incriminating information against both the FBI and the INS.

NOTE: As part of the Counterintelligence—Border Coverage Program San
Diego was previously authorized to interview [8-10 characters redacted] under
pretext of the U.S. Immigration and Naturalization Service check point at San
Isidro, California. Arrangements were made for [3 characters redacted, perhaps
"her"] Border Crossing card to be picked up because [3 characters redacted,
perhaps "she"] highly valued that card, and it was expected that through [3
characters redacted, perhaps "her"] resentment at losing that card [3 characters
redacted, perhaps "she"] might bring pressure to bear on [11-12 characters
redacted] to disrupt [4 characters redacted] Communist Party activities. (p.1)

The top and last paragraphs of the following page are entirely redacted.
The middle section paragraph is worth quoting entirely given its continued
self-incrimination by the FBI and INS:

Local Liaison with INS in the San Diego area is excellent and for many
years San Diego has been able to use INS interview facilities for discreet
pretext interviews with subjects of security interest. It is believed San Diego's
plan to utilize INS interview facilities in this case is sound, and this appears
to be an effective opportunity. (p.2)

Not only does this specific memo approve and commend this tactic of
extortion and blackmail by both federal agencies but also indicates that "for
many years San Diego has been able to use INS interview facilities for discreet pretext interviews with subjects of security interest." This tactic then
predates the initiation of the Border Coverage Program. Moreover, it is held
up to be sure as a model to replicate at every border entry point, at least with
Mexico if not other border crossings then and perhaps now.

A follow-up three-page memo between the same two parties of June
27 has many redacted paragraph to render it useless for analytical and

insightful historical review of BOCOV activity; however, one line on page 2 is of interest because it name a new organization but without any description or further detail unless it is behind the redacted material. This reads as follows:

> For this reason, the Bureau is requested to authorize the San Diego Office to carry out these counterintelligence measures against the National liberation Movement when the occasion arises.[11]

R.O. L'Allier, reporting to his boss, William C. Sullivan, the 3rd man down in the chain of command at the FBI was the assistant director of Domestic Intelligence Operations from 1961 to 1971. As such, he was in charge of BOCOV and all the COINTELPRO operations. On June 27, 1961, L'Allier wrote to Sullivan a two-page report about a new right-wing group forming in Mexico that should be of interest to the FBI. L'Allier made reference to a prior report of June 16, 1961 (not released) captioned "Anti-Communist Activities in Mexico, Foreign Political Matters," that came from the Legat in Mexico City. This report stated that the National Action Party (PAN) and the National Sinarquist Union (UNS), both acronyms in Spanish, joined with "various Catholic groups to combat communism" and "Mexico City suggested possibility of using that organization to harass and disrupt the communists." The first two organizations were described as "the extreme right in Mexican politics and at various times during World War II were reported to be pro-Fascist." Reportedly, "Special Agent Sheldon W. Parks was introduced to the principal leaders of the new organization by [remaining line redacted] informant who is [remaining line redacted] Attorney [name redacted] one of the principal figures in the new organization" (p.1). This new group of principal figures asked the FBI Mexico City office to help them "throw out the corrupt political machines which have held Mexico back for years and to overcome communist influence in Mexico." The new group also claimed credit for a 100,000-person anticommunist demonstration in Puebla, Mexico (p.1). According to this report the "Legal Attache suggests use of this organization to leak information concerning communist activities and pending demonstrations for use in the press or for counterdemonstrations" (p.2). In the last two paragraphs of this last page under "OBSERVATIONS:" and "ACTION:" some cautious words are used to recommend holding off on any direct contact with the new group and not use them "for communist harassment purposes." And, this should and was put into an "attached letter be sent to Mexico advising that . . ." (p.2). This letter was not released nor made part of this report; but more reports on this developing organization were requested. "Mexico" did respond, and it was the Foreign Liaison Desk writing to director, FBI which I assumed was part of the FBI's Legal Attache team housed in the US Embassy; however, just below the letterhead is typed

"San Diego, California." Reading the heavily redacted pages and noting the withheld pages, apparently, the San Diego FBI field office had such a desk as part of its BOCOV operations. The date of this seven-page response is July 10, 1961; three pages were withheld entirely, and two others have the page number redacted so it is not known what correct sequence to read the transmission. What can be gleaned from information left readable is that another local file was opened on [redacted name] and "the Bureau will be asked for authority to talk to [name redacted] along the same lines as the approached used on [name redacted]." And, San Diego will seek "to have published in the local newspapers of Baja California the thesis entitled '*Cooperacion Bade Para El Buen Funcionamiento de la Ley.*'" The next page, but not numbered has two large blocks of redacted material and in between them is this message: "It is not known if [redacted name] has other family members who hold border crossing cards." The last page released has much redacted but for a closing sentence: "The San Diego office will continue to give this important function aggressive and energetic thought and every possible avenue to this project will be utilized subject to Bureau approval" (p.7). We must all continue to wonder what they actually did in Tijuana, Baja California, and rest of Mexico.

SAC, El Paso chimes in after the summer is past on September 21, 1961, with a one-page memo to the director, FBI referenced prior letters in the year and their report which was not released. Apparently, El Paso was waiting on the Bureau for instruction, more like authorization, and had not received any hence, "Pending further instructions from the Bureau, no action is being taken in this matter." Unlike El Paso, the director, FBI did respond to the SAC, San Diego, however, on October 4, 1961, about their suggestions in a four-page memo of which only two pages were released. The first paragraph is redacted so we are in the dark about who or what is being discussed. In the next paragraph, we learn Hoover is willing to let San Diego forward but he requests, "that you advise the Bureau whether [name redacted] is considered to have any informant potential which would be destroyed if his status as a CP leader were to be undermined." The next paragraph is also entirely redacted but Hoover promises to look at what they have in mind, but only after, "receipt of your reply relative to [redacted name] informant potential." Obviously, Hoover is most concerned with keeping the roster of informants viable over new initiatives that could jeopardize that source of information and their counterintelligence activity.

SAC, El Paso on October 9, 1961, receives a "personal attention" short one-page note from the director, FBI acknowledging a submission of tactics to be used against [redacted name and entire paragraph following to end the message]. Ten days later, SAC, El Paso submitted some piece of literature for approval by the director to be disseminated. The opening paragraph is redacted, and the remaining sentences given more redacted names or pronouns, She, He, Her, Him, etc. are not intelligible. The last line of the note suggests the planned tactic involved a book store or magazine/newspaper stand because, [redacted 4-5 words] "currently displays the flag bearing the words, 'Viva Cuba.'"

## Who Is Julio Prado Valdez?

The front page of this next memo was not released, or the second page dated but seems to be a recommendation of a tactic, a flyer or handbill, about a person named Julio Prado Valdez to be distributed.[12] The memo was sent to Assistant Director William Sullivan, previously identified by an unidentified FBI staffer recommending "San Diego's counterintelligence proposal be approved." It was approved because it was distributed but that exchange of memos on this tactic was not released. The bilingual, double-spaced, all capitalized handbill is entirely quoted here for the full flavor of its creative and inciting verbiage to be appreciated as well as the bilingual incapacity of FBI personnel involved this endeavor. It is single-spaced here:

JULIO PRADO VALDEZ
WHO IS JULIO PRADO VALDEZ? IS HE A DOCTOR? IT HE A FRIEND
OF THE POOR? IS HE A COMMUNIST? DOES HE BELIEVE IN JUS-
TICE FOR ALL?
NO! THE TRUTH IS
JULIO PRADO IS RICH. HE IS A LANDLORD. HE HAS BUSINESSES.
HE HAS A CLINIC. HE HAS NO INTEREST IN THE POOR. PRADO IS
ONLY INTERESTED IN HIMSELF.
NO ONE CAN BELIEVE WHAT PRADO SAYS. NO ONE LIKES THIS
MAN BECAUSE HE IS A MILLIONAIRE AND SEEKS HIS WAY OF
LIFE FROM A PARTY THAT DOES NOT EXIST. IT IS A FANTASY.

## Organized Committee of Baja California

JULIO PRADO VALDEZ
? QUIEN ES JULIO PRADO VALDEZ? ? ES MEDICO? ? ES AMIGO DEL
POBRE?
? ES COMUNISTA? ? CREE EN JUSTICIA PARA TODOS?
!NO! LA VERDAD ES
JULIO PRADO VALDEZ ES RICO. ES CASA TENIENTE. TIENE
NEGOCIOS.
TIENE UNA CLINICA. NO TIENE INTERES EN LOS POBRES. PRADO
TIENE INTERES EN SI MISMO.

LO QUE PRADO DICE NADIEN LE CREE. NADIEN QUIERE A ESTE
  HOMBRE PORQUE
ES UN CRESCO Y BUSCA SU MEDIO DE VIVIR DE UN PARTIDO QUE
  NO EXISTE. ES UN FANTASMA.

Comite Organizada de Baja California. (p.3)

Someone at the FBI did catch some errors in the copy submitted for
approval and was approved with only one correction: "Note that in the
Spanish language the question marks appear at the beginning and ending of
a sentence. The question mark at the beginning of the sentence is inverted."
This someone forgot to include the same rule for an exclamation point.
Several words in English are not translated correctly such as "fantasy" at
the end of the message. *Fantasma* is a phantom not a fantasy. "Organized
Committee" is not *"Comite Organizada,"* that is a literal translation; it
should be *"Comite Organizador.* And, most importantly to my view, why is
the English version at the top of the hand bill? Why even include an English
portion if it was to be distributed in Baja California among Mexicans not
English-speaking tourists?

## Into the Next Year: 1962

SAC, San Diego let half a year pass, unless more files were withheld, before
they sent their decoded copy of a two-page teletype dated May 26, 1962, to
the director, FBI about BOCOV. Again, a heavily redacted first paragraph
begins the teletype and proceeded to warn. Of a student demonstration
that took place the night before in front of City Hall in Tijuana and then
walked over to the United States-Mexico border crossing area. The protestors chanted "Cuba Si Yanqui No!" and "We Want Water." The police shot
into the air and then resorted to tear gas which broke up the demonstration.
The police arrested forty students and the teletype indicates all were released
"half hour later" (p.1). Apparently, the US media picked up the story and
gave it "wide publicity in San Diego area newspapers and through medium
of radio" (p.2). A month later on June 28, SAC, San Diego sent a single-page
memo to the director, FBI attention the Foreign Liaison Desk. I assume now
that every border FBI office and the Bureau headquarters all had such a staff
person with this title tied the BOCOV COINTELPRO. This memo reported
on the aftermath of the student protest and police action as being a very successful one in that "the Guerra Montemayor Cell has been disbanded and
some degree of confusion and distrust still exists." Regrettably, half of the
memo is redacted. The closing informed Hoover that they would "be alert
to such incidents and will follow the procedure of immediately advising the
interested U.S. Government agency." Perhaps, this means other agencies like
INS were also involved in drawing benefit from BOCOV. SAC, San Diego a

week later on July 6, 1962, is being overly cautious about some matter. Like the prior communication, the first half of the one-page memo is redacted. All that remains is the cautious wording:

> The San Diego office, however, wishes to hold in abeyance making any recommendation regarding this matter until it is in receipt of the Legat, Mexico's observation regarding the effect such a letter might have on their operations.

The letter alluded to was not released but it did come from Hoover and dated June 22, 1962. Whatever the subject matter was about a successful tactic, it pleased Hoover because he responded to SAC, San Diego a week later on July 13 asking for names of anyone in operations "handled by personnel of your office merit commendation, you should advise the Bureau with your recommendations."

## The Albuquerque BOCOV Conference

Events slowed for the overall BOCOV Program over the remainder of the summer of 1962. In the fall, Hoover called his border agents from all field office to a conference held in Albuquerque, New Mexico on November 13 and 14. The topic was a letter sent to the Bureau from SAC, San Diego but not released. The content is not known and the redacted paragraph which is the bulk of the three-page memo further obscures what the message could have been about. The redacted material continues into two-thirds of the second page. In the last paragraph of this page, however, the San Diego office requested advance authorization to "carry out these counterintelligence measures against the National Liberation Movement when the occasion arises." Surely, "these counterintelligence measures" were described in the redacted material. On the last page, 3, whatever it was being requested for approval had to do with disrupting and causing dissention in the ranks of the groups "vying for power within the MLN in the State of Lower California."

I was unable and continue to be in obtaining the program of these various BOCOV conferences and list of attendees.

## The Case of Robert Mayhew in 1963

D.J. Brennan alerted Assistant Director William Sullivan on March 14, 1963, by a two-page memo that "Robert Mayhew was to institute classes to teach the English language at the State Public Library in Mexicali." Brennan picked that up from an open source, "the Mexicali newspaper, 'ABC'." Mayhew must have been of interest to the top echelons of the FBI for other reasons because only three lines quoted above are unredacted in the first page of this memo. Mayhew's teaching apparently had to be disrupted and prevented from taking place. Brennan wrote, "continuing consideration is being given this matter, particularly as to the possibility of exploiting the subject's alleged frequent drunkenness. As instructed, Bureau authority will be requested before implementing any proposed counter intelligence" (p.2).

Between dealing with Mayhew's classes to teach English and the pending Julio Prado Valdez flyer, SAC, El Paso receives a two-paragraph teletype note from the director, FBI on March 3, 1963. The opening paragraph is entirely redacted. The second reads:

> give careful consideration to this situation with the possibility in mind of working out some counterintelligence tactic which could be utilized not only to eliminate the possible use of those bombs for terroristic purposes but also to embarrass the Communist Party and thereby assist in curtailing its continued operations in Juarez.

There was no prior information released as to who had bombs or what type bombs anyone had in Juarez, Mexico across from El Paso, Texas.

The Mayhew case came up again in a one-page memo from the SAC, San Diego to the director, Attention: Foreign Liaison Desk dated April 30, 1963. However, the entire page is redacted but for a single closing line about advising the Bureau if any other developments take place. The next memo is disturbing. Dated May 10, 1963, surely not a happy Mother's Day for Robert Mayhew, Hoover notified the SAC, San Diego that it had read its letter of April 30, advising "that the English language classes formerly held by [name redacted, but it was stated previously] the State Public Library in Mexicali have been discontinued." The remaining page material is entirely redacted. Robert Mayhew's classes were "neutralized."

A year later, April 9, 1964, Hoover contacted the SAC, San Diego via a two-page memo about the national presidential elections in Mexico but the exact narrative is redacted. This lone sentence is situated between redacted paragraphs on the first page, "Based on your assurance that no embarrassment to the Bureau would ensue as a result of [redacted remainder of partial sentence] in this activity" [Redacted 2 more sentences and remainder of page]. The second page again alludes to the national election again and states "close supervision has been given [redacted lines] insure [*sic*] that no embarrassing situations would develop." Obviously, the FBI did not want to be caught by Mexican authorities or the Mexican press trying to influence the outcome of the Mexican national election of 1964.

In 1965, the state and municipal elections took place in Mexico and these were of interest to Hoover. He cautioned again and referenced the 1964 letter to be careful with tactics by single-page memo dated April 21, 1965.

SAC, San Diego responded to that 1964 letter advising Hoover that "thus far activities of the PCM with regard to the political campaign appear to be ineffectual and it is not believed that a counterintelligence project in this connection would serve any useful purpose." Clearly, the FBI under the BOCOV Program had plans to undermine Mexican elections, national and state and local, but opportunities did not present themselves. Again on June 22, 1965, SAC, San Diego alerts Hoover Attention: Nationalities Intelligence Section, a name not previously encountered in FBI documents, by one-page memo that the elections will take place in July 1965. In closing, he added, "San Diego will continue to be alert for any opportunity to implement the counterintelligence program. No action will be taken without prior Bureau authority." Beginning the new year, 1966, SAC, San Diego notified Hoover that all is calm and has been since after the elections in July past. The SAC observed that the activities of the PEP, the PCM, and "other related organizations" are presently seeking to revive themselves "after their low ebb of activity at the end of the political campaign." Throughout the year, memos went back and forth between SAC, San Diego, the center of most BOCOV activity, and FBI headquarters stating the same: nothing much happening but each memo had heavy redacting. By the beginning of 1967, SAC, San Diego repeated the news of no news on the BOCOV front. The same type of report was sent on August 18, 1967, with only one new item, the formation of a Communist Youth Group in the Tijuana area. By November 8, however, SAC, San Diego does request approval for a tactic to be employed but the matter is all redacted. A portion was not redacted properly, and it reads, "The projector and film were returned to the U.S. Consulate on 10/24/1967. It is pointed out to the Bureau that the San Diego Office is most cognizant of the sensitive nature of this program [redacted and unreadable two sentences follow]."

On February 3, 1968, SAC, San Diego sent a two-page memo Hoover Attention the Latin American Section (another term not found in prior documents). The first page is heavily redacted but the second contains a telling phrase in the closing paragraph: "The San Diego Office is, of course, attempting to find out the identity of this individual in order that appropriate action can be taken." Who, what, when, why are all in the air given no other disclosure. The subsequent memos between San Diego and Hoover dated May 7, July 26, July 29, and October 25, do not add anything new to the analysis here. However, on November 29, the Julio Prado Valdez handbills were about to be distributed. On January 29, 1969, ten copies of the handbill were sent to the Bureau by the SAC, San Diego and a copy to the Legat, Mexico. That same day, W.R. Wannall wrote a one-page memo to William Sullivan, his boss of the FBI's Domestic Intelligence Division, lauding the success of the Prado Valdez handbill operation. He wrote:

we have now learned the distribution of the handbill has caused additional dissent among PCM followers and is causing considerable concern on part of Prado as to strength of his leadership. Despite intense efforts by Prado to determine originator of handbill, our operation continues to remain completely secure. Prado now blames dissatisfied Mexican leftist students and dissident members of his own group for this disruptive action.

W.R. Wannall also reported that the results and effect of this handbill tactic as part of the BOCOV Program "have been disseminated to Department of State, Central Intelligence Agency and the military without identifying our participation in the operation."[13]

SAC, San Antonio chimes in after a long period of inactivity with BOCOV on March 6, 1969 with a three-page memo to Hoover. Regrettably, like other documents, the heavy redacted portions do not leave much information to analyze but for a dismal short blurb about "there is some indication of personality clashes between one or two local leaders at Rio Bravo" (p.1). The following page begins with "connections between the PCM in the two towns and [redacted name] reduce our informants opportunity to gather information." The remaining entire page is redacted (p.2). In this redacted material, however, San Antonio is asking Hoover to approve a tactic. This is the top line of the page wording while the remainder of the page is also redacted: "Accordingly Bureau authority is requested to employ the tactic mentioned above against [redacted remainder of sentence] (p.3).

SAC, San Diego reported to the director, FBI for several months on these dates: 3/27/69, 4/3/69, 9/29/69, and 7/3/69 that due to the lack of activity during this time, the San Diego office had not originated any additional projects in connection with the BOCOV Program. Not until the following year on March 4, 1970, did the San Diego field office alert Hoover in a one-page memo about the "forthcoming national elections in the Republic of Mexico." And, it warned that the "Communist Party of Mexico in the State of Lower California is carrying out all of its activities with a great deal of caution for fear of governmental reprisal." The next and final paragraph on the solo page is redacted. That same month on the 23rd, SAC, El Paso reported the leftist groups in the Juarez area "have such attendance as to be almost completely negligible." El Paso states it will not take any disruptive action under these circumstances.

SAC, San Diego repeated their "lack of activity" by communists in Baja California and their fear of government reprisals has kept things inopportune to employ BOCOV tactics in a one-page memo dated June 11, 1970, to Hoover. Again on September 9, 1970, to December 2, 1970, basically the same message between these parties was sent. The next year, according to the first memo between San Diego and Hoover, dated February 23, 1971, was the same. By May 5, San Diego SAC only reported that the MCP was only engaged in a "national fund raising campaign." These 1970–1971 memos seem to indicate the BOCOV Program was over in terms of actual tactics being implemented and employed.

## BOCOV Resurrects in 1975

It is quite possible that the BOCOV Program was in hibernation during the early 1970s but it is also quite possible it wasn't; and, the files simply were not released or destroyed. After Hoover died on May 2, 1972, and the following month that the Watergate scandal broke with arrests of the "burglars" on June 17, 1972, the FBI did go into a cover-up mode. The US Senate and House both began investigations into this FBI wrongdoing. The January 8, 1975, memo from SAC, San Diego to the new Director, FBI indicates the thought of cover-up by utilizing their power to reclassify documents to avoid release under FOIA. The entire portion of this memo related to this issue reads as follows:

> During review of Counterintelligence Program (COINTELPRO) files necessitated by Freedom of Information Act (FOIA) request at FBIHQ, the above captioned file came to the attention of the San Diego Division. This file, while not of the primary COINTELPRO files, is a closely related file.
>
> Review of this file reveals that numerous serials contain information which, if disclosed, would be expected to cause damage to relations between the United States and a friendly foreign government.
>
> It is not clear whether this file is one of those which might become subject to public disclosure, but if this is the case, it should be reviewed for classification purposes.
>
> REQUEST OF THE BUREAU
>
> The Bureau is requested to advise whether above captioned case is subject to public disclosure with other COINTELPRO files under FOIA request.

The "above captioned file" was "(100-12363) (P*)."

The new FBI director, Clarence Kelley, responded to SAC, San Diego on March 14 that HQ was busy "in the process of classifying appropriate material in HQ files. When this has been completed, you will be furnished instructions relating to the classification of material in your file." Full panic mode followed in Kelley's terse four-page memo dated April 25, 1975 to SACs in "Albuquerque, El Paso (105-788), Phoenix (100-6654), San Antonio (100-9500), San Diego (100-12363), LEGAT, Mexico City (100-434445)." He wrote instructions,

> ReBuairtel to Albany and all offices 12/23/74, captioned "Communist Party, USA; Counterintelligence Program; IS-C," which advised that documents

relating ot that program had become subject to a Freedom of Information Act request, and instructed recipients to classify their copies of Cointelpro documents classified at FBIHQ. In addition, recipients were to review their Cointelpro files for any additional classifiable documents located in those files, classify them, and notify other offices having copies to likewise classify their copies. (p.1)

Director Kelley enclosed a "work paper" that listed documents classified at FBIHQ so each office would do likewise (p.2). Kelley wanted this "completed by 5/30/75" (p.3). The more bright light on disclosure, classification, and secreting, my words, was directed by Kelley in the remaining pages of this memo under the subheading "NOTE:" which is copied here entirely:

Captioned program was implemented in the early 1960s among the southwestern filed offices and Legat, Mexico City, and very little activity was conducted. Although no indication was located in Bureau files that the program was formally concluded, neither was any indication located that any activities have been conducted under this program since 1968 or early 1969. (underline emphasis mine) (p.3).

NOTE CONTINUED:

A broad request has been made by the media for documents relating to our Cointelpros, and although BOCOV was not specifically mentioned in this request, it is felt it would be encompassed by a request for Cointelpro material; therefore, classifiable documents contained in the FBIHQ files concerning this program have been classified, and copies of these documents appearing in other FBIHQ files will also be classified.

> By letter of 4/21/75 to the Attorney General, we advised the Department of the existence of BOCOV, along with the four other recently-discovered Cointelpros (Yugoslav, Cuban, Puerto Rican Nationalists and Hoodwink), and indicated that we were presently classifying, as appropriate, material appearing in our files pertaining to these programs. (underline emphasis mine). (p.4)

On April 30, 1975, the Bureau began a review of all COINTELPRO files and released to me thirteen pages of records on each file reviewed in the San Diego office. Each page contains ten entries by file number with few exceptions, prepared by Special Agent Rex I. Shroder. Mexico City, Legat, responded to Kelley on May 22, 1975, that their review was completed on BOCOV but for five communications it sought Bureau for instructions. Between May 28 and June 9, 1975 all the southwestern field office reported to the director, FBI having completed their review and classification of BOCOV files. A June 9, 1975, Airtel from Kelley to all the offices handling BOCOV files informed them that the USAG had by letter dated May 17 notified Representative Don Edwards, heading up the House Subcommittee on Civil Rights and Constitutional Rights that "the five recently discovered Cointelpros" and listed them as identified and underlined by me above, that the AG's letter was going to be classified "Secret" because "disclosure of references to the Mexican, Puerto Rican, Yugoslavian, and Cuban operations could damage relations in those areas."

The last memos from June 1975 ending with one on the 30th, all deal with follow-up queries about completion of classification except this last two-page one. It simply stated in closing to include the FBI's FOIPA Reading Room for review and classification (p.2). The final memo dated July 1, 1975, on BOCOV files released to me is from the director, FBI to the SAC, El Paso is repeating that this field office now has "all work papers relating to referenced Bureau Airtel and communications" on the reclassification of files. So, end the BOCVO files.

Clearly and deliberately the FBI directors from Hoover to Kelley withheld information from the public and Congress when FOIA requests were made and during the investigations underway at that time. Leading the US Senate investigation about forty-five years ago was Idaho's Frank Church (D) during 1975 into 1976. His work probed the violations of the Fourth Amendment of the US Constitution and section 605 of the Communications Act of 1934 against telephone taps during the presidential administrations of Kennedy, Johnson, and Nixon by the FBI and other national security agencies. The "Church Committee" as it became popularly known, produced fourteen reports on abuses by the FBI, CIA, NSA, and included assassination attempts of foreign leaders.[14]

## NOTES

1. Lars Schoulz, *Beneath the United States: A History of U.S. Policy toward Latin America* (Cambridge: Harvard University Press, 1998): xii.

2. *Ibid.,* Preface: xiv–xvii.

3. Eugene H. Schied, CBP Senior Accountability Officer, Department of Homeland Security, "U.S. Customs and Border Protection SBI*net* Development Border Technology, Southwest Border Recovery Act Plan," Department of Homeland Security, Washington, DC: Government Printing Office

4. The numbers in parenthesis following the name of the city are part of the file numbers which must be added after 100-434445 to get the BOCOV file maintained at that FBI field office. Example: San Antonio 100-434445-45 would be the number to ask for in attempting to obtain these files via FOI/PA. These numbers were provided on page 5 of the first document under scrutiny dated January 9, 1961.

5. Co-author Leon Andrew Immerman, *Are You Now or Have You Ever Been in the FBI Files: How to Secure and Interpret Your FBI Files* (New York: Grove Press, 1981), 194.

6. See Chapter 17, "Homeland Security: The Phoenix Comes Home to Roost," in *The CIA as Organized Crime: How Illegal Operations Corrupt America and the World* (Atlanta: Clarity Press, 2017), 293–314 for his analysis and comparison of the FBI's COINTELPRO operations and the CIA's Phoenix Program to current activities of the Department of Homeland Security; and, also see pages 195–201 for the collaborative work of the CIA and the Drug Enforcement Agency (DEA) in Mexico involving assassinations and cover-ups.

7. In my recent work *Tracking King Tiger* this surveillance is presented from primary sources of FBI documents.

8. Oropeza, *The King of Adobe*, 151–152, 197, 257–258 and for Chapa interview, 346.

9. Belmont died at the age of seventy-nine in 1977 having retired from the FBI in 1965, according to his obituary at www.washingtonpost.com/archive/local/1977/08/02/alan-h-belmont-retired-from-number-3-position-in-fbi/a9604b34-a15b-b03b0013b10d/ accessed February 6, 2020.

10. Gerald K. Haines and David A. Langbart, both with lengthy service at the National Archives and Records Administration's (NARA) FBI Task Force, wrote *Unlocking the Files of the FBI: A Guide to Its Record and Classification System* (Lanham, MA: Rowman and Littlefield, 1993), which is most useful in understanding how to read and interpret FBI files. The Mary Ferrell Foundation, "How to Read an FBI File" article is also useful in understanding specific acronyms, abbreviations, numbering system and the like used in almost every FBI document. This article can be found at www.maryferrell.org/archive/ accessed February 6, 2020.

11. In Spanish and in Mexico about this time, the late 1950s to early 1960s when the BOCOV allegedly was launched as part of the FBI family of COINTELPROs, the *Movimiento de Liberacion Nacional* (MLN) was formed comprised of various leftist political groupings. Some argue it began with the Committee to Promote Peace (CIP in Spanish) founded by Lazaro Cardenas, former Mexican president, founded on August 5, 1961. The founding groups were the National Peasant Confederation (CNC), the Confederation of Mexican Workers (CTM), the Institutional Revolutionary Party (PRI), and the Popular Socialist Party (PPS); all the acronyms in Spanish. Read about this in Dan La Botz, *Democracy in Mexico: Peasant Rebellion and Political Reform* (Boston: South End Press, 1995) for general review; Kathleen Bruhn, *Taking on Goliath: The Emergence of a New Left Party and the Struggle for Democracy in Mexico* (University Park: Pennsylvania State University Press, 1996), 49–53; and, Donald Hodges and Ross Gandy, *Mexico Under Siege: Popular Resistance to Presidential Despotism* (London: Zed Books, 2002), 82–87.

12. In the 1970s, Cesar E. Chavez of the United Farmworkers Union of America, contracted with Dr. Julio Prado Valdez in Mexicali to provide medical services for his members from that area of Mexico. See my work, *The Eagle Has Eyes: The FBI Surveillance of Cesar Estrada Chavez of the United Farm Workers Union of America, 1965–1975* (E. Lansing: Michigan State University Press, 2019), 129–131, 215.

13. W. Raymond Wannall died at the age of ninety-two, January 29, 2011. He served in the FBI's Intelligence Division for many years. His obituary can be accessed at https://www.legacy.com/obituaries/washingtontimes/obituary.aspx?pid=148309988/.

14. Stuart Taylor, Jr., *The Big Snoop: Life, Liberty, and the Pursuit of Terrorists*, and eBook from Brookings Institute Press, Washington, DC, 2014 accessible at https://www.kobo.com/us/es/ebook/the-big-snoop-4/.

# Conclusion

The material covered in this volume relied to a great extent on actual physical observation by agents, informant reports, data collection via photographs, recordings, mail interception, and telephone taps. It is called surveillance in this book, but the practice of spying with the advent of improvements in electronic transmission of data and the internet has moved to another level—that of dataveillance. Dataveillance also depends on self-reporting as opposed to an agent or informant watching and listening; a target self-reports by using the cell phone, credit card, opening email, driving a car with a GPS application or monitor (rental cars all have them), and accepting cookies be placed on their computer.

## SPY SCHOOLS

The Powell Memo was written decades ago by former Justice Lewis Powell as a working paper for the US Chamber of Commerce before he was appointed to SCOTUS. The memo is credited with laying out of an intellectually strategic plan for the rise of conservative policy initiatives.[1] One such initiative was the creation of think tanks and campus-based student organizations as part of a master plan for the radical right to develop its adherents in support of their public policies. Nancy MacLean relates this history in her work, *Democracy in Chains: The Deep History of the Radical Right's Stealth Plan for America.*[2] These think tanks and campus organizations have been created.

The next step taken was to fund curriculum by the Department of Defense (DOD) on college and university campuses on national security. These programs and departments are busy imparting the virtues of national security over privacy and civil rights taught in various courses in the humanities.

More importantly, these programs and departments are a breeding ground for personnel trained in modern dataveillance and national security programs that DOD contractors long for as employees. The DOD has more independent contractors on payroll and subsidy than regular employees. Much of this development is covered by Daniel Golden in *Spy Schools: How the CIA, FBI, and Foreign Intelligence Secretly Exploit American Universities.*[3]

## REAR VIEW MIRROR TO THE
## NATIONAL SECURITY AGENCY

On November 4, 1952, the area of communications had expanded into unimaginable technology components, so much that the federal government put all its branches doing such intelligence work into one, the National Security Agency (NSA). Within years it became the largest of all US intelligence agencies. George F. Howard, the historian for the NSA for fifteen years, published the first history of this agency, which for some time was classified and secret, used only internally.[4] Along came James Bamford, another experienced journalist who was able to utilize the Freedom of Information Act (FOIA) process early on to produce the first authoritative work on the NSA. Like Wise and Ross and Snowden, currently with his new publication, Bamford had to fight off the Reagan administration, which was trying to intimidate him with criminal prosecution for violating the Espionage Act for seeking to publish classified material, which it was not, if FOIA released it and won. He also had other fights to win and he did, before the public could read his first of four major works, all best sellers, on the NSA.[5] More current is the 2009 work by Matthew M. Aid on the NSA.[6]

Bamford opened the NSA for public inspection into its work. Briefly stated, the NSA has monitored and collected data on every communication of any kind coming in and out of the United States for decades. It has the largest employee workforce and most warehouse locations, not to mention the actual computer centers, than any other intelligence agency to store all its data. The NSA has made physical surveillance, the actual watching, eavesdropping, tapping phones, mail intercepts, taking photos, copying license plates, hiring informants, and relying on snitches almost obsolete. The NSA has ushered in the era of dataveillance, learning about everyone by electronic means whether they use a credit or debit card, use email, have a smartphone or an iPhone, or even by radio signal to monitor what that person is doing. With the advent of social media, such as Facebook, Twitter, Instagram, WhatsApp, and email, who provide their data on everyone using their services to the federal government's intelligence agencies, primarily NSA, physical surveillance is on the wane. We report to these intelligence agencies on our own; the concern over national security has overridden privacy and civil rights.

## TECHNOLOGY TO COME

Facial recognition is the new thing in tracking all peoples probably dating to 2002, when movie producer Steven Spielberg released his film, *The Minority Report*. In that sci-fi movie, every entry point and transit center in the country had such technology in place, taking photo images of every person. This method aided the control freaks in that society to monitor the movements of every person. In 2020, this technology is somewhat developed and affordable in the form of ubiquitous surveillance cameras in homes, businesses of all types, schools, transit centers, traffic intersections, government buildings, police cars, and border check points. At border crossing centers and inland check points, cameras are in use as is the still digital photography of documents, such as a Global Entry card, passport, and driver license, for example. The existing system will be enhanced and in place at border crossings and inland check points by December 2020, with California and Texas as the first sites. A first contract for this technology was let to Northrup Grumman Corporation in 2013 for a multi-million-dollar amount. This biometric software is in place and in use at fifteen major airports in the United States. The goal is to have it in place in every airport of the country by 2021. The plan of the new contract is to "see" the documents and facial image of everyone before reaching the border or check point. If the facial or document image is of someone that should not be allowed entry or arrested and detained for prior offenses or suspicions of imminent criminal activity once crossed, the border agents have time to prepare for that confrontation. The United States is looking for contractors to develop this technology to higher levels of sophistication among three major corporations—Microsoft, Amazon, and Google. Amazon Web Services, a subsidiary company of Amazon, currently has the contract to maintain the biometric software system used by the US Customs and Border Patrol (CBP) in 2019. Amazon Web Services helped CBP track over a million persons and 280,000 vehicles daily that year. The test phase of such prototype is being allocated $960 million for a first contract to run through 2025. This spying protocol is big business. The goal is the use of that imagery instead of fingerprints, voice pattern recognition, DNA, or eyewitness to identify a person. Police departments at the local level are anxious for this technology to arrive so they can in Spielberg-terms use it to detain and arrest people for "pre-crimes," that is, before a crime is committed. The pre-crime criteria will be based on an algorithm of propensity toward violence or crime and past criminal history regardless of seriousness of past offense such as traffic tickets or protesting. The database of facial images run through the algorithm will reveal those targets.[7]

If cameras taking your photograph without your consent are not invasive enough, how about your faucets and toilets also being used to listen to your conversations? Delta and Kohler companies, two of several such manufacturers, are developing smart faucets and toilets with the help of Alexa, the device marketed by Alexa Internet Incorporated, which is a wholly owned subsidiary of Amazon. Amazon has over a dozen devices run via Alexa Internet Inc. offered for sale to the unsuspecting public. These devices use VoiceIQ technology, which records your voice to identify you from others. The content of such voice imprints is also kept by the company, so they know what you said, when, to whom, and for what purpose. Delta is incorporating Alexa into their faucets so you can control it: how much water you want, how hot or cold, and when to run. Kohler makes toilets, among other products, including faucets, and it is adding Alexa to toilets so you can tell it when to flush and how much water to use, plus listen in on all you, and perhaps others, say while in the vicinity of a toilet so equipped, like a shower or tub where two persons may share to save water.[8] Amazon does not back away from the claim of listening to your conversations and storing them, often sharing that data with the federal government; they insist it is to improve voice recognition technology and service.[9]

## CYBERSPACE

New frontiers for espionage and warfare in outer space are beckoning all in the twenty-first century. In 2010 when the Stuxnet worm was detected, which can attack and immobilize industrial control systems, the US intelligence community grew by another agency with focus on cyberspace security; and, a joint cyber command with some allied nations was also created then. As early as the 1990s, intelligence analysts under the Clinton administration began forecasting such a scenario—war in outer space. Already satellites high above the planet monitor movements not just for purposes of weather but for detection of military, naval, and logistical maneuvers of all nations as preemptive measures to be on alert and avoid an electronic-directed Pearl Harbor. A US Naval War College professor complied a broad subject anthology on such cyberspace security.[10] The word "cyberspace" came from a short story written in 1982 and later made commonplace with the movie *The Matrix*.[11] The first uses of the internet were by the US military and that history was also kept secret until recently by Yasha Levine, who detailed those developments in his work.[12] As the number of subscribers to the various internet providers for access into World Wide Web increases, so does the danger posed by cyberspace. As Patrick Jagoda at the University of Chicago posits, "lack of digital literacy—the ability to read, write, and understand computer processes—represents a greater threat to cybersecurity than any single computer virus."[13] Our ignorance of this ever-growing and invading technology is the problem; it is ignorant to us. And, in the near future, Chicanos and others will be the people working against our civil rights and interests as paid agents of private contractors and governments.

## NOTES

1. The history of the Powell Memo is well developed and related by Mark Schmitt on April 27, 2005, at https://prospect.org/legend-powell-memo/. Accessed January 9, 2020.

2. Nancy MacLean, *Democracy in Chains: The Deep History of the Radical Right's Stealth Plan for America* (New Brunswick, Australia: Scribe Publications, 2017).

3. Daniel Golden, *Spy Schools: How the CIA, FBI, and Foreign Intelligence Secretly Exploit American Universities* (New York: Henry Holt & Company, 2017).

4. "The Early History of the NSA," SECRET, at www.nsa.gov/portrals/70/d ocuments/news-features/declassified-documents/cryptologic-spectrum/early_history _nsa/pdf/. Accessed September 30, 2019.

5. The first book was *The Puzzle Palace: A Report on NSA, America's Most Secret Intelligence Agency* (New York: Houghton Mifflin, 1982), a Penguin books edition was in 1983; *Body of Secrets: Anatomy of the Ultra-Secret NSA, From the Cold War to the Dawn of a New Century* (New York: Doubleday, 2001); *A Pretext for War: 9/11, Iraq, and the Abuse of America's Intelligence Agencies* (New York: Doubleday, 2004); and, his most recent work, *The Shadow Factory: The Ultra-Secret NSA from 9/11 to the Eavesdropping on America* (New York: Doubleday, 2008).

6. *The Secret Sentry: The Untold Story of the National Security Agency* (New York: Bloomsbury Press, 2009).

7. David Beyer, "Facial Recognition Technology Is Here," *Gringo Gazette*, September 2, 2019, 3–6.

8. See https://www.zerohedge.com/technology/smart-faucets-and-toilets-use-ale xa-listen-your-conversations/. Accessed September 29, 2019.

9. Go to www.amazon.com/gp/help/customer/display-html?nodeld=201602230/ for a series of FAQs that address this issue and more. Accessed September 29, 2019.

10. Derek S. Reverson, ed. *Cyberspace and National Security: Threats, Opportunities, and Power in a Virtual World* (Washington, DC: Georgetown University Press, 2012).

11. Reverson, *Cyberspace and National Security*, 5.

12. Yasha Levine, *Surveillance Valley: The Secret Military History of the Internet* (New York: PublicAffairs, 2018).

13. Reverson, *Cyberspace and National Security*, 225.

# Bibliography

## THE NAMES OF FBI FILES CITED IN THE BOOK

Rosalio Muñoz
Rubén Salazar
*Catolicos por la Raza*
Francisco "Pancho" Villa
Francisco Madero
Victoriano Huerta
John "Black Jack" Pershing
Joseph Swing
Operation Wetback
Woodrow Wilson
Donald Trump
Andres Manuel Lopez Obrador
Enrique Peña Nieto
Venustiano Carranza
Cesar Estrada Chavez*
Reies Lopez Tijerina
Lyndon Baines Johnson*
William "Bill" Clinton*
George W. Bush
Barack Obama
Raymond Telles
Delfina Telles
Zoot Suit Riots
Operation Ajax
Operation PBSUCCESS
Bay of Pigs
U2 Spy Plane

Daniel Berrigan*
Chelsea Manning
Edward Snowden
Allen W. Dulles
Plant Production Section
Industrial Workers of the World
U.S. Army Military Intelligence Division
John F. Kennedy*
National Security Agency
Luisa Moreno
Blanca Rosa Rodriguez
Gabriela Mistral
Lucila Godoy Alcayaga
Luis Moreno
Luisa Capetillo
Diego Rivera
Frida Kahlo
Leon Trotsky*
Communist Party USA*
Marlon Brandon
Francisco "Pancho" Medrano
Baldemar Huerta aka Freddy Fender
Texas Farm Workers Union
Antonio "Tony" Orendian
Raquel Orendain
American G. I. Forum
Joe Molina
J. Edgar Hoover*
Herbert Hoover
Cartha DeLoach*
Douglas MacArthur
William Sullivan*
Patrick J. Hurley
Sen. Joseph (Joe) McCarthy*
The Ku Klux Klan*
Gray Bemis
Congress of Industrial Organizations
United Cannery Agricultural Packing and Allied Workers of America
Roberto Galvan
Ernesto Galarza
Bert Corona
Alfred Renton "Harry" Bridges
Carey McWilliams
Franklin Delano Roosevelt
Cordell Hull

International Longshoremen's Association
National Rifle Association*
Harlon Carter*
*Congreso de Pueblos de Habla Español*
Weather Underground (Weathermen)*
FBI's Explanation of Exemptions*
Clyde Tolson*
Jerry Garcia*
COINTELPRO*
Sleepy Lagoon Defense Committee
"Jack" Tenney
California Committee on Un-American Activities
U.S. House Committee on Un-American Activities
National Labor Relations Board
William A. Godfrey
Workers Alliance Pecan Shellers Union, Local #172
Thomas Ryan Walsh
Owen Kilday
San Juana Flores
Sister Superior Leonille, St. Michael's Academy
James Sagar
Monsignor Thomas Moczygemba
Vaughn I. Parry
Hubert H. Finkel
George Mink
Nancy Reed
James Wimason
James W. Mason
Jacob Shaffer
Ward Wight, Jr.
Henry A. Wallace*
Lewis F. Powell, Jr.*
Carol Winter
Carol King
Edwin O. Haudsep
Mrs. Matthew Barkley
George H. Scatterday
Carl winter
Max Silver
Pettis Perry
George Sandy
Henry Steinberg, Jr.
Arturo Mata.
A.E. Edgar
Richard Lynden

Vernon D. Jensen
Peter Harislades
Dr. Paul Crouch
W. Albert Stewart, Jr.
Norman S. Higson
Miles J. Johnson
Phil Ougensky
American National Mexican Association
William E. Dettweiller
W.G. McGee
American Committee for the Protection of the Foreign Born
Miles J. Johnsen
Nat Honig
John Foster Dulles
Valdimir Lenin
Robert W. Kenny
Edward J. Kirby
Charlene Barrett
Francis D. O'Brien
Ralph G. Harder
Lee M. Fallan
Donald Wiberg Kuno
Richard M. Nixon*
President Richard M. Nixon FBI Application*
Whittaker Chambers*
Alger Hiss*
W. H. Dettekiles, Jr,
William Schneiderman
Archie Brown
Pedro J. Gonzalez
Buron Fitts
Dora Versus
Philip Usquiano
John Quimby
Virginia Vera Goodrow
W. Albert Stewart, Jr.
Al Gayton
Augusto Charnaud MacDonald
Richard E. Coombs
Steve Murdock
Richard T. Winterman
George M. Gibson
Milton K. Wells
Ignacio Lopez
Jaime Gonzalez

Richard Ibañez
William G. Marshaw
Dixie Tiller
Ben Harrison
Henry Grattan
James S. Bower
B. H. Kirk
Arnold D. Orrantia
Enrique Abañil
Harry Steinmetz
U.L. Press
Edward Bordeaux Szekely
Asa Katz
Samuel J. Novick
George F. Munro
Carmen Otero y Gama
Vicente Lombardo Toledano
John Christensen
Nathan Buchwald
Naftula Buchwald
Mexican American Youth Organization
La Raza Unida Party
Rodolfo "Corky" Gonzales
Luis Echevarria Alvarez
Gerald Ford
Jorge Bustamante
Robert F. Ryan
Pan American Union
Ernesto Galarza
D.F. Bryant
National Archives and Records Administration
Luis Quintanilla
Equal Employment Opportunity Commission
White House Cabinet Committee Hearings, El Paso, Texas
George W. Crump
J.E. Lawler
G.A. Nicholson
L.S. Rowe
William Griffin
Guy Hottel
Helen Waters
Concha Romero James
L. M. C. Smith
Custodial Detention Index
Security Index

C.A. Evans
R. Howard Calhoun
H.L. Bobbitt
R.C. Kopriva
B.E. Primm
Dorothy Nichols
Kathyrn Briker
Marquise M. Childs
R.W. Meadows
Edward J. Murtagh
Evelyn Wheaton
Mrs. John Adikes
Jerry Voorhis
James Patton
Louis Post
Frances Biddle
Hugh B. Cox
Di Giorgio Fruit Corporation
National Farm Labor Union
William Rhodes Davis
John L. Lewis
Morris L. Ernst
Jacob Landau
Lee Pressman
Xavier Icaza
Lázaro Cárdenas
Leon Freeman
*Confederacion de Trabajadores Mexicanos*
R.W. Ware
Ismael C. Falcon
Raymond F. Farrell
Bernard A. Harrison
Lawyer's Committee on American Relations With Spain
Linn Gale
Albert C. Hayden, Jr.
Mrs. Mildred Steagall
Marvin Watson
Sidney Kossen
Ronald Reagan
Raymond Telles
Richard Telles
Delfina Telles
Dennis Chavez
Albert A. Peña. Jr.
Henry B. Gonzales

Vicente Ximenes
Clark Clifford
Robert F. Kennedy
Sargent Shriver
Hector P. Garcia
Reynaldo Garza
Sharon Day
Harris H. Huston
Clarence M. Kelley
James E. Barrett
Willard D. Watson
Mrs. Maude E. Roll
William H. Nimmins
Thomas B. White
P. Kenneth O'Donnell
Melville E. Blake, Jr.
A.E. Walton
C. H. Cravens
Harry Zucher
Robert F. Woodward
Alex A. Cohen
Charles R. Burrows
William D. McKee
Fernando Lara Bustamante
Glyn T. Brymer
Howard Vaught
Douglas M. Smith
Woodrow Seals
William Crockett
G. Marvin Gentile
Denman F. Stanfield
Patrick M. Rice
Joseph Burks
William Ryan
Henri G. Grignon
David H. McCabe
John M. Steeves
William Ryan Justice
Harold Reis
Clarence A. Boonstra
Louis M. Marrano
John R. Ellis
Frederick W. Trabsand
Alexander P. Butterfield
Robert H. Haynes

Ernest Guinn
Ralph Yarborough
William Farah
Arturo G. Constantino
Lloyd Bentsen
Richard C. White
Edward F. Berliner
Jack Fant
J.W. Wally Fields
James Moran
Cecilia Moran
Julián Nava
Jimmy Carter
Maury Page Kemp
Baldemar Huerta
Ann Richards
John Wayne
Heuy Meaux
Leo Fender
Andy Russell
Andres Rabago
Vikki Carr
Ritchie Valens
Bob Keane
Anthony Quinn
Rita Hayworth
Raquel Welch
Lynda Carter
Ted Williams
Jim Plunkett
Joe Kapp
Robert Redford
Ferdinand Marcos
Joe Brown Enterprises LTD
Jerry Garcia*
The Grateful Dead*
Gilberto Padilla
Agricultural Workers Association
Community Services Organization
Bill Kircher
Larry Itliong
Philip Vera Cruz
Andy Imutan
Schenley Industries
Eugene Nelson

John Connally
Othal Brand
C.L. Miller
David M. Hardy
Gus Hall
Texas Farm Workers Union
Ford Foundation
Nation of Islam
Black Panther Party
Pete Torres
Chicano Moratorium
Charles Grace
Ralph Yarborough
Crusade for Justice
Young Workers Liberation League
Clay Zachary, Jr.
Fausto Hernandez
Juventino Balderas
R.S. Bowe
Efrain Fernandez
Maria Magallan
David Magallan
Mateo Sandoval
Gilbert Zuniga
Alfredo Ramírez
Guadalupe Lucio Salinas
Manuel Mata
Alfredo Ramirez
Alfred Y. Allee
Jack Dean
Alfonso "Poncho" Flores
Robert Johnson
David Fishlow
Brown Berets
Claudio Castañeda
Clay Zachary, Jr.
J. Meyers Cole
MHCHAOS
James B. Adams
Fred Dawson
Ramiro Raul Casso
Benito Rodriguez
Kathy Baker
Francisco "Pancho" Medrano
Joe Bernal

Robert Hall
Chris Dixie
Eugene E. Harden
Irma Mireles
Rita Martinez
Julio Cordero
Maria Salas
Julio Coreño
Claudio Ramirez
Jose Rodriguez
March of Human Rights of 1977
Jesus Moya
David Sandoval
Drew S. Days, III
Charles Wetegrove Corporation
Roy Fernandez
Oscar Correa
Sabas Garza, Jr.
William P. Clements
Julián W. De La Rosa
Daniel K. Hedges
League of United Latin American Citizens
American G. I. Forum
Gustavo Garcia
Carlos Cadena
George I. Sanchez
Carlos Castañeda
Joe Montoya
Don Contreras
Office of Naval Intelligence, 8th Naval District, New Orleans, Louisiana
Felix Longoria
Beatriz Longoria
Tom Kennedy
Edward "Ed" Idar, Jr.
Cris Alderete
Cleotilde Garcia
Antonio Garcia
Viva Kennedy Clubs
Viva Johnson Clubs
Bracero Program
Mexican American Political Association
Political Association of Spanish Speaking Organizations
David H. Stowe
Mrs. Adela Elliott
Congress of Mexican and Spanish-American People of the United States

Frank Church
James M. McInerney
FBI Undercover Operations*
Mexican Mafia*
Adolph Hitler
Alan Shivers
People's Institute of Applied Religion
Willard Kelly
Ramon Gonzalez
Gilbert C. Garcia
Richard M. Casillas
William F. Tompkins
José "Joe" Rodriguez Molina
Soledad Palomo
Texas School Book Depository
Gloria Calvary
Lee Harvey Oswald
Felix Botello
James Wood
Margarita Landin
Joe Landin
Ruth Lowery
William James Lowery, Jr.
Augustin Estrada
R.L. Thornton
National Association for the Advancement of Colored People
A.Raymond Switzer
Eugene F. Petrakis
William Gannaway
Jack Revill
Will Fritz
John Stanford
O.V. Campbell
H.M. Hart
Jesse Curry
Dan Yarborough
Elwood Ross
Roy S. Truly
Arthur K. Sayre
Bess P. Coville
Thelma Logan
R.T. Summer
Malvin E. Shugart
Jerry Shinley
Selena Quintanilla

Henry "Hank" Leyvas
José Diaz
Culbert Olson
Luis Valdez
Zoot Suit Riots
Mrs. Fred Holley
Ed Gossett
Frank Knox
R.O. Smith
Alfredo Elias Calles
David W. Bagley
C. B. Horrall
Al Capp
Charles C. Dail
Earl Warren
Maxwell Murray
E. Robert Anderson
w. J. Decker
T.L. Caudle
Manuel Sorola
Joaquin Jack Garcia
Helen Gandy
Joseph Lash
Andrea Perez
Sylvester Davis
*Alianza Hispano Americana*
Pedro Gonzalez
Robert H. Scott
Fletcher Brown
The *Cristero* Wars
Screen Writers Guild
Orson Wells
Mrs. Will Rogers, Jr.
Steven Spielberg
Patrick Jagoda
Note: Asterisk denotes files posted online at FBI website (see https://vault.fbi.gov/) and or under the FBI's Name Check Program. All other files are in the author's possession obtained from others or www.fbi.gov/foia/.

## SECONDARY SOURCES

Acuña, Rodolfo. 2019. *Occupied America: A History of Chicanos*, 9th edition. London: Pearson.

Afasiabi, Peter. 2016. *Burning Bridges: America's 20-Year Crusade to Deport Labor Leader Harry Bridges*. Brooklyn: Thirlwere Books.

Aid, Matthew M. 2009. *The Secret Sentry: The Untold History of the National Security Agency*. New York: Bloomsbury Press.

Allsup, Carl. 1982. *American G.I. Forum: Origins and Evolution*. Austin: University of Texas Press.

Alonzo, Armando C. 1998. *Tejano Legacy: Rancheros and Settlers in South Texas, 1734–1910*. Albuquerque: University of New Mexico Press.

Ambrose, Stephen E. 1983. *Eisenhower: Soldier, General of the Army and President-Elect*, Vol. 1. New York: Simon & Schuster.

———. 1984. *Eisenhower: The President*, Vol. II. New York: Simon & Schuster.

Arkin, William M. 2005. *Code Names: Deciphering US Military Plans, Programs, and Operations in the 9/11 World*. Hanover, New Hampshire: Steerforth Press.

Balderrama, Francisco and Raymond Rodriguez. 1995, 2006. *Decade of Betrayal: Mexican Repatriation in the 1930s*. Albuquerque: University of New Mexico Press.

Bamford, James. 1982. *The Puzzle Palace: A Report on NSA, America's Most Secret Intelligence Agency*. New York: Houghton Mifflin; Penguin edition 1983.

———. 2001. *Body of Secrets: Anatomy of the Ultra-Secret NSA from the Cold War to the Dawn of a New Century*. New York: Doubleday.

———. 2004. *A Pretext for War: 9/11m Iraq, and the Abuse of America's Intelligence Agencies*. New York: Doubleday.

———. 2008. *The Shadow Factory: The Ultra-Secret NSA from 9/11 to the Eavesdropping on America*. New York: Doubleday.

Bardacke, Frank. 2012. *Trampling Out the Vintage: Cesar Chavez and the Two Souls of the United Farm Workers*. London: Verso.

Barger, W. K. and Ernesto M. Reza. 1994. *Social Change and the Farm Labor Movement in the Midwest: Adaptation Among Migrant Farmworkers*. Austin: University of Texas Press.

Barrera, James. 2004. "The 1968 Edcouch-Elsa High School Walkout: Chicano Student Activism in a South Texas Community," *Aztlan, Journal of Chicano Studies*, 29:2: 93–102.

Becker, Marc. 2017. *The FBI in Latin America: The Ecuador Files*. Durham: Duke University Press.

Beyer, David. September 2, 2019. "Facial Recognition Technology Is Here," *Gringo Gazette*, Tijuana, Mexico.

Blackstock, Nelson. 1975, 1988, 2011. *COINTELPRO: The FBI's Secret War on Political Freedom*. New York: Pathfinder Press.

Blaisdale, Lowell L. 1962. *The Desert Revolution: Baja California, 1911*. Madison: University of Wisconsin Press.

Bobrow-Strain, Aaron, 2019. *The Death and Life of Aida Hernandez*. New York: Farrar, Straus and Giroux, 2019.

Bruhn, Kathleen. *Taking on Goliath: The Emergence of a New Left Party and Democracy in Mexico*. University Park: Pennsylvania State University Press, 1967.

Buitrago, Ann Mari and Leon Andrew Immerman. 1981. *Are You Now or Have You Ever Been in the FBI Files? How to Secure and Interpret Your FBI Files.* New York: Grove Press.

Bustamante, Jorge A. 1990, *Historia de la Colonia Libertad.* Tijuana: Colegio de la Frontera Norte.

Calavita, Kitty. 1992. *Inside the State: The Bracero Program, Immigration, and the I.N.S.* New Orleans: Quid Pro Books.

Calbillo, Carlos. 2002. "The Chicano Movement in Houston and Texas: A Personal Memory," *Houston History Magazine*, 9:1: 26–29.

Cannato, Vincent J. 2010. *American Passage: The History of Ellis Island.* New York: Harper Perennial Books.

Carr, Barry. 1992. *Marxism and Communism in Twentieth-Century Mexico.* Lincoln: University of Nebraska Press.

Carrigan William D. and Clive Webb. 2013. *Forgotten Dead: Mob Violence against Mexicans in the U.S., 1848–1928.* New York: Oxford University Press.

Carroll, Patrick J. 2003. *Felix Longoria's Wake: Bereavement, Racism, and the Rise of Mexican American Activism.* Austin: University of Texas Press.

Chalkley, John F. 1998. *Zach Lamar Cobb: El Paso Collector of Customs and Intelligence During the Mexican Revolution, 1913–1918.* El Paso: Texas Western Press.

Charles, Douglas M. 2015. *J. Edgar Hoover and the Anti-Interventionists.* Columbus: The Ohio State University Press.

———. 2015. *Hoover's War on Gays: Exposing the FBI's "Sex Deviates" Program.* Lawrence: University Press of Kansas.

———. 2012. *The FBI's Obscene File: J. Edgar Hoover and the Bureau's Crusade against Smut.* Lawrence: University Press of Kansas.

Chavez, John R. 1984. *The Lost Land: The Chicano Image of the Southwest.* Albuquerque: University of New Mexico Press.

Chavez-Garcia, Miroslava. "Intelligence Testing at Whittier School, 180–1920." *Pacific Historical Review*, 76:2: 193–228.

Churchill, Ward and Jim Vander Wall. 1990. *The COINTELPRO papers: Documents from the FBI's Secret Wars Against Domestic Dissent.* Boston: South End Press.

Correa, Jennifer G. 2006. "Chicano Nationalism: The Brown Berets and Legal Social Control," Master's Thesis, Oklahoma State University.

———. 2011. "The Targeting of the East Los Angeles Brown Berets by a Racial Patriarchal Capitalist State: Merging Intersectionality and Social Movement Research," *Critical Sociology* 37: 83–101.

Culleton, Claire A. 2004. *Joyce and the G-Men: J. Edgar Hoover's Manipulation of Modernism.* New York: Palgrave Macmillan.

Davis, James Kirkpatrick. 1992. *Spying on Americans: the FBI's Domestic Counter-Intelligence Program.* Westport: Praeger.

D'Este, Carlo. 2002. *Eisenhower: A Soldier's Life.* New York: Henry Holt and Company.

De Leon, Arnoldo. 1989. *Ethnicity in the Sunbelt: A History of Mexican Americans in Houston.* Houston: Mexican American Studies, University of Houston.

DeVoto, Bernard. Ed. 1997. *The Journals of Lewis and Clark*. New York: Houghton and Mifflin Company.

Douglas, James W. 2008. *JFK and the Unspeakable: Why He Died and Why it Matters*. New York: Touchstone Books.

Dray, Philip. 2011. *There Is Power in a Union: The Epic Story of Labor in America*. New York: Anchor Books.

Dunbar, Roxanne Ortiz. 2007. *Roots of Resistance: Land Tenure in New Mexico, 1680–1980*. Norman: University of Oklahoma Press.

———. 2014. *An Indigenous Peoples' History of the United States*. Boston: Beacon Press.

Dunn, Timothy J. 1996. *The Militarization of the U.S.-Mexico Border, 1978–1992: Low Intensity Conflict Doctrine Comes Home*. Austin: University of Texas Press.

Englehardt, Tom. 2014. *Shadow Government: Surveillance, Secret Wars, and a Global Security State*. Chicago: Haymarket Books.

Erlich, Paul R., Loy Bilderbach and Anne H. Erlich. 1979. *The Golden Door: International Migration, Mexico, and the United States*. New York: Ballantine Books.

Ernesto Galarza. 1971. *Barrio Boy*. Notre Dame University Press.

Escobar, Edward J. "The Dialectics of Repression: The Los Angeles Police Department and the Chicano Movement, 1968–1971," *Journal of American History* (March 1993) 79:4: 1483–1514.

Faris, Wendy B. 1983. *Carlos Fuentes*. New York: Ungar Publishing.

Fernandez-Armesto, Felipe. 2014. *Our America: The Spanish History of the United States*. New York: W.W. Norton.

Ferris, Susan and Ricardo Sandoval. 1997. *The Fight in the Fields: Cesar Chavez and the Farmworkers Movement*. New York: Harcourt, Brace & Company.

Feuerlicht, Roberta Strauss. 1971. *America's Reign of Terror*. New York: Random House.

Fields, Rona M. 1970. "The Brown Berets: A Participant Observation Study of Social Action in the Schools of Los Angeles," PhD. Dissertation, University of Southern California, Los Angeles, California1970.

Fisch, Louise Ann. 1996. *All Rise: Reynaldo G. Garza, the First Mexican American Federal Judge*. College Station: Texas A & M University Press.

Fishlow, David. February 26, 1971. "Poncho Flores is Dead," *The Texas Observer*, 1.5.16.

Fried, Albert. 1997. ed. *McCarthyism: The Great American Red Scare*. New York: Oxford University Press.

Galarza, Ernesto. 1956. *Strangers in Our Fields*. New York: Fund for the Republic.

———. 1964, 1972. *Merchants of Labor: The Mexican Bracero Story*, Santa Barbara: McNally and Loftin.

———. 1970. *Spiders in the House and Workers in the Fields*, Notre Dame: University of Notre Dame Press.

———. 1977. *Tragedy at Chualar*, Santa Barbara: McNally and Loftin.

Gallo, Ruben. 2010. *Freud's Mexico: Into the Wilds of Psychoanalysis*. Cambridge and London: The MIT Press.

Ganz, Marshall. 2009. *Why David Sometimes Wins: Leadership, Organization, and Strategy in the California Farm Worker Movement*. New York: Oxford University Press.

Garcia, Ignacio M. 2002. *Hector P. Garcia: In Relentless Pursuit of Justice*. Houston: Arte Publico Press.

———. 2008. *White But Not Equal: Mexican Americans, Jury Discrimination, and the Supreme Court*. Tucson: University of Arizona Press.

Garcia, Joaquin "Jack". *Making Jack Falcone: An Undercover FBI Agent Takes Down a Mafia Family*. New York: Touchstone Books.

Garcia, Juan Ramon. 1980. *Operation Wetback: The Mass Deportation of Mexican Undocumented Workers in 1954*. Westport: Praeger.

Garcia, Mario T. 1991. *Mexican Americans: Leadership, Ideology, and Identity, 1930–1960*. New Haven: Yale University Press.

———. 1994. *Memories of Chicano History: The Life and Narrative of Bert Corona*. Los Angeles: University of California Press.

Garcia, Mario and Sal Castro. 2011. *Blowout! Chicano Walkout and the Struggle for Educational Justice*. Chapel Hill: University of North Carolina Press.

Garcia, Matt. 2012. *From the Jaws of Victory: The Triumph and Tragedy of Cesar Chavez and the Farm Worker Movement*. Berkeley: University of California Press.

Garrison, James. 1998. *On the Trail of the Assassins: One Man's Quest to Solve the Murder of President Kennedy*. New York: Sheridan Square Publications.

Gentry, Kurt. 1991. *J. Edgar Hoover: The Man and the Secrets*. New York: W. W. W. Norton & Company.

Ghodsee, Kristen, 2015. *The Left Side of History: World War II and the Unfulfilled Promise of Communism in Eastern Europe*. Durham: Duke University Press.

Giblin, James Cross. 2009. *The Rise and Fall of Senator Joe McCarthy*. Boston: Clarion Books.

Gittell, Marilyn. 1980. *Limits to Citizen Participation: The Decline of Community Organization*. Beverley Hills: Sage Publications.

Golden, Daniel. 2017. *Spy Schools: How the CIA, FBI, and Foreign Intelligence Secretly Exploit American Universities*. New York: Henry Holt & Company.

Gonzalez, Gilbert G. July 1982. "Racial Intelligence Testing and the Mexican People," *Education in Ethnic Studies*, 5:2: 36–49.

Goodwin, Robert. 2019. *América: The Epic Story of Spanish North America, 1493–1898*. New York: Bloomsbury Publishing.

Grandin, Greg. 2011. *The Last Colonial Massacre: Latin America in the Cold War*. Chicago: University of Chicago Press.

———. 2019. *The End of Myth: From the Frontier to the Border Wall in the Mind of America*. New York: Metropolitan Books.

Grebler, Leo, Joan W. Moore and Ralph C. Guzman. 1970. *The Mexican American People, the Nation's Second Largest Minority*. New York: Free Press.

Griswold del Castillo, Richard. 1990. *The Treaty of Guadalupe Hidalgo*. Norman: University of Oklahoma Press.

Guardiola, Gloria and Yolanda Garza Birdwell, 1971. *La Mujer: Destrucción de Mitos Formación y Practica del Pensamiento Libre*. Houston: self-published pamphlet.

Gutierrez, Jose Angel. 1986. "Chicanos and Mexicans Under Surveillance: 1940–1980," *Renato Rosaldo Lecture Series Monograph*. Tucson: Mexican American Studies & Research Center, 2: 39–43.

———. 2017. *Albert A. Peña, Jr.: Dean of Chicano Politics*. E. Lansing: Michigan State University Press.

———. 2017. Oral History Interview with Yolanda Garza and Walter Birdwell, 40 pages, September 7, Laguna Vista, Texas.

———. 2019. *The Eagle Has Eyes: The FBI Surveillance of César Estrada Chávez of the United Farm Workers Union of America, 1965–1975*. E. Lansing: Michigan State University Press.

———. 2019. *Tracking King Tiger: Reies López and the FBI*. E. Lansing: Michigan State University Press.

Hernandez, Kelly Lytle. 2006. "The Crimes and Consequences of Illegal Immigration: A Cross-Border Examination of Operation Wetback, 1943–1954," *The Western Historical Quarterly*, 37:4: 421–444.

———. 2017. *City of Inmates: Conquest, Rebellion, and the Rise of Human Caging in Los Angeles, 1771–1965*. Chapel Hill: University of North Carolina Press.

Herrera, Hayden. 1984. *Frida: A Biography of Frida Kahlo*. New York: Perennial Harper Collins.

Hoover, J. Edgar. 1958. *Masters of Deceit: The Story of Communism in America and How to Fight It*. New York: Henry Holt and Company.

———. 1969. *On Communism*. New York: Random House.

Immerwahr, Daniel. 2019. *How to Hide and Empire: A History of the Greater United States*. New York: Farrar, Strauss and Giroux.

Jayco, Margaret. 1988, 2009. *FBI on Trial: The Victory of the Socialist Workers Party Suit Against Government Spying*. New York: Pathfinder Press.

Jensen, Joan. 1991. *Army Surveillance in America, 1775–1980*. New Haven: Yale University Press.

Jensen, Merrill. 1959. *The Articles of Confederation: An Interpretation of the Social-Constitutional History of the American Revolution, 1774–1781*. Madison: University of Wisconsin Press.

Jerome, Fred. 2002. *The Einstein File: J. Edgar Hoover's Secret War Against the World Most Famous Scientist*. New York: St. Martin's Press.

Johnson, Benjamin Heber. 2005. *Revolution in Texas: How a Forgotten Rebellion and Its Bloody Suppression Turned Mexicans into Americans*. New Haven: Yale University Press.

Johnson, David K. 2004. *The Lavender Scare: The Cold War Persecution of Gays and Lesbians in the Federal Government*. Chicago: University of Chicago Press.

Joyner, Brian D. 2009. *Hispanic Reflections on the American Landscape: Identifying and Interpreting Hispanic Heritage*. Washington, DC: U.S. Government Printing Office.

Kahlenberg, Richard D. and Moshe Z. Marvitt. 2012. *Why Labor Organizing Should Be a Civil Right: Rebuilding a Middle-Class Democracy by Enhancing Worker Voice.* New York; The Century Foundation Press.

Kanellos, Nicolas. 2002. *Hispanic American Almanac.* Farmington Hills: Gale.

Kells, Michelle Hall. 2018. *Vicente Ximenes, LBJ's Great Society, and Mexican American Civil Rights Rhetoric.* Carbondale: Southern Illinois University Press.

Kessler, Ronald. 2002. *The Bureau: The Secret History of the FBI.* New York: St. Martin's Press.

Kettenmann, Andrea. 1997. *Diego Rivera, 1886–1957: A Revolutionary Spirit in Modern Art*, Cologne, Germany: Benedikt Taschen Verlag GmbH.

Kiloch, John. November 5, 1942. "Mexicans Face Police Terror Round-Ups: Vile Press Slur," *The California Eagle*: 1A,7B.

Klehr, Kyrill, M. Anderson and John Earl Haynes. 1998. *The Soviet World of American Communism.* New Haven: Yale University Press.

Knight, Alan. 1987. *U.S.-Mexico Relations, 1910-1940: An Interpretation.* San Diego: Center for U.S.-Mexican Studies, University of California, San Diego, Monograph 28.

Kreneck, Thomas H. 2001. *Mexican American Odyssey: Felix Tijerina, Entrepreneur and Civic Leader, 1905–1965.* College Station: Texas A & M University Press.

Larrowe, Charles P. 1972. *Harry Bridges, the rise and fall of radical labor in the U.S.* Rochester: L. Hill Publisher.

Lehr, Dick. 1988. "The Information Underworld: Police Reliance on Criminal Informants Is a Dangerous Game for Both," *The Boston Globe*: A27, October 16.

Lerner, Lee and Brenda Wilmoth Lerner, 2004. eds. *Encyclopedia of Espionage, Intelligence, and Security,* 3 Volumes. Farmington Hills, MI: Gale Publishing Group.

Levario, Miguel Antonio. 2012. *Militarizing the Border: When Mexicans Became the Enemy*, College Station: Texas A & M University Press.

Levine, Yasha. 2018. *Surveillance Valley: The Secret Military History of the Internet.* New York: PublicAffairs.

Levy, Guenter. 1997. *The Cause That Failed: Communism in American Life.* New York: Oxford University Press.

Levy, Jacques E. 1975. *Cesar Chavez: An Autobiography of La Causa.* New York: W.W. Norton & Company.

Lofgren, Michael. 2014. *The Deep State: The Fall of the Constitution and the Rise of a Shadow Government.* New York: Penguin Books.

Lopez, Ian F. Haney. 2003. *Racism on Trial: The Chicano Fight for Justice.* Cambridge: Belknap Press.

Lord, Clifford L. 1968. ed. "The Mexicans in America: A Student's Guide to Localized History." *Localized History Series.* New York: Columbia University Press.

Loza, Steven. 1993. *Barrio Rhythm: Mexican American Music in Los Angeles.* Champaign: University of Illinois Press.

MacLean, Nancy. 2017. *Democracy in Chains: The Deep History of the Radical Right's Stealth Plan for America.* New Brunswick, Australia: Scribe Publications.

MacLachlan, Colin M. 1991. *Anarchism and the Mexican Revolution: The Political Trials of Ricardo Flores Magon in the United States.* Berkeley and Los Angeles, University of California Press.

Markham, Felix. 1963. *Napoleon.* New York: Mentor/Penguin Group.

Marquez, Benjamin. 1973. *LULAC: The Evolution of a Mexican American Political Organization.* Austin: University of Texas Press.

———. 2014. *Democratizing Texas Politics: Race, Identity, and Mexican American Empowerment.* Austin: University of Texas Press.

Marroquín, Héctor. 1978. *Mi Historia, La Lucha Por el Asilo en Los Estados Unidos.* Los Angeles: Totalitarian Press.

Maxwell, William J. 2015. *F. B. Eyes: How J. Edgar Hoover's Ghostreaders Framed African American Literature.* Princeton: Princeton University Press.

———. 2017. ed. *James Baldwin: The FBI File.* New York: Arcade Publishing, 2017.

Mazon, Mauricio. *The Zoot-Suit Riots: The Psychology of Symbolic Annihilation.* Austin: University of Texas Press.

Meier, Matt S. 1988. *Mexican American Biographies: A Historical Dictionary, 1836–1987*, Westport: Greenwood Press.

Meier, Matt S. and Feliciano Ribera. 1972. *The Chicanos: A History of Mexican Americans,* New York: Hill and Wang.

———. 1994. *Mexican Americans/American Mexicans: From Conquistadors to Chicanos.* New York: Hill and Wang.

Miller, Robert J., Jacinta Ruru, Larissa Behrendt, and Tracey Lindberg. 2010. *Discovering Indigenous Lands: The Doctrine of Discovery in the English Colonies.* New York: Oxford University Press.

Mize, Ronald L. an Alicia C. S. Swords. 2011. *Consuming Mexican Labor from the Bracero Program to NAFTA.* Toronto: University of Toronto Press.

Montejano, David. 2012. *Sancho's Journal: Exploring the Political Edge with the Brown Berets*, Austin: University of Texas Press.

Murphy, James. 2019. *Saints and Sinners in the Cristero War: Stories of Martyrdom from Mexico.* San Francisco: Ignatius Press.

National Archives and Records Administration, 8601 Adelphi Road, College Park, Maryland, 20740-6001.

Natapoff, Alexandra. 2009. *SNITCHING: Criminal Informants and the Erosion of American Justice.* New York: New York University Press.

Nava, Julián. 2002. *Julian Nava: My Mexican Journey.* Houston: Arte Publico Press.

Nava, Michael, January 2, 2020. "Big Lit Meets the Mexican Americans: A Study in White Supremacy," *Los Angeles Review of Books.* Los Angeles, California.

Navarro, Armando. 1990. *The Mexican American Youth Organization, Avant Garde of the Chicano Movement in Texas.* Austin: University of Texas Press.

Olivas, Michael A. 2006. *Colored Men and Hombres Aqui: Hernandez v. Texas and the Emergence of Mexican American Lawyering.* Houston: Arte Publico Press.

Pagan, Eduardo Obregon. 2003. *Murder at the Sleepy Lagoon: Zoot Suits, Race and Riots in Wartimes.* Chapel Hill: University of North Carolina Press.

Paget, Karen M. 2015. *Patriotic Betrayal: The Inside Story of the CIA's Secret Campaign to Enroll American Students in the Crusade Against Communism.* New Haven: Yale University Press.

Palace, Steve. 2018. "Ronald Reagan's Early Role as an FBI Informant," *The Vintage News* at www.thevintagenews.com/2018/09/06/young-ronald-reagan/, September 8.

Pawell, Miriam. 2014. *The Crusades of Cesar Chavez: A Biography.* New York Bloombury Press.

Perales, Alonso. 1937. Vol. I and II. *En Defensa de Mi Raza.* San Antonio: Artes Graficas.

Perez, Juan M. 2014. *Through Brown Eyes: A Short History of the Texas Brown Berets Organization and the Chicano Movement from my Point of View*, self-published, ISBN13-978-1537156446 and 10-1537156446.

Perkins, Clifford Alan. 1978. *Border Patrol: With the U.S. Immigration Service on the Mexican Boundary, 1910–1954.* El Paso: Texas Western Press.

Piess. Katie. 2014. *Zoot Suit: Enigmatic Career of an Extreme Style.* Philadelphia: University of Pennsylvania Press.

Pitt, Leonard. 1971. *The Decline of the Californios: A Social History of the Spanish-Speaking Californios.* Los Angeles: University of California Press.

Powell, Jim. 2005. *Wilson's War: How Woodrow Wilson's Great Blunder Led to Hitler, Lenin, Stalin, & World War II.* New York: Crown Forum.

Priest, Dana and William Arkin. 2011. *Top Secret America: The Rise of the New American Security State.* New York: Little Brown and Company.

Prignitz-Poda, Helga. 2015. *Frida Kahlo and Diego Rivera; Mexican Modern Art.* New York: Skira Rizzoli Publications.

Pycior, Julie Leininger 1997. *LBJ & Mexican Americans: The Paradox of Power.* Austin: University of Texas Press.

———. 2014. *Democratic Renewal and the Mutual Aid Legacy of U.S. Mexicans.* College Station: Texas A & M University Press.

Rafalko, Frank J. 2011. *MH/CHAOS: The CIA's Campaign Against the Radical Left and the Black Panthers.* Annapolis: Naval Institute Press.

Ramirez, Catherine R. 2009. *The Women in the Zoot Suits: Gender, Nationalism, and the Cultural Politics of Memory.* Durham: Duke University Press.

Ramirez, Henry M. 2013. *A Chicano in the White House: The Nixon No One Knew*, self-published, 2013. ISBN 13:9781497545823.

Ramos, Henry A. 1998. *The American G.I. Forum: In Pursuit of the Dream, 1948 and 1983.* Houston: Arte Publico.

Ratt, Dirk W. 1987. "U.S. Intelligence Operations and Covert Action in Mexico, 1900–1947," *Journal of Contemporary History*, 22:4: 615–638.

Reeve, Richard. 1969. *An Annotated Bibliography on Carlos Fuentes, 1949–1969.* Walled Lake, MI: Association of Teachers of Spanish and Portuguese.

Reverson, Derek S. 2012. ed. *Cyberspace and National Security: Threats, Opportunities, and Power in a Virtual World.* Washington, DC: Georgetown University Press.

Richardson, Peter. 2019. *American Prophet: The Life and Work of Carey McWilliams.* Oakland: University of California Press.

Rivera, Diego with translation by Gladys March. 1991. *My Art, My Life: An Autobiography*. New York: Dover Publications.

Robbins, Natalie. 1992. *Alien Ink: The FBI's War on Freedom of Expression*, New York: William Morrow and Company.

Rosales, Arturo. 2006. *Dictionary of Latino Civil Rights History*. Houston: Arte Publico Press.

Rosenbaum, Robert J. 1998. *Mexicano Resistance in the Southwest*. Dallas: Southern Methodist University Press.

Ross, Steven T. 2002. *American War Plans, 1890–1939*. New York: Frank Cass Publishers.

Ruiz, Vicki. 2006. "Nuestra America: Latino History as United States History," *Journal of American History*, 93:3: 664–671.

Ruiz, Vicki and Virginia Sanchez Korrol. 2006. *Latinas in the United States*. Bloomington: Indiana University Press.

Saenz, Rogelio and Dudley I. Poston, Jr., January 9, 2020, "Children of Color Already Make Up the Majority of Kids in Many US States," *The Conversation Blog*.

Salinas, Lupe S. 2015. *U.S. Latinos and Criminal Justice*. E. Lansing: Michigan State University Press.

Samora, Julian, Albert Peña, and Joe Bernal. 1979. *Gunpowder Justice: A Reassessment of the Texas Rangers*. Notre Dame: Notre Dame University Press.

Sanchez, David. 1978. *Expedition Through Aztlan*. La Puente, CA: Perspectiva Publications.

Sanchez, George J. 1995. *Becoming Mexican American: Ethnicity, Culture, and Identity in Chicano Los Angeles, 1900–1945*. New York: Oxford University Press.

Sanders, Lyle and Olen Leonard. 1951. *The Wetback in the Lower Rio Grande Valley of Texas*. Austin: University of Texas Press.

Sandoval, Moises. 1979. *The First Fifty Years: Half Century of Community Leadership, 1929–1979*, Washington, DC: National Office, 52–62.

Sanford, Amy Aldridge, 2020. *From Thought to Action: Developing a Social Justice Orientation*. San Diego: Cognella.

San Miguel, Jr., Guadalupe. 1991. "'The Community Is Beginning to Rumble,' The Origins of Chicano Educational Protest in Houston," *The Houston Review: History and Culture of the Gulf Coast*, 13:3: 127–147.

———. 2007. *Brown, Not White: School Integration and the Chicano Movement in Houston*, College Station: Texas A & M University Press.

Schrecker, Ellen. 1994. *The Age of McCarthyism: A Brief History with Documents*. Boston: Bedford Books.

Schultz, Randy. "The Ku Klux Klan Revisited," *SAM Houston's Metropolitan Magazine*, (Feb/Mar 1976), 1: 4: 16–18.

Seigle, Larry, Farrell Dobbs and Steve Clark. 2014. *50 Years of Covert Operations in the US*. New York: Pathfinder Press.

Shenon, Philip. September 11, 1988. " Hispanic FBI Agents' Suit Reflect Sense of Betrayal," *New York Times*: Section1:26.

Shino, Enrijeta. 2011. "Brown Berets: A Story of Continuous Surveillance," *European Journal of Social Sciences*, 19:3: 450–464.

Shockley, John S. 1974. *Chicano Revolt in a Texas Town.* Notre Dame: Notre Dame University Press.

Sirvent, Roberto and Danny Haiphong, 2019. *American Exceptionalism and American Innocence: A People's History of Fake News—From the Revolutionary War to the War on Terror.* New York: Skyhorse Publishing.

Sloss-Vento, Adela. 1997. *Alonso S. Perales: His Struggle for the Rights of Mexican-Americans.* San Antonio: Artes Graficas.

Smith, Jeff. June 22, 2011 and July 13, 2011, "The California Whirlwind, Part One" and "Rosa/Luisa: The California Whirlwind, Part Two," respectively, *San Diego Reader,* San Diego, California.

Smith, Ryan. 2018. "Guatemalan Immigrant Luisa Moreno Was Expelled from the U.S. for her Ground Breaking Labor Activism," *Smithsonian Magazine,* Washington, DC, July 15.

Sobarzo, Alejandro. 1996. *Deber y conciencia; Nicolas Trist, el negociador norteamericano en la Guerra del 47.* Mexico, DF: Fondo de Cultural Economica.

Sonenstein, Brian. 2019. "ICE Retalliates Against Immigrant Rights Activists by Suspending Visitation Program in Alabama," *Shadow Proof Blog,* December 19.

Spence, Mark David. 1999. *Dispossessing the Wilderness: Indian Removal and the Making of the National Parks.* New York: Oxford University Press.

Subcommittee on Constitutional Rights of the Committee on the Judiciary of the U.S. Senate. 1972. *Army Surveillance of Civilians: A Documentary Analysis,* Washington, DC: Government Printing Office.

St. John, Rachel. 2011. *Line in the Sand: A History of the Western U.S.-Mexico Border.* Princeton: Princeton University Press.

Stout, Jr., Joseph A. 2012. *Spies, Politics and Power: El Departamento Confidencial en Mexico, 1922–1946.* Fort Worth: TCU Press.

Street, Richard Steven. 2004. *Beasts of the Fields: A Narrative History of California Farmworkers, 1769–1913.* Stanford: Stanford University Press.

Sullivan, William C. with Bill Brown. 1979. *The Bureau: My Thirty Years in Hoover's FBI.* New York: W.W. Norton.

Suth, John Edward. 2012. *Eisenhower in War and Peace.* New York: Random House.

Swing, Joseph, 1954. *Annual Report of the Immigration and Naturalization Service, End of Fiscal Year 1954,* Washington, DC: Department of Justice, Government Printing Office.

Texas State Historical Association, *Handbook of Texas Online,* Austin. Httpsd:// tshaonline.org/

The National Geographic Society. 1984. *A Guide to Our Federal Lands,* Rockville: Holladay-Tyler Printing Corporation.

Theoharis, Athan. 1991. *From the Secret Files of J. Edgar Hoover.* Chicago: Ivan R. Dee Publisher.

———. 2006. *The Central Intelligence Agency: Security Under Scrutiny.* Westport: Greenwood Press.

Tuchman, Barbara. 1971. *The Zimmerman Telegram.* New York: Bantam Books.

U.S. Commission on Civil Rights, Mexican Americans and the Administration of Justice in the Southwest. 1970, *A Report of the United States Commission on Civil Rights*, Washington, DC: Government Printing Office.

United States House of Representatives. 2013. *Hispanic Americans in Congress, U.S. House of Representatives, 1822–2012.* Washington, DC: Government Printing Office.

Utley, Robert M. 2007. *Lone Star Lawmen: The Second Century of the Texas Rangers.* New York: Berkley Books.

Valdés, Ernesto. 2007, Houston, Texas, Oral History Interview with Yolanda Birdwell, 41 pages, May 4. Repository URL: http://info.lib.uh.edu/about/campus -libraries-collections/special-collections/.

Van Cleve, George William. 2017. *We Have Not a Government: The Articles of Confederation and the Road to the Constitution.* Chicago: University of Chicago Press.

Vigil, Ernesto. 1999. *The Crusade for Justice: Chicano Militancy and the Government's War on Dissent.* Madison: University of Wisconsin Press.

Villanueva, Jr., Nicolas. 2017. *The Lynching of Mexicans in the Texas Borderlands.* Albuquerque: University of New Mexico Press.

Walker, Wayne T., April 1982. "Gus Jones: From Texas Ranger to Special Agent-In-Charge," *Real West: True Real West Adventures,* eCRATER STORE at 184: 25: 20-22, 54 at www.craterstore.com/.

Wannall, W. R. 2000. *The Real J. Edgar Hoover: For the Record,* Paducah: Turner Publishing Company.

Washington, Mary. 2014. *The Other Blacklist: The African American Literary and Cultural Left of the 1950s.* New York: Columbia University Press.

Weeks, Douglas O. 1929. "The League of United Latin American Citizens," *The Southwestern Political and Social Science Quarterly,* X:3: 257–278.

Weiner, Tim, 2012. *Enemies: A History of the FBI.* New York: Random House.

Weitz, Mark A. 2010. *The Sleepy Lagoon Case; Race Discrimination and Mexican American Rights.* Lawrence: University Press of Kansas.

Wilson, Joan Hoff. 1992. *Herbert Hoover, Forgotten Progressive.* Prospect Heights: Waveland Press.

Wolfe, Patrick. 1963. "Settler Colonialism and the Elimination of the Native," *Journal of Genocide Research,* 8:4: 387–409.

Yanez, Angelica Maria. 2010. "Chicano and Black Radical Activism of the 1960s: A Comparison Between the Brown Berets and the Black Panther Party in California," Master's thesis. University of California, San Diego, San Diego, California.

Young, Alice G. 2015. *Mexican Exodus: Emigrants, Exiles, and Refugees of the Cristero War.* New York: Oxford University Press.

Zamora, Emilio. 2008. *Claiming Rights and Righting Wrongs in Texas: Mexican Workers and Job Politics During World War II.* College Station: Texas A & M University Press.

Zlotnik, Jack. 1964. *National Security Management: National Intelligence.* Washington, DC: Industrial College of the Armed Forces.

Zuboff, Shoshana. 2019. *The Age of Surveillance Capitalism: The Fight for a Human Future at the New Frontier of Power.* New York: PublicAffairs.

# Index

Academic Support Program (ASP), 106

ACFPFB. *See* American Committee for the Protection of the Foreign Born (ACFPFB)

ACLU. *See* American Civil Liberties Union (ACLU)

activists, 186

activities: centers of, 187; militant, 124; subversive, 6, 166

Acuña, Rodolfo, 97

Administrative Index (ADEX), 117

affidavits, 172, 173

AFL. *See* American Federation of Labor (AFL)

agencies, US, 182

Agency for International Development (AID), 86

AGIF. *See* American GI Forum (AGIF)

Agricultural Workers Organizing Committee (AWOC), 41

AID. *See* Agency for International Development (AID)

Aid, Matthew M., 206

Albuquerque, New Mexico, 195

Alcayaga, Lucila Godoy, 2

Alexa Internet Incorporated, 208

aliases, 32; Fender, F., 129, 137; Moreno, 11, 13, 14; Telles, Ramón "Raymond," 71–72

Allee, Alfred. Y., 145

allegations, 75, 76–77, 80–81

ambassador, US, 65, 68–70

American Civil Liberties Union (ACLU), 104

American Committee for the Protection of the Foreign Born (ACFPFB), 26

American Council of Spanish Speaking People, 160

American Federation of Labor (AFL), 4

American GI Forum (AGIF), 147, 148, 171, 172, 175–76, 177n30; Americanism, 156; Communist ties, 159–61, 165–67; dissension, 155; FBI file, 157–59, 163–67; growth, 157; Hoover, J., on, 161–62; incorporation, 153; Molina on, 169–70; network, 154

American National Mexican Association (ANMA), 28, 29

Angel De León, Miguel, 2–3

ANMA. *See* American National Mexican Association (ANMA)

Arbenz, Jacobo, 34

Army, US, xviii–xix

*Army Surveillance in America* (Jensen), xviii–xix, xx, xxiiin26

arrest: Castro, S., 104; Moreno, 30–31

articles, 23, 24, 27–28, 155

ASP. *See* Academic Support Program (ASP)
assassination: attempts, 201; Kennedy, J., 168–70
authorization, 192
automation, 170, 173, 174
Avila, Bobby, 103
awards, 72
AWOC. *See* Agricultural Workers Organizing Committee (AWOC)

background, subversive, 170, 175
Bacon, William H., 46
bail, 104
Baja California, Mexico, 192, 193, 194, 198
Bamford, James, 206
bankruptcy, 74
Bardacke, Frank, 61n1
Barrett, Charlene, 14–15
Barrett, James E., 71
"Before the Next Tear Drop Falls," 134
Belmont, Alan, 189, 202n9
Belmont High School, 97–98
Bemis, Gray, 4, 5, 17, 18, 30–31, 33–35
Big Lit, xvi, xvii
Bin, Martha, 108–9
blackmail, 77
Blowouts, life after, 105–7
Bobbitt, H.L., 49, 51
BOCOV. *See* Border Coverage Program (BOCOV)
BOI. *See* Bureau of Investigation (BOI)
Bolivia, 51, 52
bombs, 196
Bonus Marchers, 3–4
books, 127n42
Boonstra, Clarence A., 82
Border Coverage Program (BOCOV), 181, 194, 197; FBI files, 182–83; Hoover, J., on, 186; resurrection, 199–201; Special Mail Room file, 189–93; training conferences, 184–89, 195
border crossing, 190, 192, 207

boxing, 143, 144–45
Bracero Program, 41, 45, 51–52, 155
Brennan, D.J., 195–96
Bridges, Alfred Renton "Harry," 4, 10
Brown Berets, 102, 111, 113, 114, 116, 119–20
Brownell, Herbert, 164–65
Brown Power Conference, 60
*Brown v. Board of Education*, 99
brutality, police, 164
Bryant, D.F., 43, 45, 46
Brymer, Glyn T., 78
Buchwald, Nathan, 35–36
Buitrago, Ann Mari, 185
Bureau of Investigation (BOI), 141
Burrows, Charles R., 76, 77
Bush, George H. W., 130
Bush, George W., xvi
Bustamante, Jorge, 45
Butterfield, Alexander P., 84, 94n33
Byron, Rhonda, 116–17

Calhoun, R. Howard, 48
California: HUAC equivalent hearings, 19–22; Sacramento, 41. *See also* Los Angeles, California (LA)
California State University, at Los Angeles, 97
Calvary, Gloria, 169
Campbell, O.V., 173, 174
Camp Hess Kramer, 99–101, 110
captioned program, 200
cards, border crossing, 190, 192
career, of Telles, Ramón "Raymond," 66–67
Carter, Jimmy, 130, 135
Carter, Lynda, 133
cases, domestic worker, 89–90
Castro, Annette, 97
Castro, Raul, 87–88
Castro, Salvador "Sal," 99–100, 116; arrest, 104; ASP implemented by, 106; childhood, 95–96; death, 111; FBI file, 112–14, 122–23; informants on, 122–23; lectures of,

123–24; legal persecution, 120–24; surveillance reports, 117; teacher training, 97; walkouts organized by, 101–5

Castro, Victoria M "Vickie," 109, 126n36

CDI. *See* Custodial Detention Index (CDI)

centers, of activity, 187

Central Intelligence Agency (CIA), xviii, 69, 88

Certificate of Citizenship, Galarza, E., 48

Chamber of Commerce Auditorium, San Diego, 20

charity work, Telles, D., 81, 91

Charnaud MacDonald, Augusto, 24

Chavez, Cesar E., 101, 102, 202n12

Chavez, Dennis, 67

Chavez Ortiz, Ricardo, 124

Chicano groups, xii

Chicano Latino Youth Leadership Project (CLYLP), 110–11

Chicano Movement, xi, 108, 109, 156–57

Chicano nationalists, 101

Chicano Scholarship Night, 106

Chicano Studies, xiii, 106

Chicano Youth Leadership Conference (CYLC), 100, 102, 110

childhood: Castro, S., 95–96; Galarza, E., 42; Medrano, F., 142–43; Moreno, 1; Telles, Ramón "Raymond," 66

Christensen, John, 35

Church, Frank, 201

Church Committee, 201

CIA. *See* Central Intelligence Agency (CIA)

CIO. *See* Congress of Industrial Organizations (CIO)

Citizens Military Training Corps (CMTC), 152

civil organizations, 145

civil rights, xvii, 41, 172

Clark, Ramsey, 116, 127n51

classes, of Mayhew, 196

classifications: of files, 200, 201; racial, 108

Cleveland, Ohio, 115

Clinton, Bill, xvi, 130

CLYLP. *See* Chicano Latino Youth Leadership Project (CLYLP)

CMTC. *See* Citizens Military Training Corps (CMTC)

coffee plantations, 74, 75

Cohen, Alex A., 76–77, 78–79

COINTELPRO. *See* Counterintelligence Program (COINTELPRO)

Columbia University, 43

commemorations, xi–xii

commissary, 83

Communism: AGIF ties to, 159–61, 165–67; Hoover, J., on, 141

Communist Party, 147; disorganizing, 184, 185; memorandums on terms for, 20

Communist Party of *Baja California* (PCMBC), 186–87, 198

Communist Party USA (CPUSA), 3, 9, 38n26, 141; COINTELPRO, 5–6; publications, 28

communist sympathizers, 187

Communist Youth Groups, 197

community, Mexican American, 123, 154

conditions, working, 42

conferences, training, BOCOV, 184–89, 195

confidential informants, 7, 13, 17, 34, 161

Congressional Committee on Education and Labor, 45

congress members, US, 69

Congress of Industrial Organizations (CIO), 4, 8, 9, 142

conservative policy initiatives, 205

conspiracy theorists, 168

Constantino, Arturo G., 86

consulting contracts, 84, 85

Coombs, Richard E., 25
corporations, 42, 207. *See also specific corporations*
Corpus Christi, Texas, 74, 75, 76, 153
*Corpus Christi Caller*, 165
Cory, Leonard, 118
Costa Rica, 74–75, 77
Counterintelligence Program (COINTELPRO), 112, 113, 188; CPUSA, 5–6; FOIPA and, 199–200; investigations, 186
counterintelligence tactics, 184, 196
Coville, Bess P., 174–75
Cox, Hugh B., 53–54
CPUSA. *See* Communist Party USA (CPUSA)
Cravens, Cleve, 75–76, 78, 79, 80
criminal records, Moreno, 12
Crockett, William, 79
Crump, George W., 46
Crusius, Patrick, xiv
culture, Mexican, 100
Curry, Jesse E., 172, 173, 174
Custodial Detention Index (CDI), 8; Cox on, 53–54; Galarza, E., and, 47–48, 49, 50
cyberspace, 208–9
CYLC. *See* Chicano Youth Leadership Conference (CYLC)

*The Daily Worker*, 5, 9, 11, 27, 58, 59
Dallas, Texas, 142, 165–67, 171
Dallas Independent School Board, 146
dataveillance, 183, 205, 206
Day, Sharon, 69
deals, oil, 55, 56
death: Castro, S., 111; Garcia, H., 175; threats, 107
Del Mar College, 132
demands, student, 103, 104
*Democracy in Chains* (MacLean), 205
demography, 110
demonstrations, 115, 191, 194
Department of Defense, US, 205–6

Department of Justice, US, 118
deportation, xvi–xvii, 19, 95, 155; lists for, 29; Moreno, 26–27, 30–31; warrants for, 25
desegregating, Mexican schools, 98–99
designation, racial, 99
Dettweiller, William E., 29, 30
development, of informants, 184–85
Diaz, Jaime, 34
Diaz, Porfirio, 41, 42
Diaz de Zatz, Alba, 34
dictators, 28n30, 135
DiGiorgio Fruit Corporation, 54, 61n3
digital literacy, 209
discrimination, 99, 143, 152, 166, 171–72
disorganizing, Communist Party, 184, 185
disruptive tactics, 188
dissension, AGIF, 155
districts, school, 109
Domestic Intelligence Division, FBI, 112, 115, 124
domestic worker case, of Telles, Ramón "Raymond," 89–90
dropout rates, high school: LA, 99; Texas, 132

Echevarria Alvarez, Luis, 45
economy, farm, 131
editorials, 62n20
Edwards, Don, 200–201
EEOC. *See* Equal Employment Opportunity Commission (EEOC)
Eisenhower, Dwight D., 68, 76, 155, 187
elections, Mexico, 196–97, 198
El Paso, Texas, xiv, 65, 71, 192–93, xxiin11
"The El Paso Declaration," 44–45
El Salvador, 89
empowerment, at Camp Hess Kramer, 99–101
encyclopedia, 22

Engles, Paul, 114–15
English as a second language (ESL), 108
Equal Employment Opportunity
  Commission (EEOC), 44, 84, 88
Ernst, Morris L., 55
errors, information, 7–9, 48, 134
ESL. *See* English as a second language
  (ESL)
Esparza, Montezuma, 100–101
espionage, 46, 47, 48, 208
Espionage Act, 206
Evans, C.A., 48
evidence, 16–17, 113
exemptions, FOIPA, 33
eyewitnesses, 169

facial recognition, 207–8
Falcon, Ismael C., 56, 57
Fallan, Lee M., 16
farm economy, 131
FBI. *See* Federal Bureau of
  Investigation (FBI)
FDIC. *See* Federal Deposit Insurance
  Corporation (FDIC)
Federal Bureau of Investigation (FBI),
  xi; AGIF file, 157–59, 163–67;
  BOCOV files, 182–83; Castro, S.,
  file, 112–14, 122–23; Fender, F.,
  file, 129–31, 134–38; field offices,
  23, 184, 190, 192, 195, 197; Foreign
  Liaison Desk, 189, 190, 191, 194;
  Galarza, E., file, 43–45; Medrano,
  F., file, 146–49; Mexico tactics, 183;
  Molina file, 170–74; Moreno file, 6–
  18; Nixon and, 140n30; Reagan and,
  140n32; Telles, Ramón "Raymond,"
  file, 70–74, 84–87. *See also specific
  topics*
Federal Deposit Insurance Corporation
  (FDIC), 90
Fender, Freddy (Baldemar Huerta), xxi;
  aliases, 129, 137; FBI files, 129–31,
  134–38; medical issues, 132; name
  change, 132–33; prison records, 130

Fender, Leo, 133, 139n16
field offices, FBI, 23, 184, 190, 192,
  195, 197
files: classifications of, 200, 201;
  numbers, 201n4
First Financial Enterprises, 90
fliers, 44–45
FOIPA. *See* Freedom of Information/
  Privacy Act (FOIPA)
Food Tobacco and Agricultural Workers
  (FTA), 29
Ford, Gerald, 135
Foreign Liaison Desk, FBI, 189, 190,
  191, 194
foreign policies, 181
Fox, Chris P., 73
El Francis Hotel, 81
Franco, Nicolasa Ruiz, 142, 143,
  149n12
fraud, voter, 146
Freedom of Information/Privacy
  Act (FOIPA), xviii, 62n12;
  COINTELPRO files and, 199–200;
  exemptions, 33; requests, 70, 129,
  138n1, 182; rules, 93n24
Freeman, Leon, 55–56, 58
FTA. *See* Food Tobacco and
  Agricultural Workers (FTA)
fundraising, 28, 29, 110
Fusillo, Wanda, 152, 153
future technology, 207–8

Galarza, Ernesto, xxi, 41, 60–61;
  CDI, 47–48, 49, 50; Certificate
  of Citizenship, 48; childhood of,
  42; "The El Paso Declaration"
  of, 44–45; FBI file on, 43–45;
  Hoover, J., on, 57–58; HUAC and,
  63n26; labor organizing of, 54–60;
  memorandums on, 52; naturalization
  records, 49; NFLU employment, 54;
  PAU employment, 51–52; protests
  organized by, 44; surveillance reports
  on, 45–51, 55–60

Galarza, Mae (née Taylor), 43, 49–50, 59, 61
Gale, Linn, 58–59
Galvan, Robert, 21–22, 23
Garcia, Antonio G., 151
Garcia, Cleotilde, 154–55
Garcia, Gilbert C., 166–67
Garcia, Gus, 158, 160, 162
Garcia, Hector P., 151, 154, 155–56, 160, 176n1; death, 175; letter, 157–58; medical practice of, 152–53; speech, 162
Garcia, Jerry, 138
Garcia, Jose, 151
Garcia, Maria Huerta, 132
Garcia, Mario T., 65, 101, 125n1, 127n42
Garfield High School, 99
Garrison, James, 178n47
Garza, Reynaldo, 74
Gayton, Al, 23
Gentile, G. Marvin, 79, 83
Ghetto Informant Program (GIP), 113–14, 127n51
Golden, Daniel, 206
Gonzalez, Pedro J., 19, 38n27
Gonzalez, Ramon, 165
Good Neighbor Commission, 166
government, Mexican, 181
grant, land, 65
Griffin, William, 47
Grignon, Henri G., 82
Griswold del Castillo, Richard, 36n2, 37n15
groups: Chicano, xii; Communist Youth, 197; leftist political, 202n11; minority, 141
growth, AGIF, 157
Guanjuato, Mexico, 142
Guatemala, 24, 25, 27, 32, 36, 38n30
Guatemala City, Guatemala, 31
Guatemalans, 164
guitars, 133, 139n16

Haines, Gerald K., 202n10

handbill, 193–94, 197–98
Hardesty, A.R., 142
Hardy, David M., 138nn1–2
Harislades, Peter, 28
Hart, H.M., 173
Haudsep, Edwin O., 13
Hazard Park, 103
Heads-Up letter, 165
hearsay, 61, 78
Hecht, Richard, 120
*Herald Examiner*, 116
*Hernandez v. Texas*, 158, 177n36
history: of surveillance, xvii–xviii; untold, xv–xvii
hitchhiking, 152
Honig, Nat, 26
Hoover, Herbert, 3–4
Hoover, J. Edgar, 6, 11, 22, 52–54, 92n21; on AGIF, 161–62; on BOCOV, 186; on Communism, 141; on Galarza, E., 57–58; Idar letter to, 163–64; Johnson, L. and, 140n29; letters from, 32–33
Hot Springs, Arkansas, 144
house of assignation, 76, 93n30
House Un-American Activities Committee (HUAC), 17, 56, 160; California hearings, 19–22; Galarza, E., and, 63n26
Howard, George F., 206
HUAC. *See* House Un-American Activities Committee (HUAC)
Huerta, Baldemar. *See* Fender, Freddy
Hull, Cordell, 6
Idar, Ed, 162, 163–64

identification division records, 136
identity, 101
ignorance, 209
"illegal aliens," xvi
Immigration and Naturalization Service (INS), xiv, 11–12, 19–20, 117
Imperial Records, 133
incorporation, AGIF, 153
indictments, 119

indigenous roots, 112
Industrial Workers of the World (IWW), xix
influential people, 152
informants, 11, 13, 14–15, 16, 23, 117–18; on Castro, S., 122–23; confidential, 7, 13, 17, 34, 161; development of, 184–85; GIP, 113–14, 127n51; types of, 161, 177n39
information errors, 7–9, 48, 134
initiatives, conservative policy, 205
INS. *See* Immigration and Naturalization Service (INS)
insecurity, 101
insurance, 69
interventions, US, 181
interviews, 46, 47, 50, 190
investigations, COINTELPRO, 186
*The Invisible Government* (Ross and Wise), xviii
IWW. *See* Industrial Workers of the World (IWW)

Jagoda, Patrick, 209
Jalco, Mexico, 41–42
El Jardin, 131
jazz, 105
Jensen, Joan M., xviii–xix, xx, xxiiin26
*Jesus Salvatierra vs Del Rio Independent School District*, 98
Jimenez, Esperanza, 144
Joe Brown Enterprises LTD, 135–36
Johnsen, Miles A., 20, 29
Johnson, Lyndon B., 44, 67–68, 82, 108, 135, xxiin22; Hoover, J. and, 140n29; Viva Johnson movement, 155
Joint US Mexican Commission on Border Area Development, 82
Jones, Gus T., 92n21
Jones, M.A., 118
Juarez, Benito, 181

Kapp, Joe, 134

Kelley, Clarence M., 88, 89, 161, 199, 200
Kemp, Maury Page, 90
Kennedy, John F., xx, 67–68, 70, 97, 156, 168–70
Kennedy, Robert, 104–5
Kennedy, Tom, 154
Kilday, Owen, 10
Kimball, Harry M., 18
Kirby, Edward J., 14
Kopriva, R.C., 49
Kossen, Sidney, 60
Kotzin, Tobias, 100
Kuno, Donald Wiberg, 16–17, 18

LA. *See* Los Angeles, California (LA)
"LA 13," 104, 105, 120–21, 122
labor: Mexican, 155; organizing, 54–60
*La Liga de Costureras* (League of Seamstresses), 3
L'Allier, R.O., 191
land grant, 65
Langbart, David A., 202n10
language: learning, 96; Spanish, 194
Larralde, Carlos, 36n2, 37n15
Latin American Section, 197
Latino Youth Leadership Conference. *See* Chicano Youth Leadership Conference (CYLC)
Law Enforcement Intelligence Unit (LEIU), 126n27
Lawler, J.E., 46–47
lawsuits, 98–99
leadership training programs, 110–11
leaflets, 27–28
League of Seamstresses (*La Liga de Costureras*), 3
League of United Latin American Citizens (LULAC), xx, 98, 144, 154, 156
lectures, of Castro, S., 123–24
leftist political groupings, 202n11
Legal Attaché. *See* Legat
legal persecution, Castro, S., 120–24

"legal squatters," 75, 93n29
Legat (Legal Attaché), 70, 138n5; Manila, 130, 136, 137, 138, 140n26; Mexico, 34, 35, 82–83, 187–88, 195
LEIU. *See* Law Enforcement Intelligence Unit (LEIU)
Lemon Grove, California, 98–99
Lerchenmuller, Carole, 104
letters, 79, 116–17, 118, 148, 184; Bryant, 43; Garcia, H., 157–58; Heads-Up, 165; from Hoover, J., 32–33; Hoover, J., and Idar, 163–64
lists, for deportation, 29
literacy, digital, 209
literature, 111
Local Liaison, FBI, 190
Longoria, Felix, 153–54, 176n19
Lopez, Alicia, 1
Lopez, Angela "Angelita." *See* Telles, Angela
Lopez Obrador, Andres Manual, xiv
Lorraine, Mytyl, 3, 10
Los Angeles, California (LA), 7, 19, 95; California State University, 97; school board, 104, 109
Los Angeles, California, high schools, 98; dropout rates, 99; walkouts, 101–5
Los Angeles Dodgers, 106
*Los Angeles Times*, 112, 124
Lowery, William J., Jr., 171, 176
Lozano, Mari, 107
LULAC. *See* League of United Latin American Citizens (LULAC)

MacArthur, Douglas, 157
MacLean, Nancy, 205
Mail Covers, 11, 18, 23, 30, 31
Manila, Philippines, 129, 130, 136, 137, 138, 140n26
Manuel (Moreno's gardener), 5
MAPA. *See* Mexican American Political Association (MAPA)
Marcos, Ferdinand, 135
Marrano, Louis M., 83

Mason, James W., 12
material, redacted, 32, 33, 115–16, 160, 189–90
MAYA. *See* Mexican-American Youth Association (MAYA)
Mayhew, Robert, 195–99
Mazatlan, Mexico, 95
McCarthy, Eugene, 104–5
McCarthy, Joseph, 162
McInerney, James M., 161
McKee, William D., 78–79
McTernan, John T., 20–21
McWilliams, Carey, 5, 10, 97
Meadows, R.W., 50
MEChA. *See* Movimiento Estudiantil Chicano de Aztlan (MEChA)
media, social, 206
medical issues, Fender, F., 132
medical practice, of Garcia, H., 152–53
Medrano, Francisco "Pancho," xxi, 141; childhood of, 142–43; FBI file, 146–49; memorandums on, 148–49; surveillance reasoning, 147; in UAW, 144–45
Medrano, Pauline (daughter), 146
Medrano, Roberto (son), 146
Medrano, Sabas (father), 142–43
*Medrano v. Allee*, 149n13
memorandums, 21, 29, 82, 149n12; on Communist Party terms, 20; on Galarza, E., 52; on Medrano, F., 148–49; on Moreno, 17–18, 32
Mercedes, Texas, 151
Mexican American Education Committee, 100
"Mexican American Militancy," 113, 119
Mexican American Political Association (MAPA), 156
Mexican Americans: community, 123, 154; veterans, 153, 154, 166
Mexican American Youth Association (MAYA), 114, 119, 145
Mexican Revolution, 65, 95, 131, 155, 181

Mexican schools, desegregating, 98–99
Mexico, 43; culture of, 100; elections, 196–97, 198; FBI tactics in, 183; government of, 181; labor from, 155; Legat, 34, 35, 82–83, 187–88, 195. *See also specific places*
Mexico City, Mexico, 2–3, 31, 34, 35
Miami, Florida, 35
*The Militant* (newspaper), 119
militant activities, 124
military records, 71, 72, 122, 152
military recruitment, 106–7
Milwaukee, Wisconsin, 141
mining, 51, 52
Mink, George, 8–9, 34
minority groups, 141
*Minority Report*, 207
Mistral, Gabriela. *See* Alcayaga, Lucila Godoy
Molina, Joe (Jose Rodriguez Molina), 167, 174–76, 178n45, 179n52; on AGIF, 169–70; FBI file, 170–74; testimony, 168–70
Monterrey Resident Agency, 187, 188
Moore, George C., 115, 128n53
Moreno, Luisa, xxi, 36; aliases, 11, 13, 14; arrest and deportation, 30–31; arrest warrant for, 23; articles, 24, 27–28; becoming, 2–4; childhood of, 1; criminal record, 12; deportation hearings, 26–27; FBI file on, 6–18; INS details, 11–12; memorandums on, 17–18, 32; Murdock on, 24–25; surveillance reports, 7–10, 12–14, 16–17, 34–35; testimony, 21, 22; union organizations of, 4–5
*Morgen Freiheit* (newspaper), 35–36
motorcade route, 168–69, 178n47
*Movimiento Estudiantil Chicano de Aztlan* (MEChA), 111–12
Munro, George F., 35
Murdock, Steve, 24–25

name changes, 132–34

name check program, 71–74, 93n26
NARA. *See* National Archives and Records Administration (NARA)
National Action Party (PAN), 191
National Agricultural Workers Union (NAWU), 41
National Archives and Records Administration (NARA), 43, 62n12
National Association for the Advancement of Colored People, 171
National Chicano Student Walkouts Conference, 107–8
National Economic Development Association (NEDA), 85
National Farm Labor Union (NFLU), 41, 54, 61n3
*National Guardian*, 157, 158
nationalists, Chicano, 101
National Liberation Movement, 191, 195, 202n11
National Rifle Association (NRA), 111
National Security Agency (NSA), 206–7
National Sinarquist Union (UNS), 191
naturalization records, Galarza, E., 49
Nava, Michael, xvi, xvii
Navarro, Delfina. *See* Telles, Delfina
NAWU. *See* National Agricultural Workers Union (NAWU)
NEDA. *See* National Economic Development Association (NEDA)
network, AGIF, 154
neutralization, 185, 196
newspapers, 187. *See also specific newspapers*
*New York Times*, 62n20
New Zealand, 136, 137–38
NFLU. *See* National Farm Labor Union (NFLU)
Nimmins, William H., 72
Nixon, Richard M., 17, 67, 87, 89, 135, 140n30
nobody's land (*terra bullius*), 93n29
North American Aviation, 143–44
*North from Mexico* (McWilliams), 97

Northrup Grumman Corporation, 207
NRA. *See* National Rifle Association (NRA)
NSA. *See* National Security Agency (NSA)
numbers, file, 201n4

Obama, Barack, xvi
O'Brien, Francis D., 15–16
Occidental College, 42
*Occupied America* (Acuña), 97
oil deals, 55, 56
Operation Wetback, 155
Orendain, Antonio "Tony," xxi
Orendain, Raquel, xxi
organizations, xxi, 145. *See also specific organizations*
Oswald, Lee Harvey, 170, 172, 175

PA. *See* Privacy Act (PA)
Palmer Raids, 26, 28, 126n27, 142
Palomo, Soledad, 167, 169, 170
PAN. *See* National Action Party (PAN)
Pan American Union (PAU), 46, 47, 51–52
parents, 100
Parks, Sheldon W., 191
Parry, Vaughn I., 8
PASO. *See* Political Association of Spanish Speaking Organizations (PASO)
passport, 87
Patton, James, 52–53
PAU. *See* Pan American Union (PAU)
PCMBC. *See* Communist Party of *Baja California* (PCMBC)
Pearl Harbor, 152
people, influential, 152
People's Institute of Applied Religion, 158, 162–63
*Peoples' World*, 23–24, 26, 28, 58, 59
Perez, Faustina, 151
persecution, legal, Castro, S., 120–24
personality, radio, 19
Philadelphia, Pennsylvania, 11, 12

phone bank, 101
photographs, xix–xx, 81
Piranya Coffee House, 102
plantations, coffee, 74, 75
Plant Production Section (PPS), xix, xix–xx
*The Plum Book*, 68, 92n13
police, 169, 170, 172; brutality, 164; undercover, 103, 126n27
policies: conservative initiatives for, 205; foreign, 181
Political Association of Spanish Speaking Organizations (PASO), 156
politics, 144, 145
poll tax, 67, 154
Post, Louis, 53
*Poverty in the Land of Plenty*, 41, 54
Powell, Adam Clayton, 45
Powell, Lewis, 205
Powell Memo, 205
PPS. *See* Plant Production Section (PPS)
Prado Valdez, Julio, 193–94, 197–98
Pressman, Lee, 55, 56
Primm, B.E., 49
prison records, 130
Privacy Act (PA), xviii
professors, 152
programs: captioned program, 200; leadership training, 110–11; name check, 71–74. *See also specific programs*
Proposition 187, 109
Proposition 227, 109
protests, xii, 25, 95, 109–10, 121; Galarza, E., organizing, 44; student, xiii, 194
Provinse, W. Nathan, 27
psychological tactics, 185
publications, CPUSA, 28
public schools, xiii

quarry, 143
question marks, 194
Quinn, Anthony, 133

Quintanilla, Selena, 175

racial classifications, 108
racial designation, 99
racism, 152, 153
radio personality, 19
ranch, 111
Raymond Telles Academy, 90
La Raza Unida Rump Conference,
    44–45
Reagan, Ronald, 60, 89, 108, 111, 135,
    140n32
recognition, facial, 207–8
recommendations, Telles, Ramón
    "Raymond," 86, 88
recordings, tape, 27
records: criminal, 12; identification
    division, 136; military, 71, 72, 122,
    152; naturalization, 49; prison, 130
recruitment, military, 106–7
redacted material, 32, 33, 115–16, 160,
    189–90
Red Scare, 142
refugees, 108, 151
reports, surveillance: Bemis, 33–35;
    Castro, S., 117; Galarza, E., 45–51,
    55–60; Galarza, M., 49–50, 59;
    Moreno, 7–10, 12–14, 16–17, 34–35;
    Telles, Ramón "Raymond," 80–82
requests, FOIPA, 70, 129, 138n1, 182
resurrection, BOCOV, 199–201
Reuther, Walter, 144, 145
Rice, Patrick M., 80–81
Richards, Ann, 130
Richards, E. Rhead, 117, 122
Richmond, Virginia, 45
rights, civil, xvii, 41, 172
Rio Grande Valley, 151
riots, 95, 109
riveting, 143
Rock and Roll Hall of Fame, 133
Rodriguez, Ernesto, 1
Rodriguez Lopez, Blanca Rosa. *See*
    Moreno, Luisa

Rodriguez Molina, Jose. *See* Molina,
    Joe
role, of US ambassador, 68–70
Romero James, Concho, 47
Roosevelt, Franklin Delano, 3, 4–5, 12,
    55, 158
Roosevelt High School, 121
roots, indigenous, 112
Rose, Jonathan C., 182
Ross, Thomas B., xvii–xviii
route, motorcade, 168–69, 178n47
Routing Slips, 33
Rowe, L.S., 47
rules, FOIPA, 93n24
Ryan, Robert F., 45
Ryan, William, 79–80

Sacramento, California, 41
salaries, 69
Sal Castro Foundation, 110
*San Antonio Light*, 160
San Benito, Texas, 131, 132
Sanchez, David, 122
Sanchez, George I., 162
San Diego, California: Chamber of
    Commerce Auditorium, 20; FBI field
    offices, 23, 184, 190, 192, 195, 197
*San Diego Tribune-Sun*, 22, 29
Sandoval, David, 126n36
San Jose, Costa Rica, 70, 83
SBI*net* Program, 182–83
Scatterday, George H., 13–14, 15, 16
school board, LA, 104, 109
schools: districts for, 109; Mexican,
    98–99; public, xiii; spy, 205–6. *See
    also specific schools*
Schoultz, Lars, 181
SDS. *See* Students for a Democratic
    Society (SDS)
search warrants, 173
Securities and Exchange Commission
    (SEC), 74
Security Index, FBI, 54, 55, 117
segregation, xi, 96–97, 98, 131

Seitsinger, Ralph, 86
Selective Service Board, FBI, 51
sensor technology, 183
Shanklin, J. Gordon, 148
"she," 189–90
Shell Oil Company, 15–16
Shinley, Jerry, 176, 179n52, 179n58
Shroder, Rex I., 200
Sillas, Herman, 105
Silver, Max, 32
sit-ins, 105, 114–20
sketch, thumbnail, 167
Smith, Jeff, 1, 36n1, 36n5
snitch visas, 161
Socialist Workers Party (SWP), 123
social media, 206
*Sociedad Gabriela Mistral*, 2
solidarity, 103
Solis, Dianne, 178n44
*Songs of the Homeland*, 135
Spanish language, 194
Special Inquiry, on Telles, Ramón
    "Raymond," 87–89
Special Mail Room, 189–93
speech, Garcia, H., 162
Spitz, Oscar, 93n27
spy schools, 205–6
*Spy Schools* (Golden), 206
Stanfield, Denman F., 79
Stanford University, 42–43
State Department, US, 51–52, 69
Steele, Walter S., 58–59
Steinmetz, Harry, 32–33
Stemmons Freeway, 168
stigmas, 151
stories, in 2020, xiii–xiv
Stowe, David H., 159, 177n38
*Strangers in the Field* (Galarza, E.), 54
strikes, 51, 54, 102, 163
students: demands, 103, 104; protests,
    xiii, 194
Students for a Democratic Society
    (SDS), 119, 147
subpoenas, 20
subversive activities, 6, 166

Subversive Activities Control Board,
    171
subversive background, 170, 175
Sullivan, Frank V., 31–32
Sullivan, William C., 112, 115, 141–42,
    191, 193
Summer, R.T., 175
Supreme Court, US, 27, 98, 99
surveillance, xvi; history of, xvii–xviii;
    Medrano, F. reasons for, 147; reports
    on Bemis, 33–34, 35; reports on
    Castro, S., 117; reports on Galarza,
    E., 45–51, 55–60; reports on Galarza,
    M., 49–50, 59; reports on Moreno,
    7–10, 12–14, 16–17, 34–35; reports
    on Telles, Ramón "Raymond,"
    80–82
surveys, xv, xxiin15
SWP. *See* Socialist Workers Party
    (SWP)
sympathizers, communist, 187
systems, PPS, xix–xx

tactics, FBI, 190, 192;
    counterintelligence, 184, 196;
    disruptive, 188; handbill, 193–
    94, 197–98; in Mexico, 183;
    psychological, 185
Tamaulipas, Mexico, 151
tape recordings, 27
taxes, poll, 67, 154
Taylor, Mae. *See* Galarza, Mae
teacher training, Castro, S., 97
TEC. *See* Texas Employment
    Commission (TEC)
technology: future, 207–8; sensor, 183
teletypes, 71, 73, 84, 113, 121, 136–37
Telles, Angela "Angelita" (née Lopez),
    65, 66
Telles, Delfina (née Navarro), xvii, xxi,
    66, 72; allegations against, 76–77,
    78, 80–81; charity work, 81, 91
Telles, Ramón (father), 65–66, 67
Telles, Ramón "Raymond," xvii, xxi,
    65, 69, 91; aliases, 71–72; allegations

against, 75, 76–77, 80–81; career of, 66–67; childhood of, 66; domestic worker case, 89–90; FBI file, 70–74, 84–87; recommendations, 86, 88; Special Inquiry on, 87–89; surveillance reports on, 80–82; in Washington, DC, 82–83
Telles, Richard Lopez, 65, 73, 87
terms: Communist Party, 20; defining, 125n2
*terra bullius* (nobody's land), 93n29
Terrorist Screening Database (TSDB), 117
testimony: Molina, 168–70; Moreno, 21, 22; Silver, 32
Texas, xiv, 98, 132. *See also specific places*
Texas Employment Commission (TEC), 174–75
Texas Independent Coffee Organization, Inc. (TICO), 74–75, 76, 93n27
Texas School Book Depository, 167–68, 171, 174–75
Theoharis, Athan, 140n29
theorists, conspiracy, 168
threats, death, 107
thumbnail sketch, 167
TICO. *See* Texas Independent Coffee Organization, Inc. (TICO)
Tiller, Dixie, 30
*Time*, 102
tin, 51
Toledano, Vicente Lombardo, 55, 56
Tompkins, William F., 167
training conferences, BOCOV, 184–89, 195
transition teams, US presidential, 67–68
translations, 193–94
trials, 120
Truly, Roy S., 174
Truman, Harry S., 58, 158, 159
Trump, Donald, xiii, xiv, xvi, 124
TSDB. *See* Terrorist Screening Database (TSDB)
2020: stories in, xiii–xiv; welcoming, xv

types, of informants, 161, 178n39

UAW. *See* United Auto Workers (UAW)
UCAPAWA. *See* United Cannery Agricultural Packing and Allied Workers of America (UCAPAWA)
undercover police, 103, 126n27
unions, 4–5, 6, 7, 14, 15, 41. *See also specific unions*
United Auto Workers (UAW), 141, 142, 144–45
United Cannery Agricultural Packing and Allied Workers of America (UCAPAWA), 4, 9, 14, 21
United States (US): agencies, 182; ambassador, 65, 68–70; Army, xviii–xix; congress members, 69; Department of Defense, 205–6; Department of Justice, 118; interventions, 181; Joint Mexican Commission on Border Area Development, 82; presidential transition teams, 67–68; State Department, 51–52, 69; Supreme Court, 27, 98, 99
University of Guatemala, 2
University of Texas at Arlington (UTA), 147
UNS. *See* National Sinarquist Union (UNS)
untold histories, xv–xvii
US. *See* United States (US)
Usquiano, Philip, 21–22, 29
UTA. *See* University of Texas at Arlington (UTA)

Valens, Ritchie (Ricardo Esteban Valenzuela Reyes), 133
Valentine, Douglas, 185
Valenzuela Reyes, Ricardo Esteban. *See* Valens, Ritchie
*Vencermos* Brigade (VB), 148
Vera, Fonda, 146
veterans, 153–54, 166

Villa, Francisco "Pancho," xiii–xiv, 65, 181
visas, 95, 161
Viva Johnson movement, 155
Viva Kennedy Clubs, 67–68, 156

*WALKOUT!*, 101
walkouts, xiii, 101–5, 107–8
Walsh, Thomas Ryan, 8
Wannall, W.R., 197–98, 203n13
Ware, R.W., 56, 57
warrants: for deportations, 25; for Moreno arrest, 23; search, 173
Washington, DC, 52, 82–83
"Wasted Days and Wasted Nights," 130, 134, 137–38
Waters, Helen, 47
Watson, Marvin, 59
weapons, 120
Webster, William H., 137
Wechsler, James A., 62n20
Welch, Raquel, 133
welcoming 2020, xv
Wharton, Willard D., 73

*What Price—Wetback?* (article), 155
Wheaton, Evelyn, 50
Wight, Ward, Jr., 11
Williams, Ted, 133–34
Wilson, Woodrow, xiv
Wimason, James, 9
Wise, David, xvii–xviii
witch-hunting, 162
witnesses, 20–21
Woodward, Robert F., 76
working conditions, 42
Writers' Congress, 13

Young America's Foundation (YFA), 111
Youth Education Summits (YES), 111
Ysleta, Mexico, 65

Zapata, Antonio, 96
Zatz, Asa, 34
Zia Corporation, 85
Zion, Illinois, 115
Zoot Suits, 5
Zurcher, Harry, 74–75

# About the Author

**José Angel Gutiérrez**, PhD and JD, is an Emeritus professor of political science formerly with the University of Texas in Arlington, Texas, and a licensed attorney in Texas and some federal courts. He is busy with work on subsequent volumes of this type of material and subject matter on Federal Bureau of Investigation surveillance of Mexican origin and Chicano people in the United States. He also has been a foundation executive and former elected and appointed public official in both Texas and Oregon. He is an award-winning author, whose most recent books have won first and second place in different categories for *Albert A. Peña, Jr.: Dean of Chicano Politics* (2017) and *The Eagle Has Eyes: The FBI Surveillance of César E. Chávez of the United Farm Workers Union of America, 1965–1975* (2019), respectively. He has an extensive publication history, including three children's books: *I am Olga: 1st Latina Jet Fighter Pilot*; *I am Ignacio Zaragoza*; and, *Ignacio Zaragoza, the Hero of the Cinco de Mayo* for middle grade readers.

www.ingramcontent.com/pod-product-compliance
Lightning Source LLC
Chambersburg PA
CBHW022305280326
41932CB00010B/992